LOVE MANGA?
LET US KNOW WHAT YOU THINK!

OUR MANGA SURVEY IS NOW
AVAILABLE ONLINE. PLEASE VISIT:
VIZ.COM/MANGASURVEY

HELP US MAKE THE MANGA
YOU LOVE BETTER!

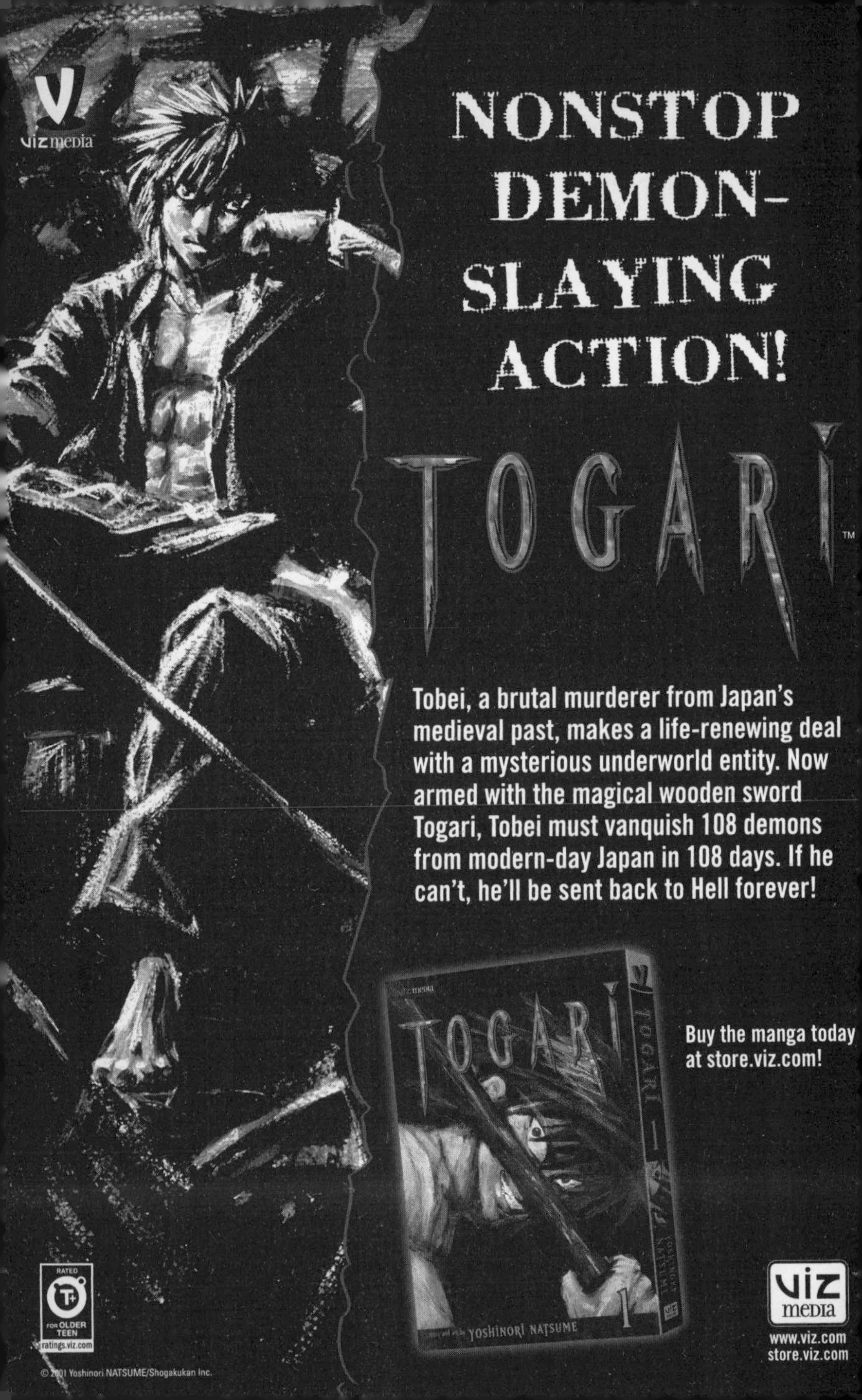
viz media
NONSTOP DEMON-SLAYING ACTION!
TOGARI™
Tobei, a brutal murderer from Japan's medieval past, makes a life-renewing deal with a mysterious underworld entity. Now armed with the magical wooden sword Togari, Tobei must vanquish 108 demons from modern-day Japan in 108 days. If he can't, he'll be sent back to Hell forever!
TOGARI
1
YOSHINORI NATSUME
Buy the manga today at store.viz.com!
RATED
T+
FOR OLDER TEEN
ratings.viz.com
viz media
www.viz.com
store.viz.com
© 2001 Yoshinori NATSUME/Shogakukan Inc.

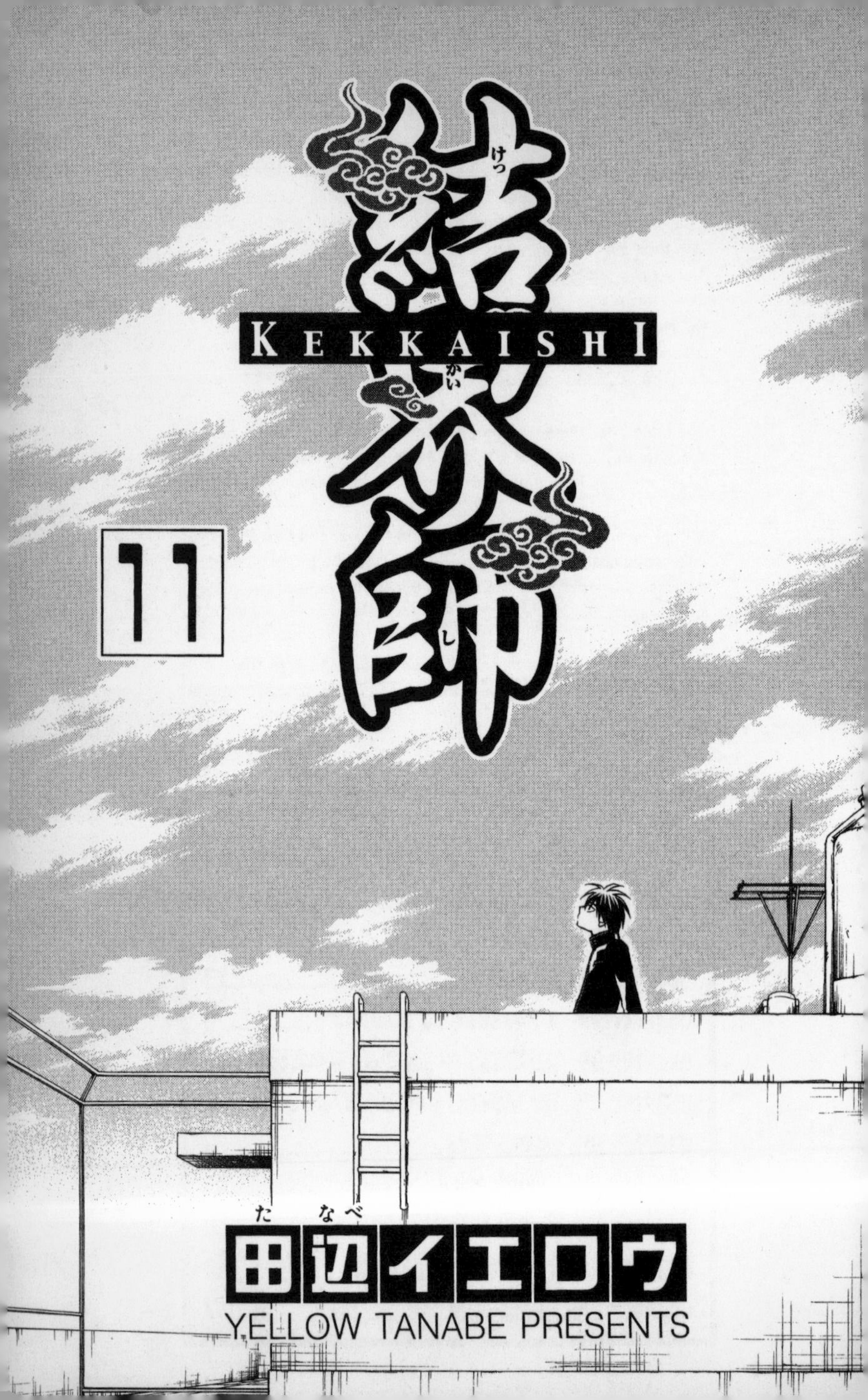
結界師
KEKKAISHI
11
田辺イエロウ
YELLOW TANABE PRESENTS

THE STORY THUS FAR

Yoshimori Sumimura and Tokine Yukimura have a special duty passed down through their families for generations—to protect Karasumori Forest from supernatural beings called *ayakashi*. People with their gift for terminating ayakashi are called *kekkaishi*, or "barrier masters."

The Night Troops, a group of outcasts within the Shadow Organization, have sent Gen Shishio, a half-ayakashi, to the Karasumori Site to assist Yoshimori and Tokine.

One fateful day the ayakashi organization Kokuboro mounts an attack on the Karasumori site, and flame-spewing equine-monster Gagin attempts to immolate Yoshimori and his allies.

As they await reinforcements, Yoshimori, Tokine, and Gen struggle valiantly against all odds. Eventually, in desperation, Gen violates the Night Troops strictest taboo, and transforms himself completely into an ayakashi.

Just when Gen is about to gain the upper hand in battle, the ayakashi Kaguro appears out of thin air and fatally slashes him with an enchanted knife…

KEKKAISHI VOL. 11
TABLE OF CONTENTS

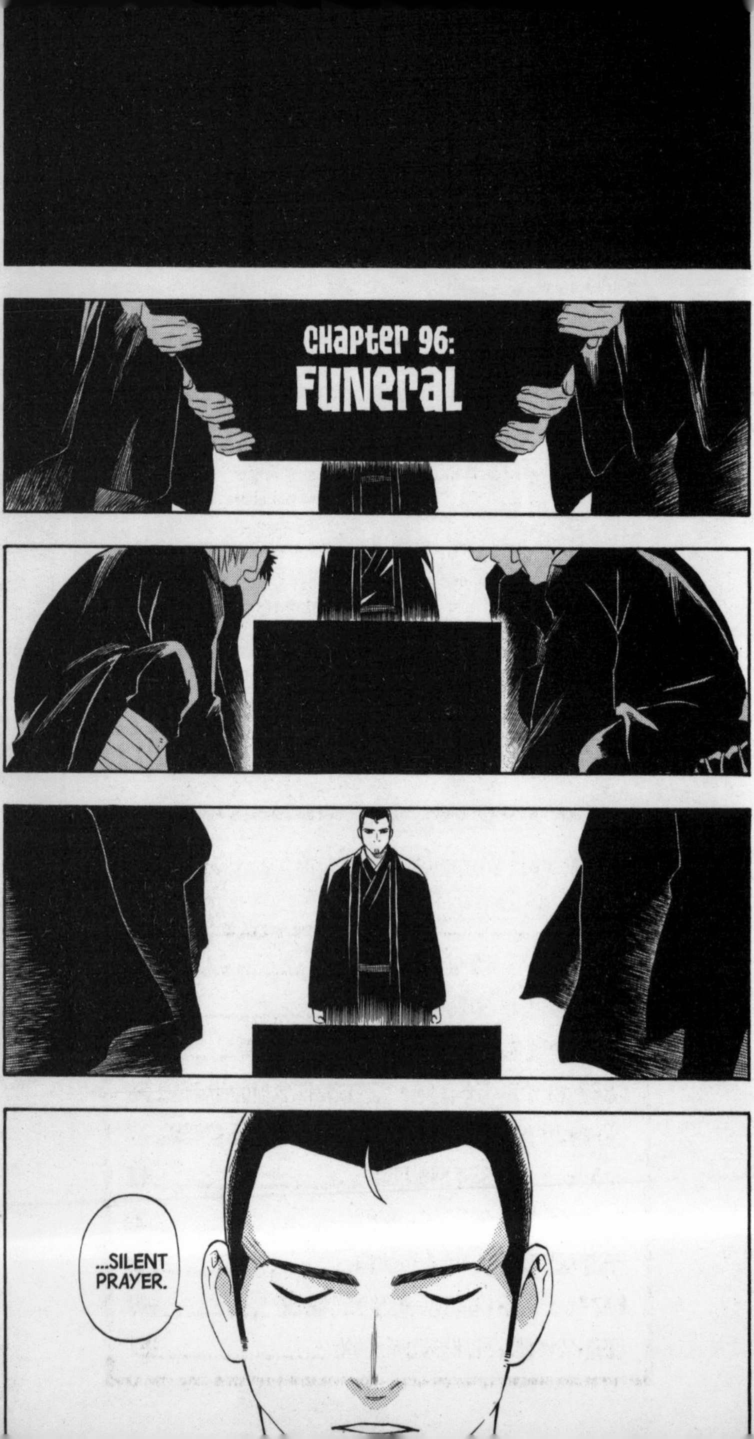
Chapter 96:
Funeral
...SILENT PRAYER.

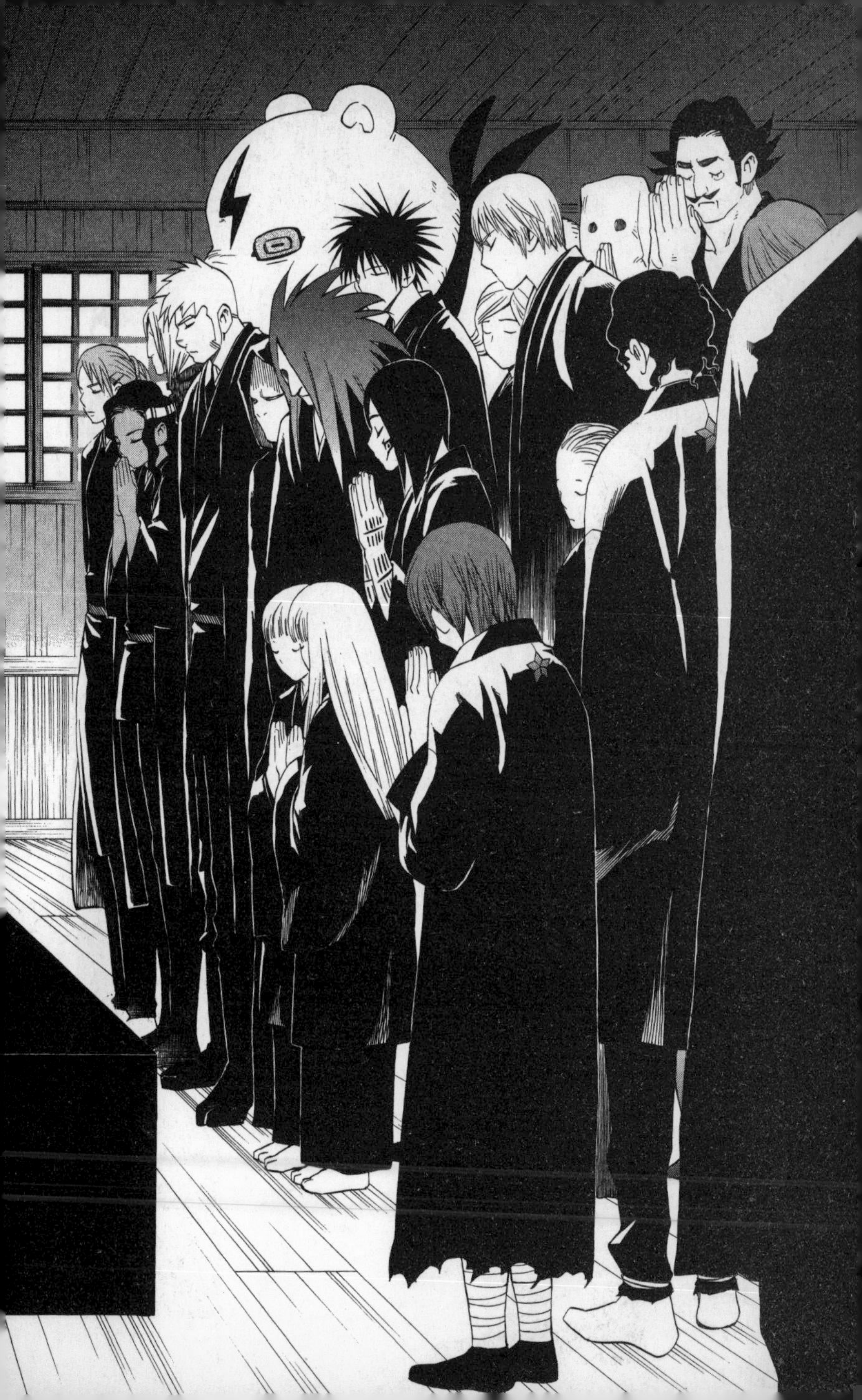

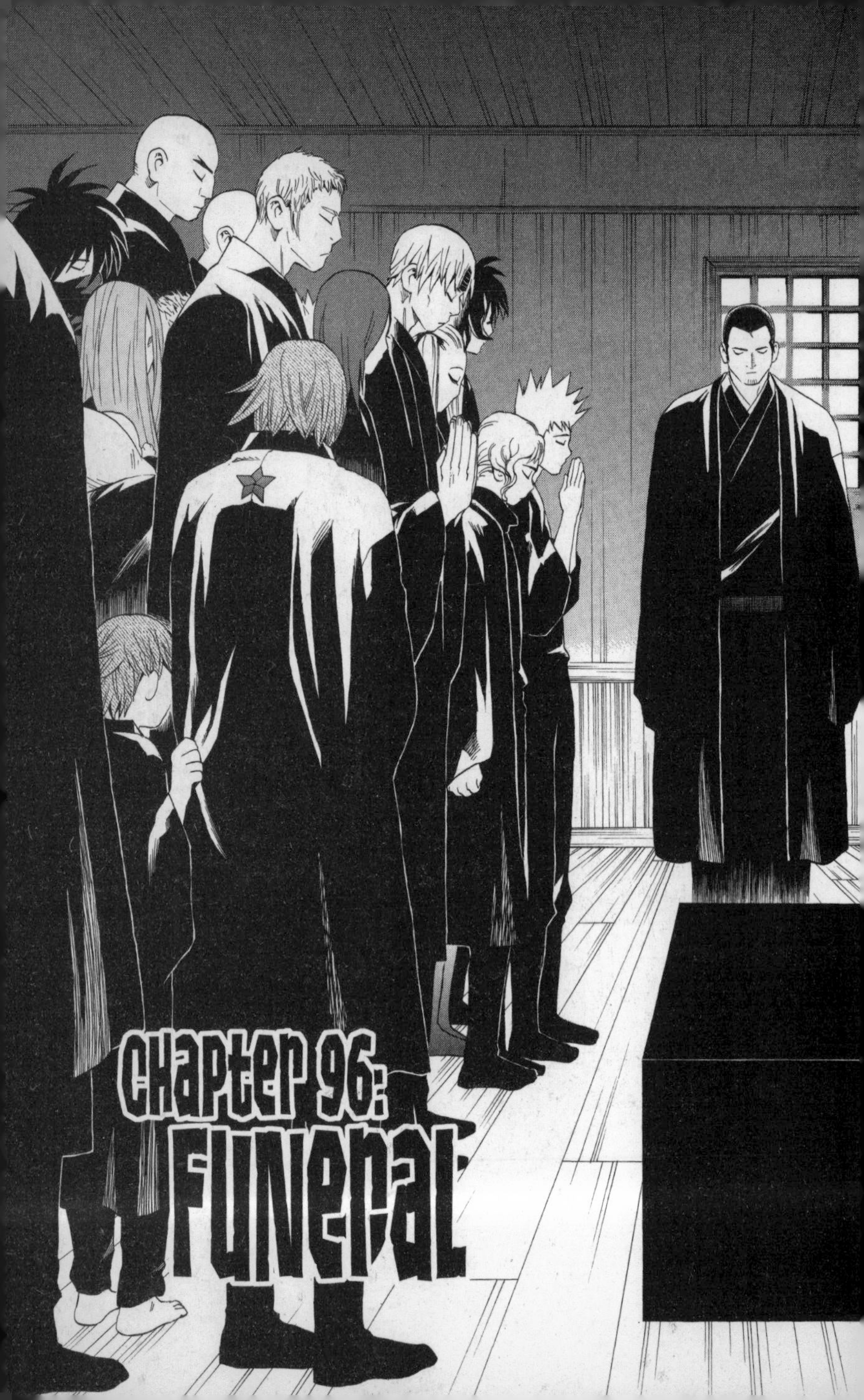
Chapter 96:
Funeral

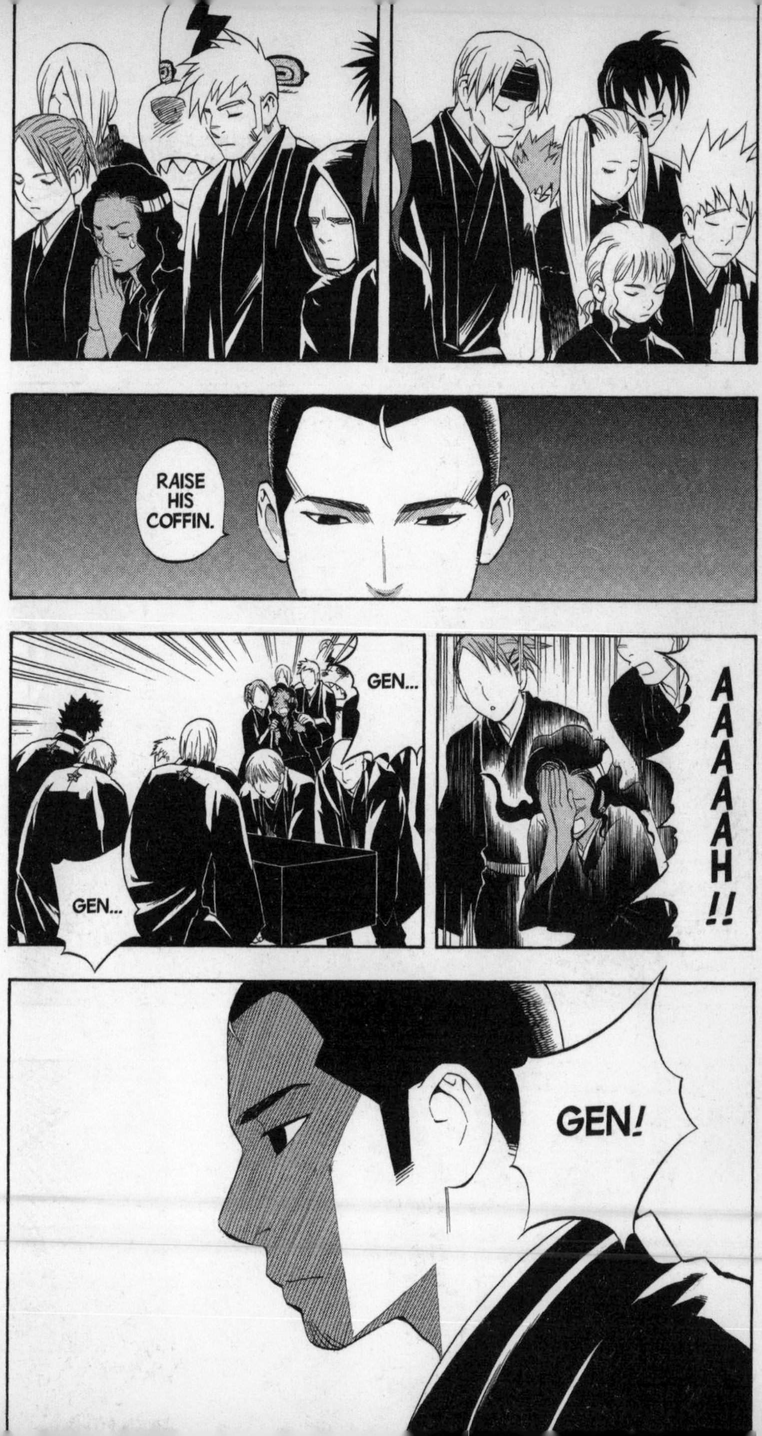
RAISE HIS COFFIN.
AAAAAH!!
GEN...
GEN...
GEN!

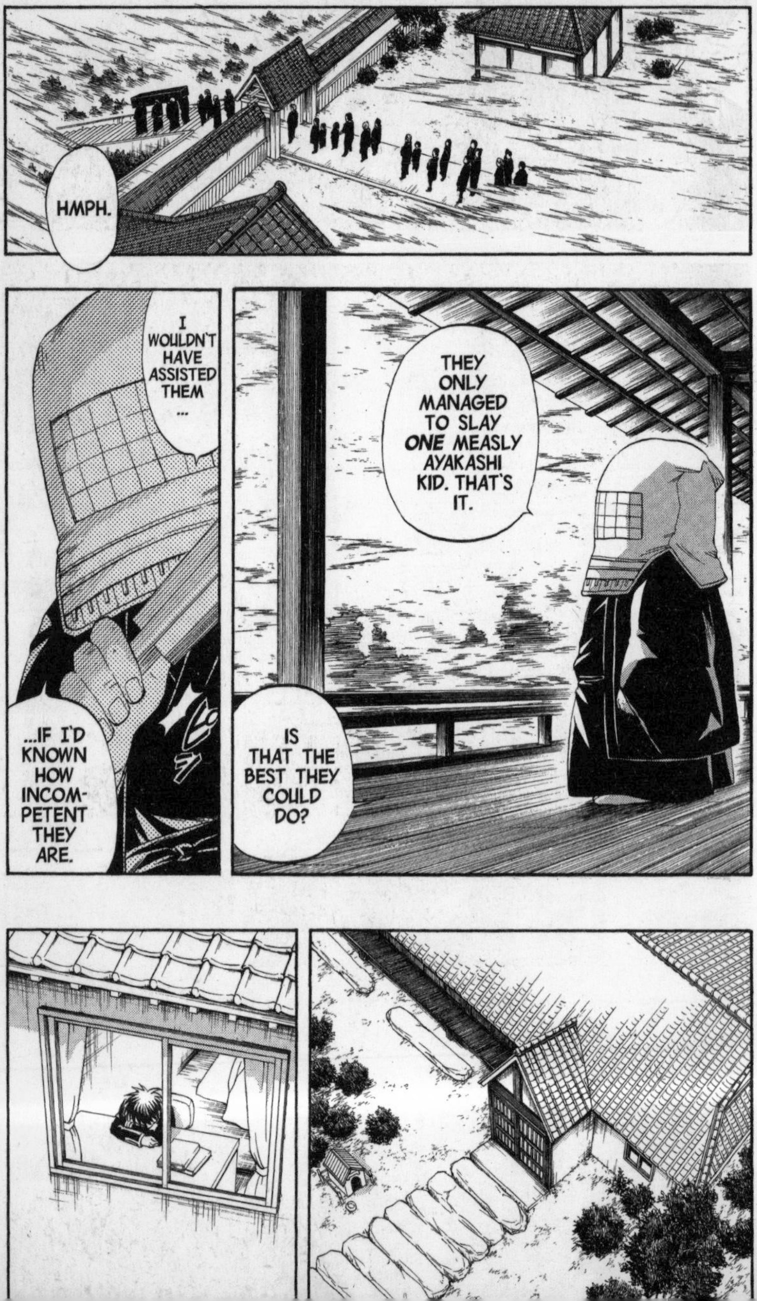
HMPH.
THEY ONLY MANAGED TO SLAY *ONE* MEASLY AYAKASHI KID. THAT'S IT.
IS THAT THE BEST THEY COULD DO?
I WOULDN'T HAVE ASSISTED THEM ...
...IF I'D KNOWN HOW INCOM-PETENT THEY ARE.

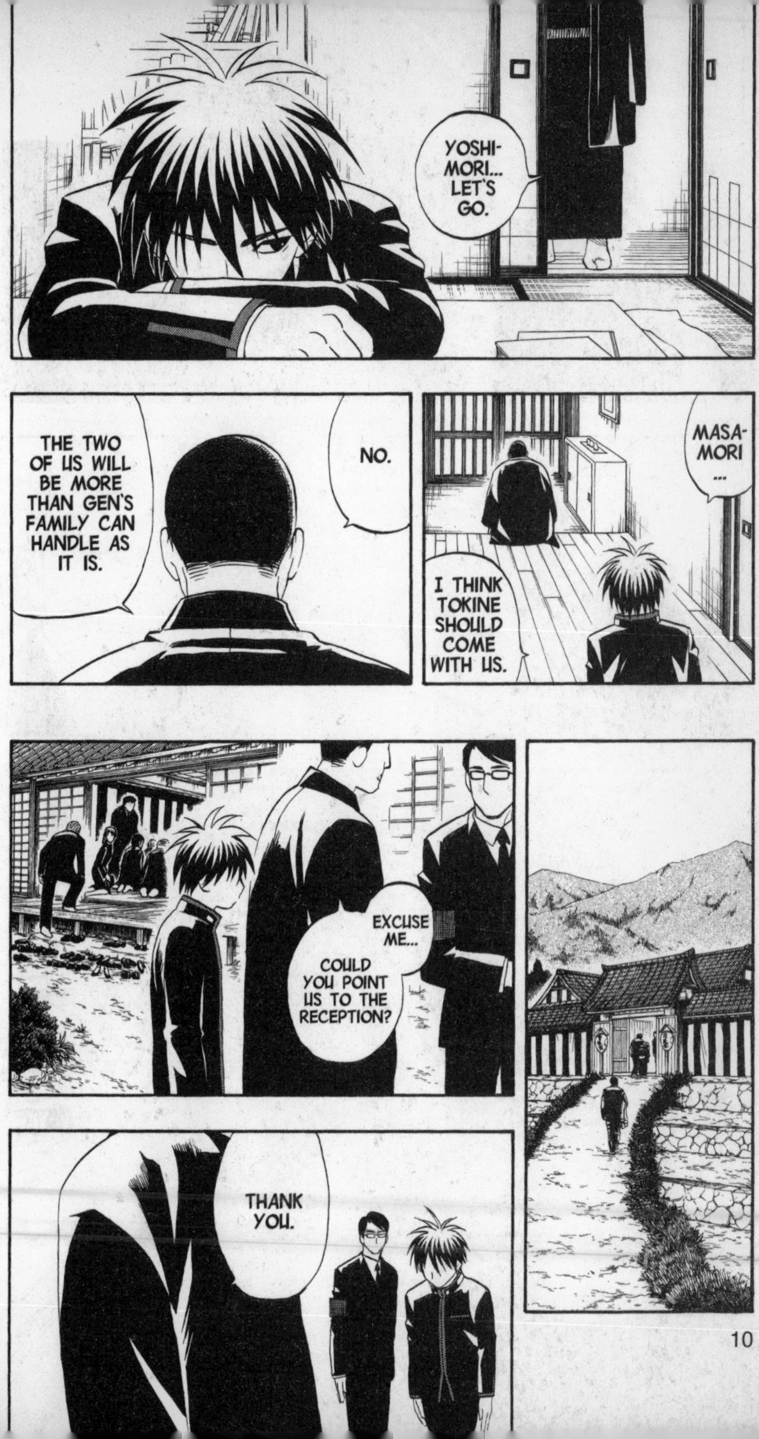
YOSHI-MORI... LET'S GO.
MASA-MORI ...
I THINK TOKINE SHOULD COME WITH US.
NO.
THE TWO OF US WILL BE MORE THAN GEN'S FAMILY CAN HANDLE AS IT IS.
EXCUSE ME...
COULD YOU POINT US TO THE RECEPTION?
THANK YOU.

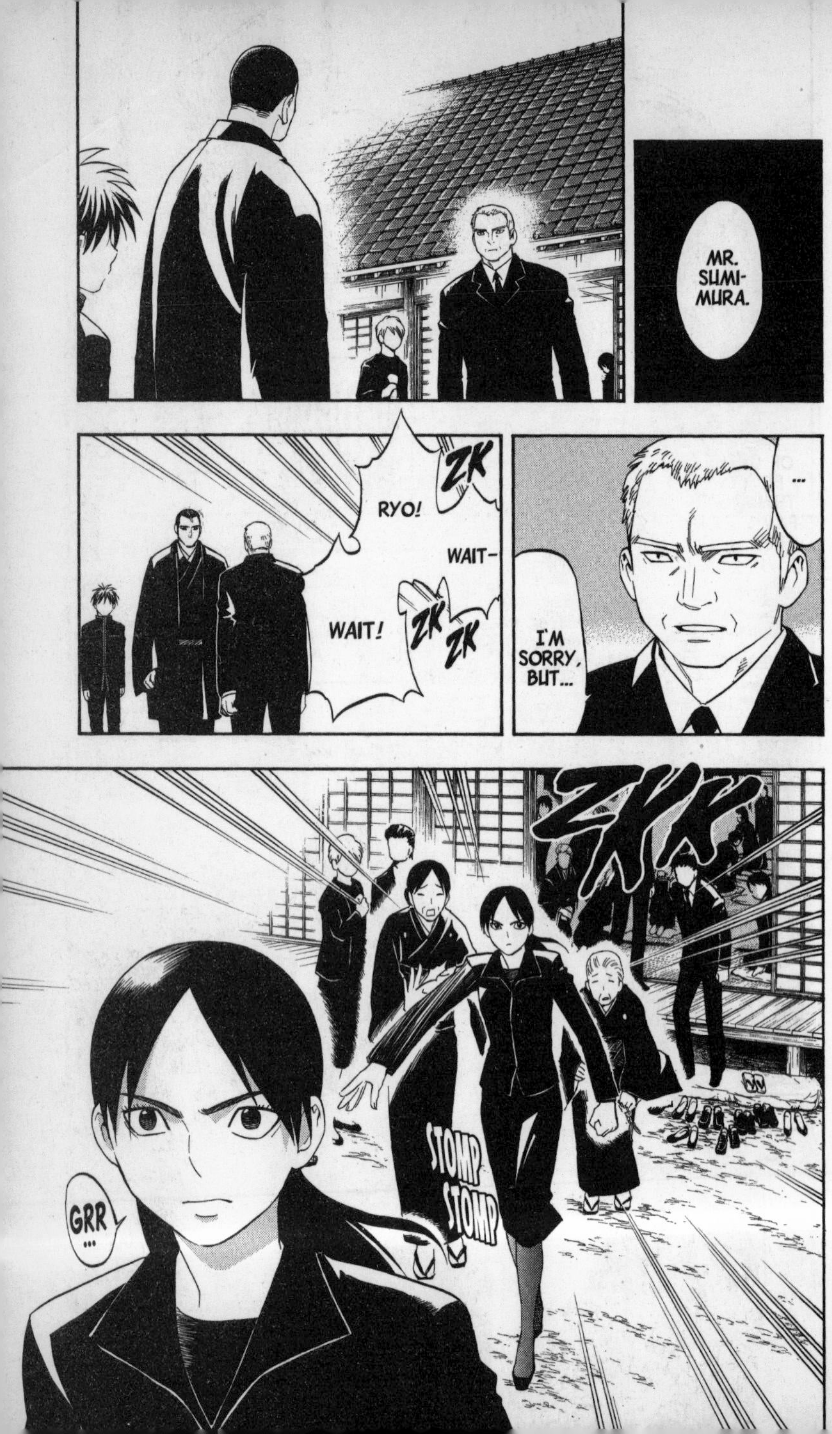
MR. SUMI-MURA.
...
I'M SORRY, BUT...
ZK
RYO!
WAIT-
ZK ZK
WAIT!
ZKK
STOMP STOMP
GRR ...

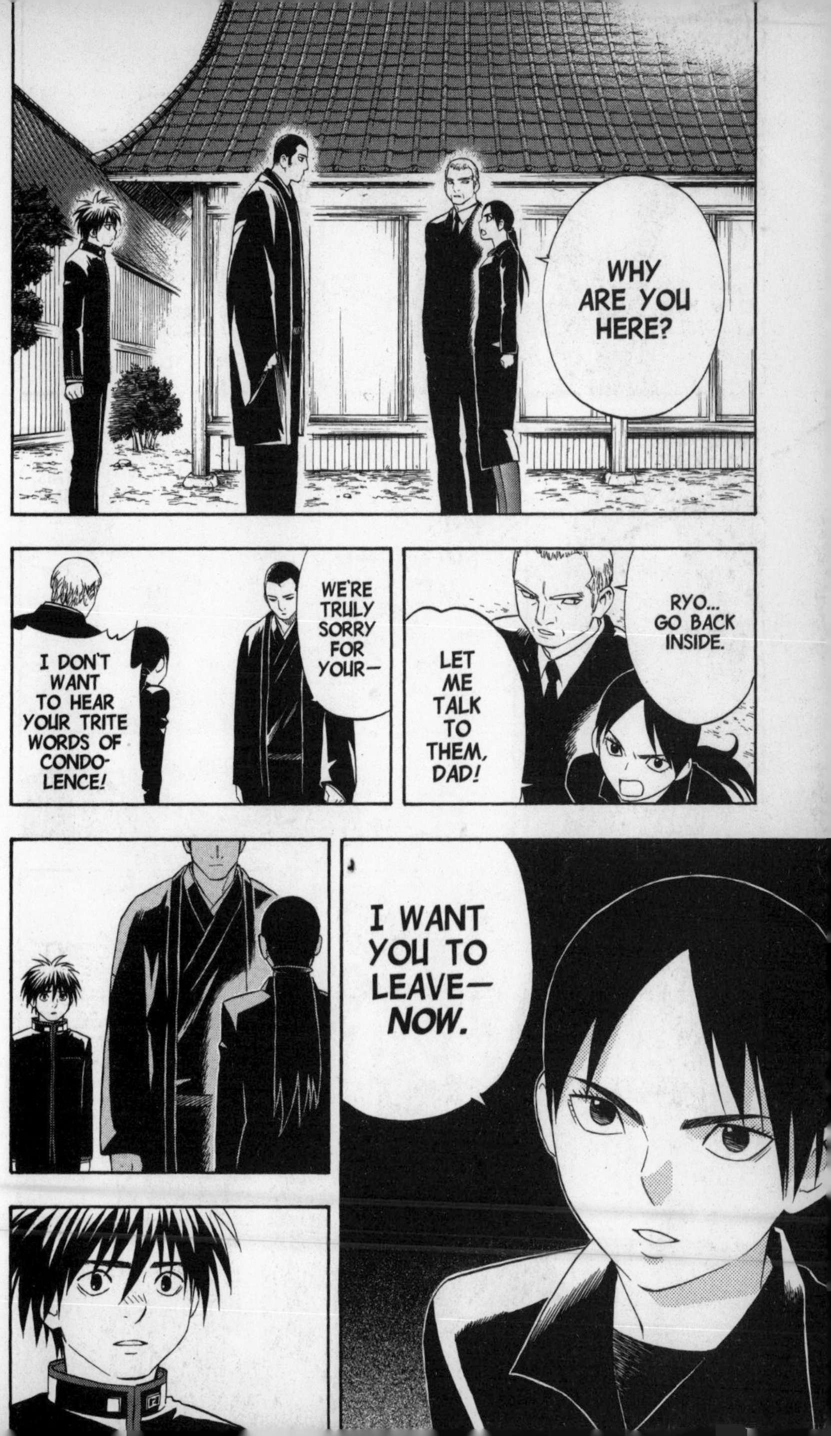
WHY ARE YOU HERE?
RYO... GO BACK INSIDE.
LET ME TALK TO THEM, DAD!
WE'RE TRULY SORRY FOR YOUR—
I DON'T WANT TO HEAR YOUR TRITE WORDS OF CONDOLENCE!
I WANT YOU TO LEAVE— NOW.

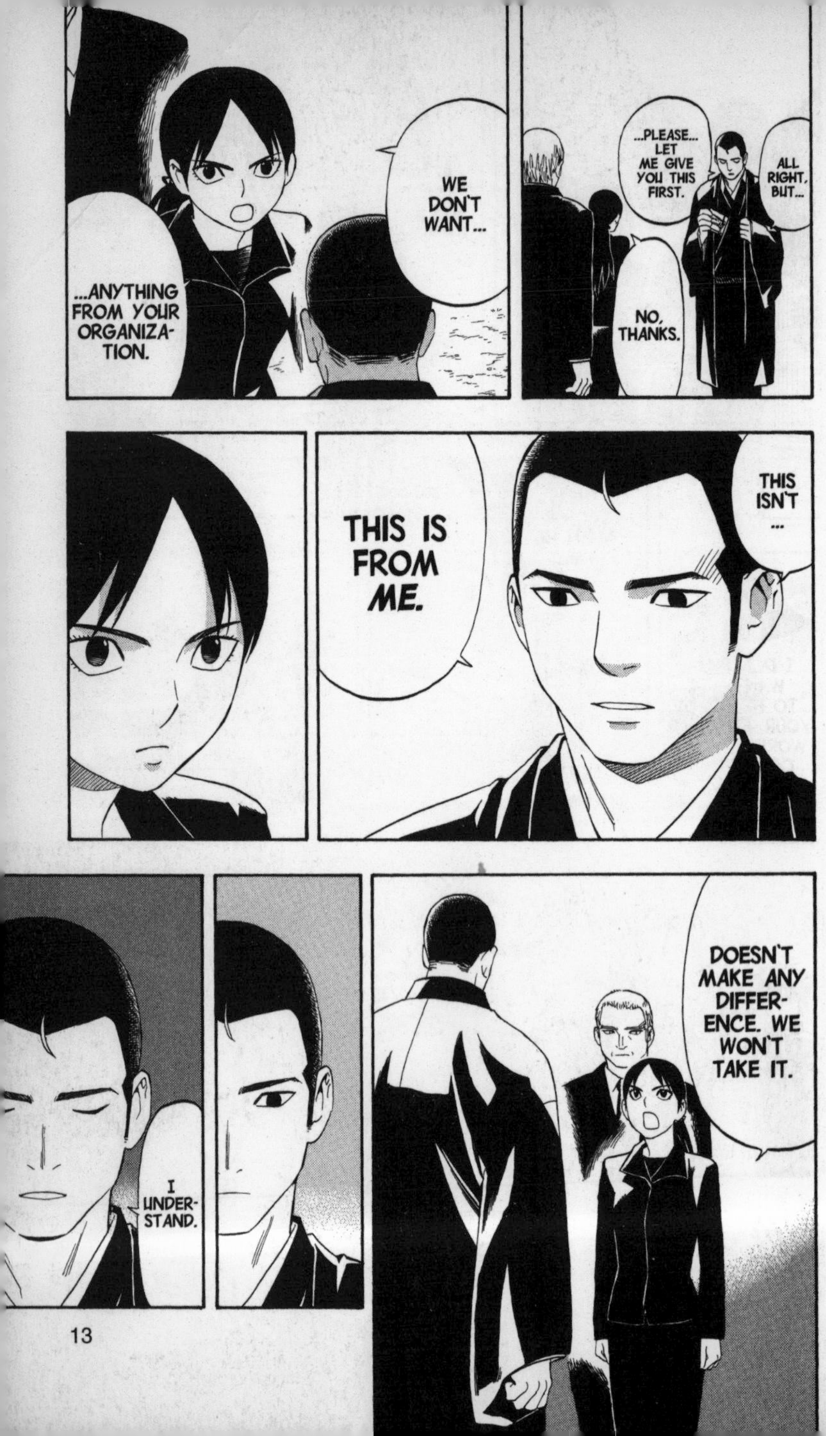
ALL RIGHT, BUT...
...PLEASE... LET ME GIVE YOU THIS FIRST.
NO, THANKS.
WE DON'T WANT...
...ANYTHING FROM YOUR ORGANIZATION.
THIS ISN'T ...
THIS IS FROM *ME.*
DOESN'T MAKE ANY DIFFERENCE. WE WON'T TAKE IT.
I UNDERSTAND.

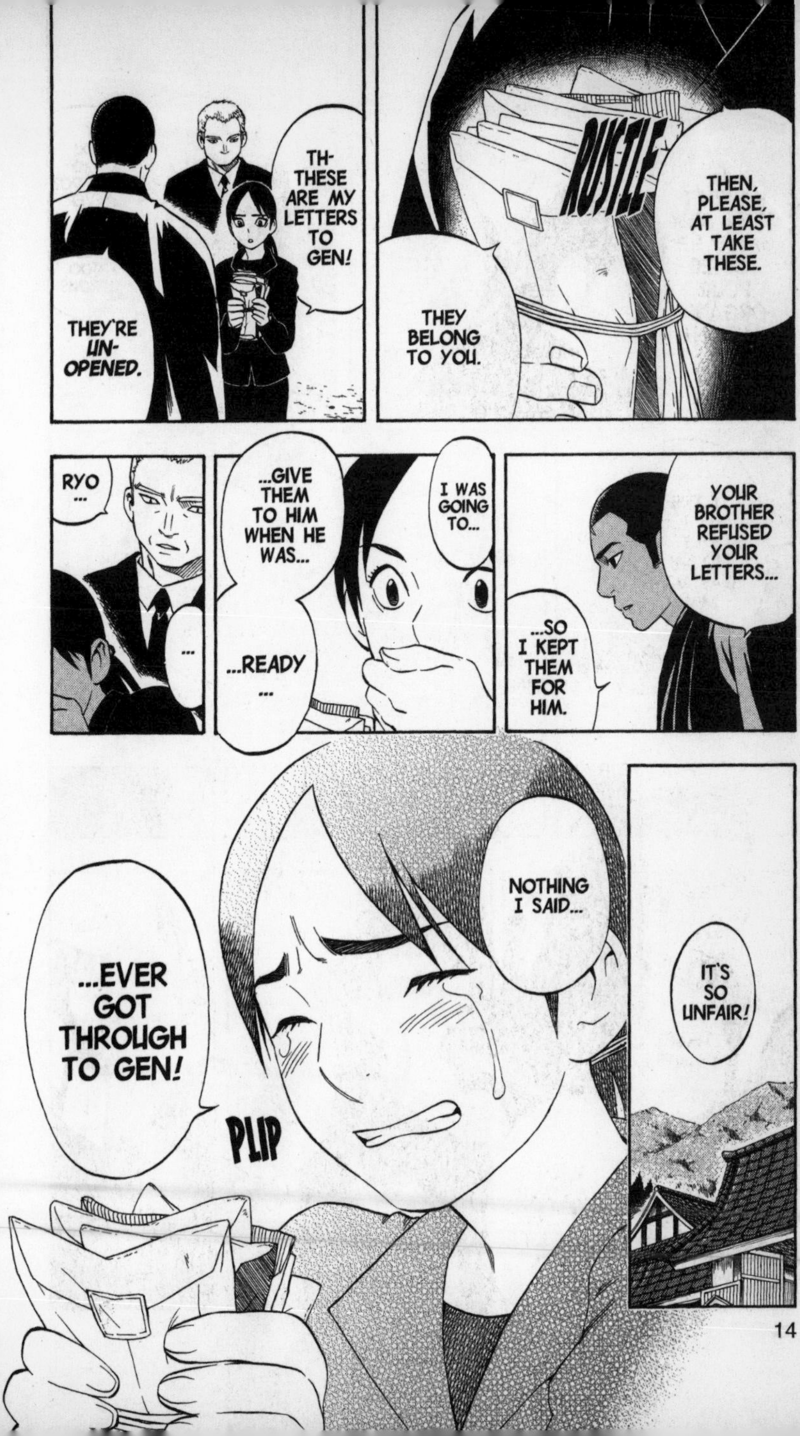
RUSTLE
THEN, PLEASE, AT LEAST TAKE THESE.
THEY BELONG TO YOU.
TH- THESE ARE MY LETTERS TO GEN!
THEY'RE UN-OPENED.
YOUR BROTHER REFUSED YOUR LETTERS...
...SO I KEPT THEM FOR HIM.
I WAS GOING TO...
...GIVE THEM TO HIM WHEN HE WAS...
...READY...
RYO...
...
IT'S SO UNFAIR!
NOTHING I SAID...
...EVER GOT THROUGH TO GEN!
PLIP

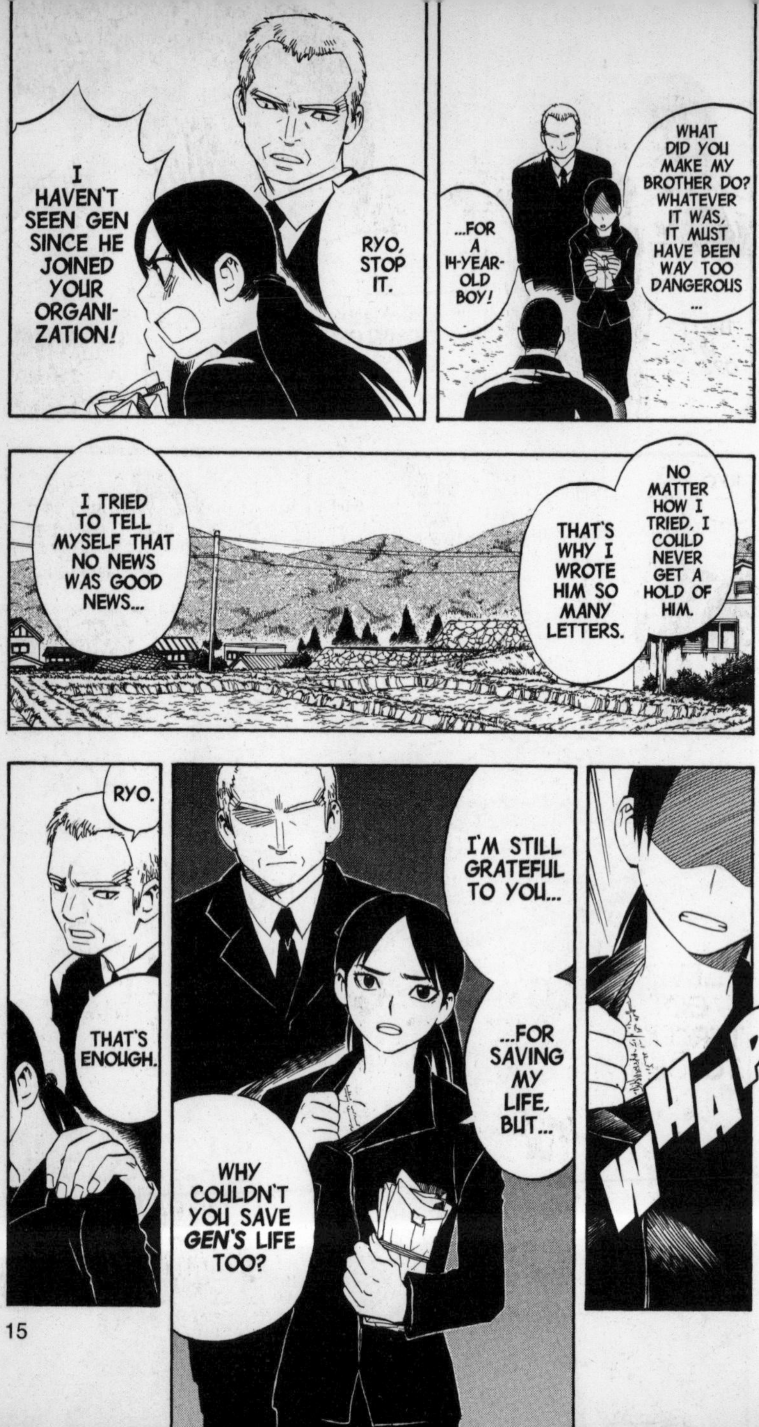
WHAT DID YOU MAKE MY BROTHER DO? WHATEVER IT WAS, IT MUST HAVE BEEN WAY TOO DANGEROUS ...
...FOR A 14-YEAR-OLD BOY!
I HAVEN'T SEEN GEN SINCE HE JOINED YOUR ORGANIZATION!
RYO, STOP IT.
NO MATTER HOW I TRIED, I COULD NEVER GET A HOLD OF HIM.
THAT'S WHY I WROTE HIM SO MANY LETTERS.
I TRIED TO TELL MYSELF THAT NO NEWS WAS GOOD NEWS...
WHAP
I'M STILL GRATEFUL TO YOU...
...FOR SAVING MY LIFE, BUT...
WHY COULDN'T YOU SAVE GEN'S LIFE TOO?
RYO.
THAT'S ENOUGH.

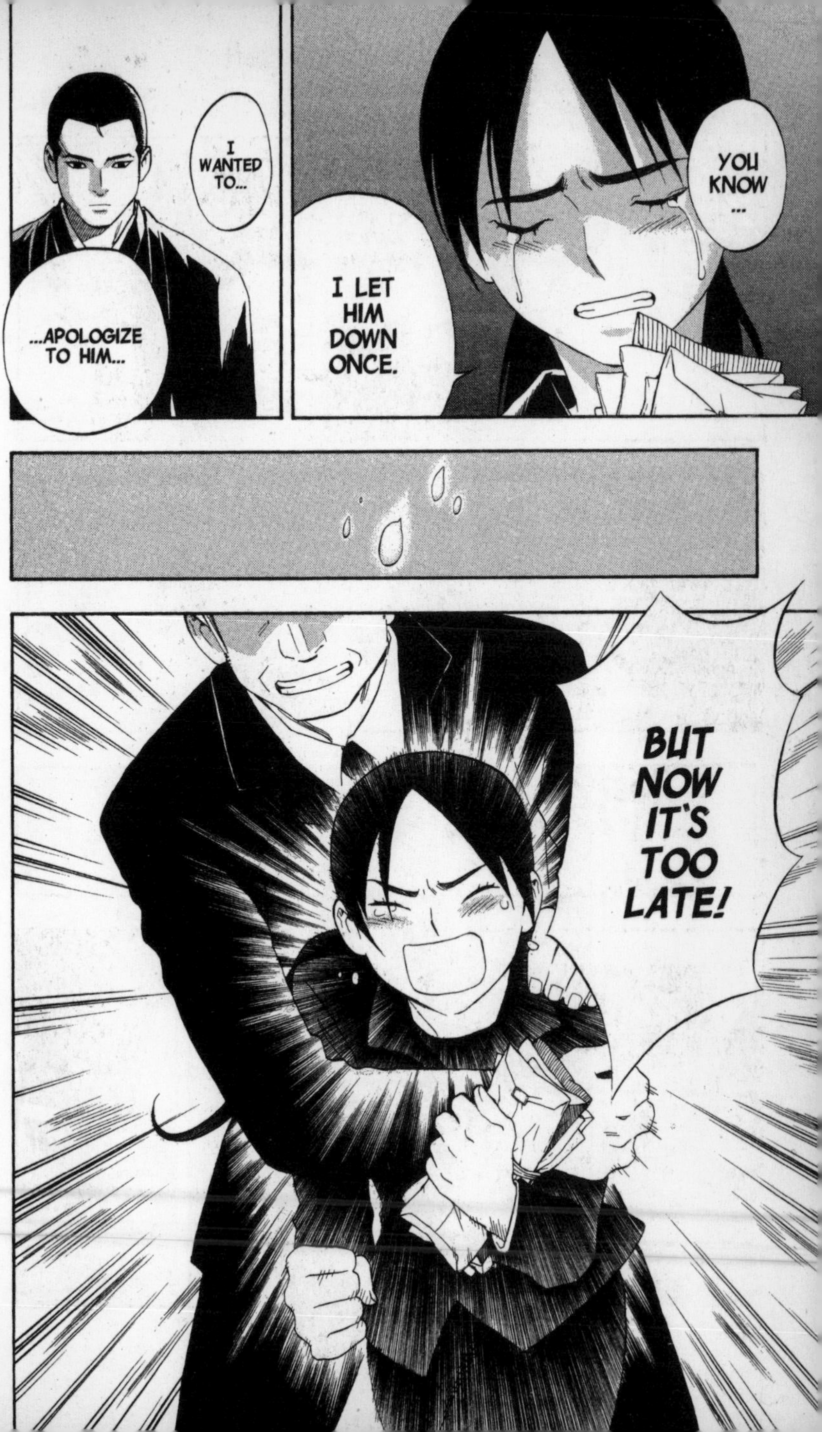
YOU KNOW ...
I LET HIM DOWN ONCE.
I WANTED TO...
...APOLOGIZE TO HIM...
BUT NOW IT'S TOO LATE!

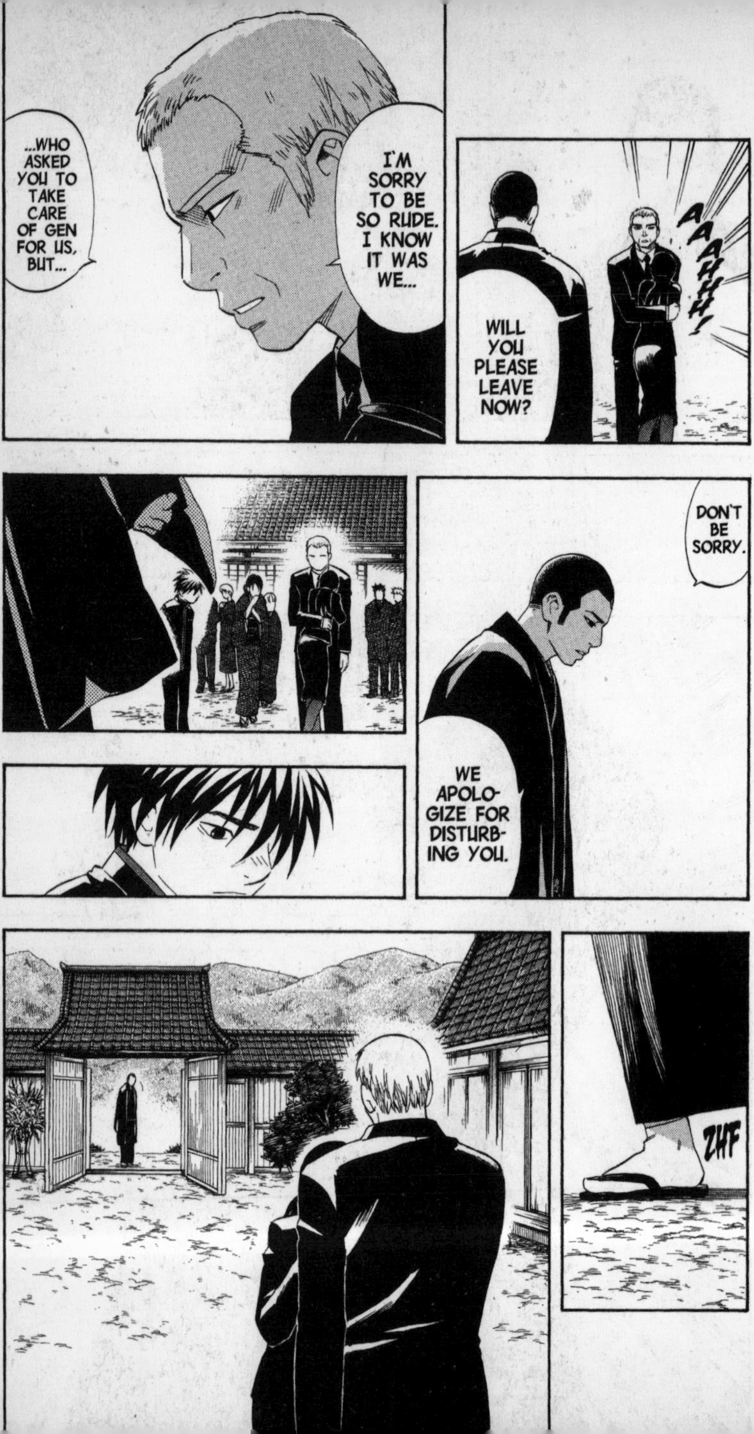
AAAHHH!
WILL YOU PLEASE LEAVE NOW?
I'M SORRY TO BE SO RUDE. I KNOW IT WAS WE...
...WHO ASKED YOU TO TAKE CARE OF GEN FOR US, BUT...
DON'T BE SORRY.
WE APOLOGIZE FOR DISTURBING YOU.
ZHF

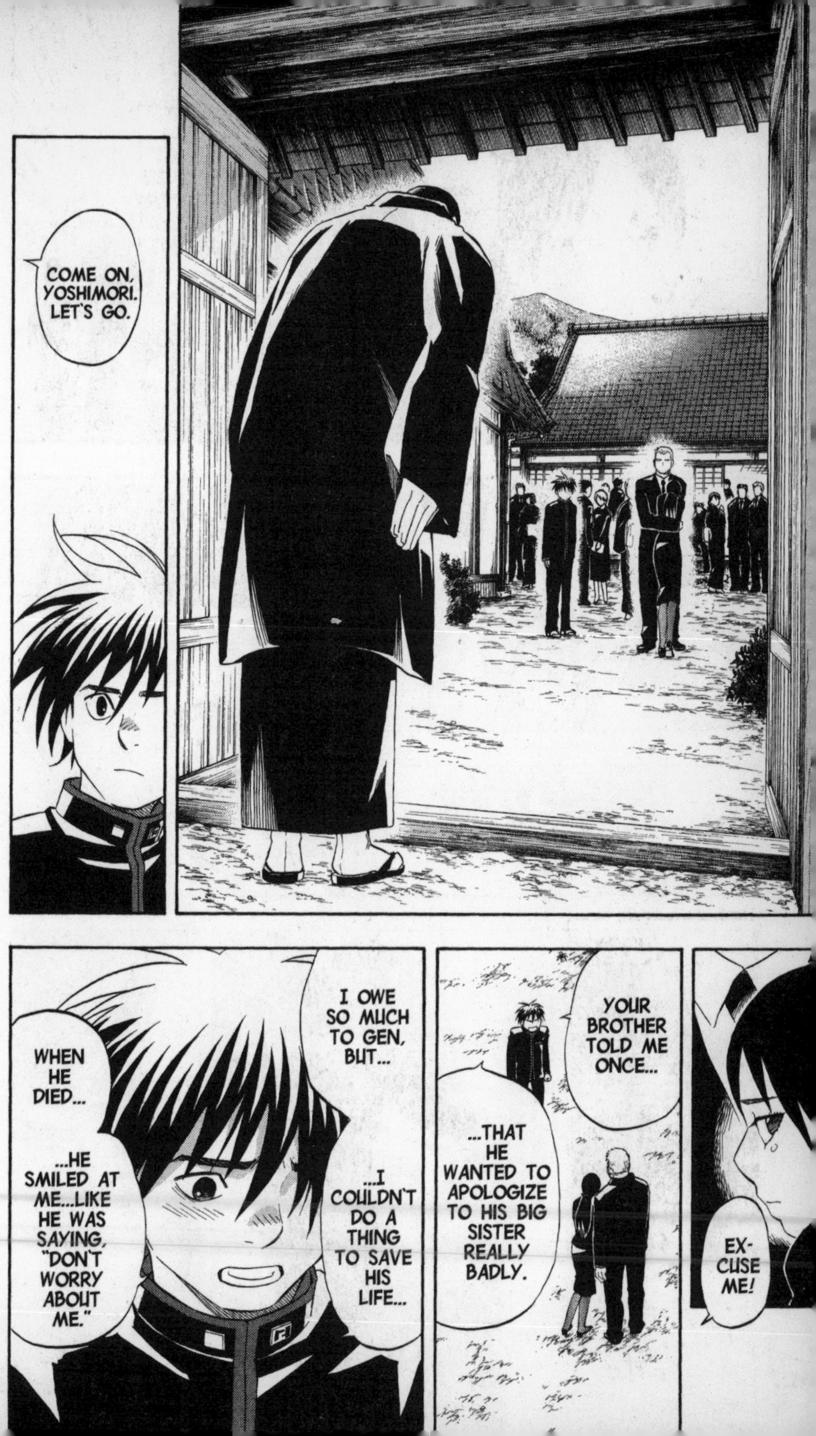
COME ON, YOSHIMORI. LET'S GO.
EX-CUSE ME!
YOUR BROTHER TOLD ME ONCE...
...THAT HE WANTED TO APOLOGIZE TO HIS BIG SISTER REALLY BADLY.
I OWE SO MUCH TO GEN, BUT...
WHEN HE DIED...
...HE SMILED AT ME...LIKE HE WAS SAYING, "DON'T WORRY ABOUT ME."
...I COULDN'T DO A THING TO SAVE HIS LIFE...

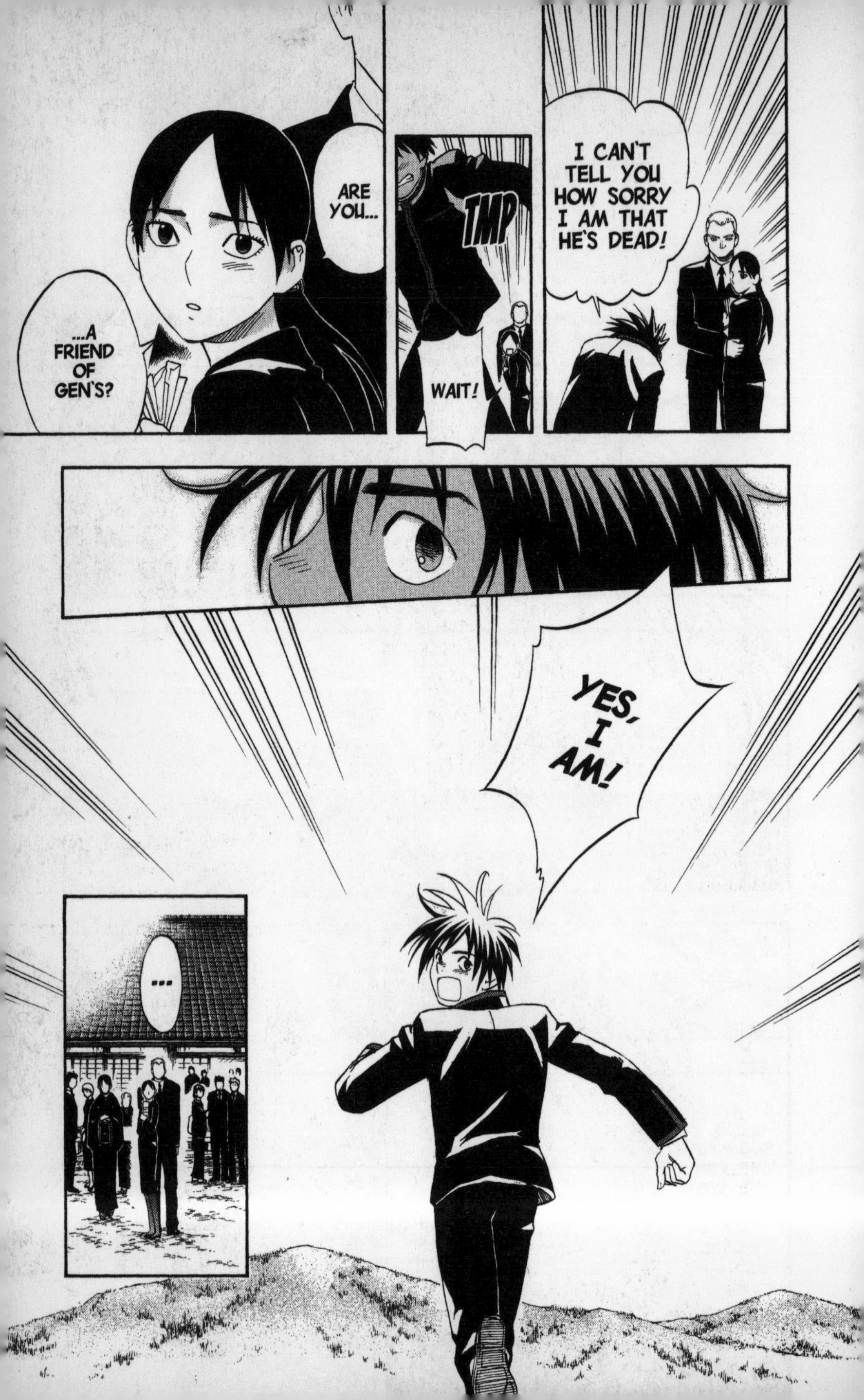
I CAN'T TELL YOU HOW SORRY I AM THAT HE'S DEAD!
TMP
WAIT!
ARE YOU...
...A FRIEND OF GEN'S?
YES, I AM!
...

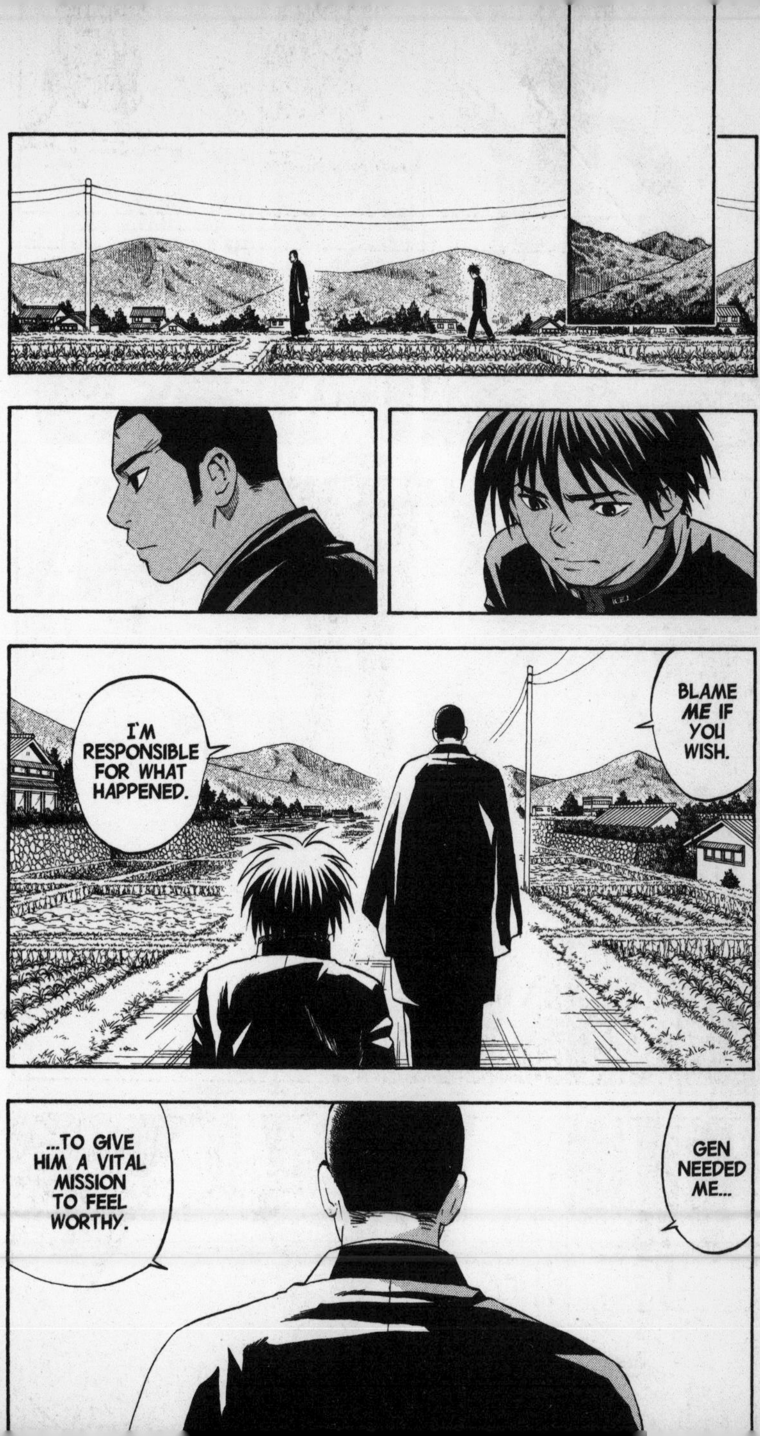
BLAME ME IF YOU WISH.
I'M RESPONSIBLE FOR WHAT HAPPENED.
GEN NEEDED ME...
...TO GIVE HIM A VITAL MISSION TO FEEL WORTHY.

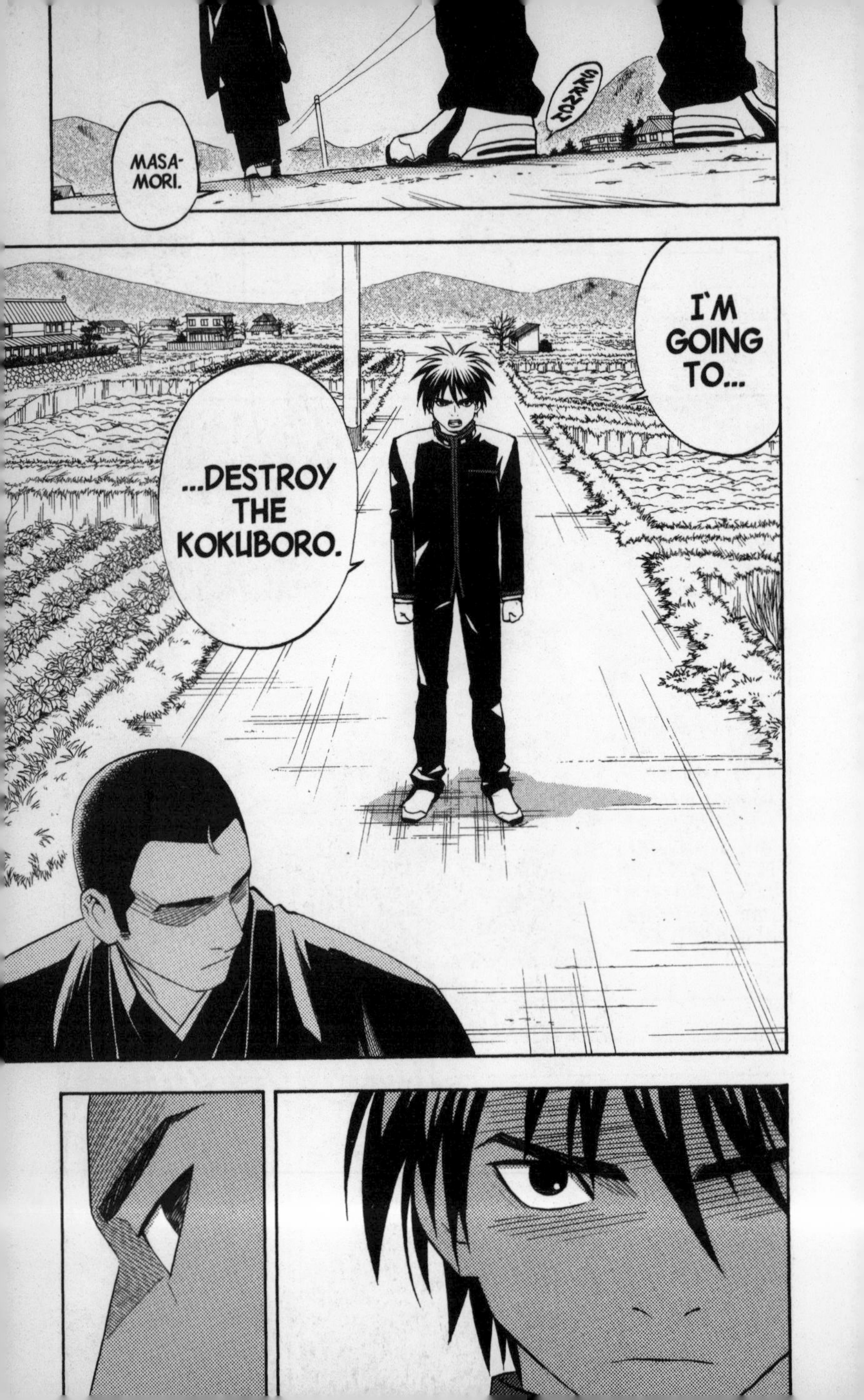
SKRNCH
MASA-MORI.
I'M GOING TO...
...DESTROY THE KOKUBORO.

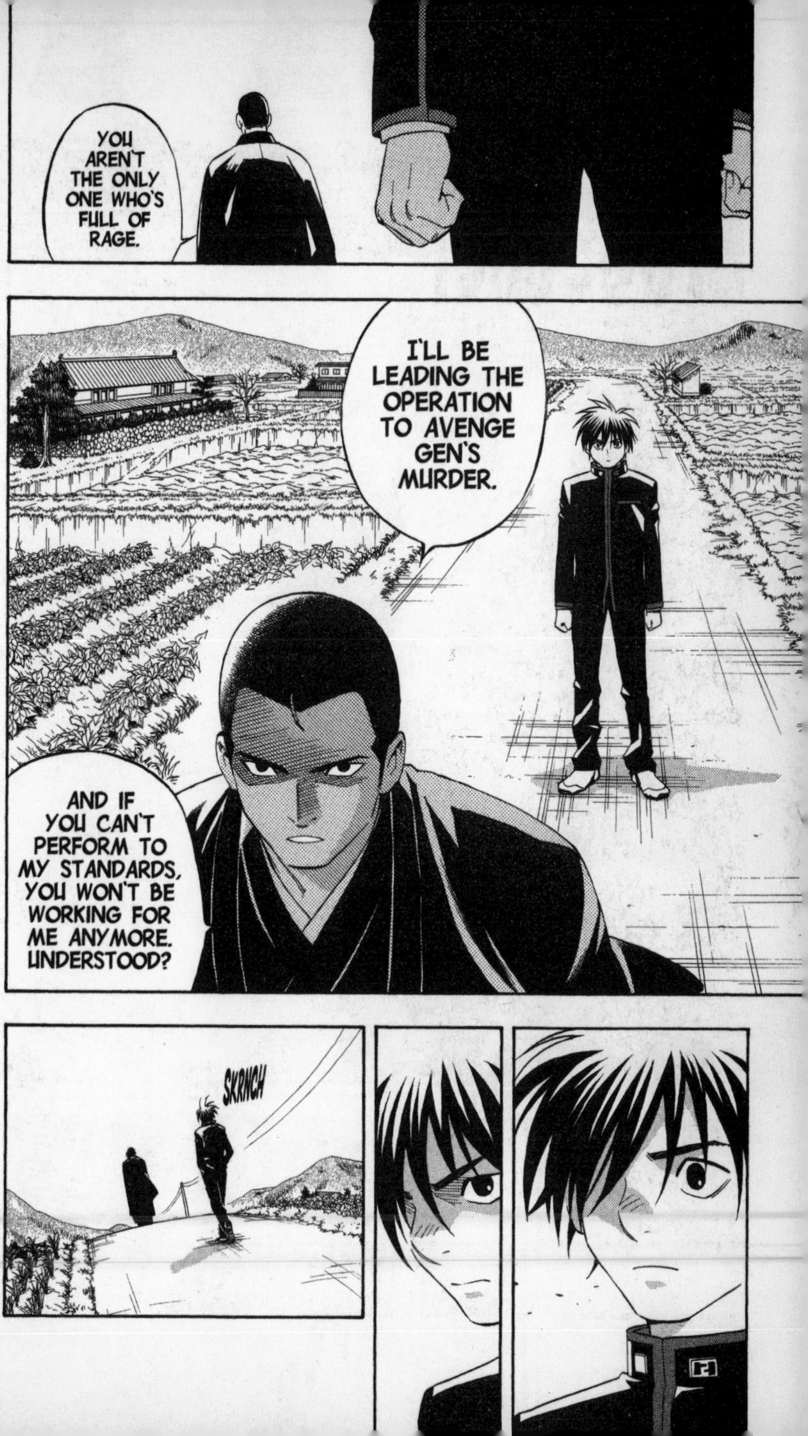
YOU AREN'T THE ONLY ONE WHO'S FULL OF RAGE.
I'LL BE LEADING THE OPERATION TO AVENGE GEN'S MURDER.
AND IF YOU CAN'T PERFORM TO MY STANDARDS, YOU WON'T BE WORKING FOR ME ANYMORE. UNDERSTOOD?
SKRNCH

Chapter 97: Together

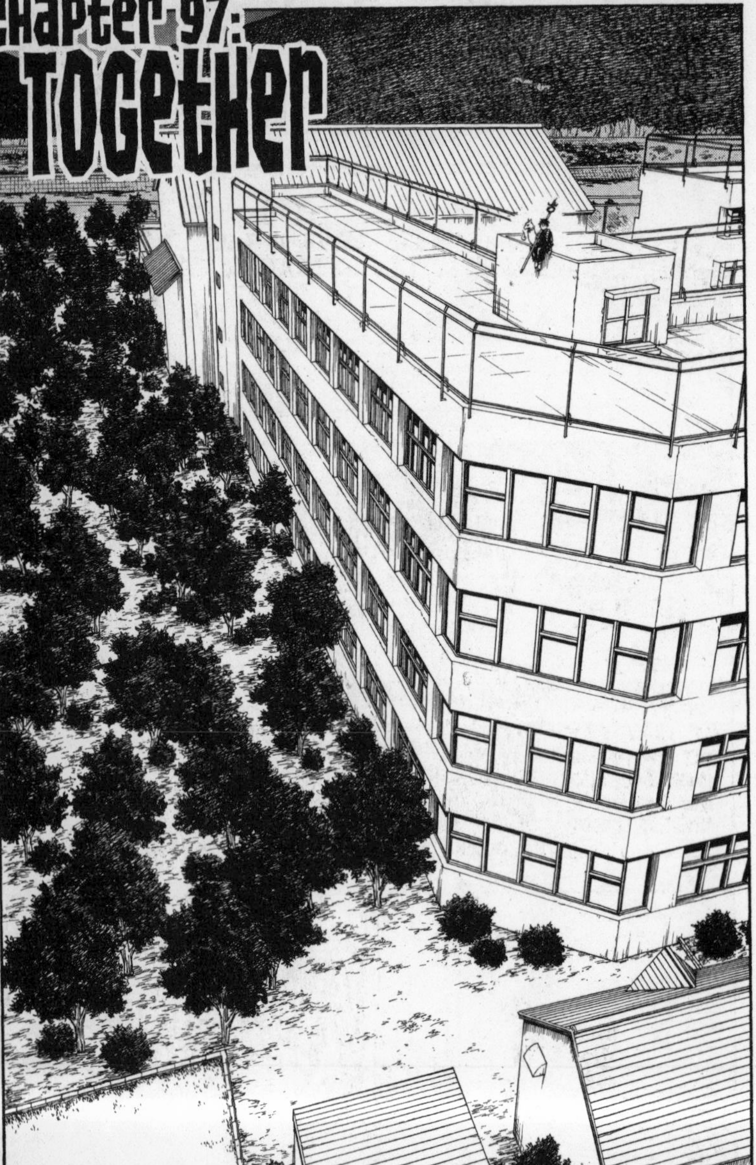

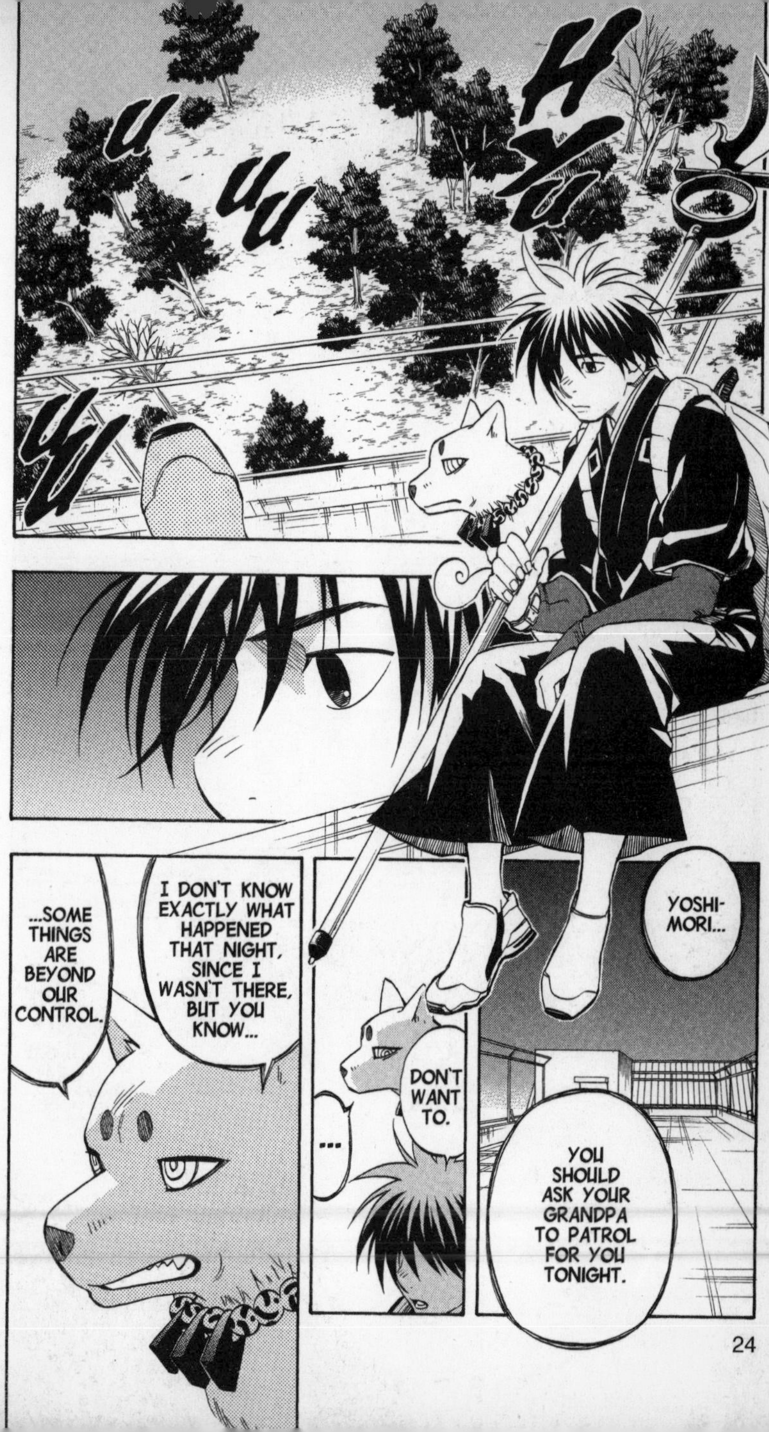
YOSHI-MORI...
YOU SHOULD ASK YOUR GRANDPA TO PATROL FOR YOU TONIGHT.
DON'T WANT TO.
...
I DON'T KNOW EXACTLY WHAT HAPPENED THAT NIGHT, SINCE I WASN'T THERE, BUT YOU KNOW...
...SOME THINGS ARE BEYOND OUR CONTROL.

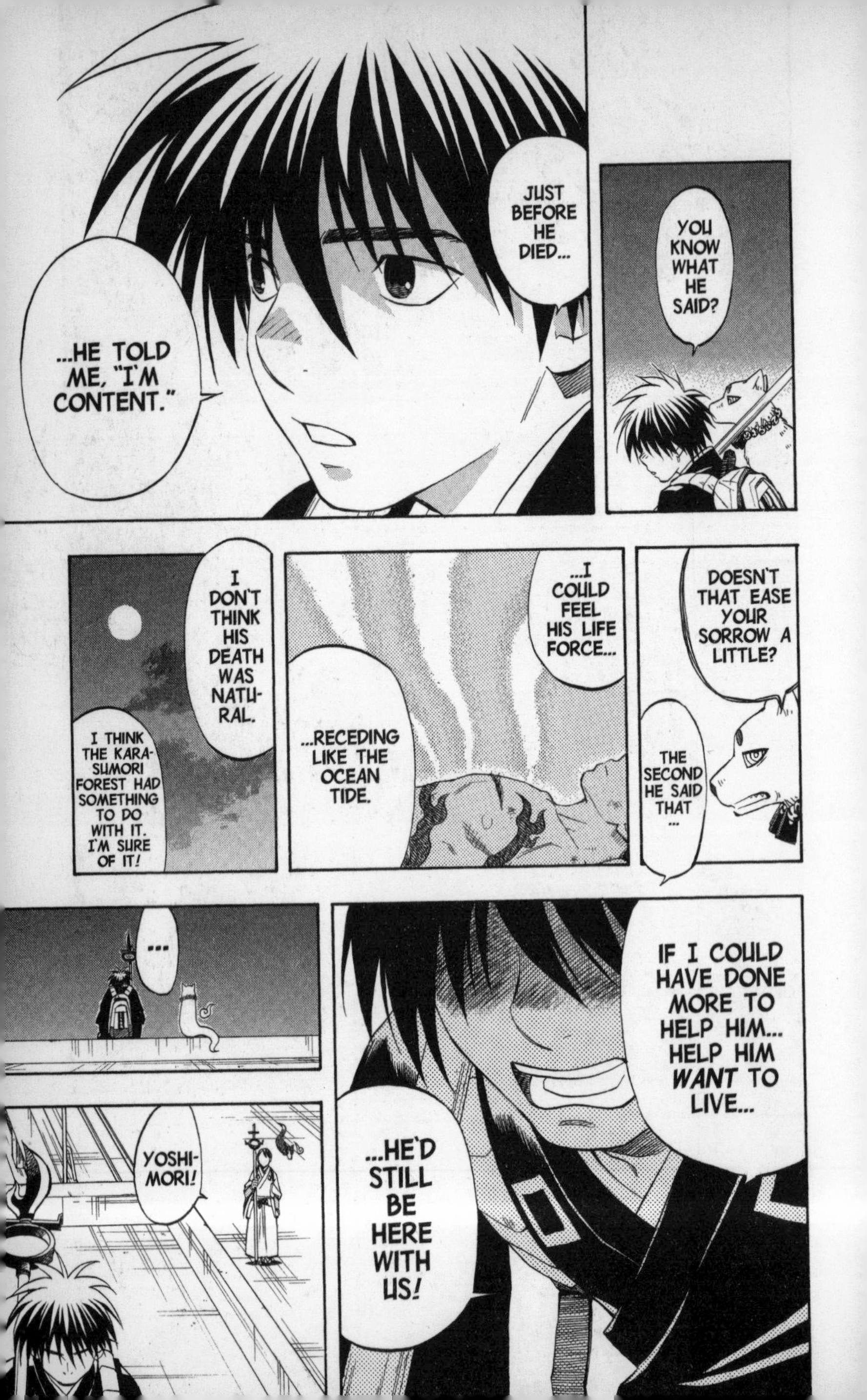
YOU KNOW WHAT HE SAID?
JUST BEFORE HE DIED...
...HE TOLD ME, "I'M CONTENT."
DOESN'T THAT EASE YOUR SORROW A LITTLE?
THE SECOND HE SAID THAT ...
...I COULD FEEL HIS LIFE FORCE...
...RECEDING LIKE THE OCEAN TIDE.
I DON'T THINK HIS DEATH WAS NATURAL.
I THINK THE KARASUMORI FOREST HAD SOMETHING TO DO WITH IT. I'M SURE OF IT!
IF I COULD HAVE DONE MORE TO HELP HIM... HELP HIM WANT TO LIVE...
...HE'D STILL BE HERE WITH US!
...
YOSHIMORI!

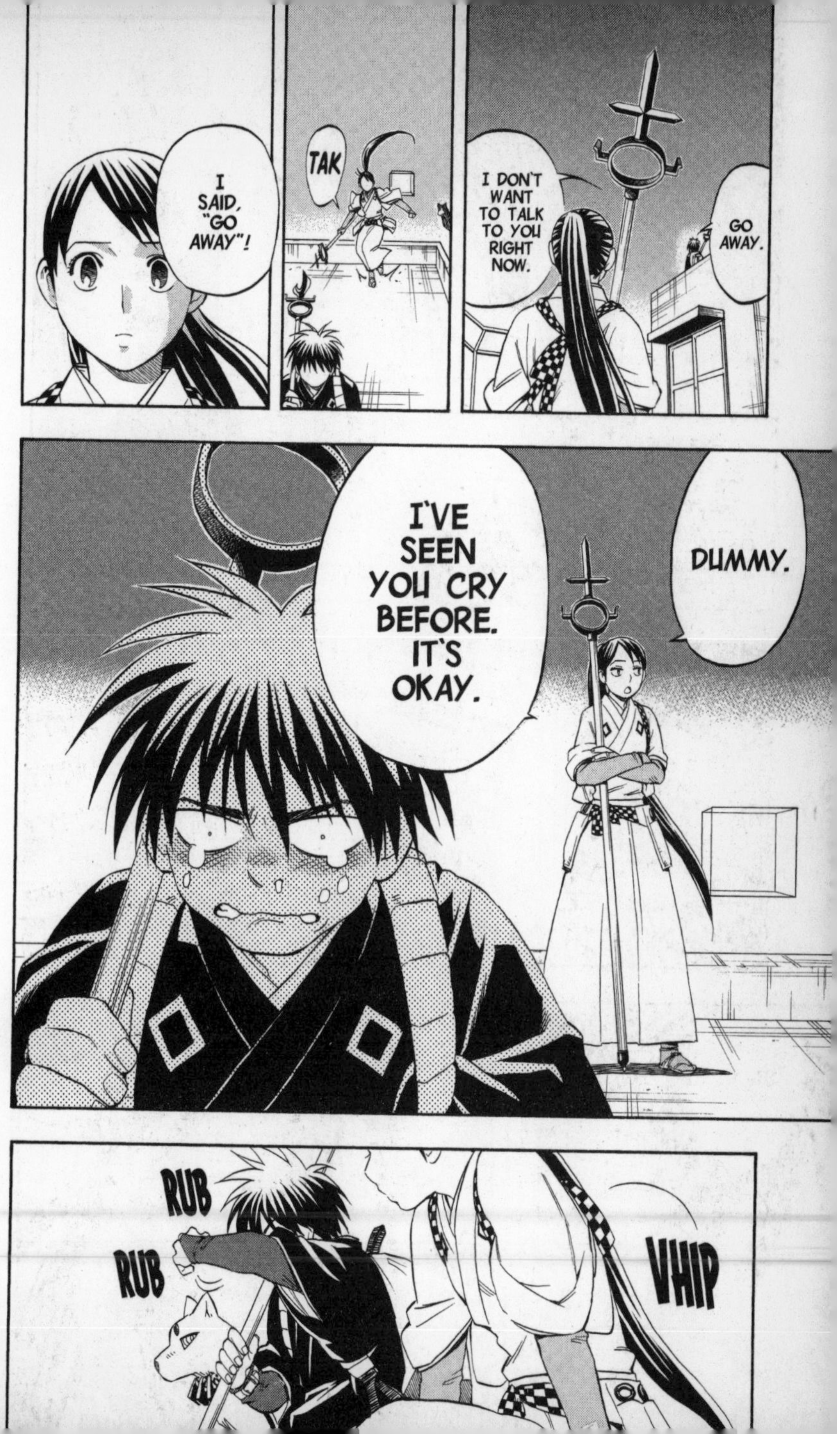
GO AWAY.
I DON'T WANT TO TALK TO YOU RIGHT NOW.
TAK
I SAID, "GO AWAY"!
DUMMY.
I'VE SEEN YOU CRY BEFORE. IT'S OKAY.
VHIP
RUB RUB

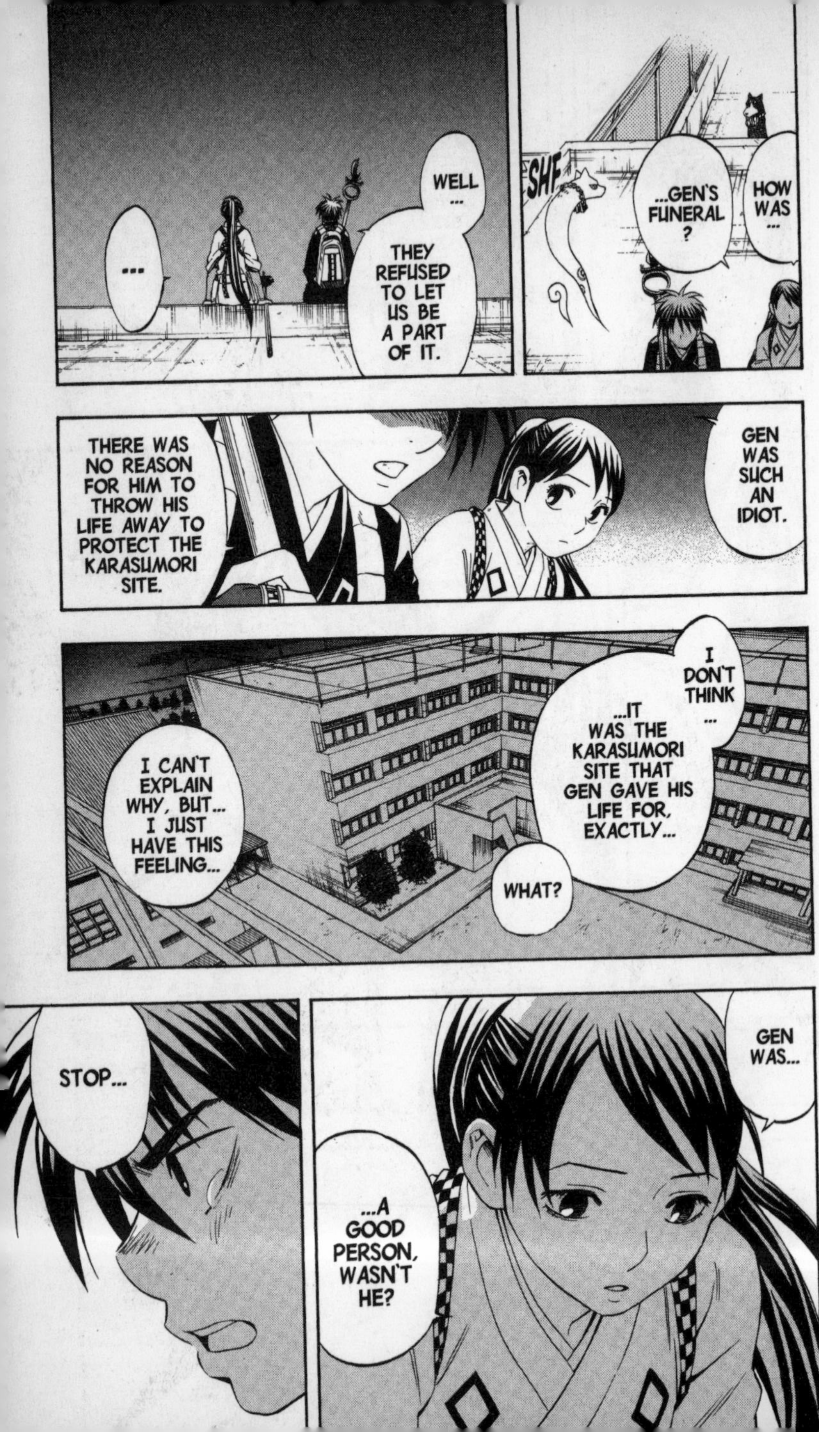
HOW WAS...
...GEN'S FUNERAL?
SHF
WELL...
THEY REFUSED TO LET US BE A PART OF IT.
...
GEN WAS SUCH AN IDIOT.
THERE WAS NO REASON FOR HIM TO THROW HIS LIFE AWAY TO PROTECT THE KARASUMORI SITE.
I DON'T THINK...
...IT WAS THE KARASUMORI SITE THAT GEN GAVE HIS LIFE FOR, EXACTLY...
WHAT?
I CAN'T EXPLAIN WHY, BUT... I JUST HAVE THIS FEELING...
GEN WAS...
...A GOOD PERSON, WASN'T HE?
STOP...

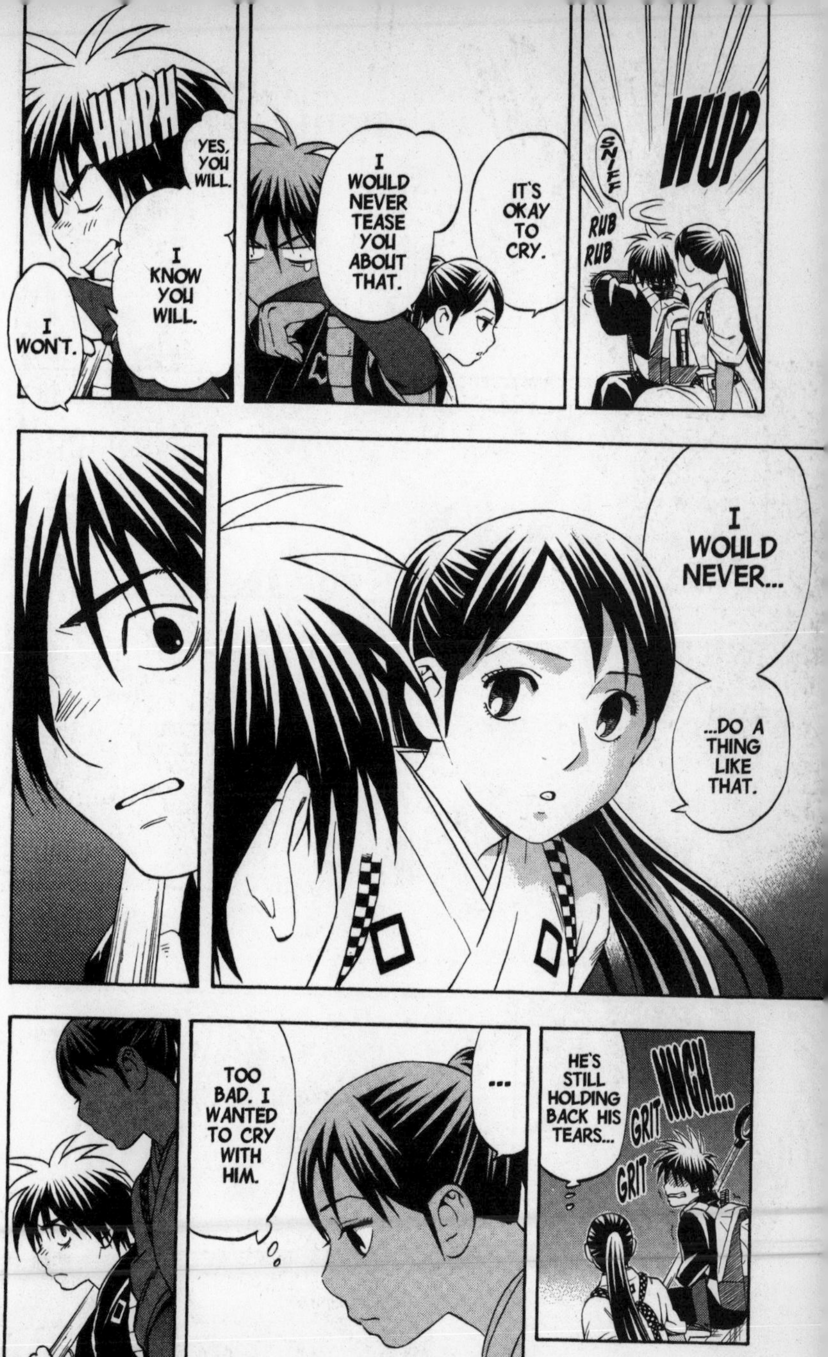
WUP
SNIFF
RUB RUB
IT'S OKAY TO CRY.
I WOULD NEVER TEASE YOU ABOUT THAT.
YES, YOU WILL.
HMPH
I KNOW YOU WILL.
I WON'T.
I WOULD NEVER...
...DO A THING LIKE THAT.
NNGH...
HE'S STILL HOLDING BACK HIS TEARS...
GRIT GRIT
...
TOO BAD. I WANTED TO CRY WITH HIM.

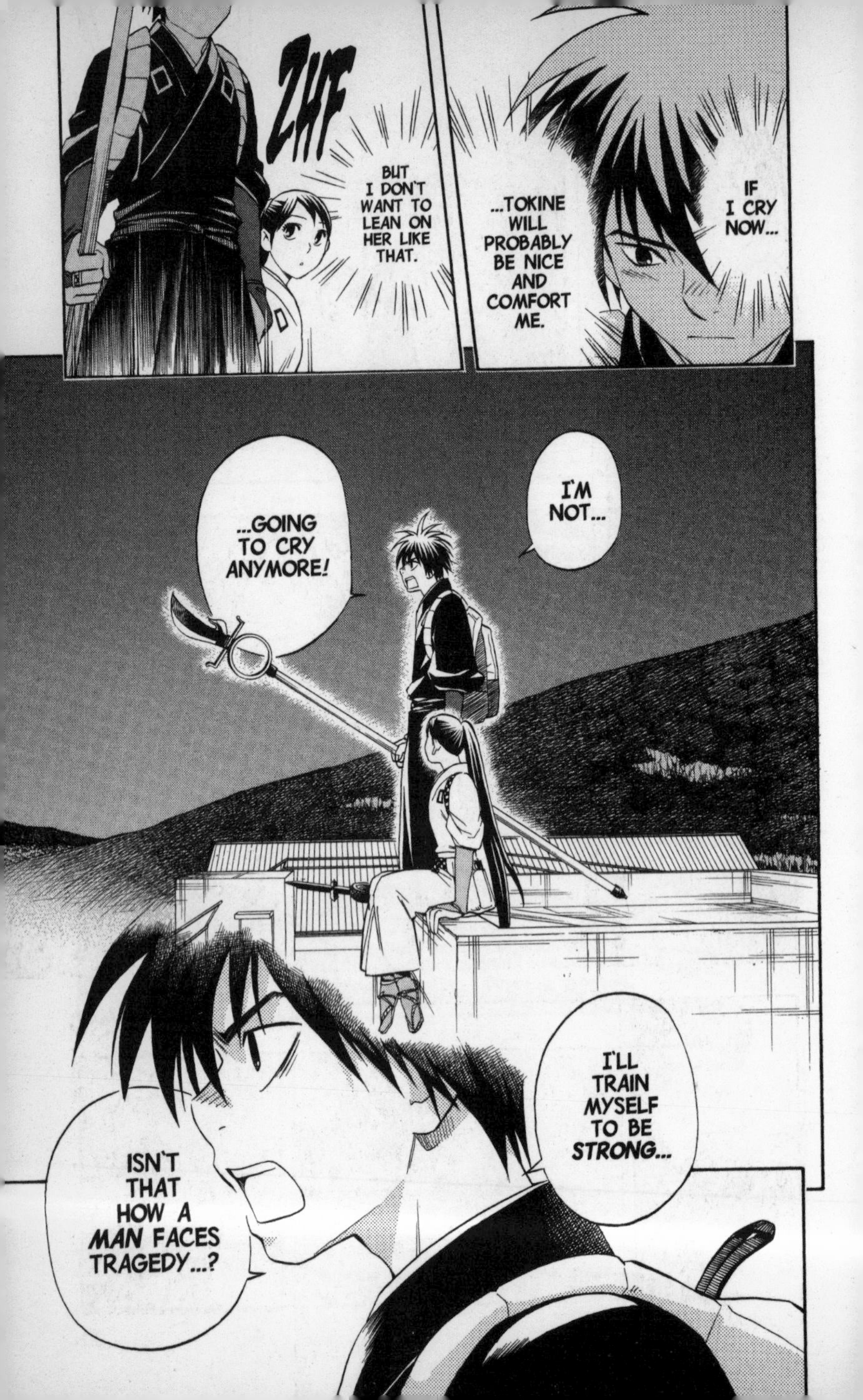

IF I CRY NOW...
...TOKINE WILL PROBABLY BE NICE AND COMFORT ME.
ZHF
BUT I DON'T WANT TO LEAN ON HER LIKE THAT.
I'M NOT...
...GOING TO CRY ANYMORE!
I'LL TRAIN MYSELF TO BE *STRONG*...
ISN'T THAT HOW A *MAN* FACES TRAGEDY...?

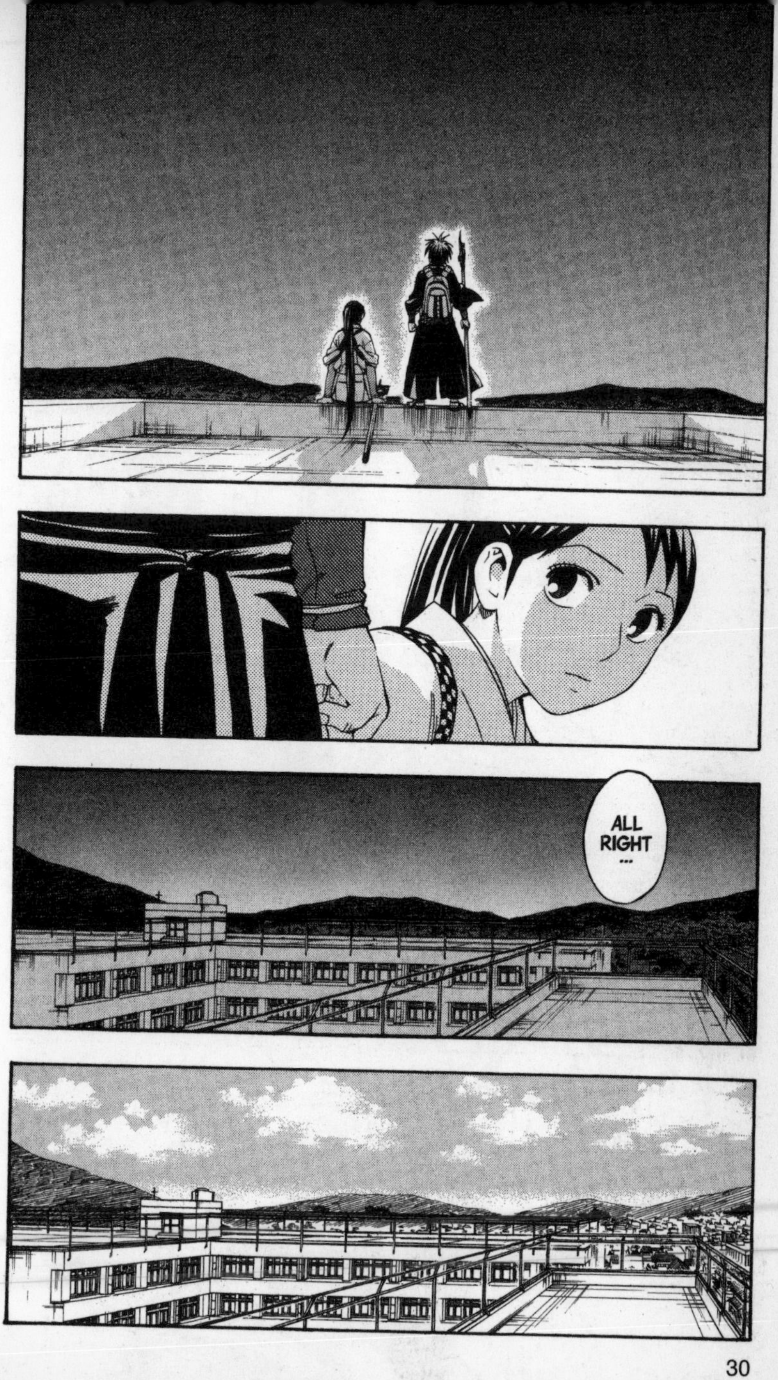
ALL RIGHT ...

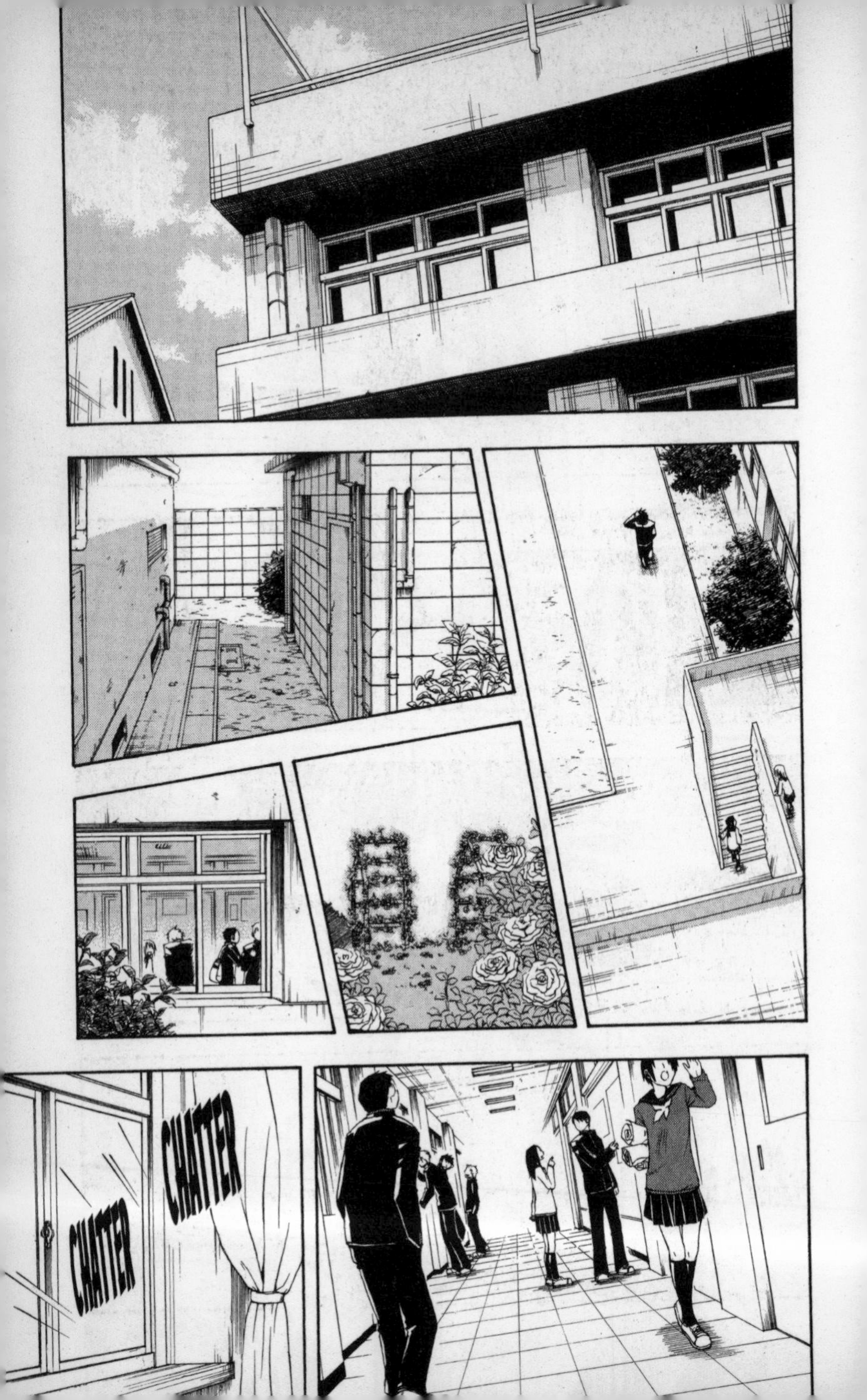
CHATTER
CHATTER

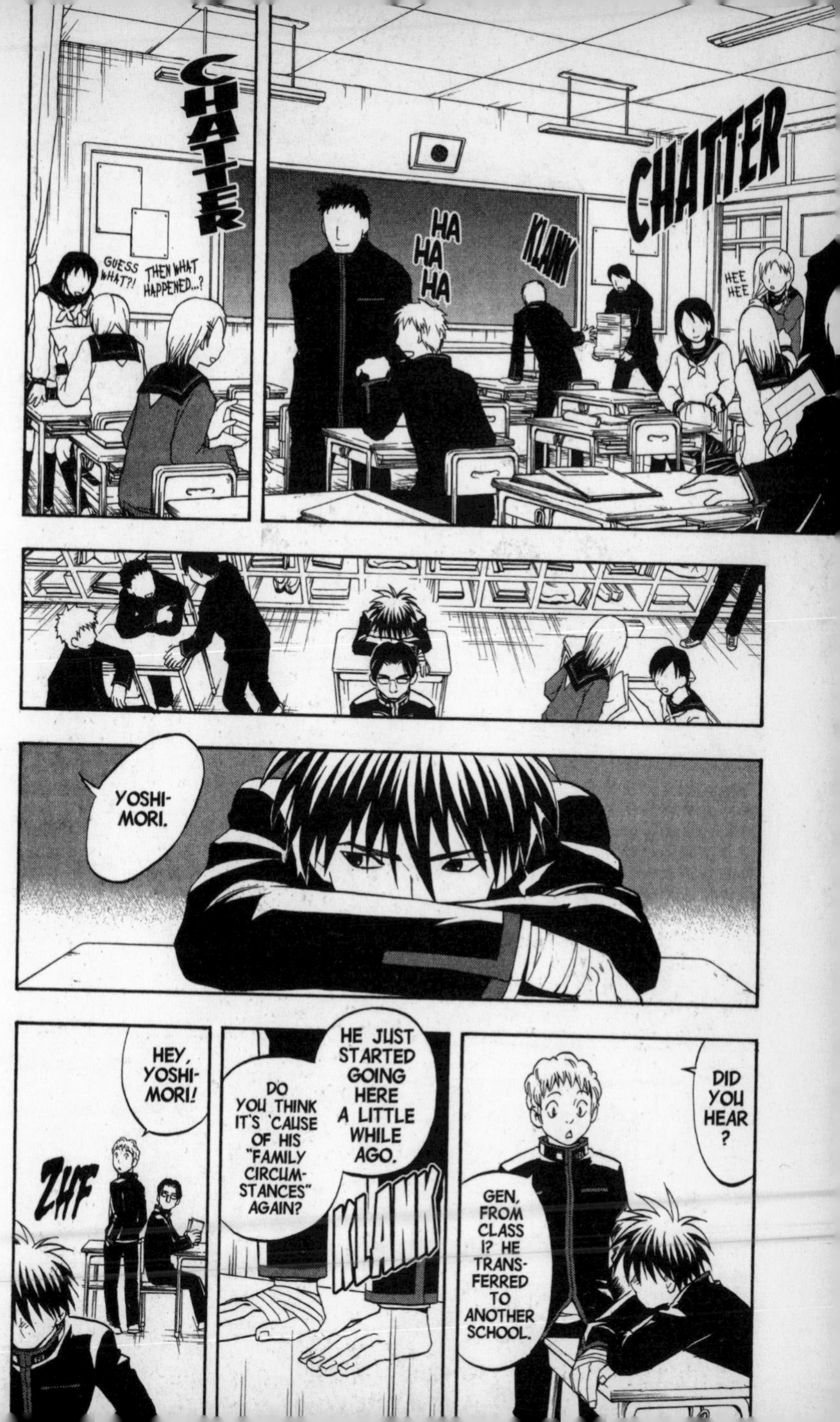
CHATTER
HEE HEE
KLANK
HA HA HA
CHATTER
THEN WHAT HAPPENED...?
GUESS WHAT?!
YOSHIMORI.
DID YOU HEAR?
GEN, FROM CLASS 1? HE TRANSFERRED TO ANOTHER SCHOOL.
HE JUST STARTED GOING HERE A LITTLE WHILE AGO.
DO YOU THINK IT'S 'CAUSE OF HIS "FAMILY CIRCUMSTANCES" AGAIN?
KLANK
HEY, YOSHIMORI!
ZHF

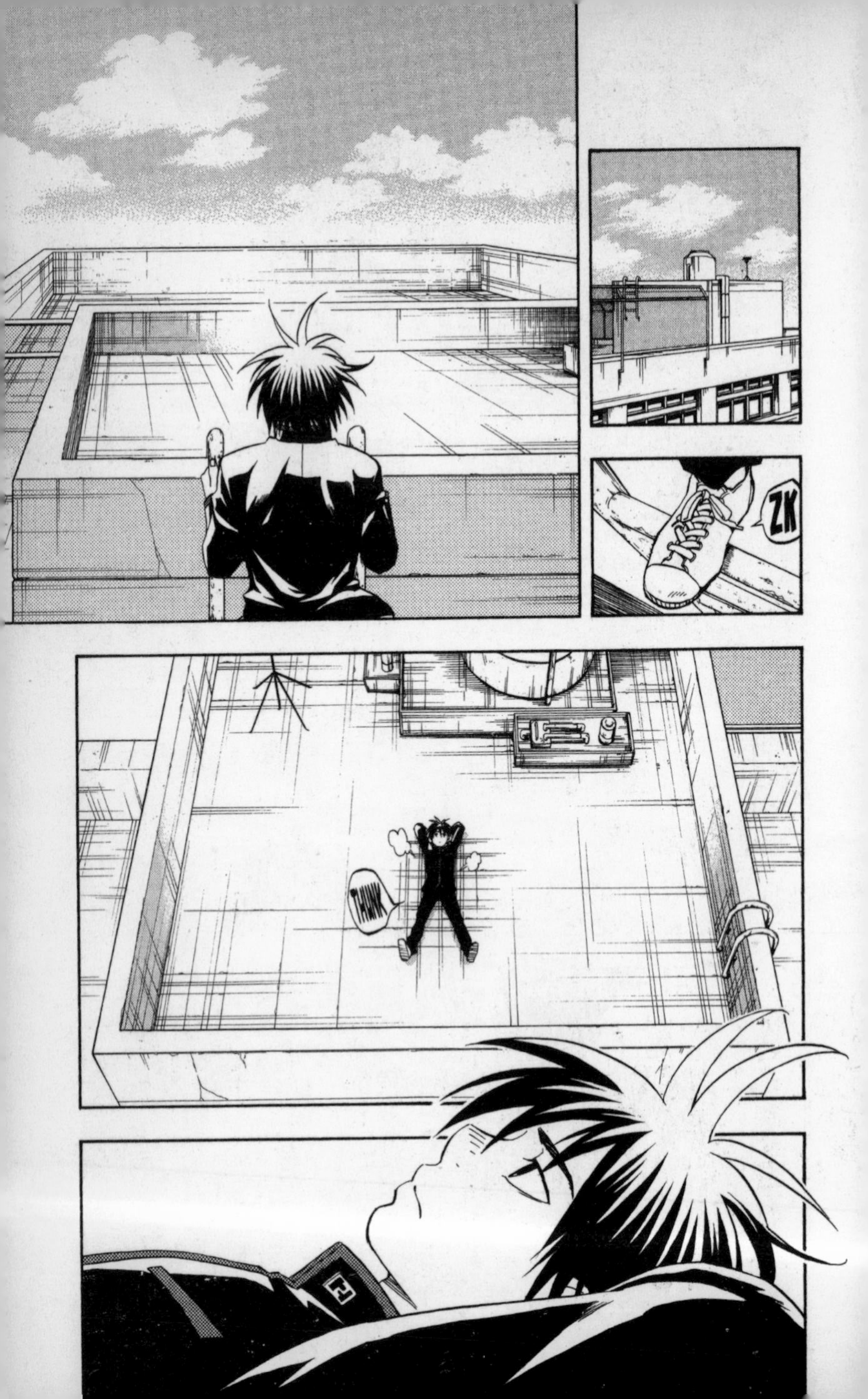
ZK
THUNK

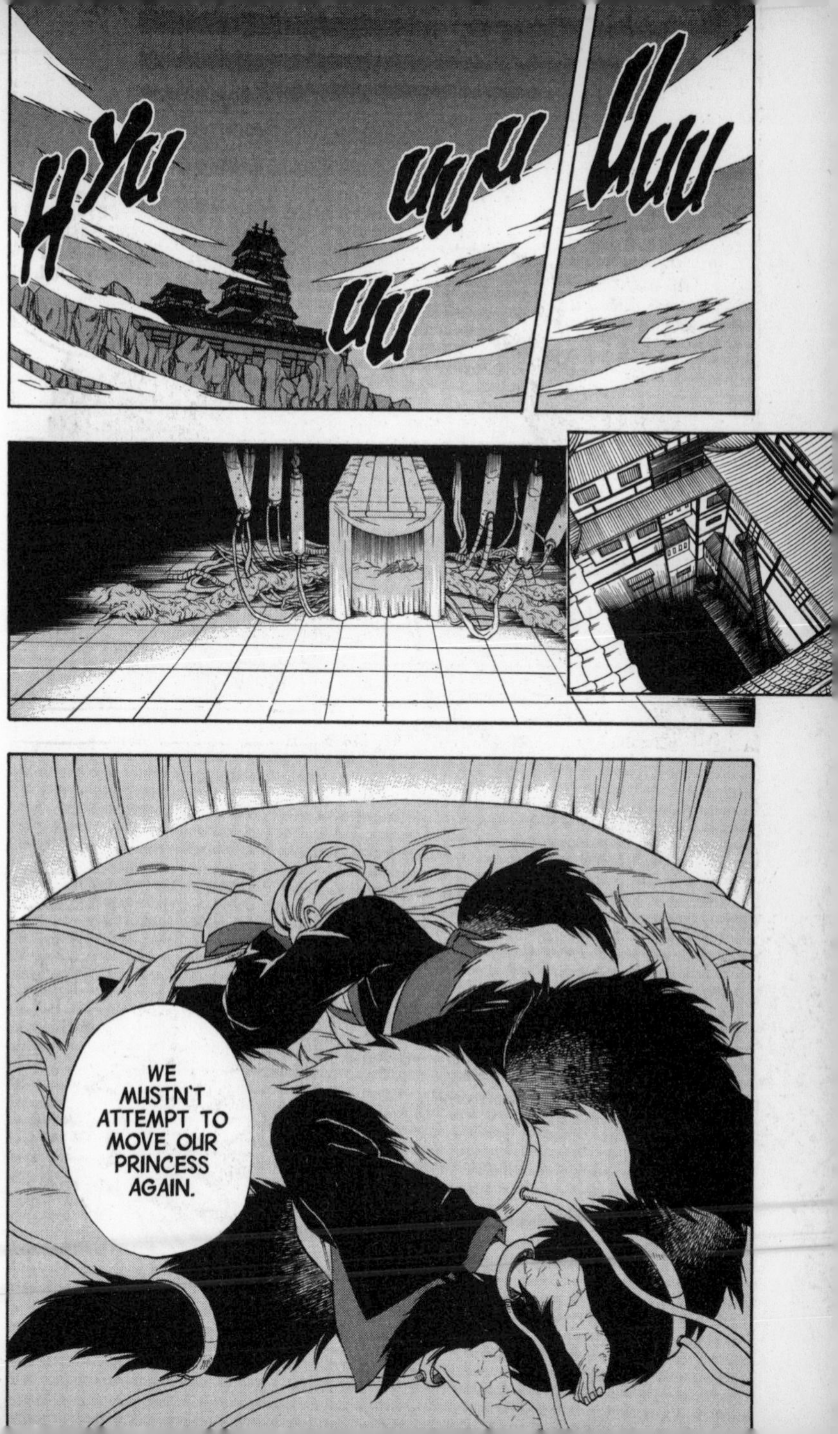
Hyu
uuru
uu
Uuu
WE MUSTN'T ATTEMPT TO MOVE OUR PRINCESS AGAIN.

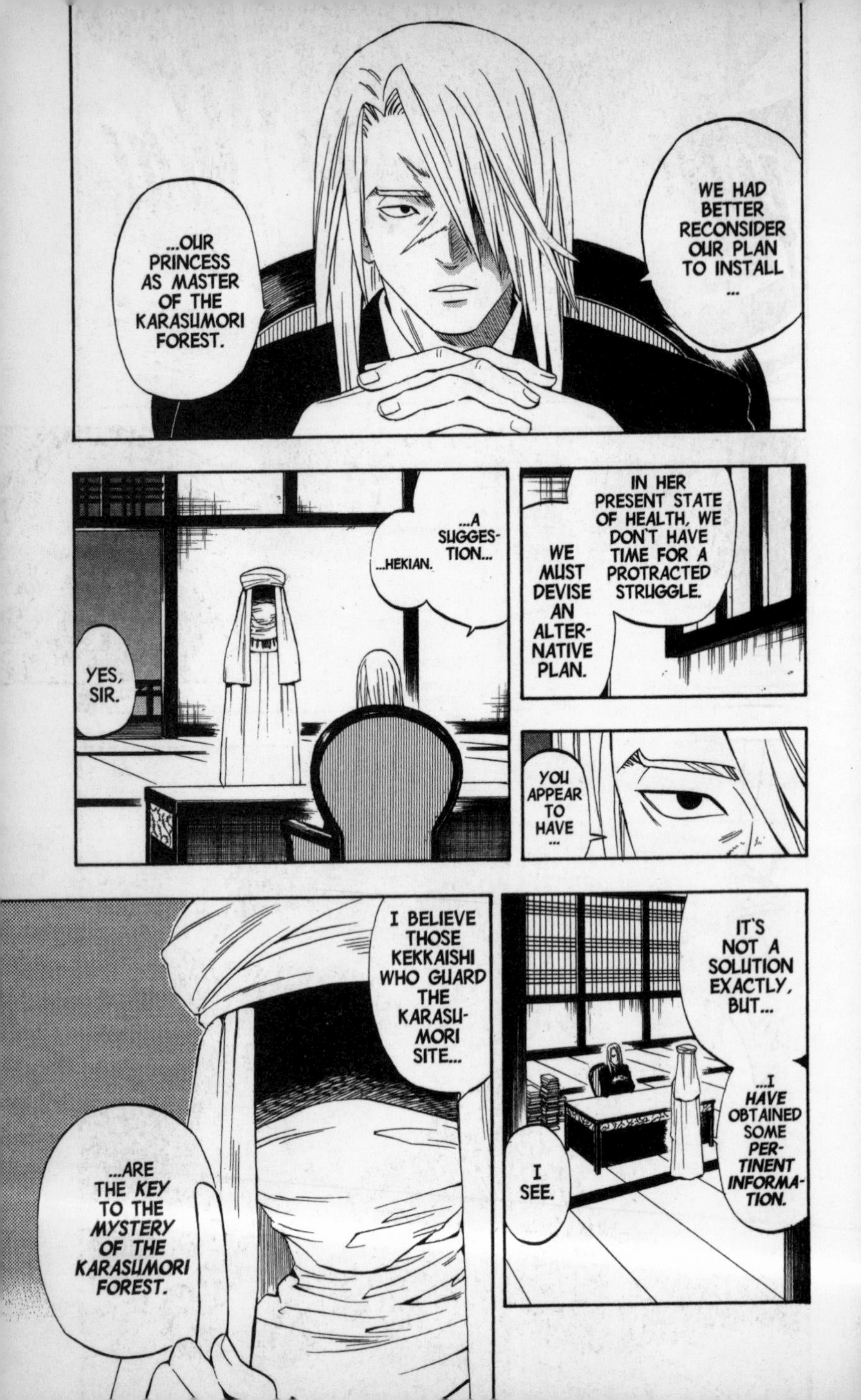
WE HAD BETTER RECONSIDER OUR PLAN TO INSTALL ...
...OUR PRINCESS AS MASTER OF THE KARASUMORI FOREST.
IN HER PRESENT STATE OF HEALTH, WE DON'T HAVE TIME FOR A PROTRACTED STRUGGLE.
WE MUST DEVISE AN ALTERNATIVE PLAN.
YOU APPEAR TO HAVE ...
...A SUGGESTION... ...HEKIAN.
YES, SIR.
IT'S NOT A SOLUTION EXACTLY, BUT...
...I *HAVE* OBTAINED SOME *PERTINENT INFORMATION.*
I SEE.
I BELIEVE THOSE KEKKAISHI WHO GUARD THE KARASUMORI SITE...
...ARE THE *KEY* TO THE *MYSTERY* OF THE KARASUMORI FOREST.

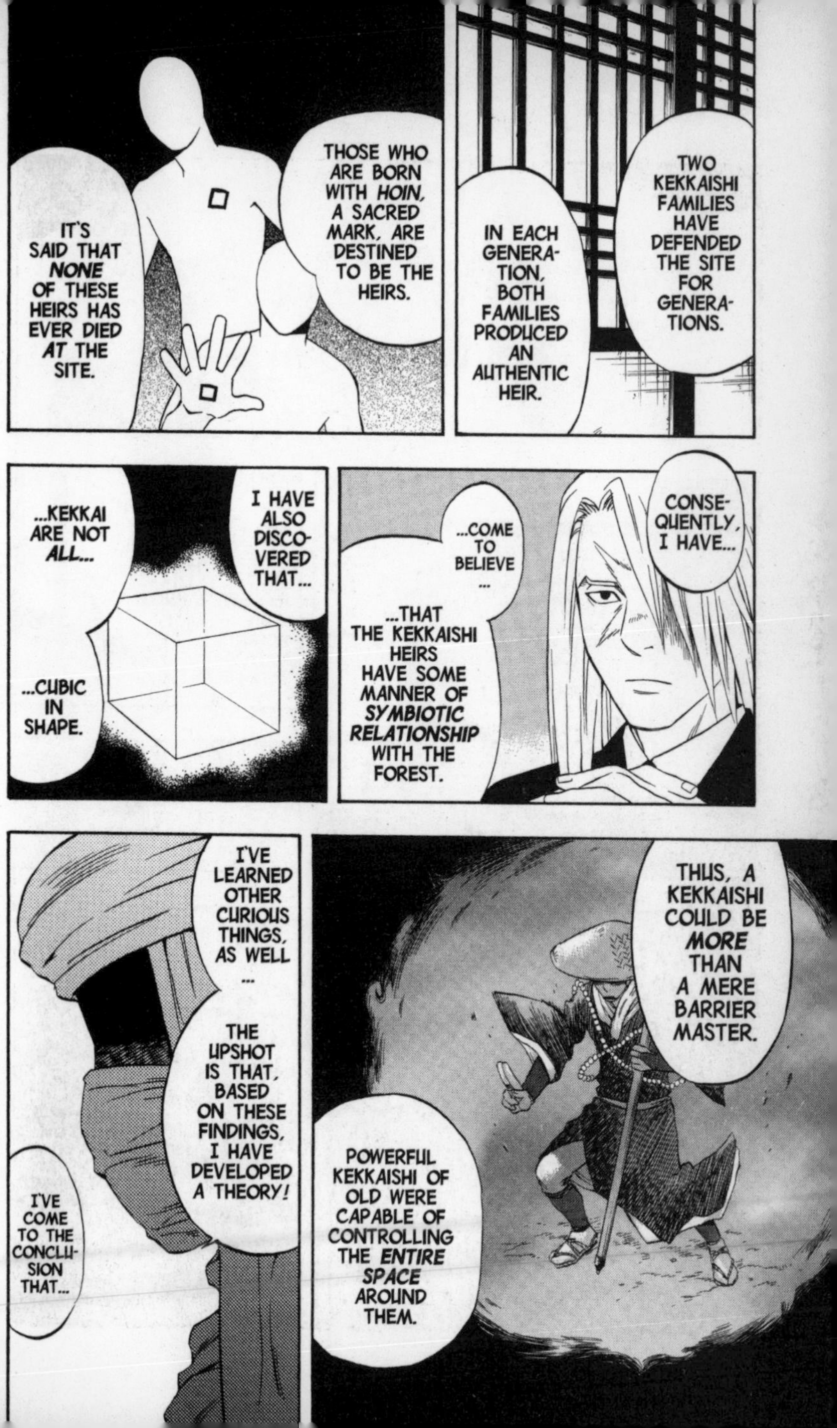
TWO KEKKAISHI FAMILIES HAVE DEFENDED THE SITE FOR GENERATIONS.
IN EACH GENERATION, BOTH FAMILIES PRODUCED AN AUTHENTIC HEIR.
THOSE WHO ARE BORN WITH HOIN, A SACRED MARK, ARE DESTINED TO BE THE HEIRS.
IT'S SAID THAT NONE OF THESE HEIRS HAS EVER DIED AT THE SITE.
CONSEQUENTLY, I HAVE...
...COME TO BELIEVE...
...THAT THE KEKKAISHI HEIRS HAVE SOME MANNER OF SYMBIOTIC RELATIONSHIP WITH THE FOREST.
I HAVE ALSO DISCOVERED THAT...
...KEKKAI ARE NOT ALL...
...CUBIC IN SHAPE.
THUS, A KEKKAISHI COULD BE MORE THAN A MERE BARRIER MASTER.
POWERFUL KEKKAISHI OF OLD WERE CAPABLE OF CONTROLLING THE ENTIRE SPACE AROUND THEM.
I'VE LEARNED OTHER CURIOUS THINGS, AS WELL...
THE UPSHOT IS THAT, BASED ON THESE FINDINGS, I HAVE DEVELOPED A THEORY!
I'VE COME TO THE CONCLUSION THAT...

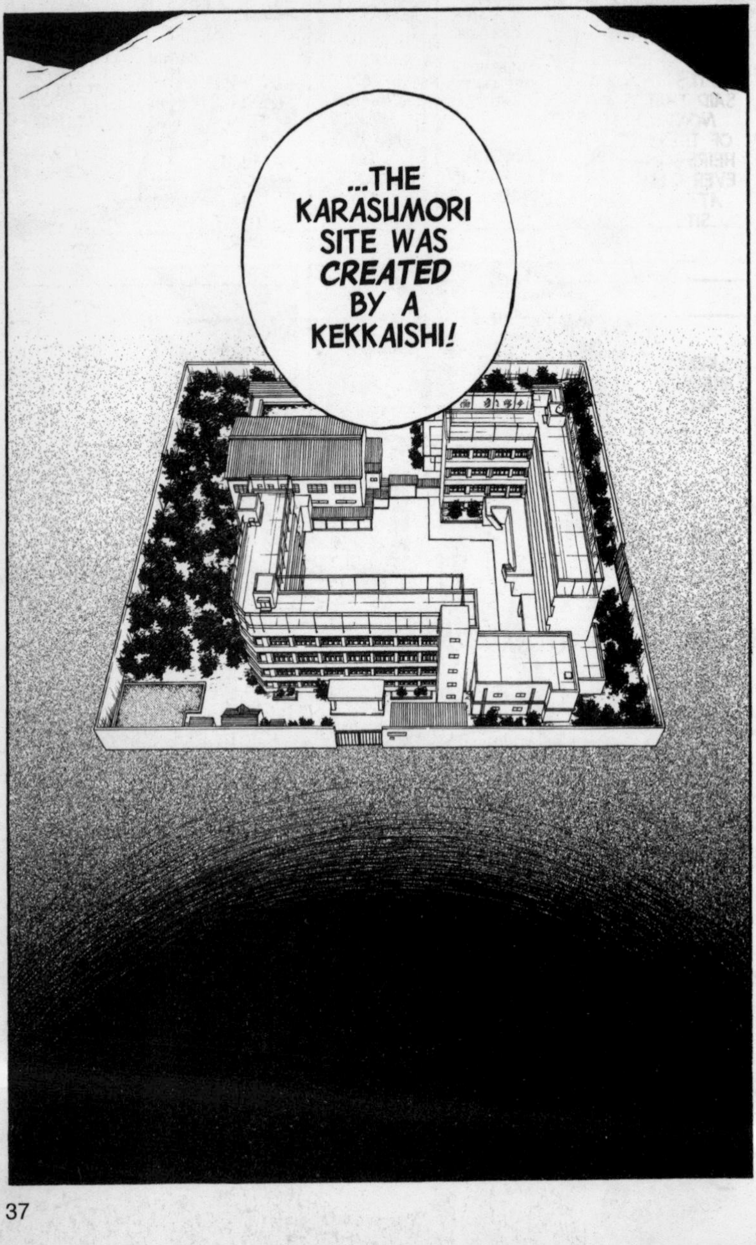
...THE KARASUMORI SITE WAS CREATED BY A KEKKAISHI!

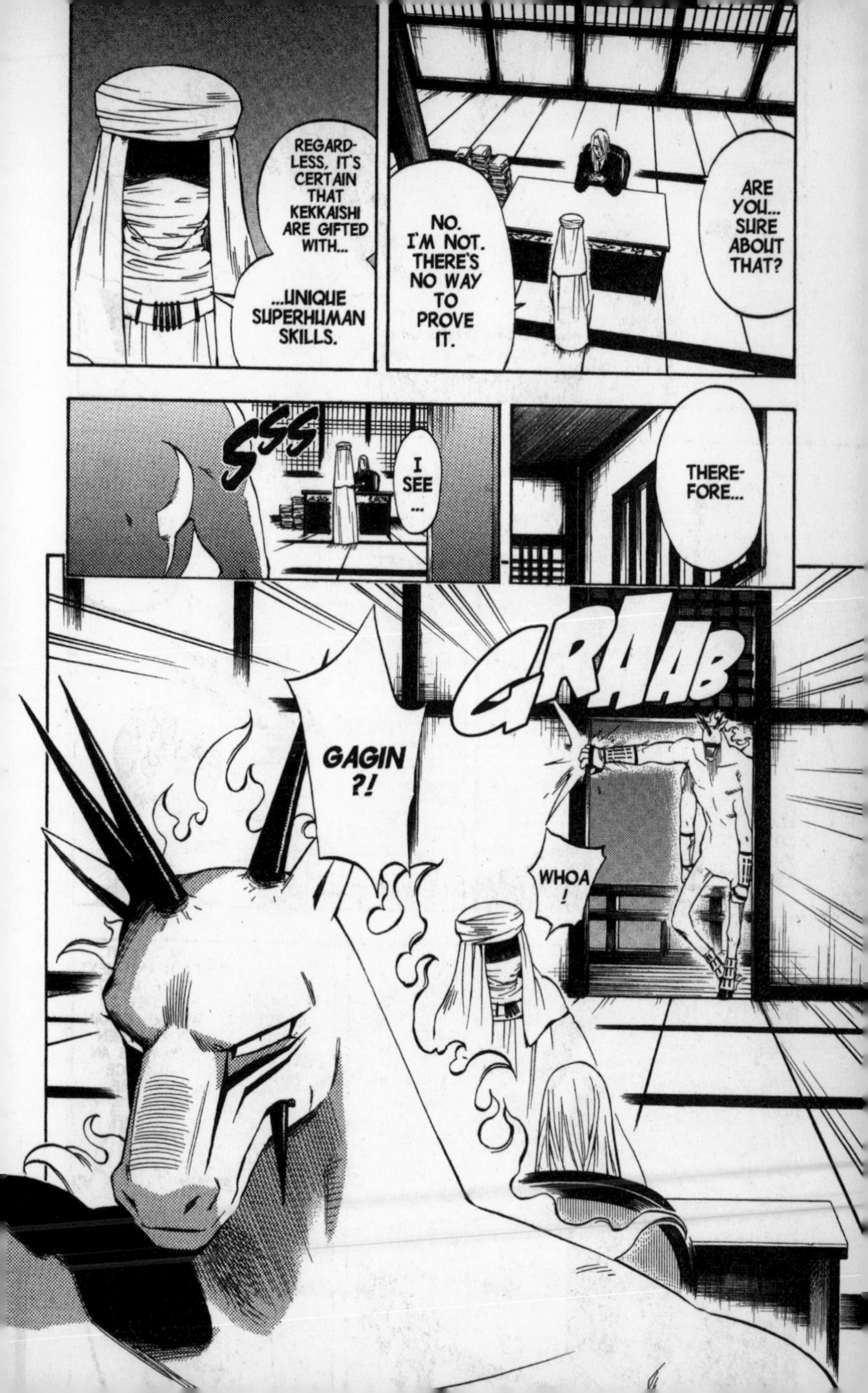
ARE YOU... SURE ABOUT THAT?
NO. I'M NOT. THERE'S NO WAY TO PROVE IT.
REGARDLESS, IT'S CERTAIN THAT KEKKAISHI ARE GIFTED WITH...
...UNIQUE SUPERHUMAN SKILLS.
THEREFORE...
SSS
I SEE ...
GRAAB
WHOA!
GAGIN ?!

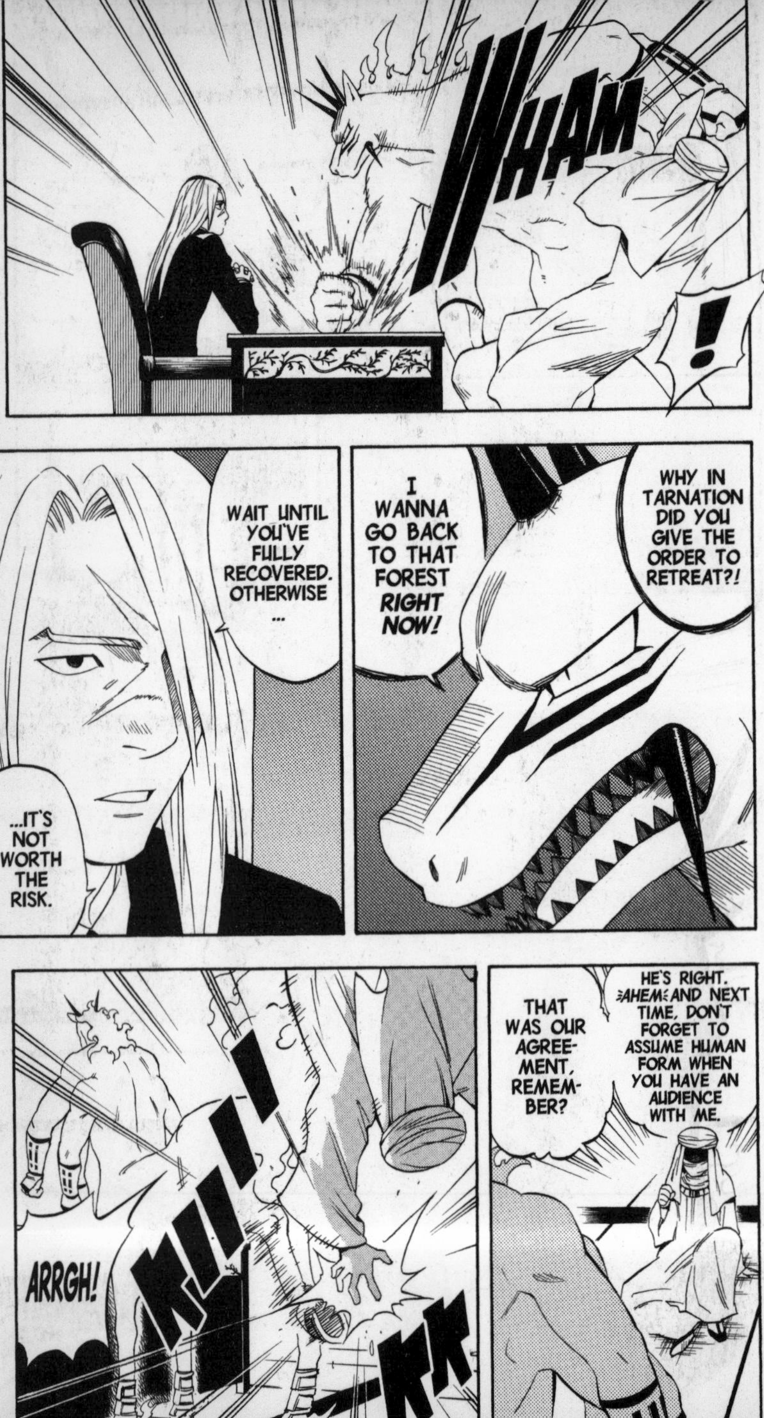
WHAM
!
WHY IN TARNATION DID YOU GIVE THE ORDER TO RETREAT?!
I WANNA GO BACK TO THAT FOREST RIGHT NOW!
WAIT UNTIL YOU'VE FULLY RECOVERED. OTHERWISE ...
...IT'S NOT WORTH THE RISK.
HE'S RIGHT. AHEM AND NEXT TIME, DON'T FORGET TO ASSUME HUMAN FORM WHEN YOU HAVE AN AUDIENCE WITH ME.
THAT WAS OUR AGREEMENT, REMEMBER?
ARRGH!

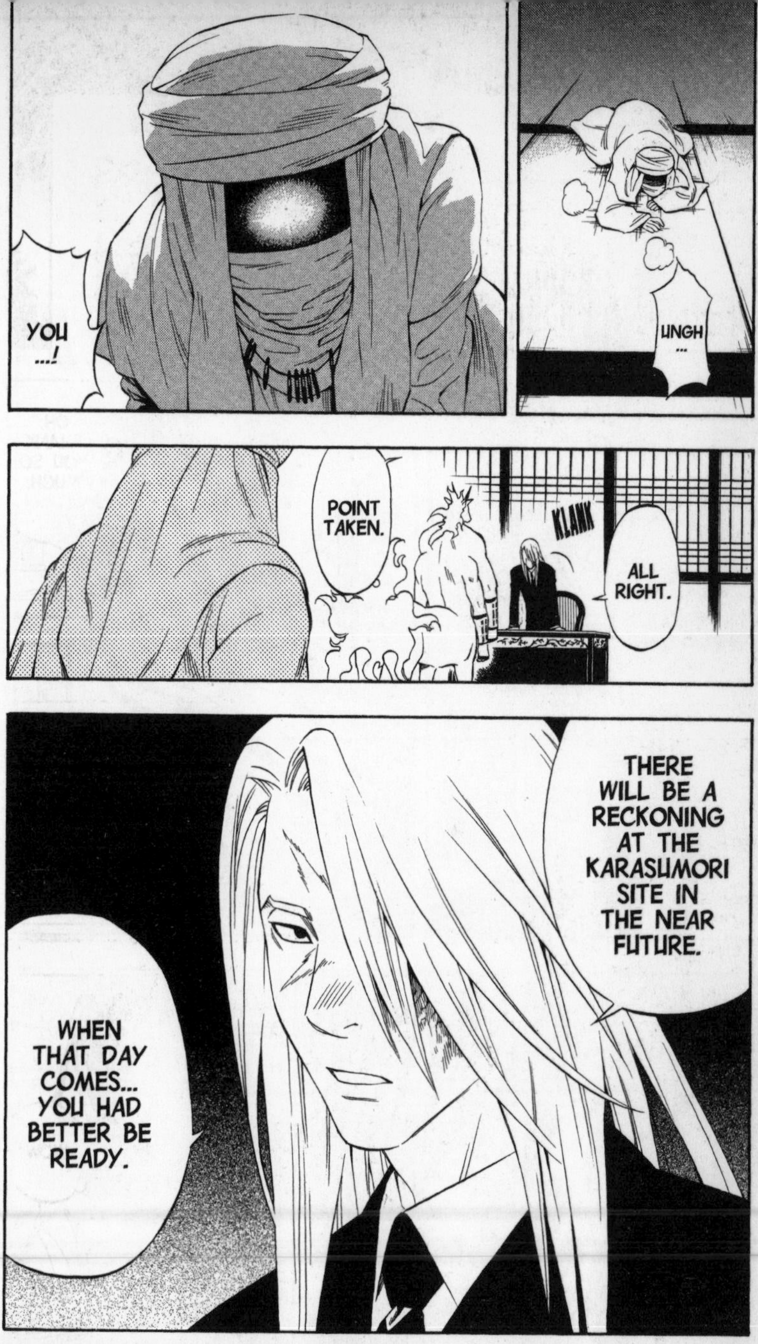
UNGH ...
YOU ...!
ALL RIGHT.
KLANK
POINT TAKEN.
THERE WILL BE A RECKONING AT THE KARASUMORI SITE IN THE NEAR FUTURE.
WHEN THAT DAY COMES... YOU HAD BETTER BE READY.

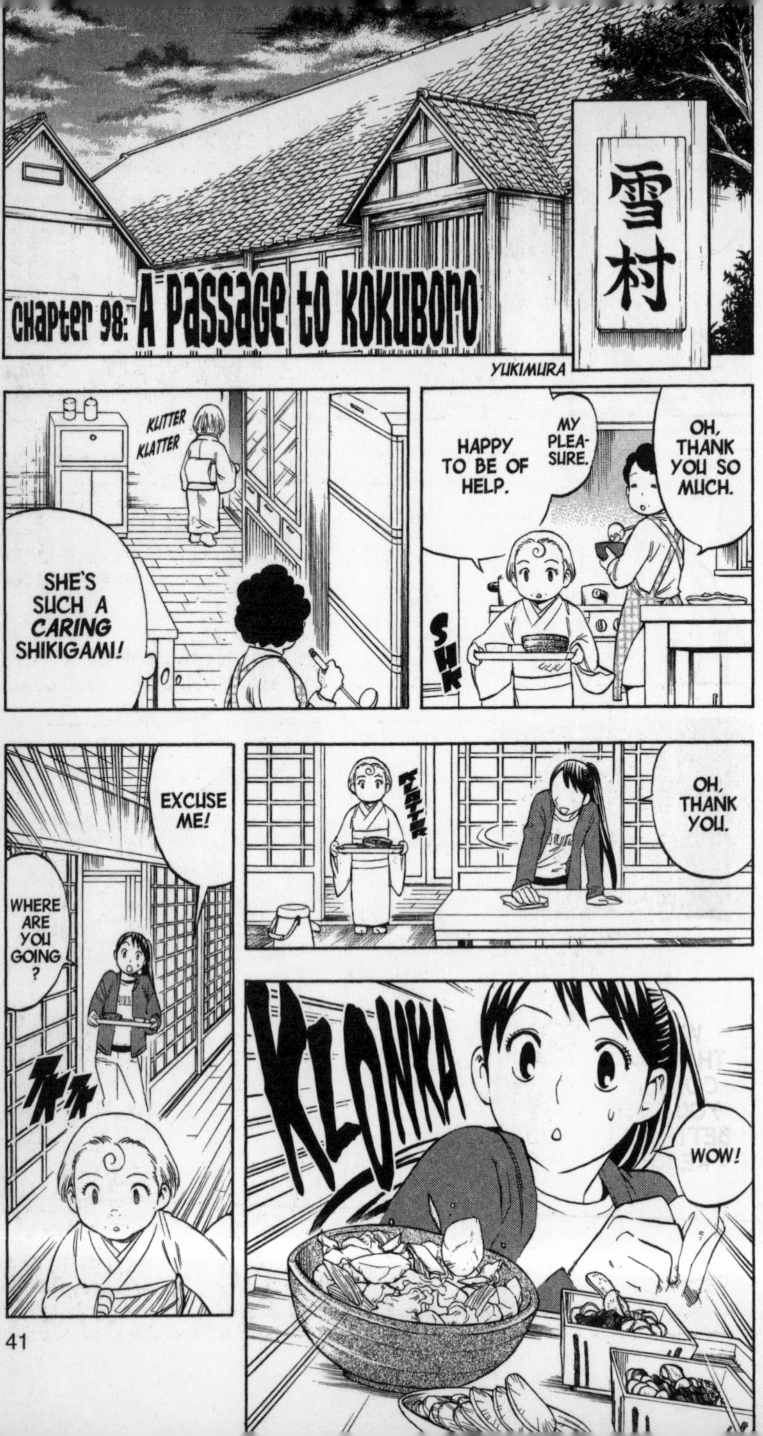
Chapter 98: A Passage to Kokuboro
雪村
YUKIMURA
OH, THANK YOU SO MUCH.
MY PLEASURE.
HAPPY TO BE OF HELP.
SHK
KLITTER KLATTER
SHE'S SUCH A CARING SHIKIGAMI!
OH, THANK YOU.
KLATTER
WOW!
KLONKA
EXCUSE ME!
WHERE ARE YOU GOING?

Chapter 98: A Passage to Kokuboro

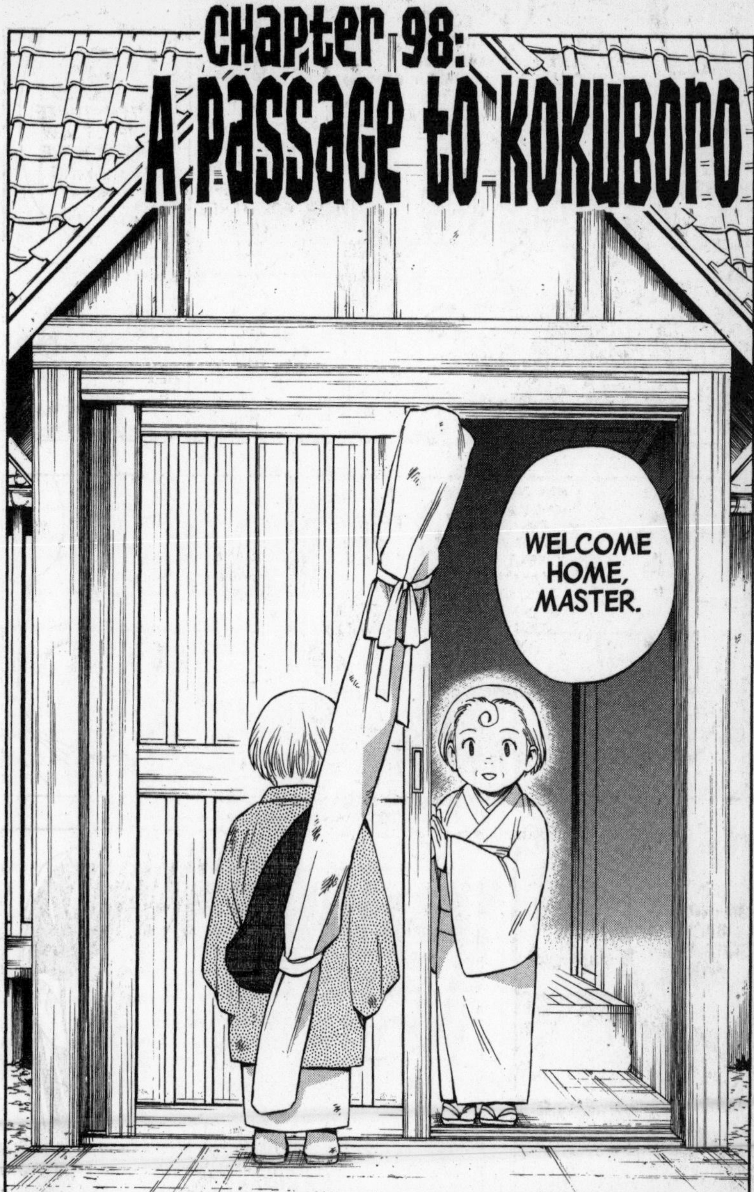
WELCOME HOME, MASTER.

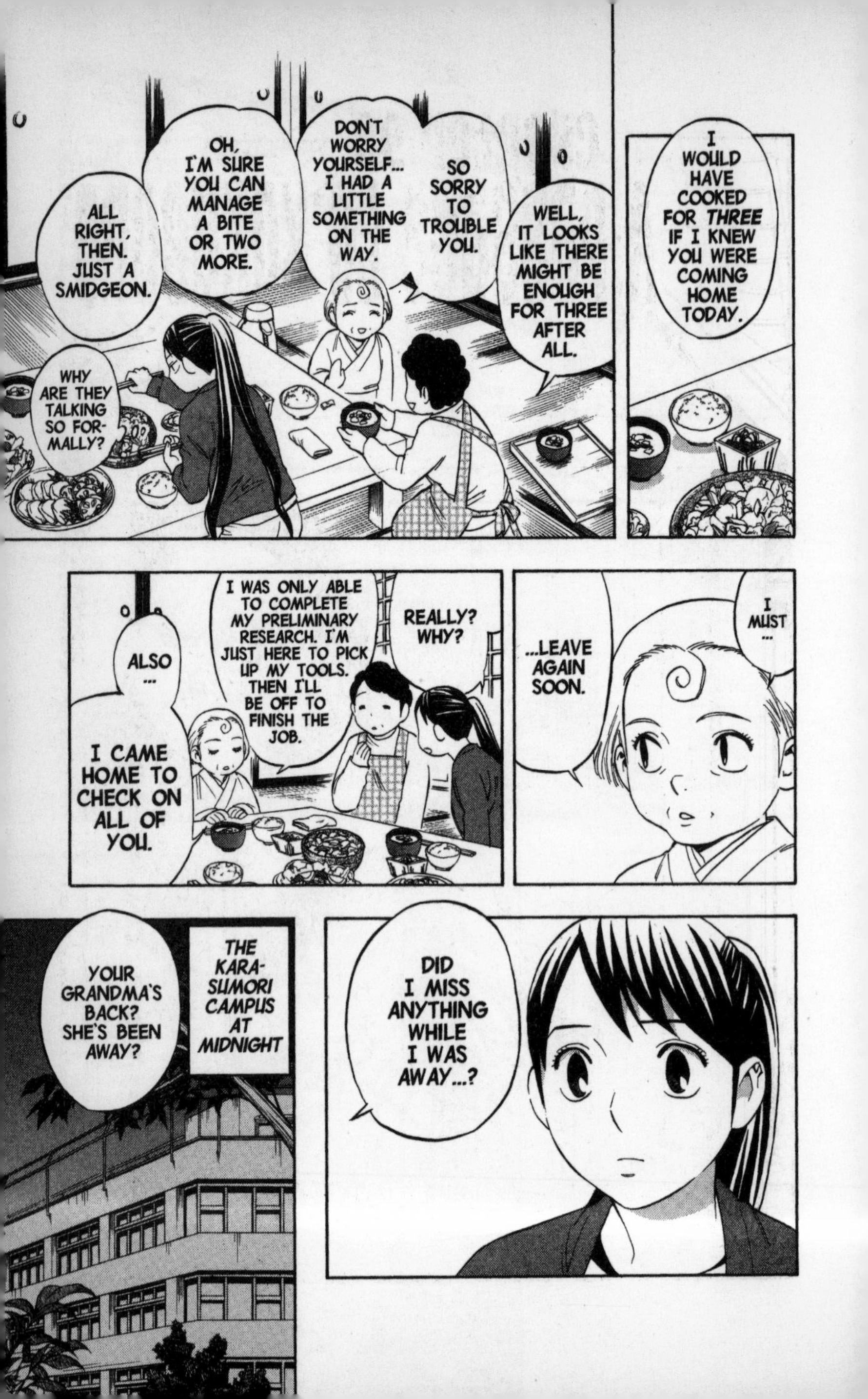
I WOULD HAVE COOKED FOR *THREE* IF I KNEW YOU WERE COMING HOME TODAY.
WELL, IT LOOKS LIKE THERE MIGHT BE ENOUGH FOR THREE AFTER ALL.
SO SORRY TO TROUBLE YOU.
DON'T WORRY YOURSELF... I HAD A LITTLE SOMETHING ON THE WAY.
OH, I'M SURE YOU CAN MANAGE A BITE OR TWO MORE.
ALL RIGHT, THEN. JUST A SMIDGEON.
WHY ARE THEY TALKING SO FOR-MALLY?
I MUST ...
...LEAVE AGAIN SOON.
REALLY? WHY?
I WAS ONLY ABLE TO COMPLETE MY PRELIMINARY RESEARCH. I'M JUST HERE TO PICK UP MY TOOLS. THEN I'LL BE OFF TO FINISH THE JOB.
ALSO ...
I CAME HOME TO CHECK ON ALL OF YOU.
DID I MISS ANYTHING WHILE I WAS AWAY...?
THE KARA-SUMORI CAMPUS AT MIDNIGHT
YOUR GRANDMA'S BACK? SHE'S BEEN AWAY?

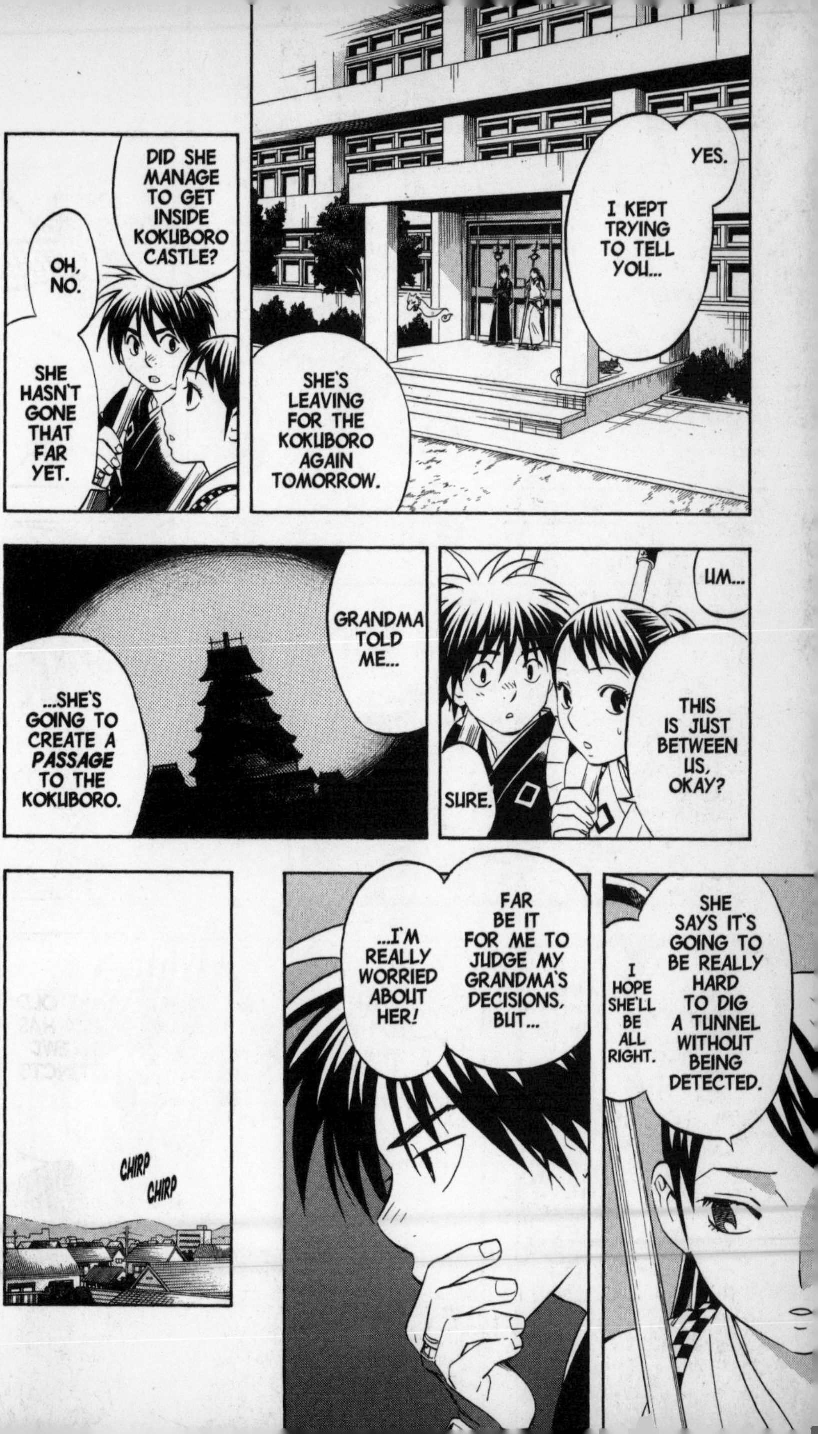
YES.
I KEPT TRYING TO TELL YOU...
SHE'S LEAVING FOR THE KOKUBORO AGAIN TOMORROW.
DID SHE MANAGE TO GET INSIDE KOKUBORO CASTLE?
OH, NO.
SHE HASN'T GONE THAT FAR YET.
UM...
THIS IS JUST BETWEEN US, OKAY?
SURE.
GRANDMA TOLD ME...
...SHE'S GOING TO CREATE A *PASSAGE* TO THE KOKUBORO.
SHE SAYS IT'S GOING TO BE REALLY HARD TO DIG A TUNNEL WITHOUT BEING DETECTED.
I HOPE SHE'LL BE ALL RIGHT.
FAR BE IT FOR ME TO JUDGE MY GRANDMA'S DECISIONS, BUT...
...I'M REALLY WORRIED ABOUT HER!
CHIRP
CHIRP

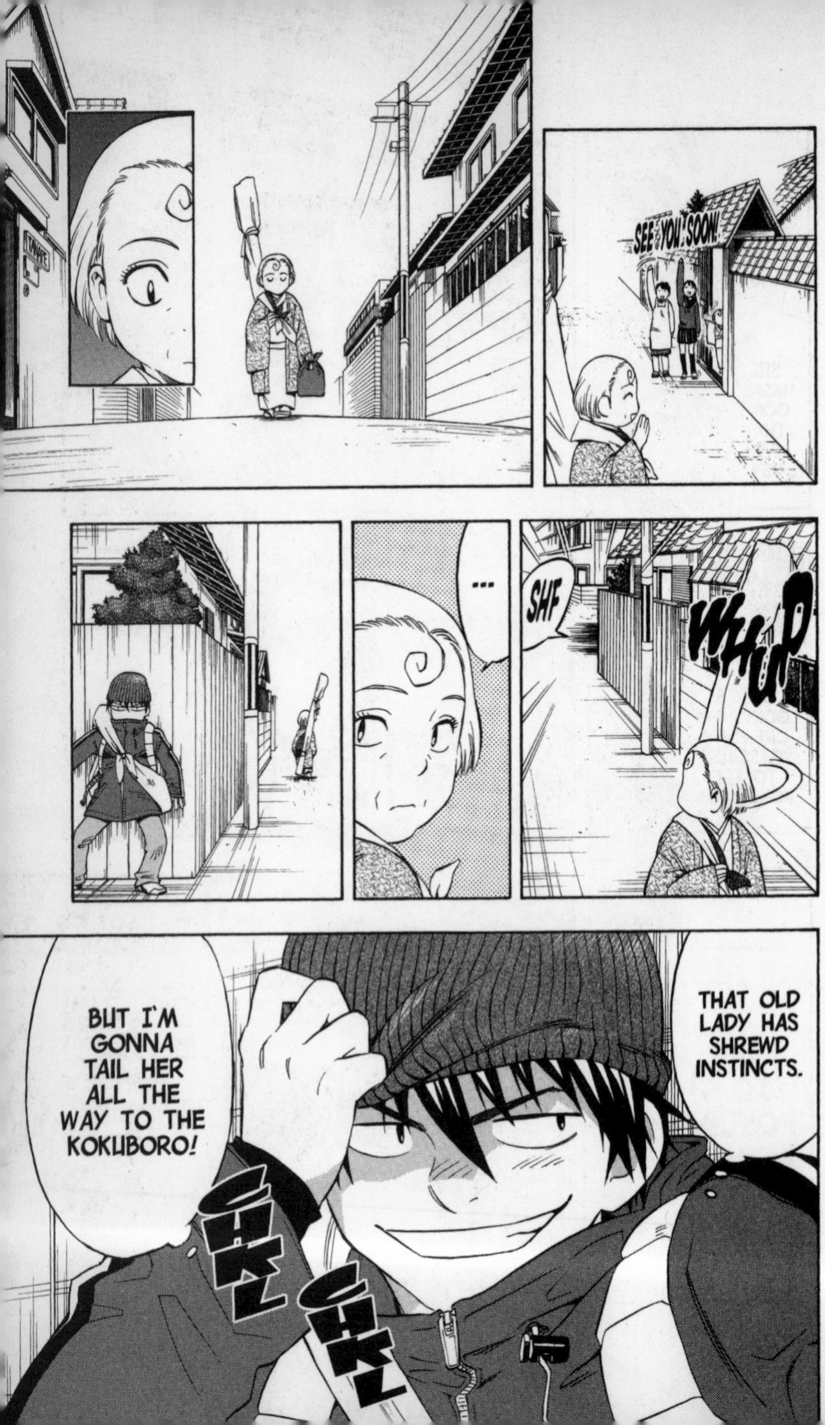

SEE YOU SOON!
SHF
WHUP
...
THAT OLD LADY HAS SHREWD INSTINCTS.
BUT I'M GONNA TAIL HER ALL THE WAY TO THE KOKUBORO!
CHKL
CHKL

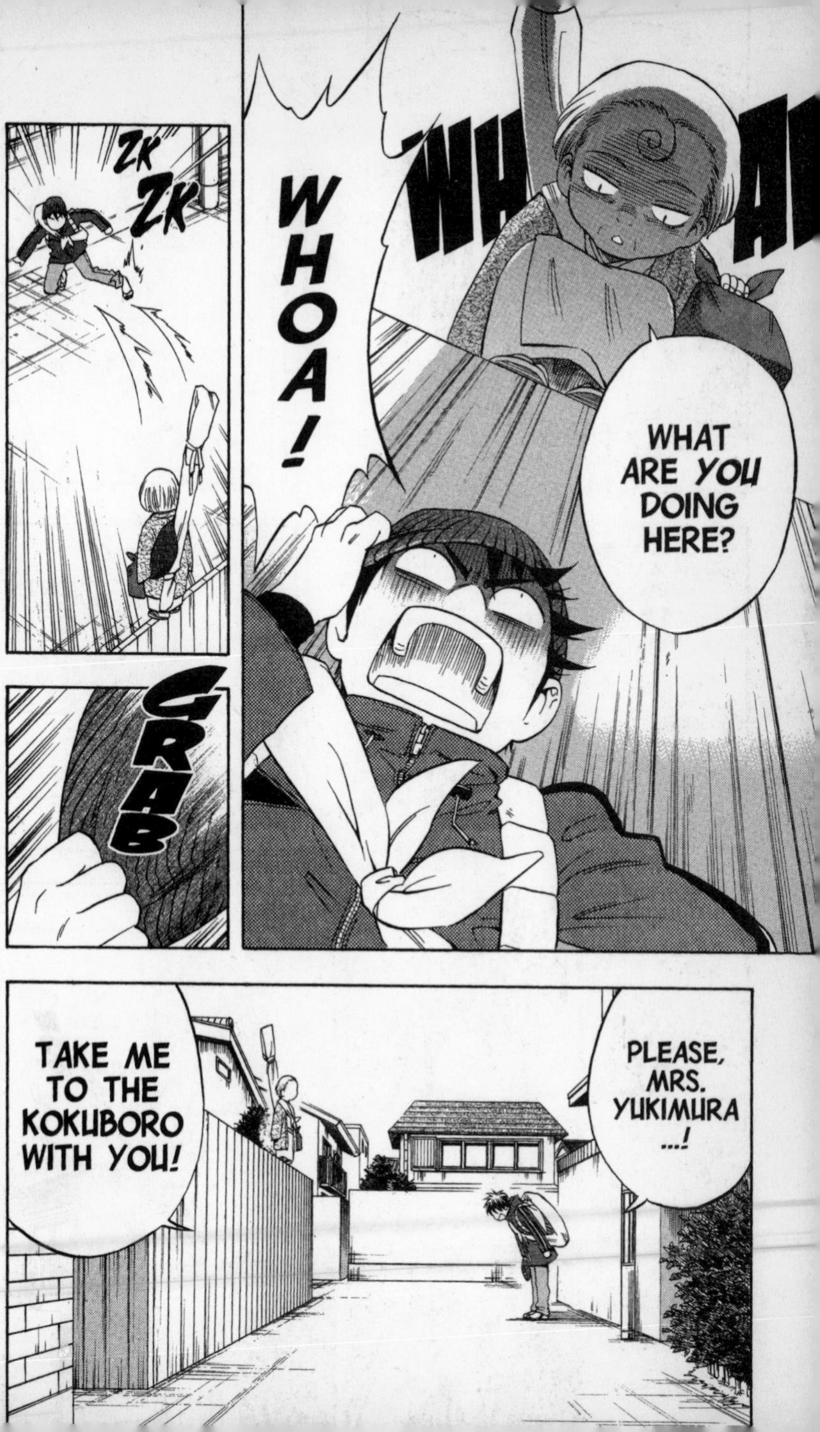
WHOA!
WHAT ARE YOU DOING HERE?
ZK ZK
GRAB
PLEASE, MRS. YUKIMURA ...!
TAKE ME TO THE KOKUBORO WITH YOU!

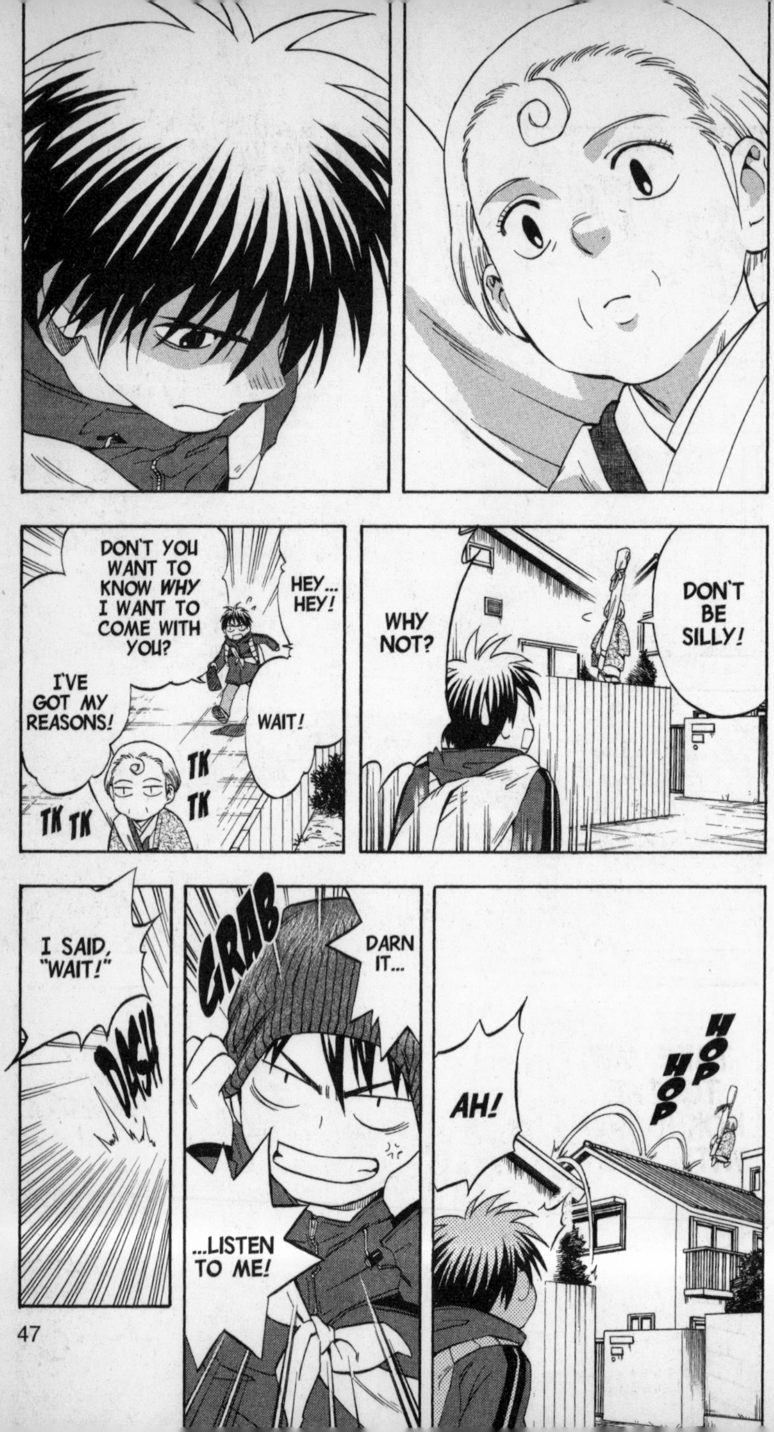
DON'T BE SILLY!
WHY NOT?
HEY... HEY!
DON'T YOU WANT TO KNOW *WHY* I WANT TO COME WITH YOU?
WAIT!
I'VE GOT MY REASONS!
TK TK
TK TK
HOP HOP
AH!
DARN IT...
GRAB
...LISTEN TO ME!
I SAID, "WAIT!"
DASH

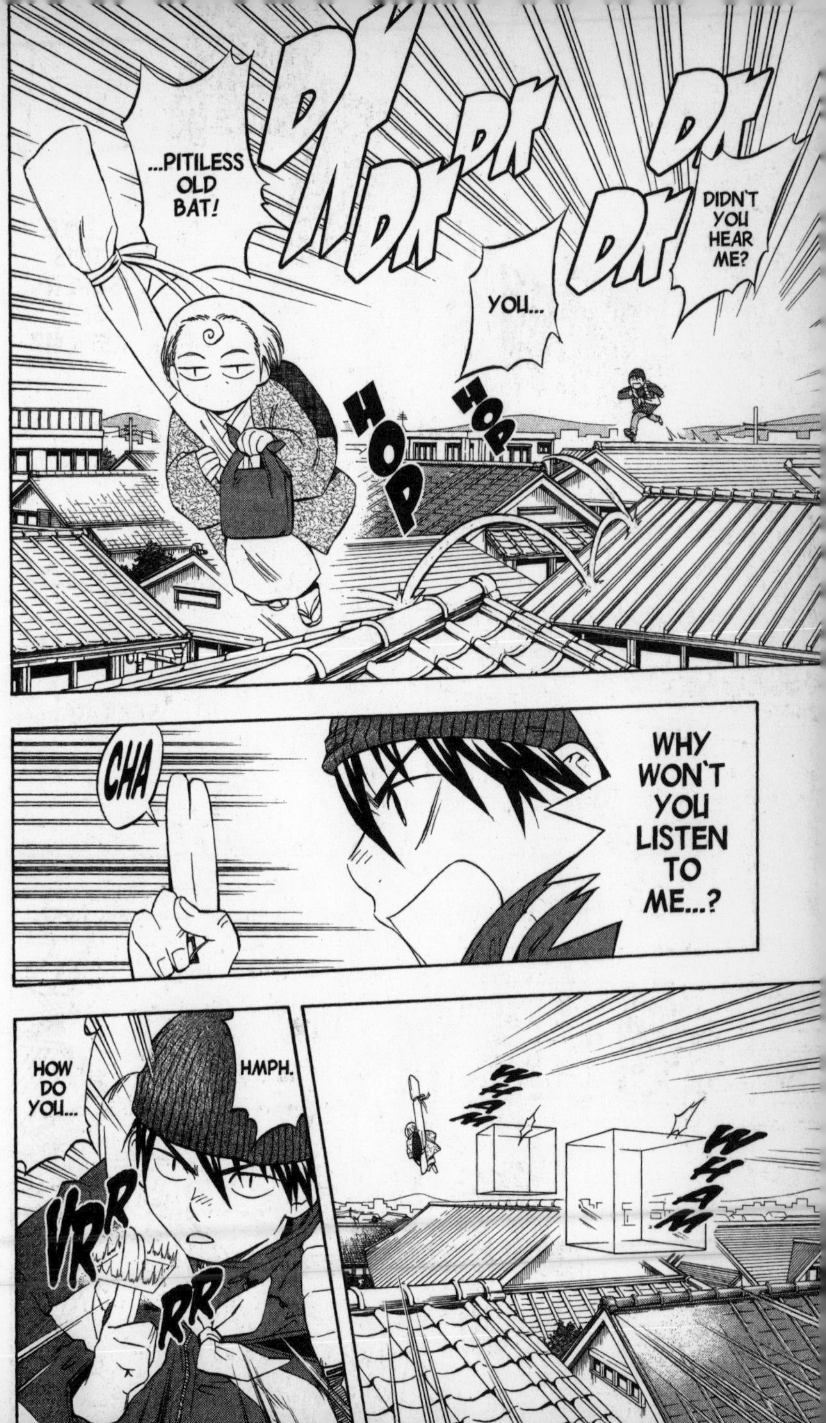
DIDN'T YOU HEAR ME?
YOU...
...PITILESS OLD BAT!
HOP
HOP
WHY WON'T YOU LISTEN TO ME...?
CHA
WHAM
WHAM
HMPH.
HOW DO YOU...
VRR
RR

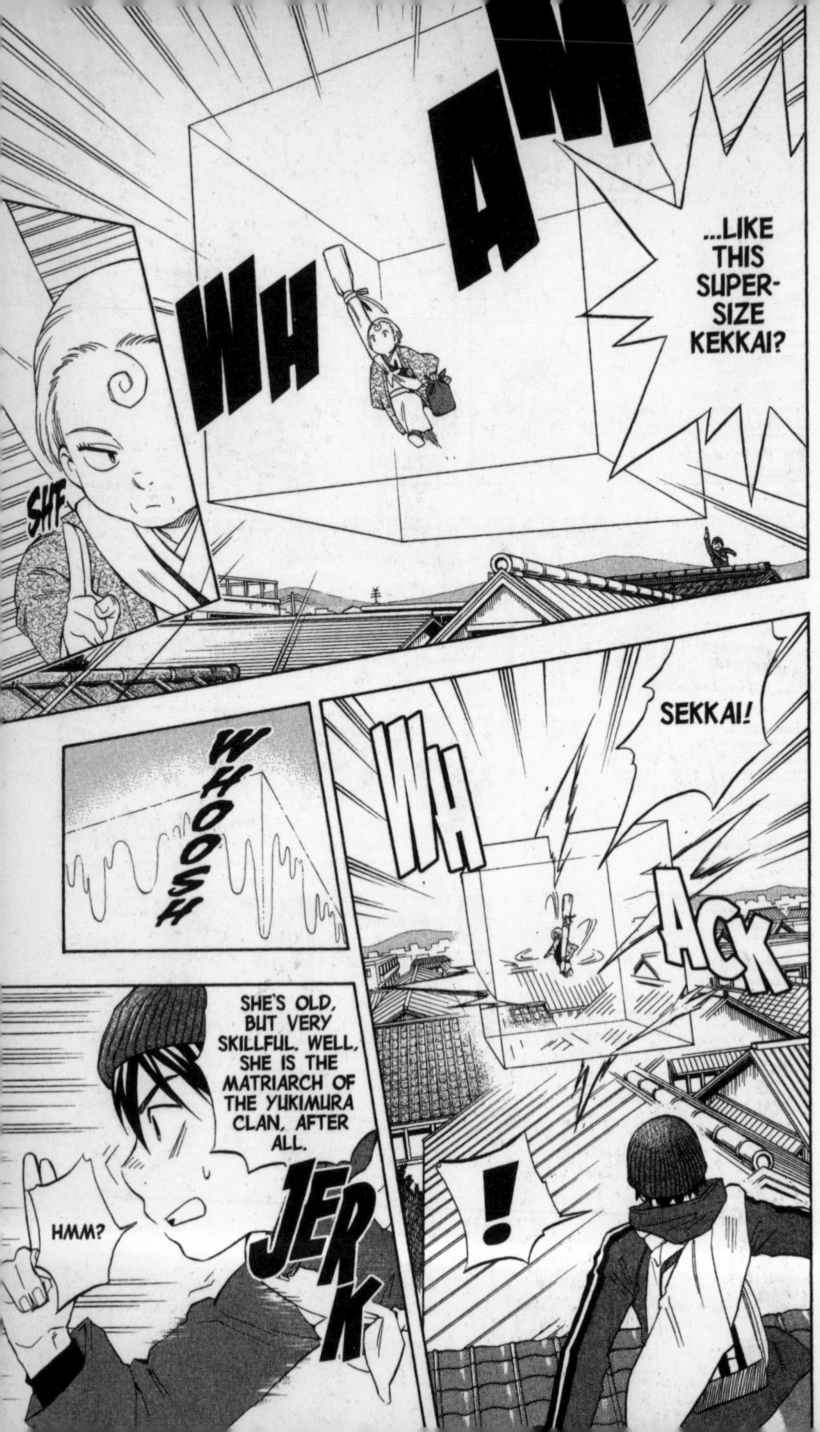
WHAM
...LIKE THIS SUPER-SIZE KEKKAI?
SHF
SEKKAI!
WHACK
!
WHOOSH
SHE'S OLD, BUT VERY SKILLFUL. WELL, SHE IS THE MATRIARCH OF THE YUKIMURA CLAN, AFTER ALL.
HMM?
JERK

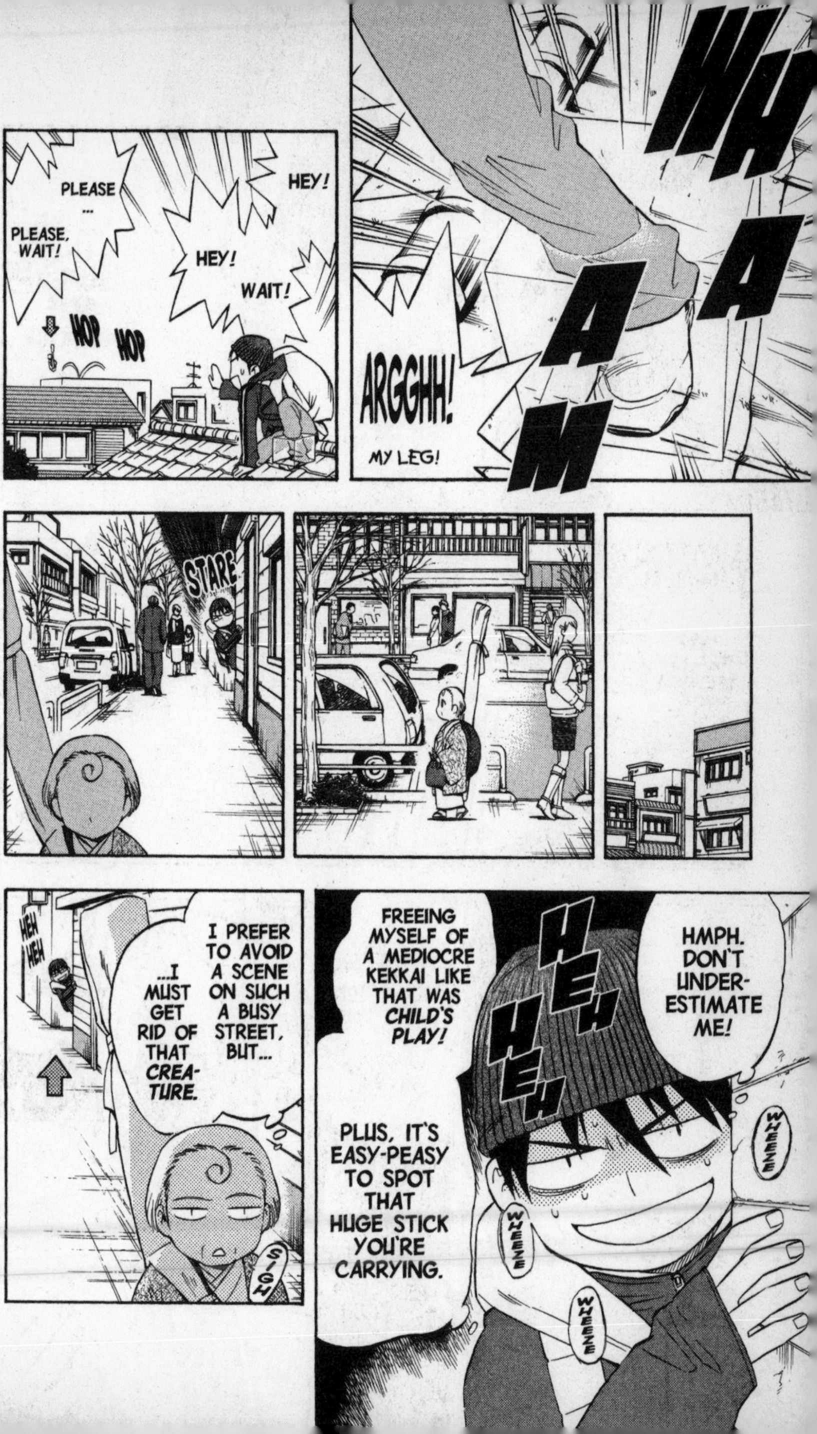
WHAAAM
ARGGHH!
MY LEG!
HEY!
HEY!
WAIT!
PLEASE ...
PLEASE, WAIT!
HOP HOP
STARE
HMPH. DON'T UNDER-ESTIMATE ME!
HEH HEH HEH HEH
FREEING MYSELF OF A MEDIOCRE KEKKAI LIKE THAT WAS CHILD'S PLAY!
WHEEZE
WHEEZE
WHEEZE
PLUS, IT'S EASY-PEASY TO SPOT THAT HUGE STICK YOU'RE CARRYING.
I PREFER TO AVOID A SCENE ON SUCH A BUSY STREET, BUT...
...I MUST GET RID OF THAT CREATURE.
HEH HEH
SIGH

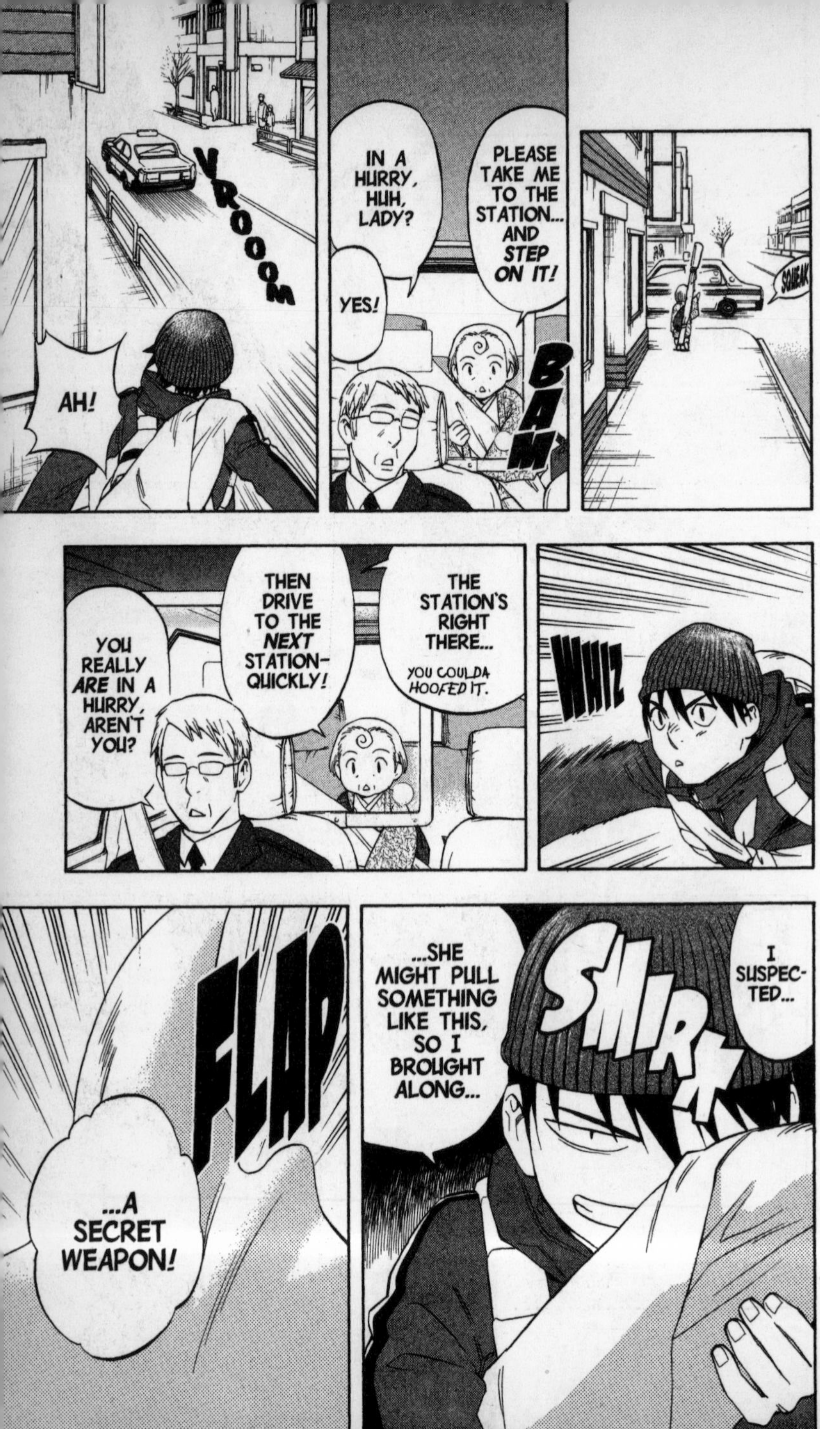
SQUEAK
PLEASE TAKE ME TO THE STATION... AND STEP ON IT!
IN A HURRY, HUH, LADY?
YES!
BAM
VROOOM
AH!
WHIZ
THE STATION'S RIGHT THERE...
YOU COULDA HOOFED IT.
THEN DRIVE TO THE NEXT STATION-QUICKLY!
YOU REALLY ARE IN A HURRY, AREN'T YOU?
I SUSPEC-TED...
SHIRK
...SHE MIGHT PULL SOMETHING LIKE THIS, SO I BROUGHT ALONG...
FLAP
...A SECRET WEAPON!

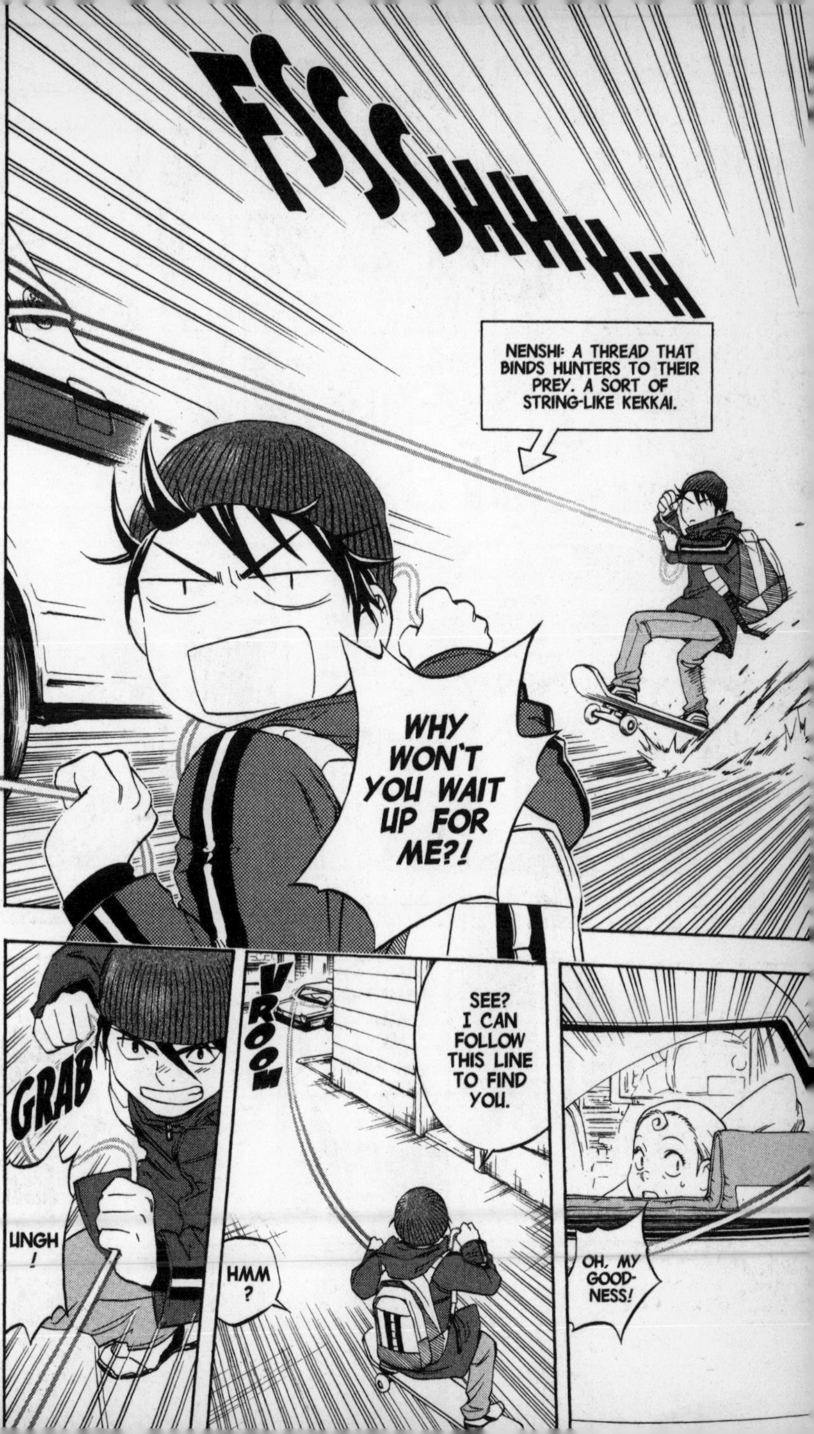

FSSSHHHHHH
NENSHI: A THREAD THAT BINDS HUNTERS TO THEIR PREY. A SORT OF STRING-LIKE KEKKAI.
WHY WON'T YOU WAIT UP FOR ME?!
OH, MY GOODNESS!
SEE? I CAN FOLLOW THIS LINE TO FIND YOU.
VROOOM
HMM?
GRAB
UNGH!

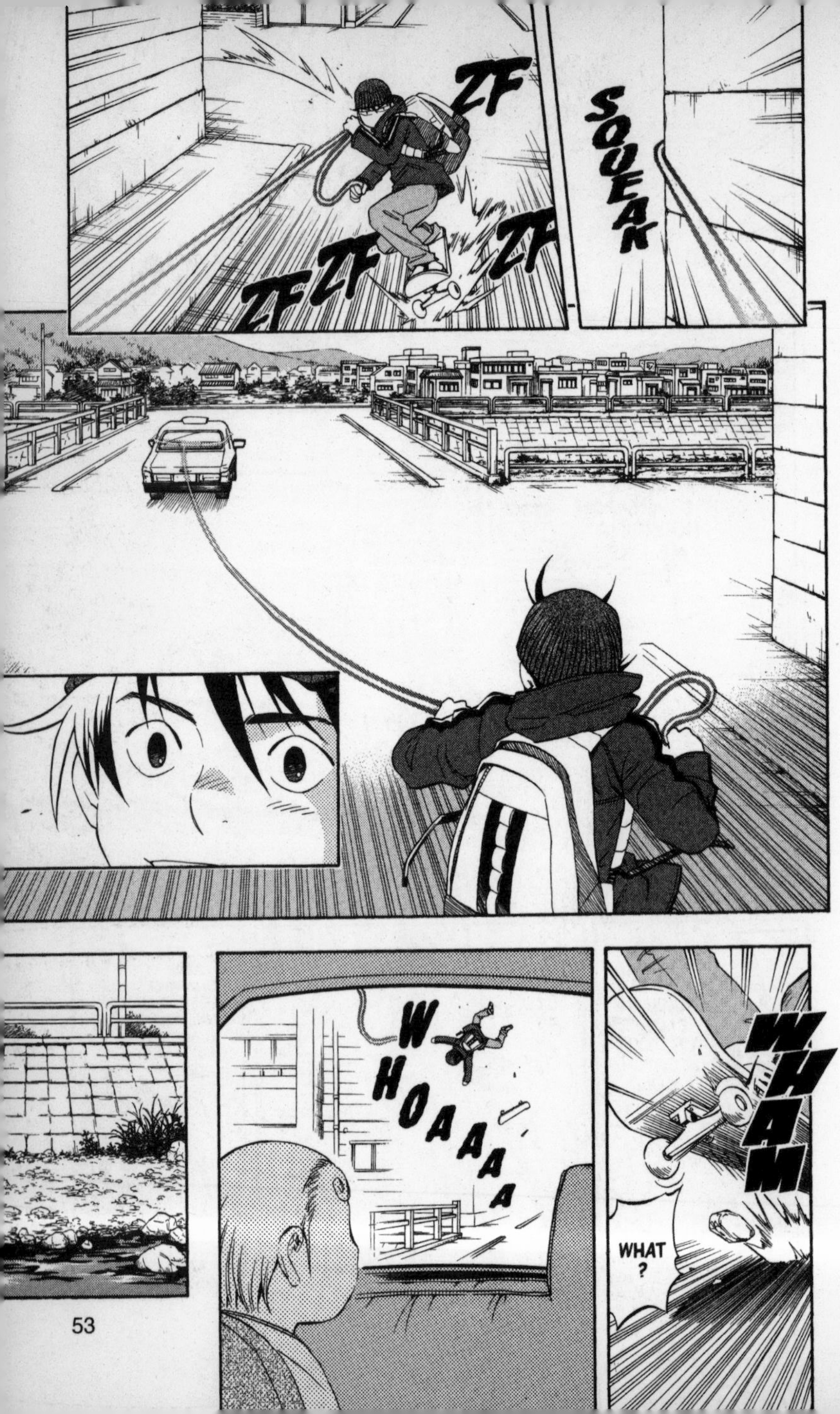
SQUEAK
ZF
ZF
ZF
ZF
WHAM
WHAT?
WHOAAAAA

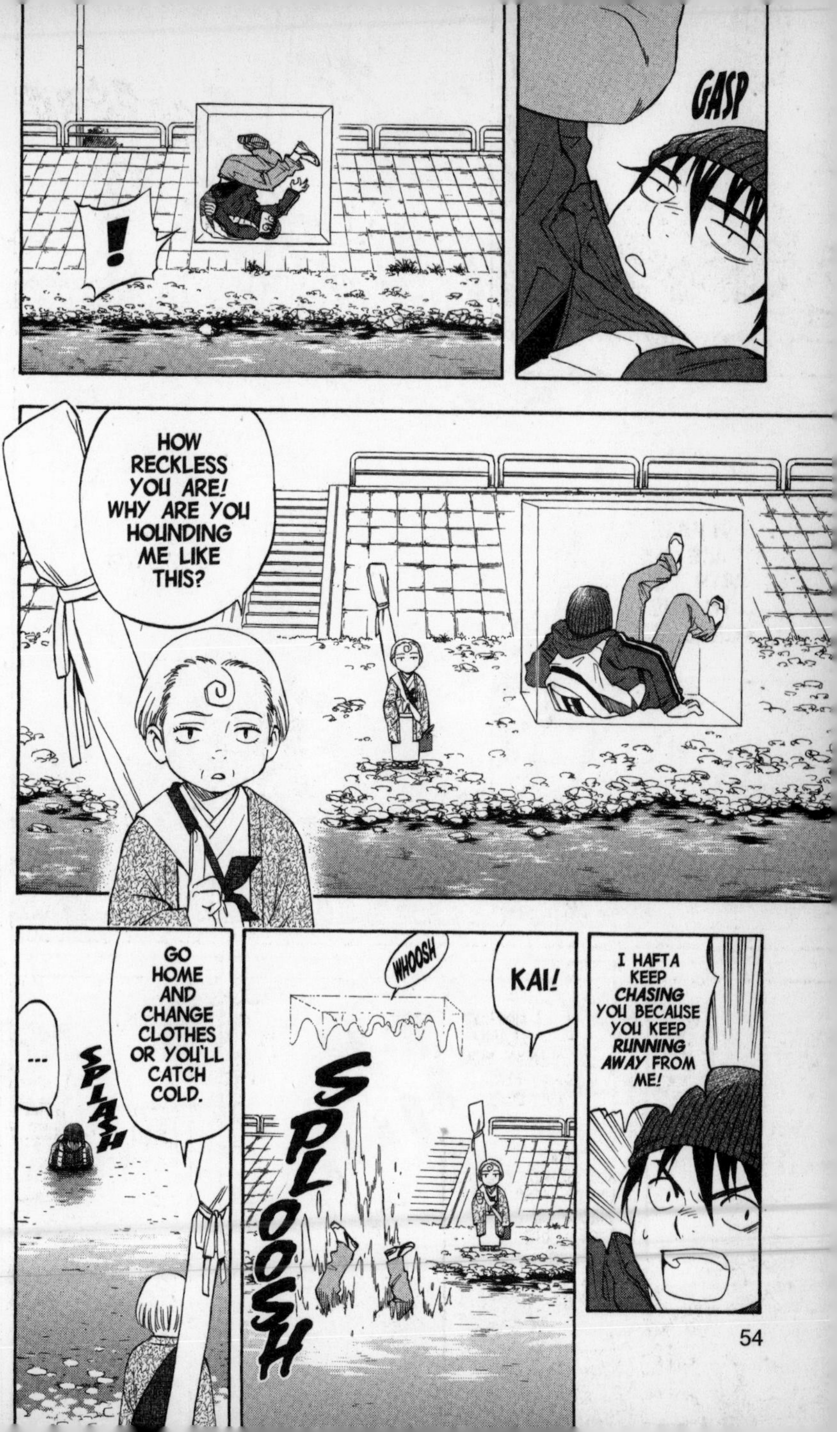
GASP
!
HOW RECKLESS YOU ARE! WHY ARE YOU HOUNDING ME LIKE THIS?
I HAFTA KEEP CHASING YOU BECAUSE YOU KEEP RUNNING AWAY FROM ME!
KAI!
WHOOSH
SPLOOOSH
GO HOME AND CHANGE CLOTHES OR YOU'LL CATCH COLD.
SPLASH
...

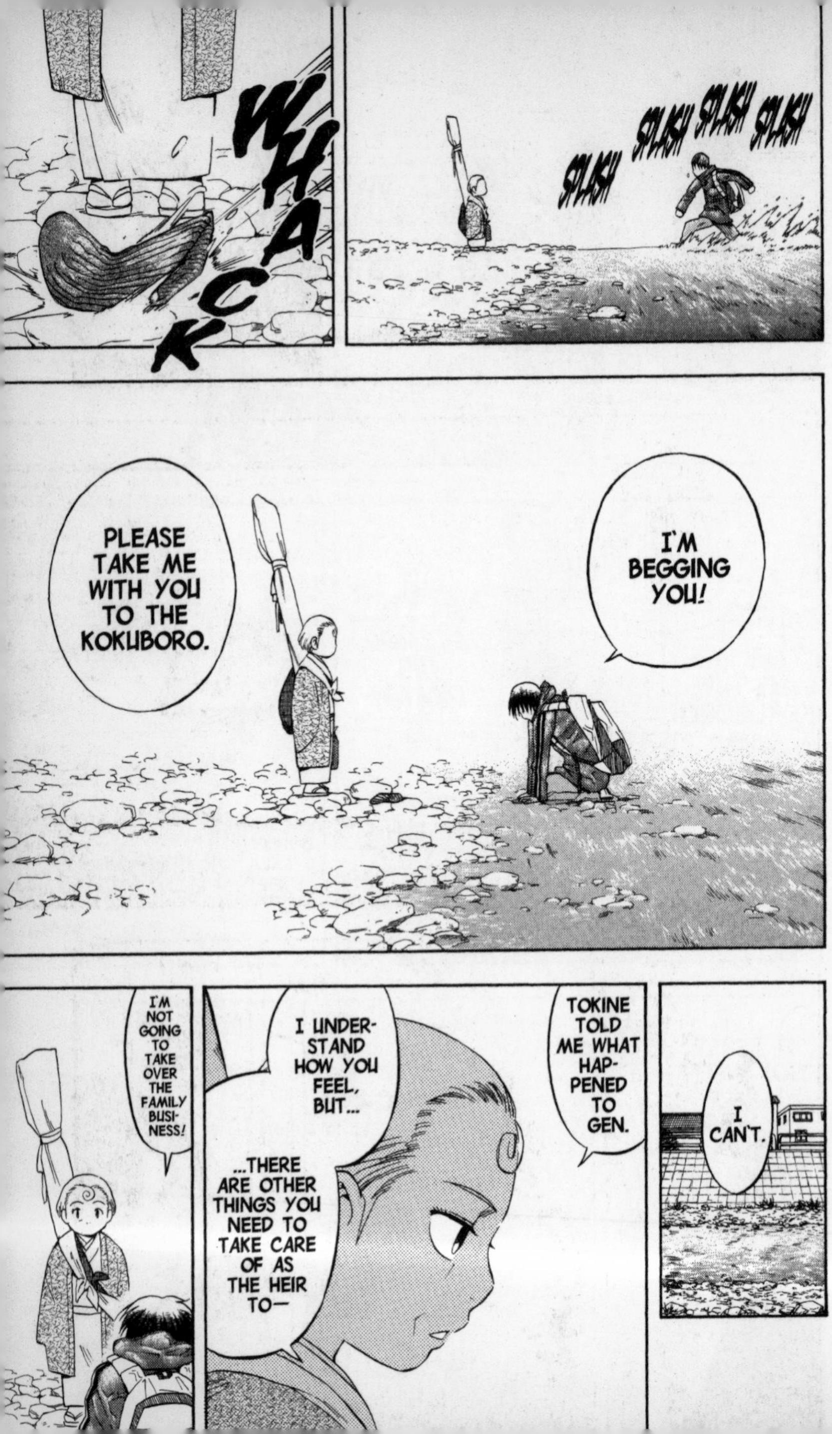
SPLASH SPLASH SPLASH SPLASH
WHACK
I'M BEGGING YOU!
PLEASE TAKE ME WITH YOU TO THE KOKUBORO.
I CAN'T.
TOKINE TOLD ME WHAT HAP-PENED TO GEN.
I UNDER-STAND HOW YOU FEEL, BUT...
...THERE ARE OTHER THINGS YOU NEED TO TAKE CARE OF AS THE HEIR TO—
I'M NOT GOING TO TAKE OVER THE FAMILY BUSI-NESS!

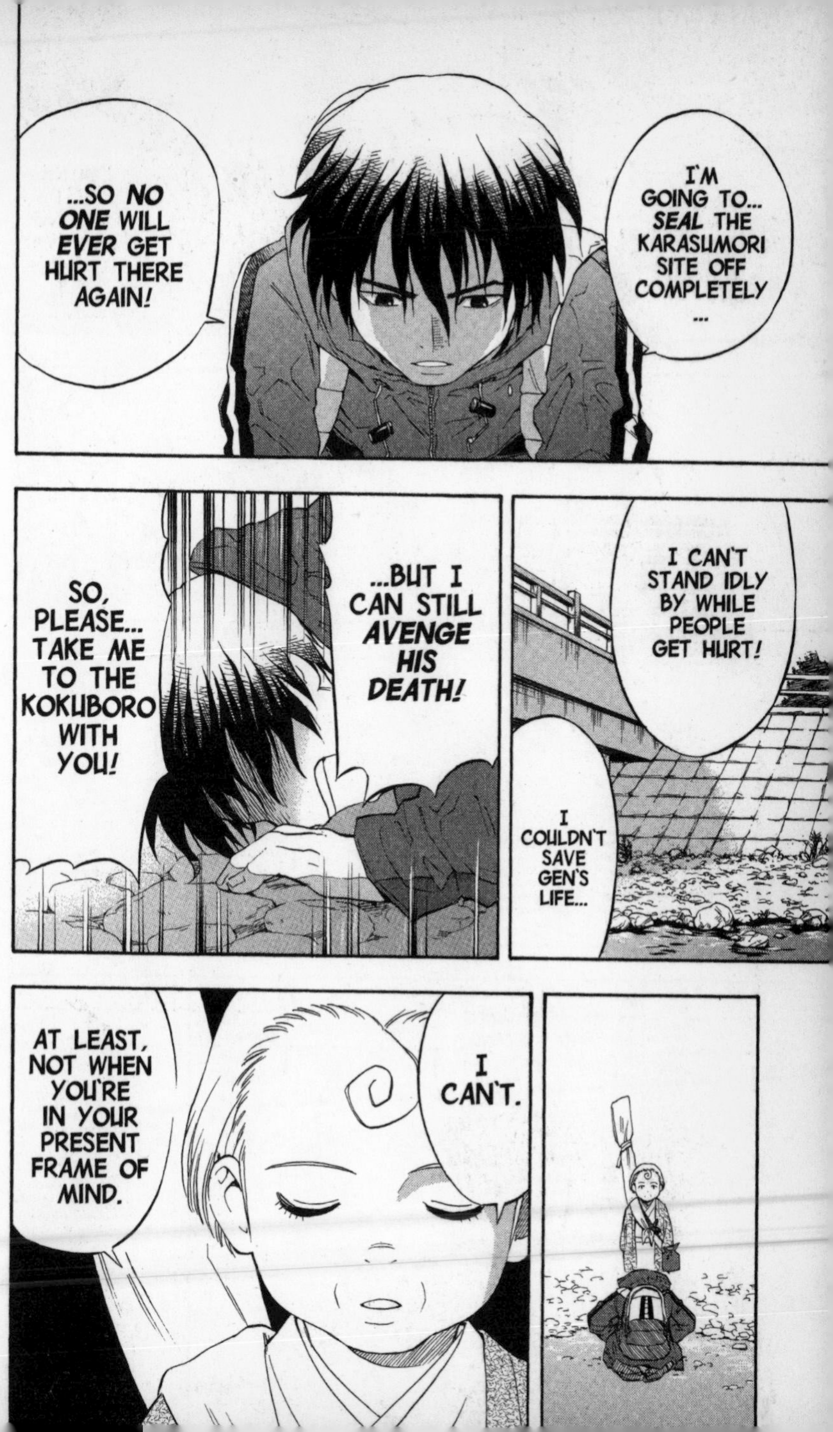
I'M GOING TO... SEAL THE KARASUMORI SITE OFF COMPLETELY ...
...SO NO ONE WILL EVER GET HURT THERE AGAIN!
I CAN'T STAND IDLY BY WHILE PEOPLE GET HURT!
I COULDN'T SAVE GEN'S LIFE...
...BUT I CAN STILL AVENGE HIS DEATH!
SO, PLEASE... TAKE ME TO THE KOKUBORO WITH YOU!
I CAN'T.
AT LEAST, NOT WHEN YOU'RE IN YOUR PRESENT FRAME OF MIND.

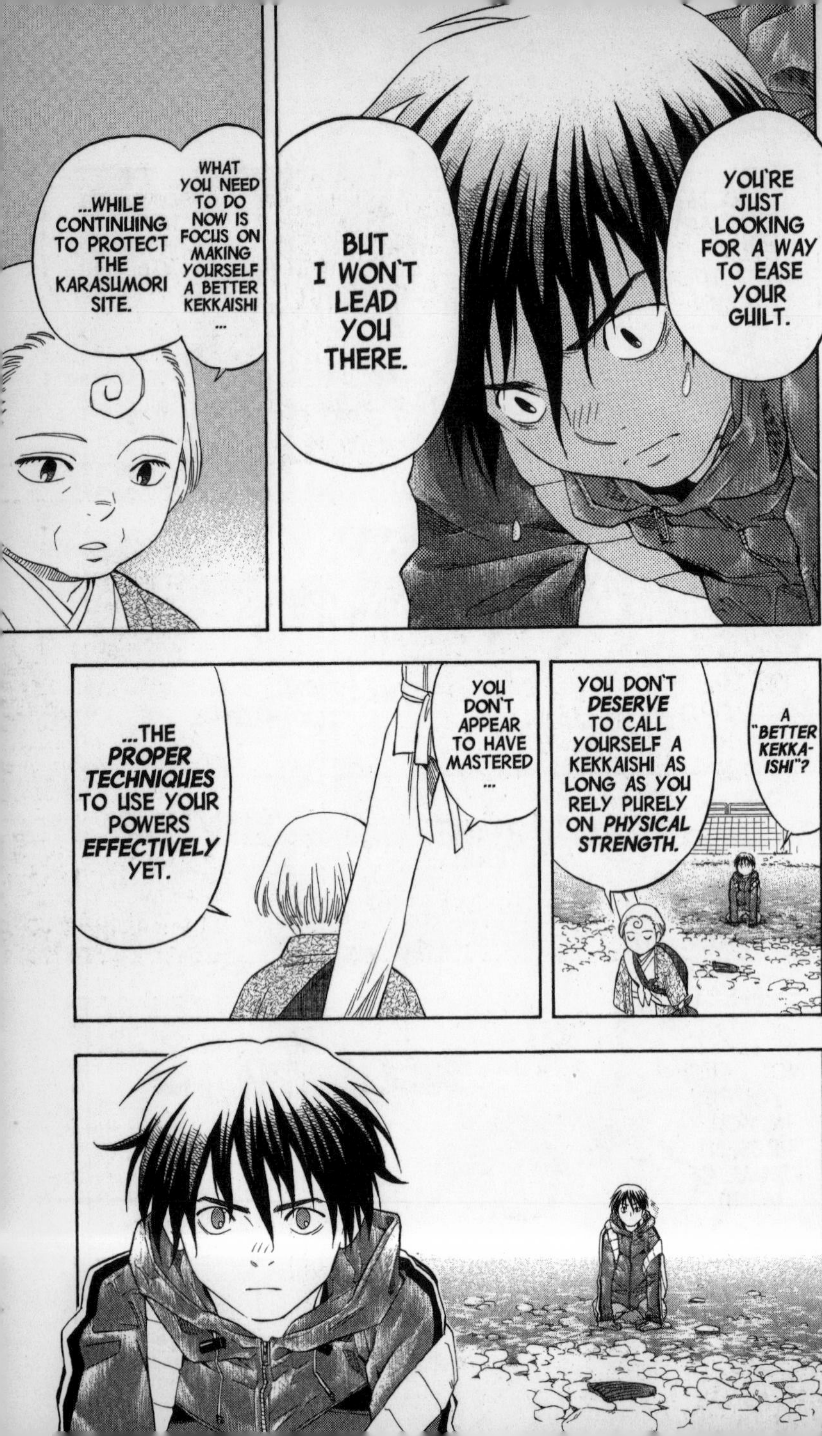
YOU'RE JUST LOOKING FOR A WAY TO EASE YOUR GUILT.
BUT I WON'T LEAD YOU THERE.
WHAT YOU NEED TO DO NOW IS FOCUS ON MAKING YOURSELF A BETTER KEKKAISHI ...
...WHILE CONTINUING TO PROTECT THE KARASUMORI SITE.
A "BETTER KEKKAISHI"?
YOU DON'T *DESERVE* TO CALL YOURSELF A KEKKAISHI AS LONG AS YOU RELY PURELY ON ***PHYSICAL STRENGTH.***
YOU DON'T APPEAR TO HAVE MASTERED ...
...THE ***PROPER TECHNIQUES*** TO USE YOUR POWERS ***EFFECTIVELY*** YET.

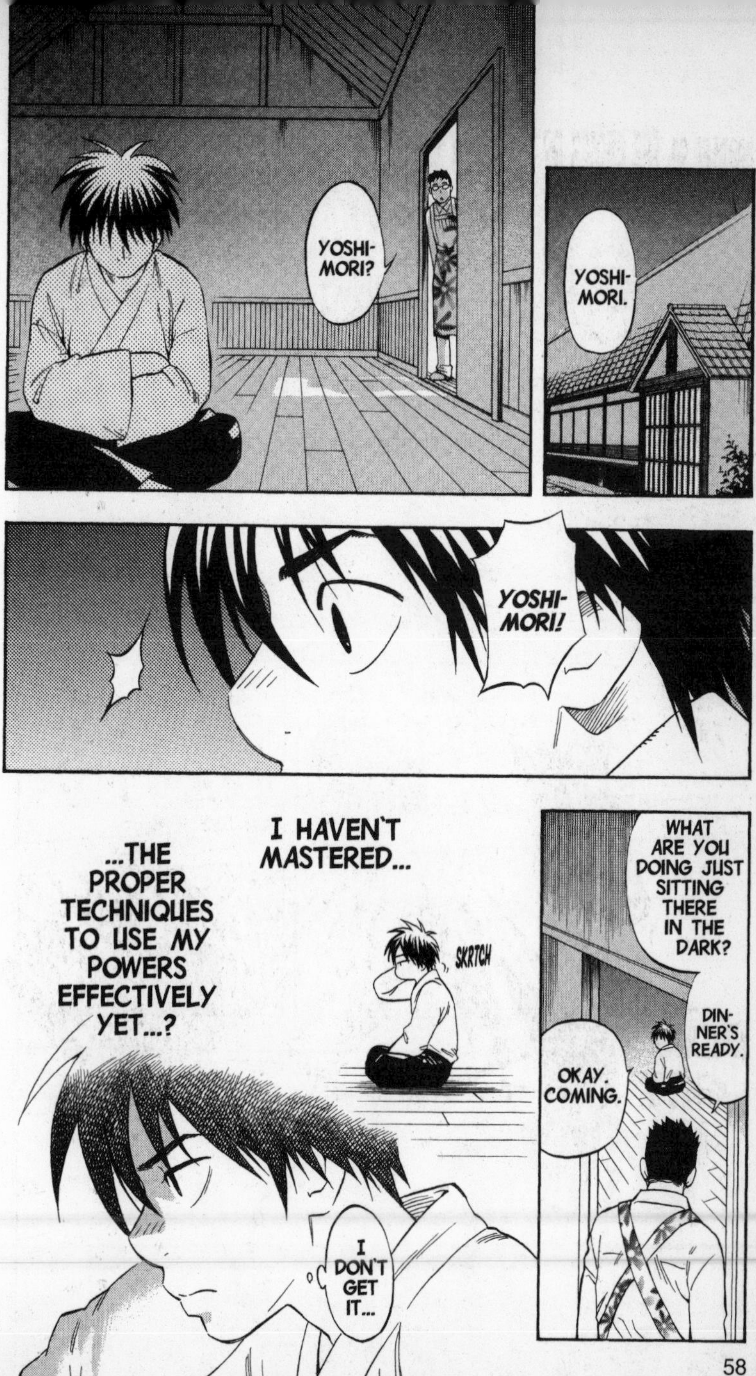
YOSHI-
MORI.
YOSHI-
MORI?
YOSHI-
MORI!
WHAT ARE YOU DOING JUST SITTING THERE IN THE DARK?
DIN-
NER'S READY.
OKAY. COMING.
I HAVEN'T MASTERED...
...THE PROPER TECHNIQUES TO USE MY POWERS EFFECTIVELY YET...?
SKRTCH
I DON'T GET IT...

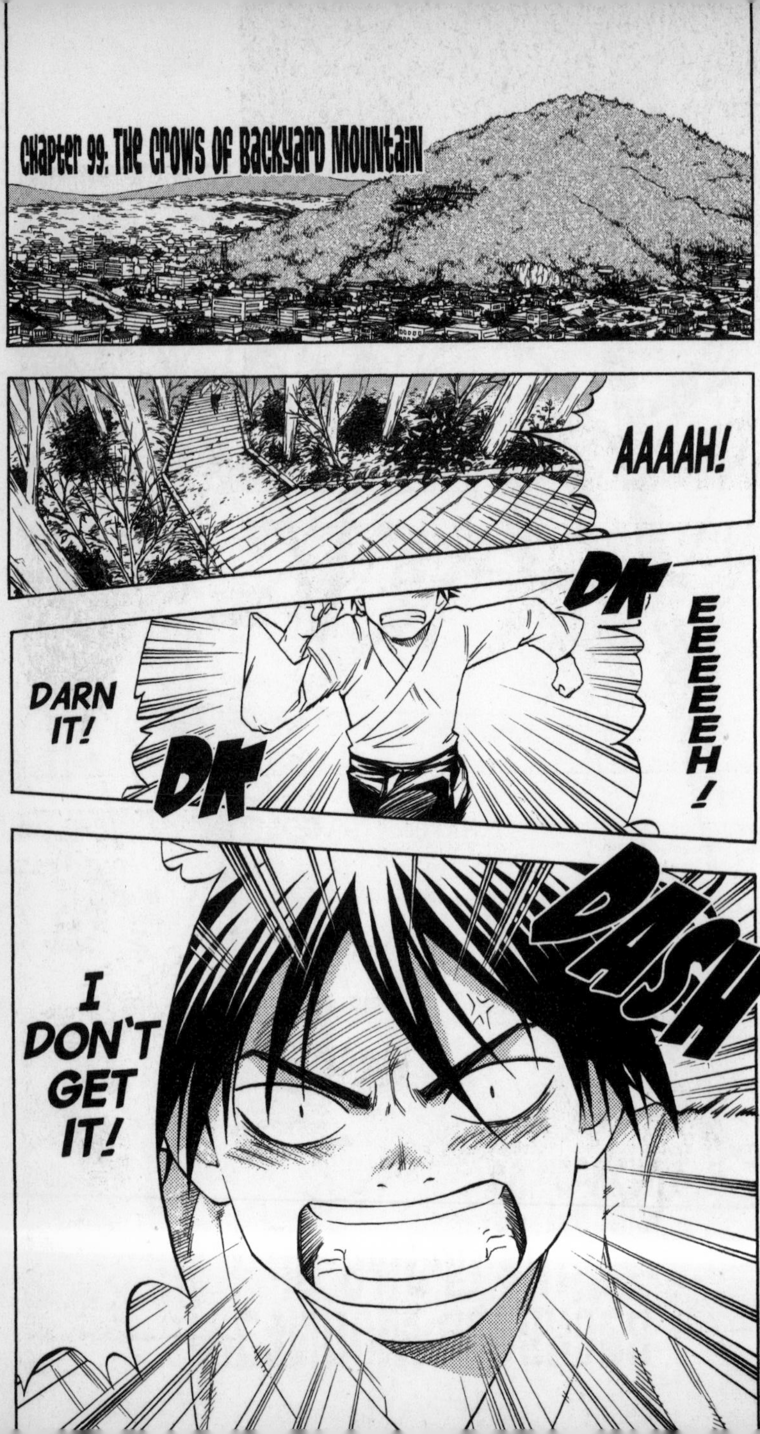
Chapter 99: The Crows of Backyard Mountain
AAAAH!
DK
EEEEEEH!
DARN IT!
DK
DASH
I DON'T GET IT!

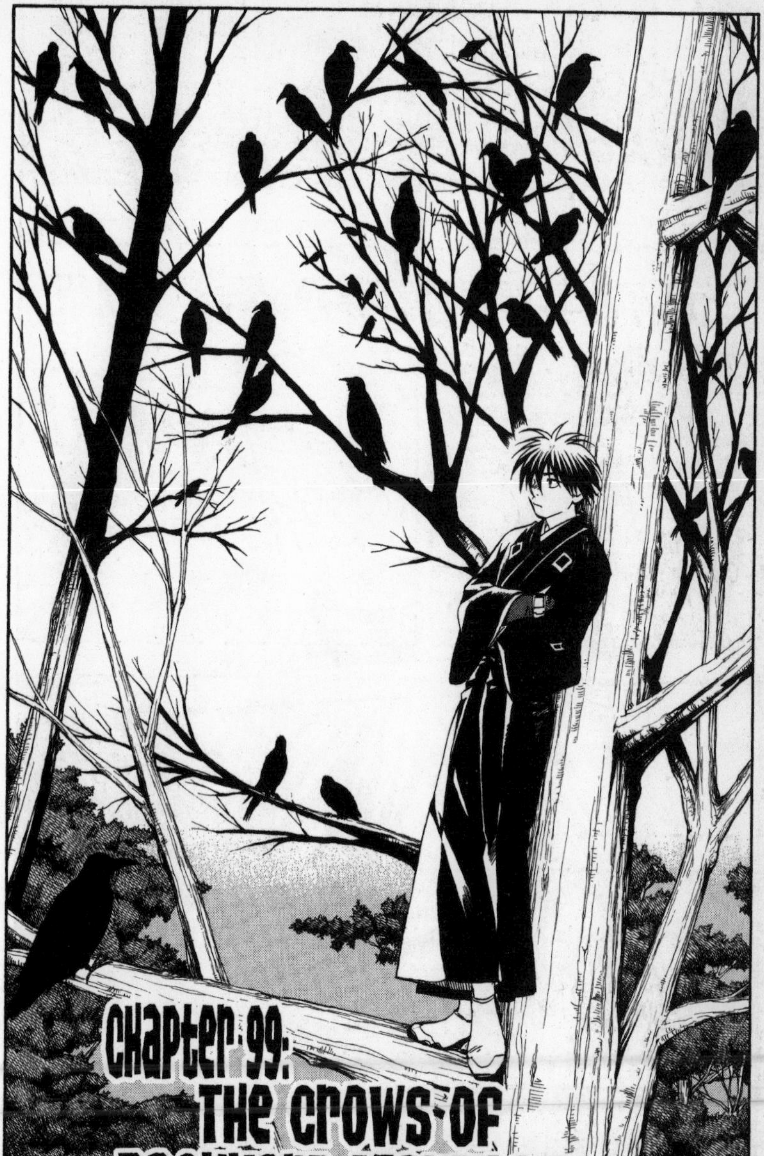
Chapter 99:
The Crows of
Backyard Mountain

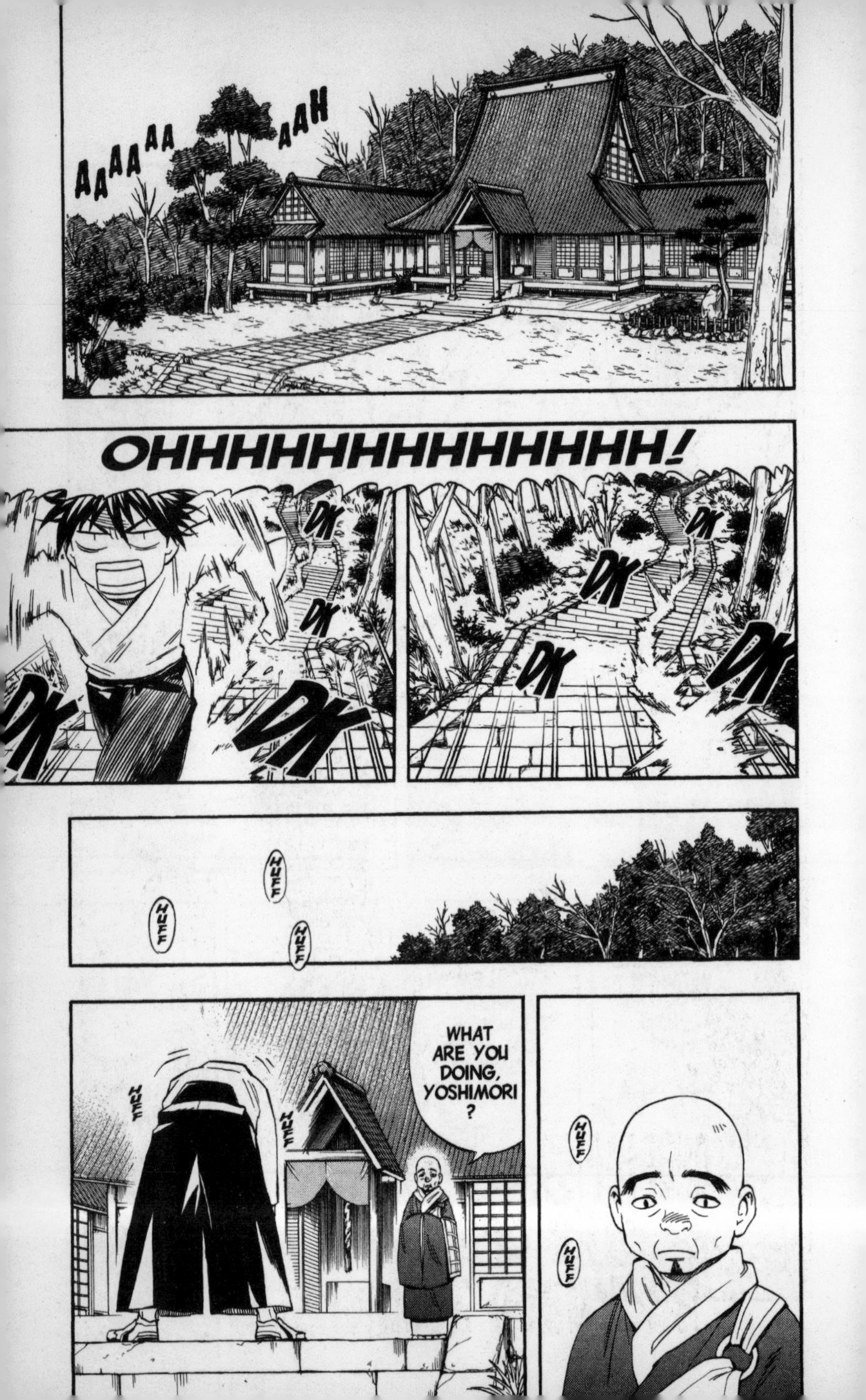
AAAAAAAAH
OHHHHHHHHHHHHH!
DK DK DK DK
DK DK DK
HUFF HUFF HUFF
HUFF HUFF
WHAT ARE YOU DOING, YOSHIMORI?
HUFF HUFF

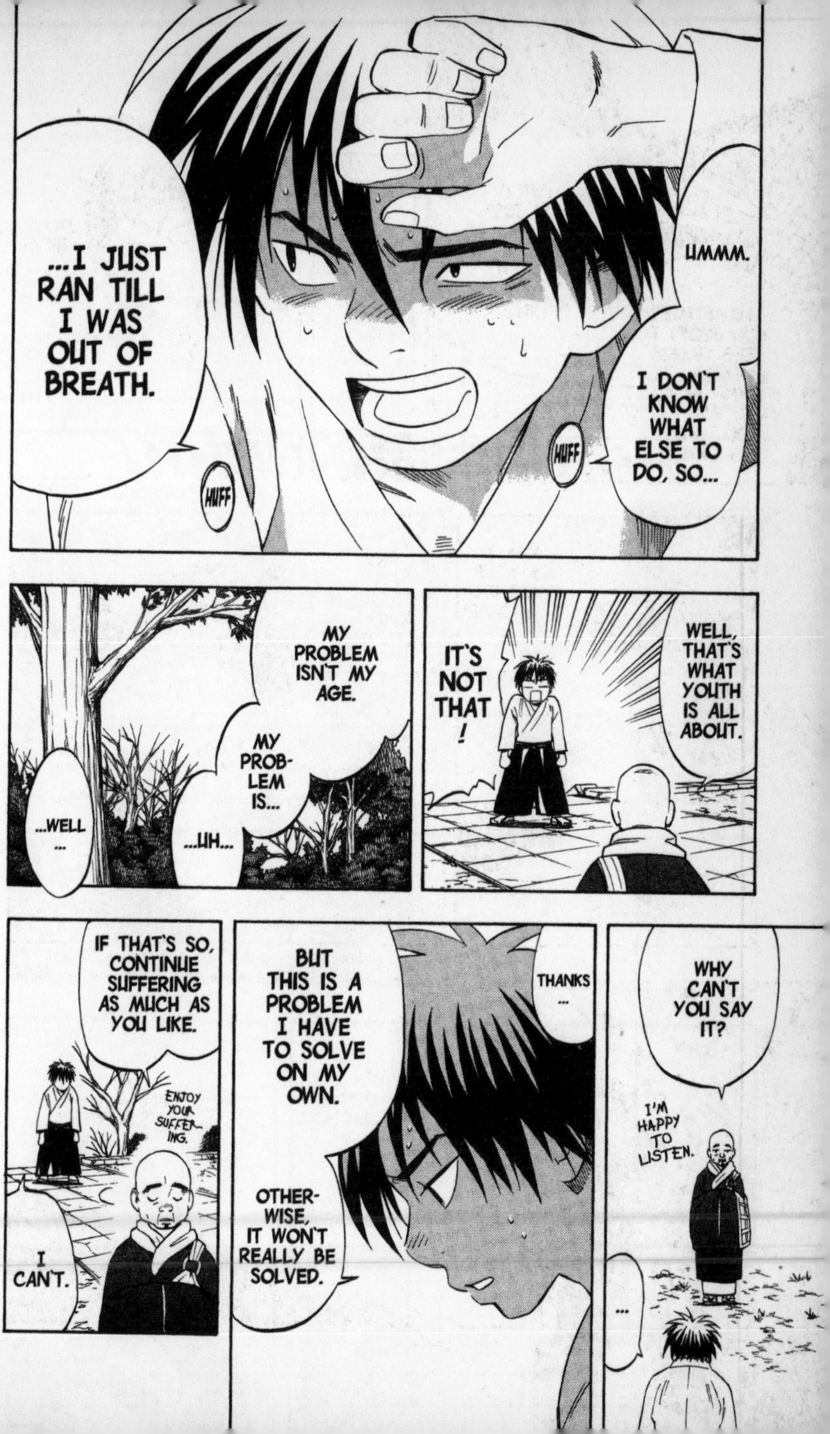

UMMM.
I DON'T KNOW WHAT ELSE TO DO, SO...
HUFF
HUFF
...I JUST RAN TILL I WAS OUT OF BREATH.
WELL, THAT'S WHAT YOUTH IS ALL ABOUT.
IT'S NOT THAT!
MY PROBLEM ISN'T MY AGE.
MY PROB-LEM IS...
...UH...
...WELL...
WHY CAN'T YOU SAY IT?
I'M HAPPY TO LISTEN.
...
THANKS...
BUT THIS IS A PROBLEM I HAVE TO SOLVE ON MY OWN.
OTHER-WISE, IT WON'T REALLY BE SOLVED.
IF THAT'S SO, CONTINUE SUFFERING AS MUCH AS YOU LIKE.
ENJOY YOUR SUFFER-ING.
I CAN'T.

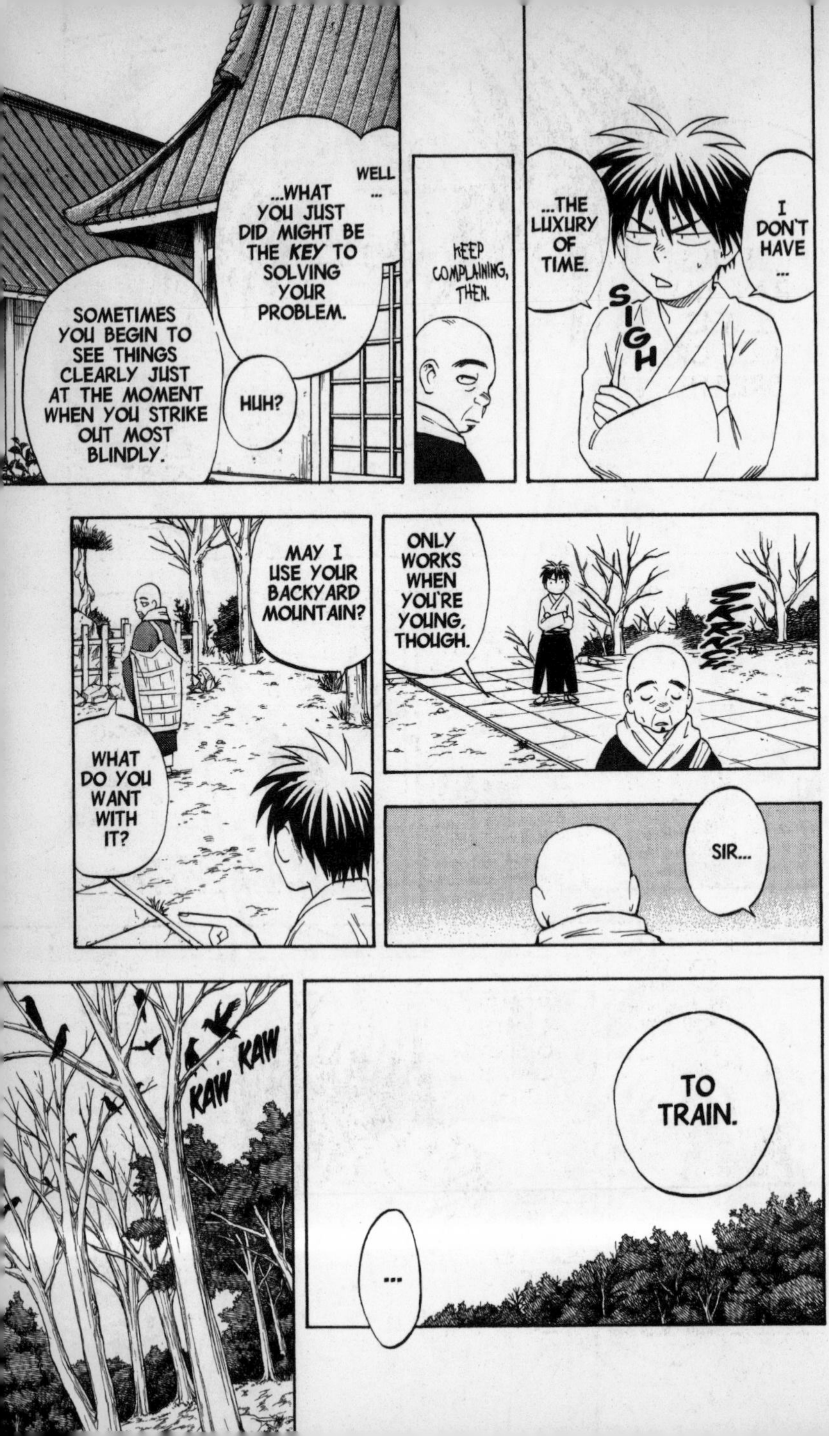
I DON'T HAVE ...
...THE LUXURY OF TIME.
SIGH
KEEP COMPLAINING, THEN.
WELL ...
...WHAT YOU JUST DID MIGHT BE THE KEY TO SOLVING YOUR PROBLEM.
HUH?
SOMETIMES YOU BEGIN TO SEE THINGS CLEARLY JUST AT THE MOMENT WHEN YOU STRIKE OUT MOST BLINDLY.
ONLY WORKS WHEN YOU'RE YOUNG, THOUGH.
SIR...
MAY I USE YOUR BACKYARD MOUNTAIN?
WHAT DO YOU WANT WITH IT?
TO TRAIN.
...
KAW KAW

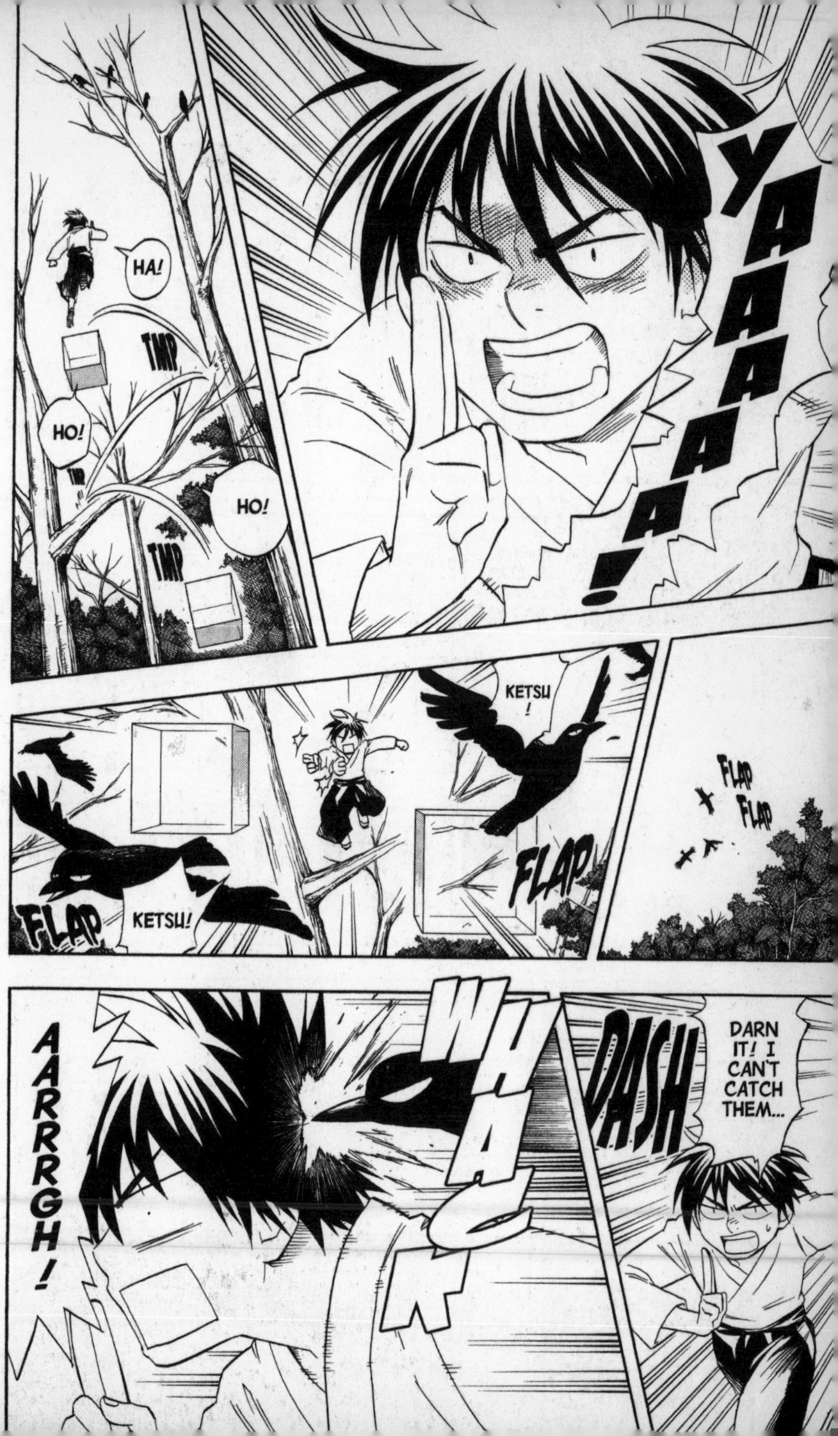
YAAAAA!
HA!
TMP
HO!
TMP
HO!
TMP
FLAP
FLAP
KETSU!
FLAP
FLAP
KETSU!
DARN IT! I CAN'T CATCH THEM...
DASH
WHACK
AARRRGH!

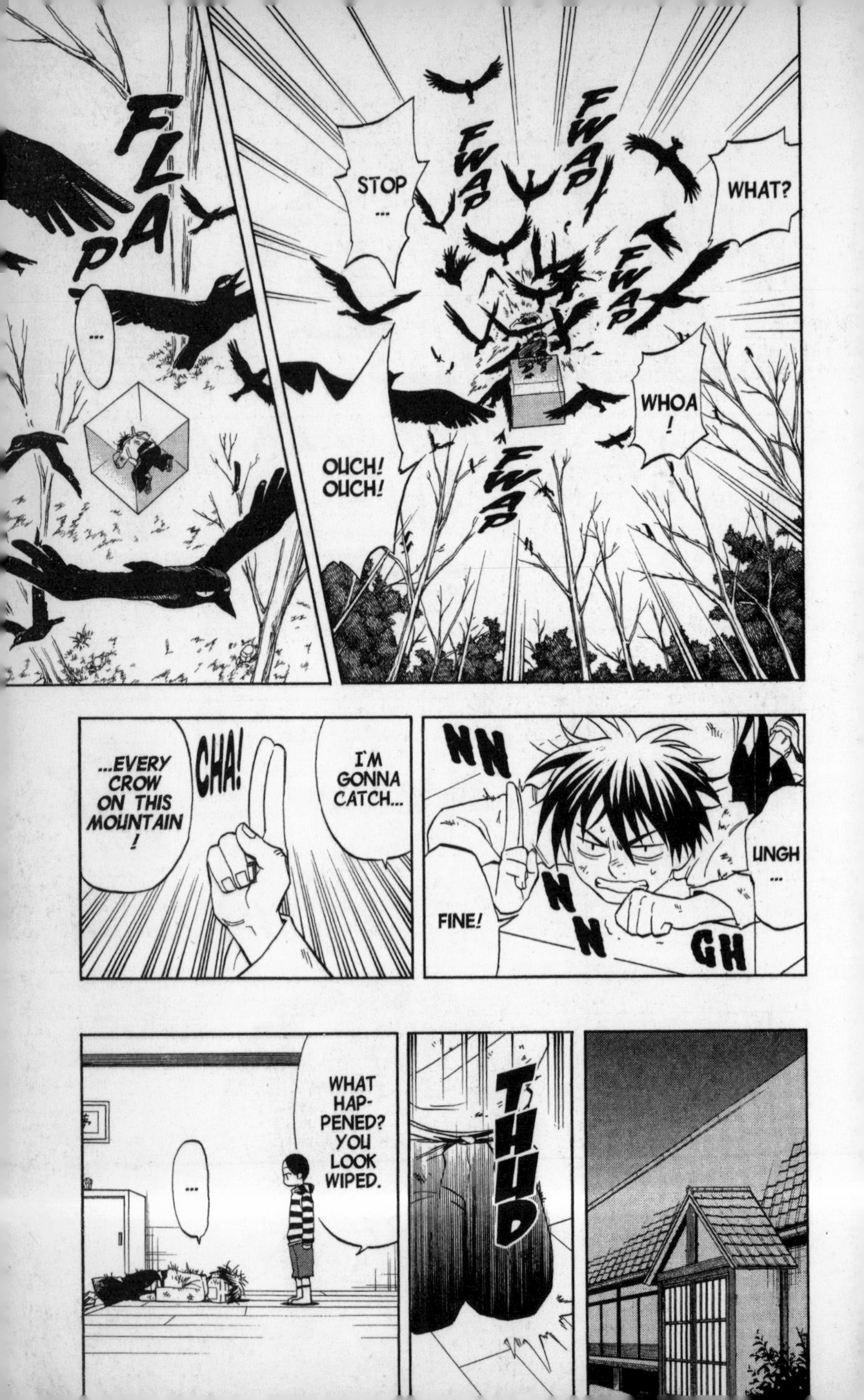
WHAT?
FWAP
FWAP
STOP ...
FWAP
WHOA!
OUCH! OUCH!
FWAP
FLAPA
...
UNGH ...
NN
FINE!
NNN
GH
I'M GONNA CATCH...
CHA!
...EVERY CROW ON THIS MOUNTAIN!
THUD
WHAT HAPPENED? YOU LOOK WIPED.
...

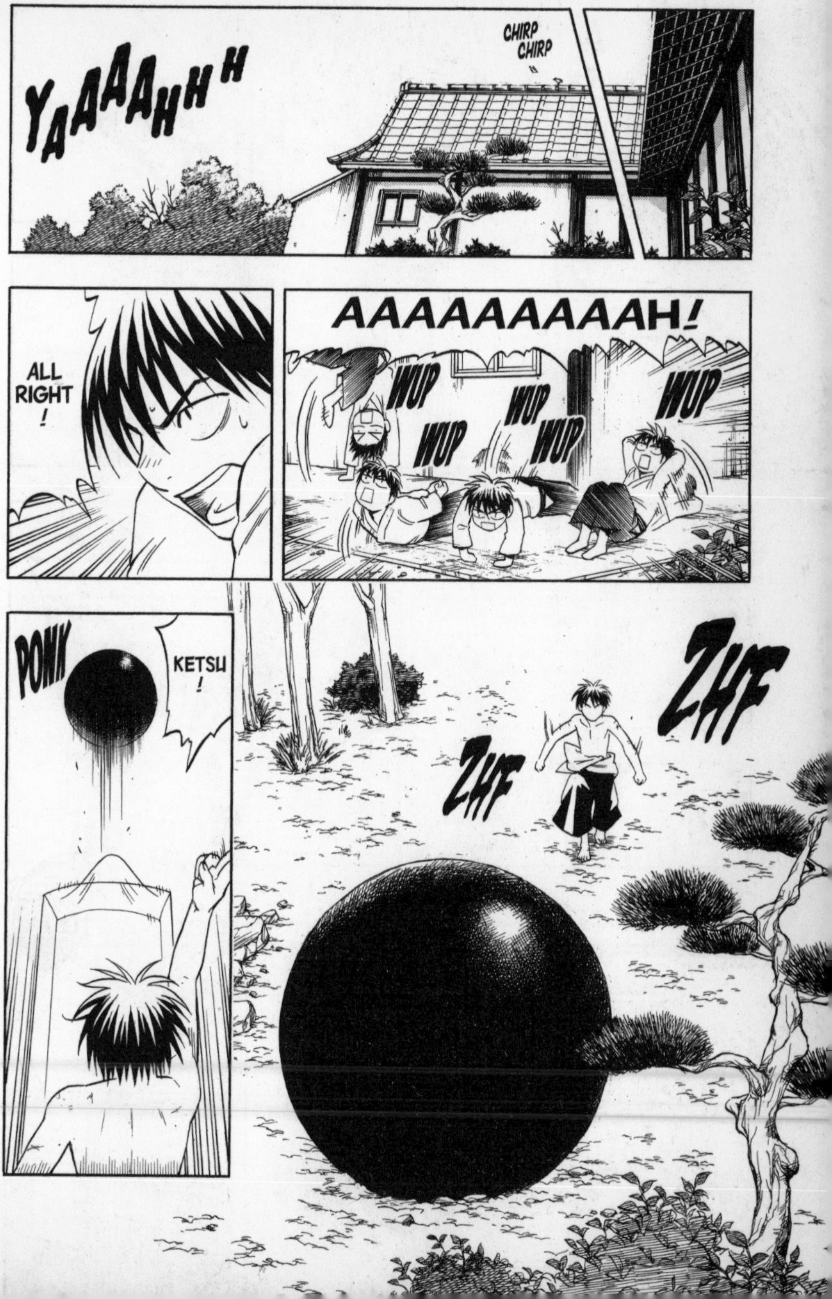
CHIRP CHIRP
YAAAAHHH
AAAAAAAAAH!
WUP
WUP
WUP
WUP
WUP
ALL RIGHT!
ZHF
ZHF
KETSU!
PONK

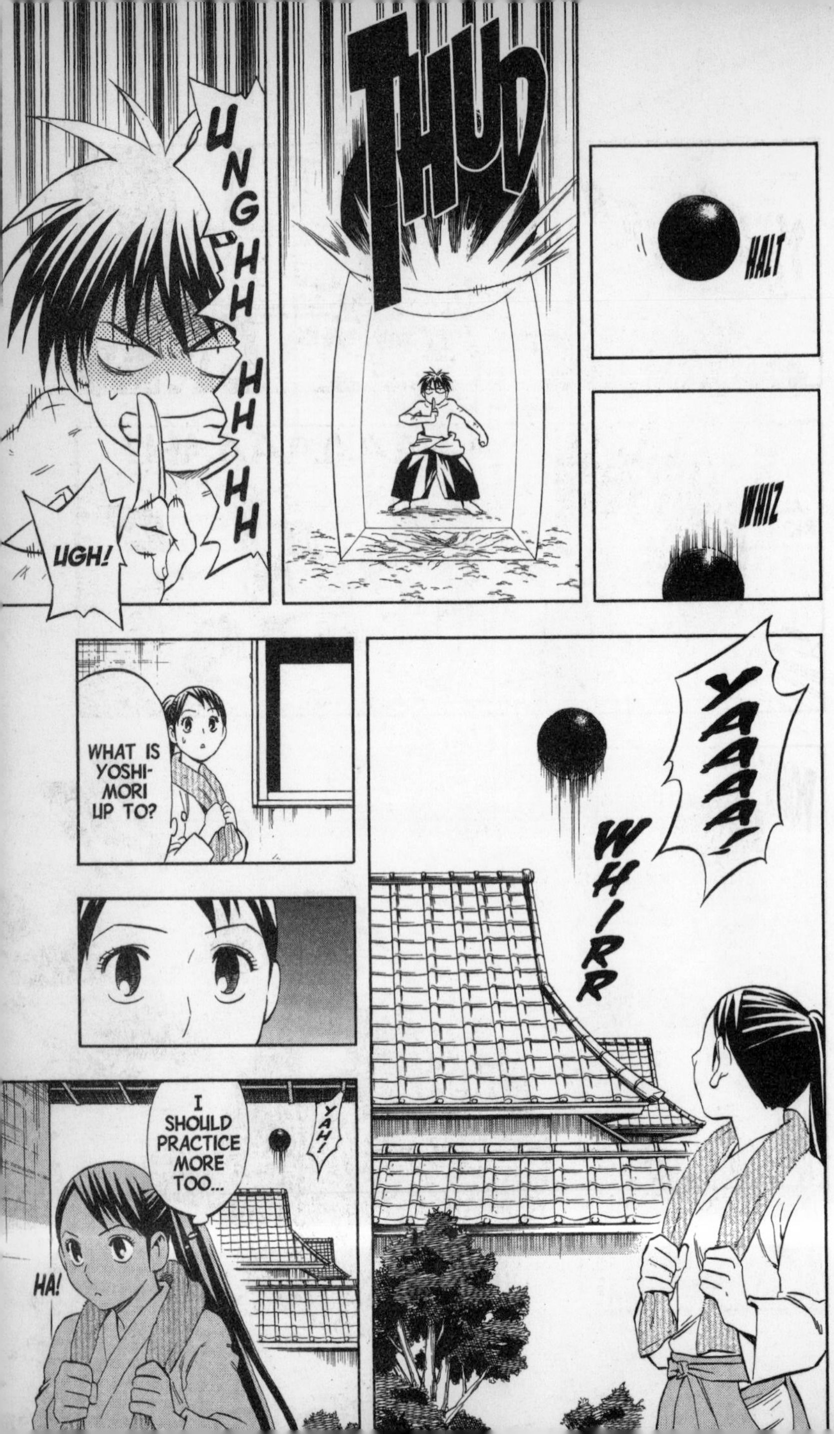
HALT
WHIZ
THUD
UNGHHHHHHH
UGH!
YAAAA!
WHIRR
WHAT IS YOSHI-MORI UP TO?
I SHOULD PRACTICE MORE TOO...
YAH!
HA!

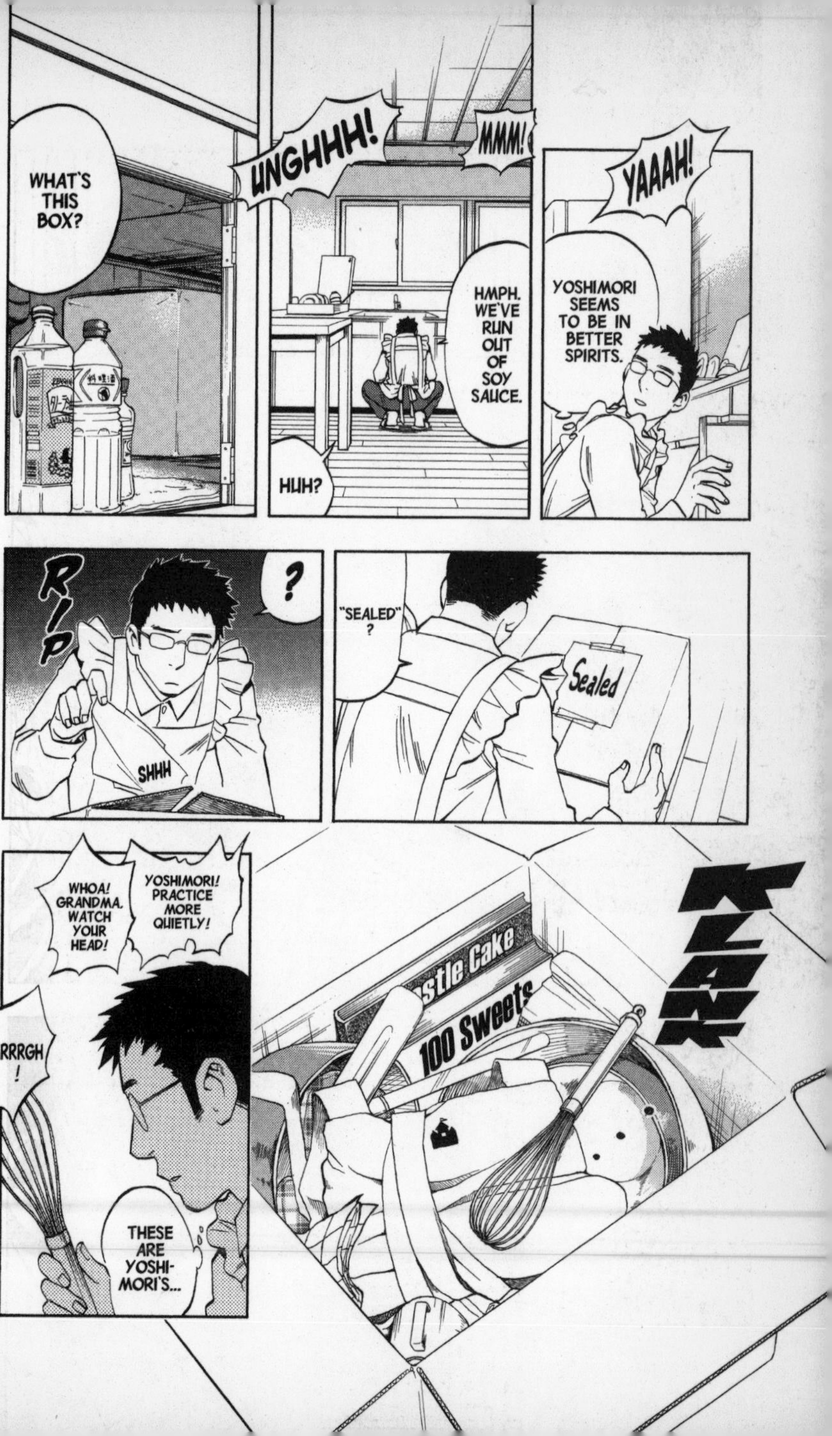
YAAAH!
YOSHIMORI SEEMS TO BE IN BETTER SPIRITS.
UNGHHH!
MMM!
HMPH. WE'VE RUN OUT OF SOY SAUCE.
HUH?
WHAT'S THIS BOX?
"SEALED"?
Sealed
?
RIP
SHHH
KLANK
stle Cake
100 Sweets
YOSHIMORI! PRACTICE MORE QUIETLY!
WHOA! GRANDMA, WATCH YOUR HEAD!
ARRRGH!
THESE ARE YOSHI-MORI'S...

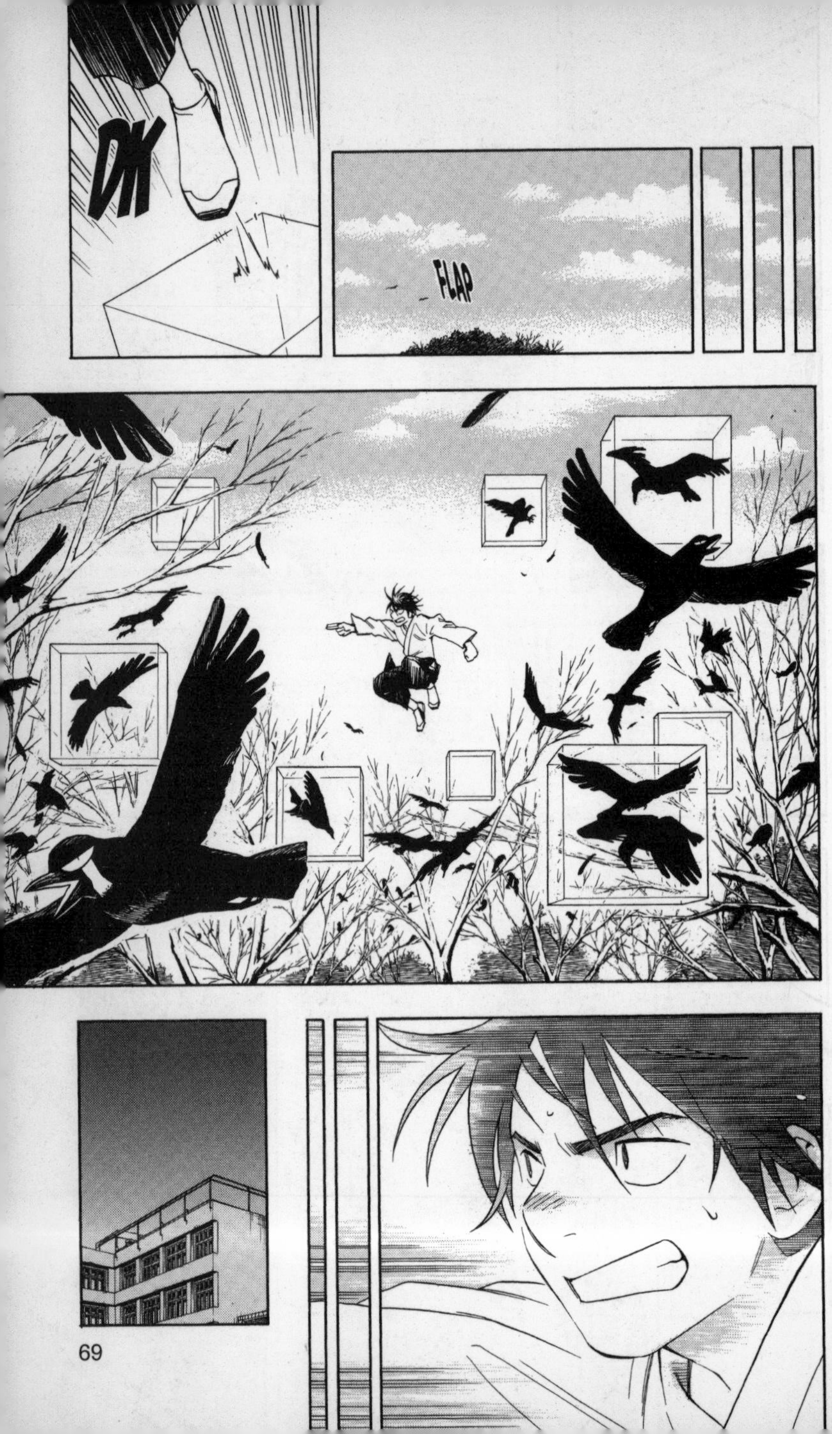
FLAP
DK

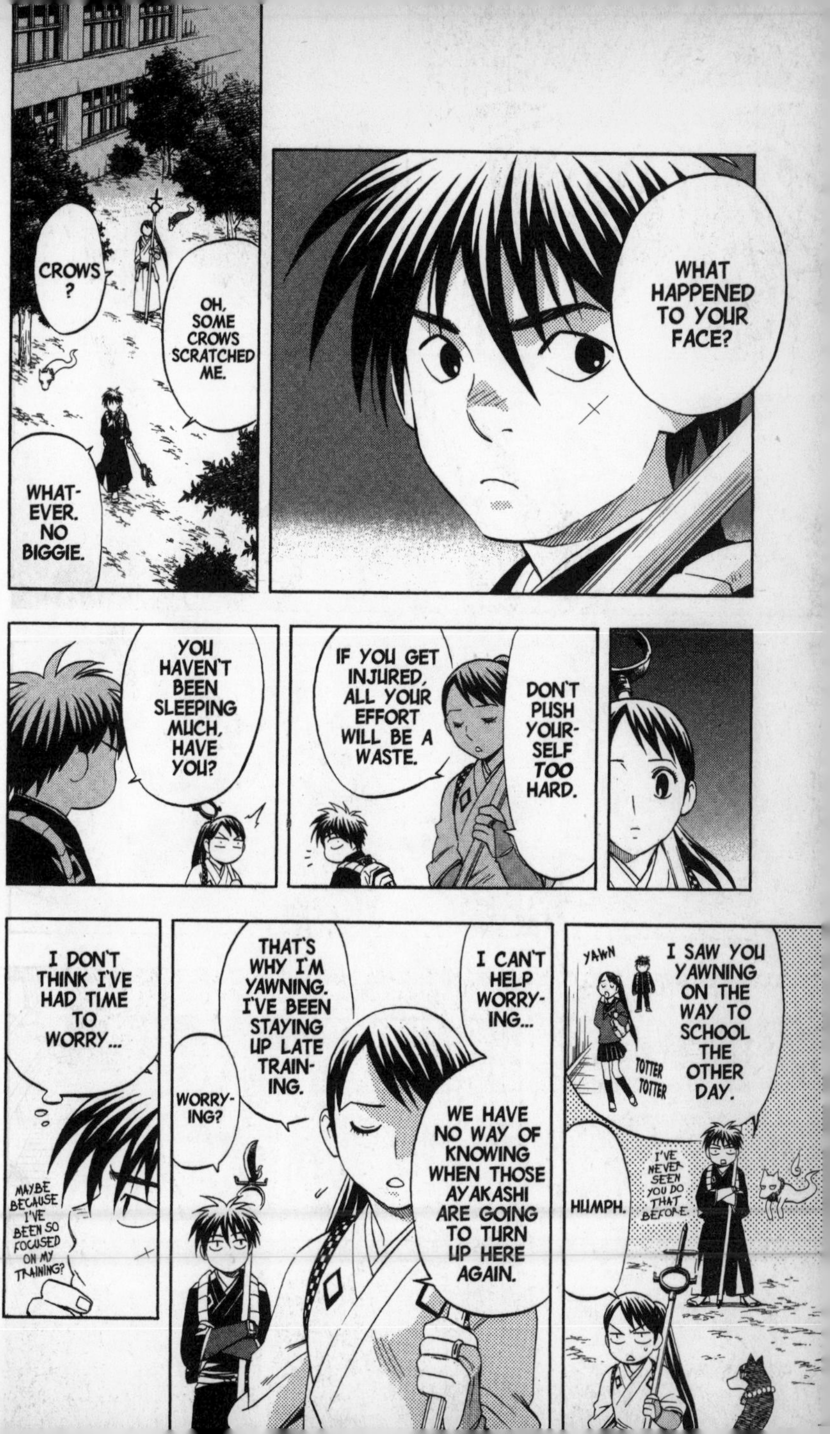
WHAT HAPPENED TO YOUR FACE?
OH, SOME CROWS SCRATCHED ME.
CROWS?
WHATEVER. NO BIGGIE.
DON'T PUSH YOURSELF *TOO* HARD.
IF YOU GET INJURED, ALL YOUR EFFORT WILL BE A WASTE.
YOU HAVEN'T BEEN SLEEPING MUCH, HAVE YOU?
I SAW YOU YAWNING ON THE WAY TO SCHOOL THE OTHER DAY.
YAWN
TOTTER TOTTER
I'VE NEVER SEEN YOU DO THAT BEFORE.
HUMPH.
I CAN'T HELP WORRYING...
WE HAVE NO WAY OF KNOWING WHEN THOSE AYAKASHI ARE GOING TO TURN UP HERE AGAIN.
THAT'S WHY I'M YAWNING. I'VE BEEN STAYING UP LATE TRAINING.
WORRYING?
I DON'T THINK I'VE HAD TIME TO WORRY...
MAYBE BECAUSE I'VE BEEN SO FOCUSED ON MY TRAINING?

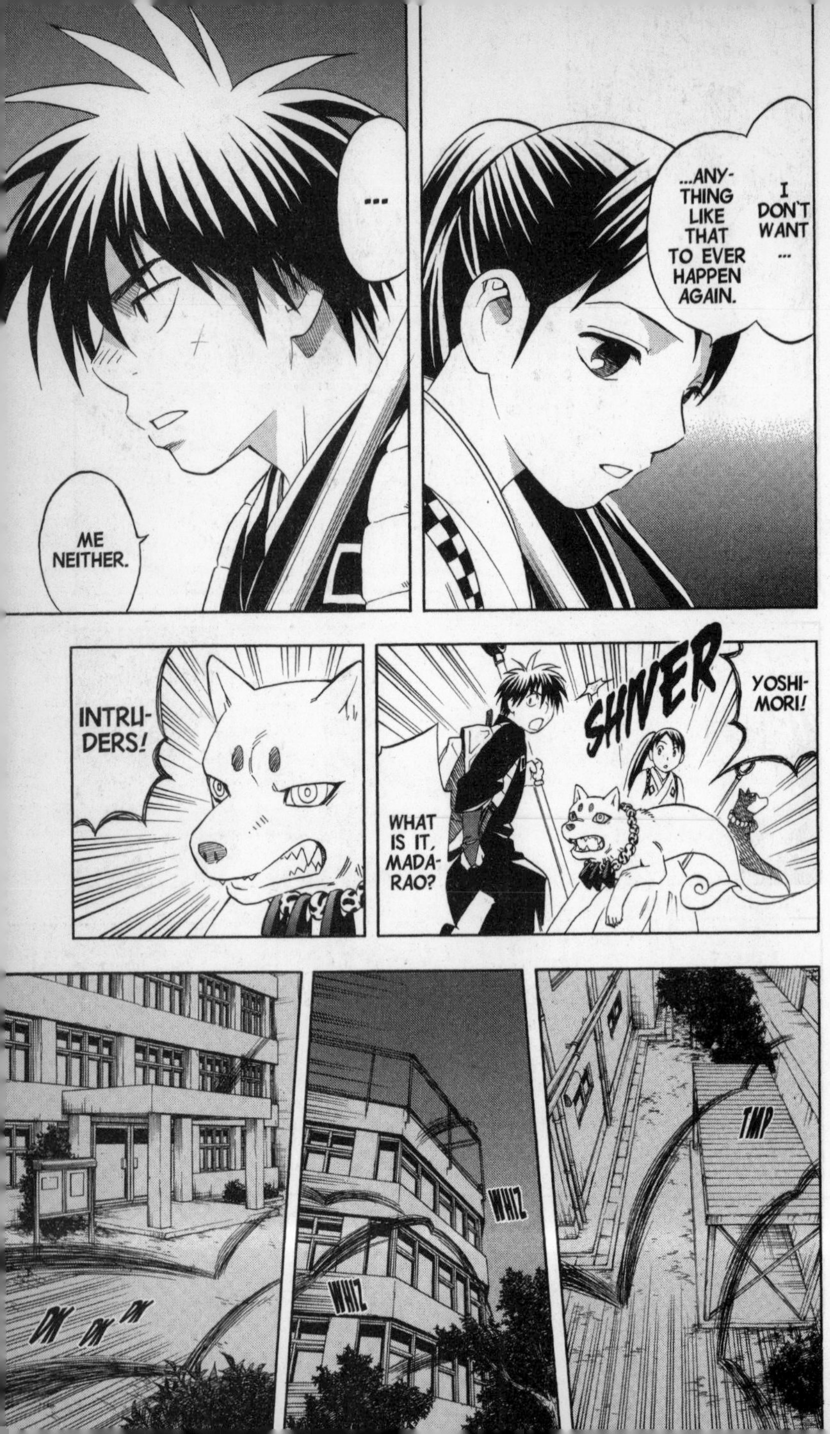
I DON'T WANT...
...ANY-THING LIKE THAT TO EVER HAPPEN AGAIN.
...
ME NEITHER.
YOSHI-MORI!
SHIVER
WHAT IS IT, MADARAO?
INTRU-DERS!
TMP
WHIZ
WHIZ
DK DK DK

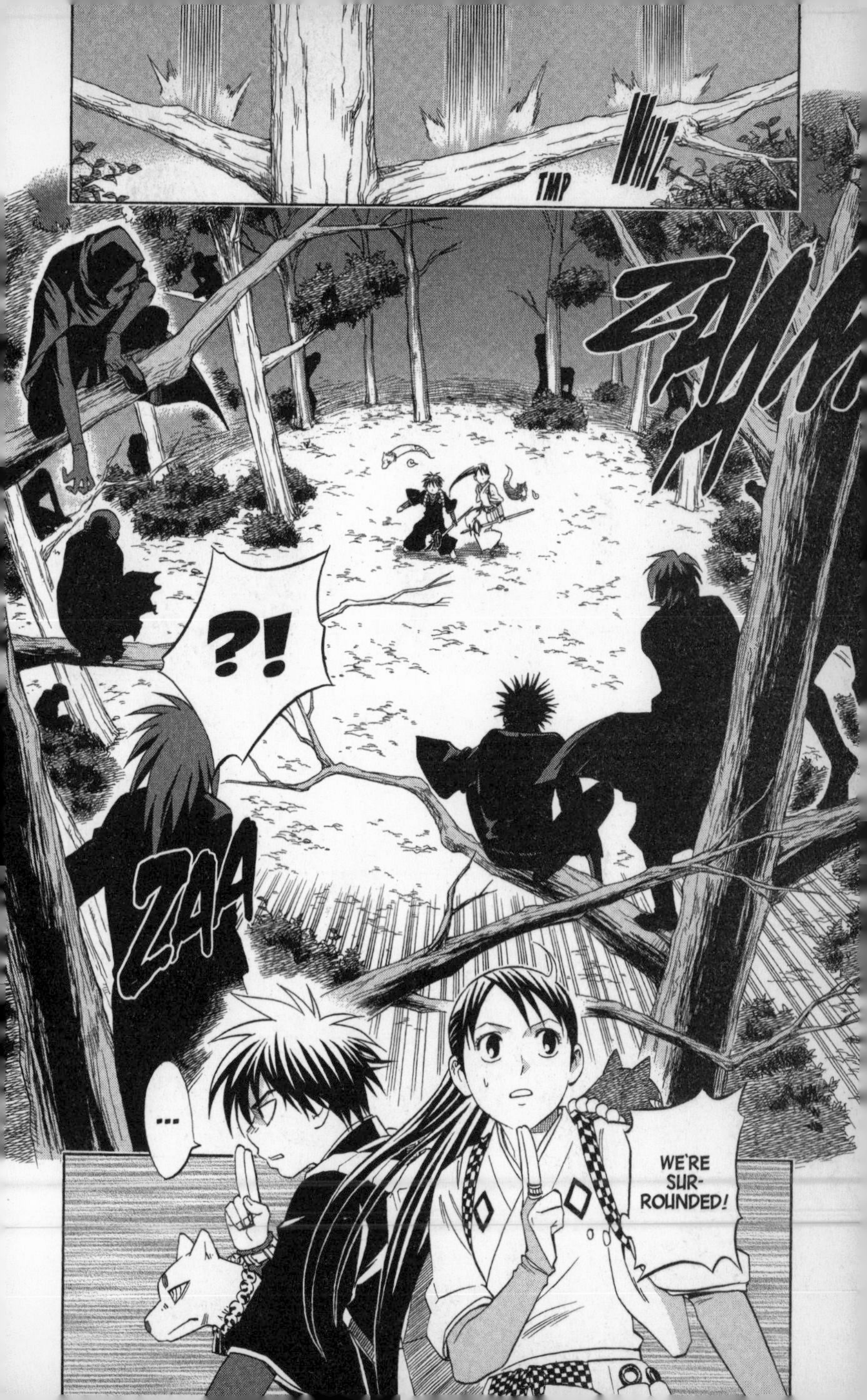
WHIZ
TMP
?!
ZAA
WE'RE SUR-ROUNDED!
...

VRRRR

WHAM WHAM WHAM WHAM

WHAM WHAM WHAM WHAM

KETSU! KETSU! KETSU! KETSU! KETSU! KETSU! KETSU! KETSU!

WHAM

WHAT THE...?

YAH!

ZIP

YOSHI-MORI?!

WOW! HIS SPEED AND HIS ACCURACY HAVE BOTH IMPROVED A LOT!

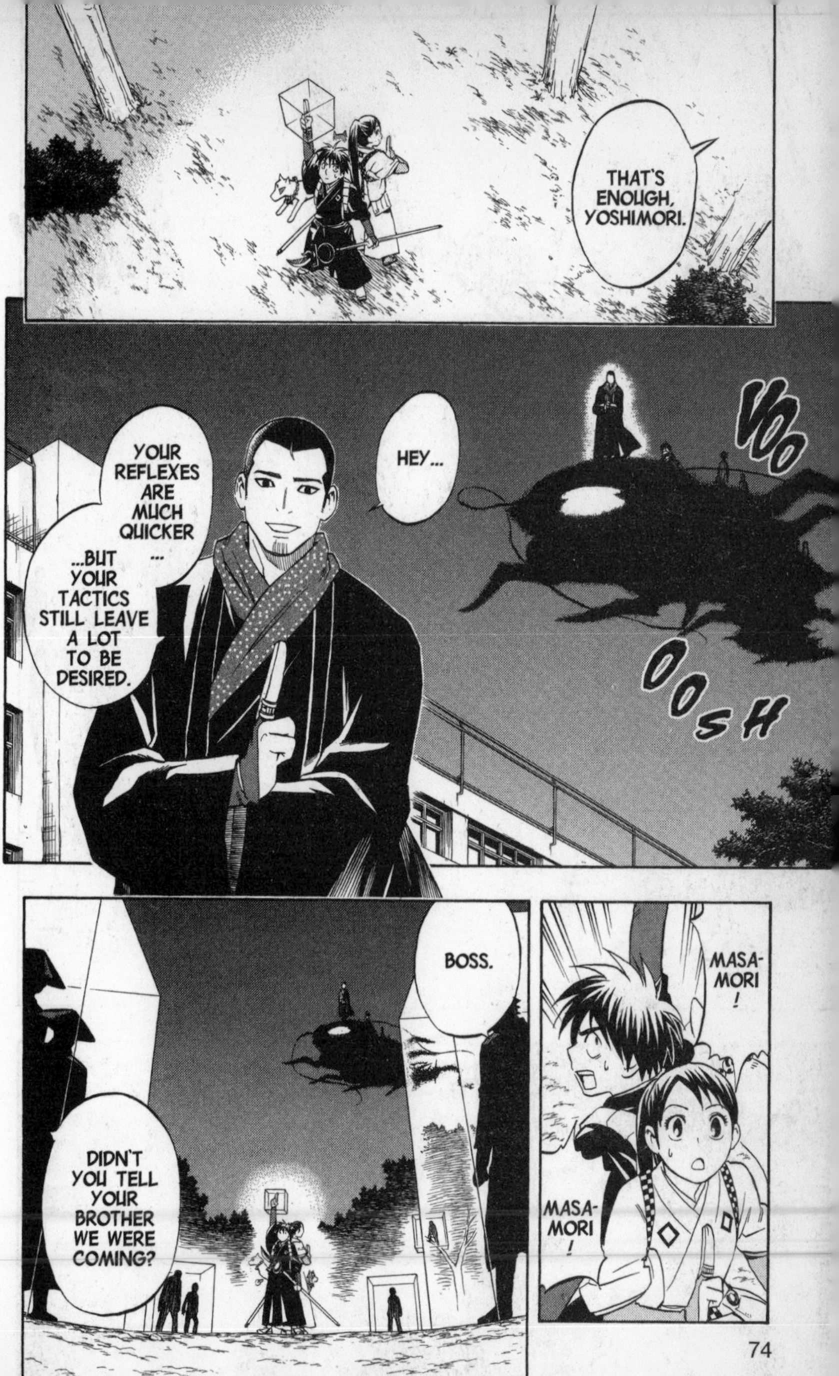
THAT'S ENOUGH, YOSHIMORI.
VOOOOSH
HEY...
YOUR REFLEXES ARE MUCH QUICKER...
...BUT YOUR TACTICS STILL LEAVE A LOT TO BE DESIRED.
MASA-MORI!
MASA-MORI!
BOSS.
DIDN'T YOU TELL YOUR BROTHER WE WERE COMING?

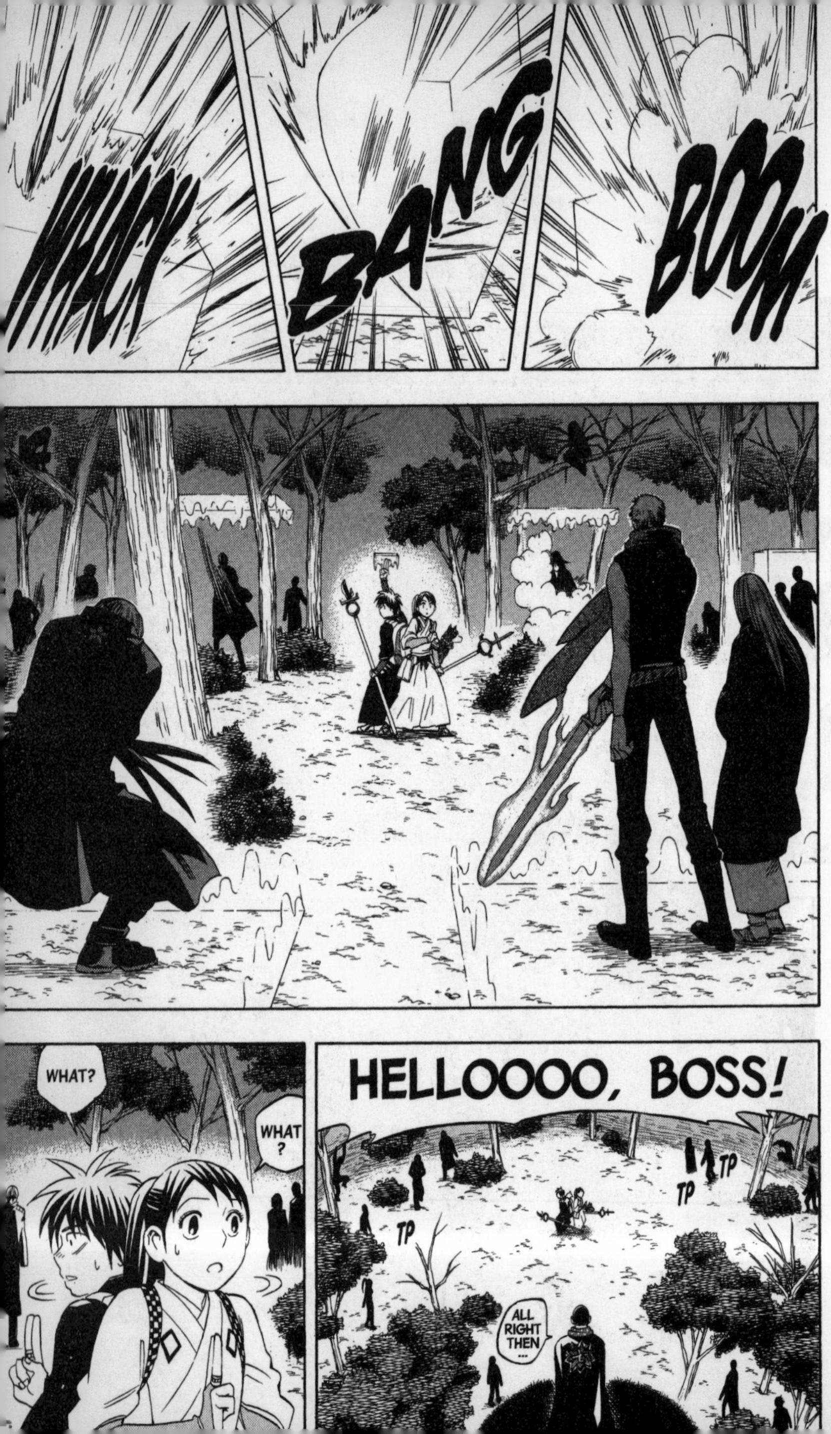
BOOM
BANG
WHACK
HELLOOOO, BOSS!
TP
TP
TP
ALL RIGHT THEN...
WHAT?
WHAT?

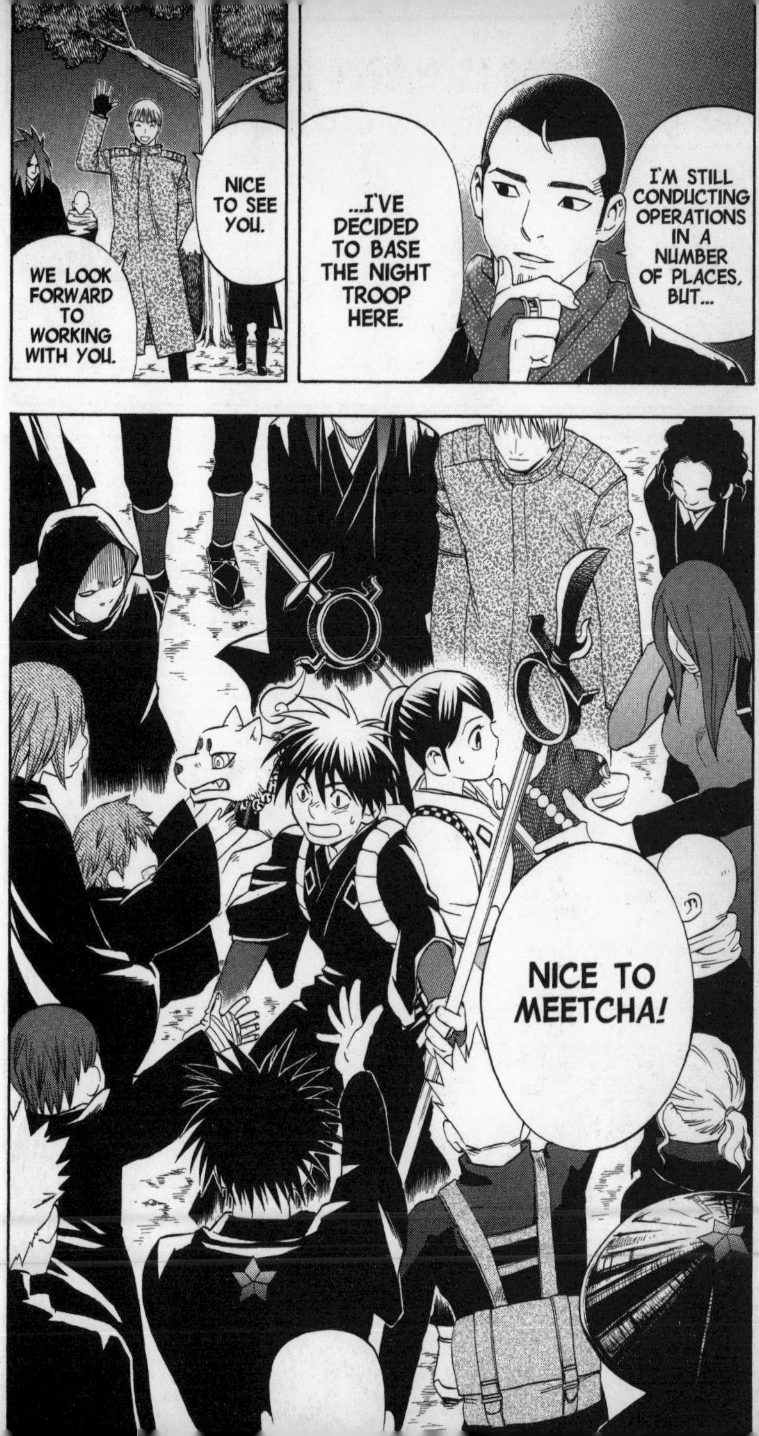
I'M STILL CONDUCTING OPERATIONS IN A NUMBER OF PLACES, BUT...
...I'VE DECIDED TO BASE THE NIGHT TROOP HERE.
NICE TO SEE YOU.
WE LOOK FORWARD TO WORKING WITH YOU.
NICE TO MEETCHA!

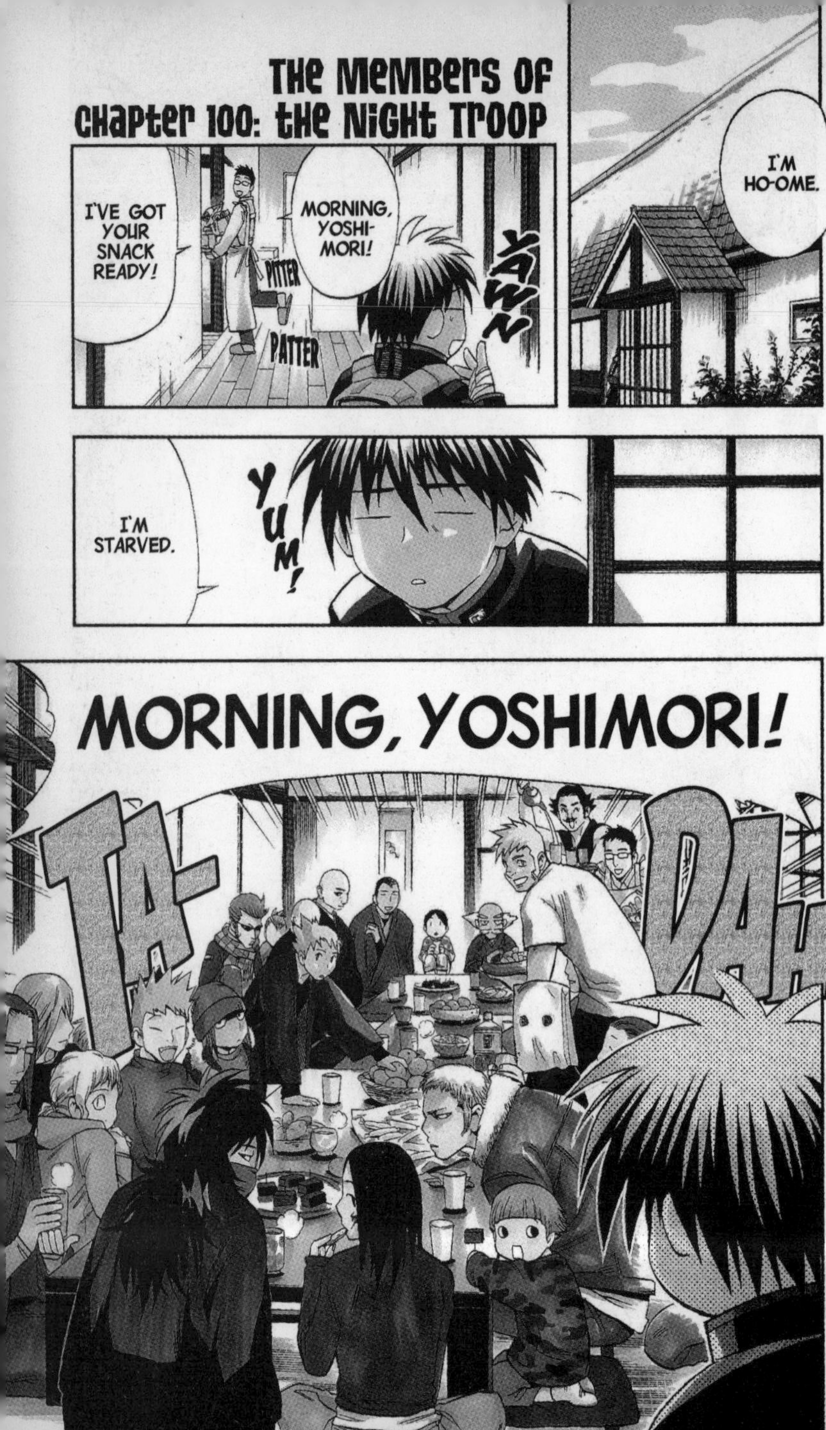
Chapter 100: The Members of the Night Troop
I'M HO-OME.
YAWN
MORNING, YOSHI-MORI!
PITTER
PATTER
I'VE GOT YOUR SNACK READY!
YUM!
I'M STARVED.
MORNING, YOSHIMORI!
TA-
DAH

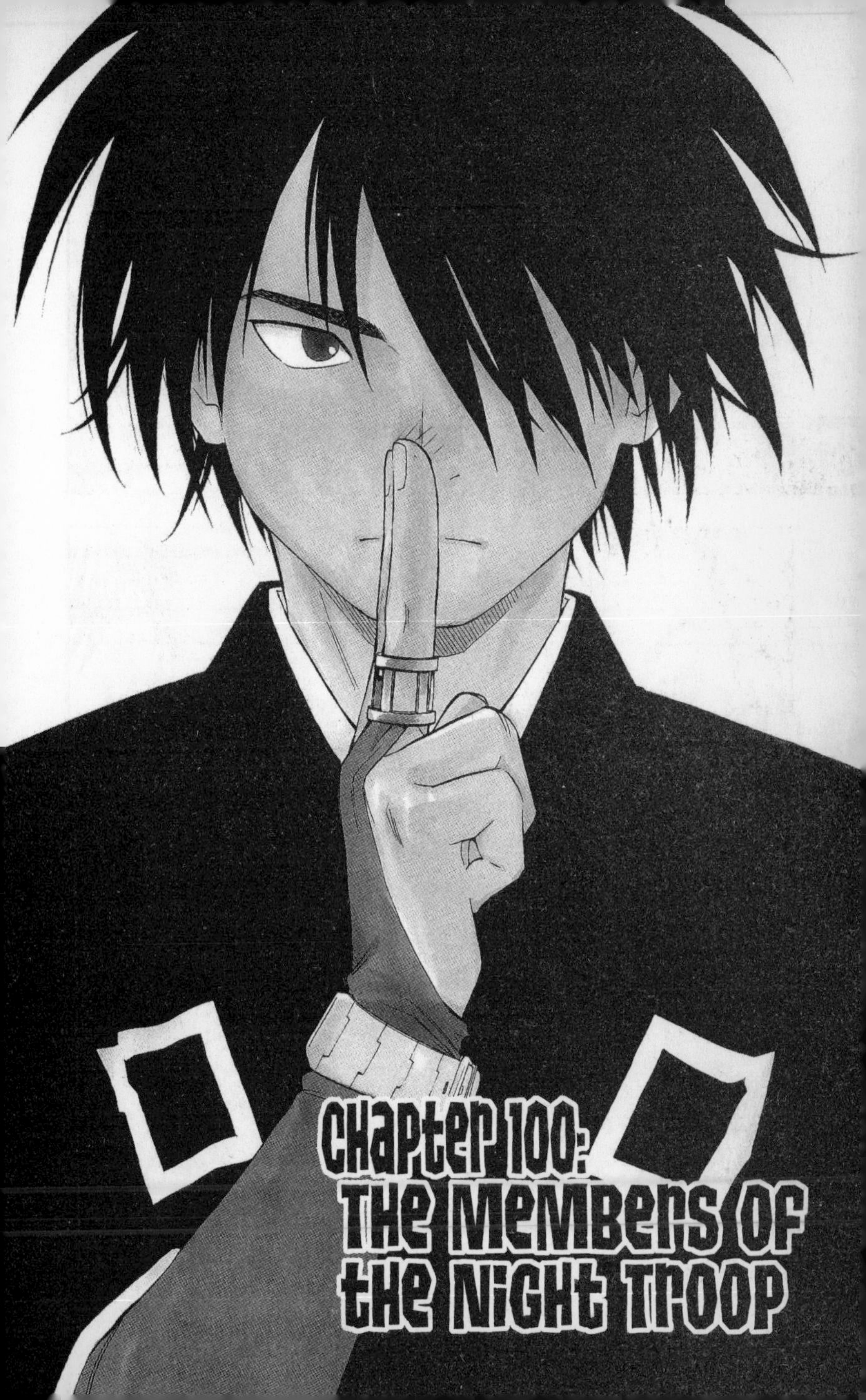

CHAPTER 100:
THE MEMBERS OF
THE NIGHT TROOP

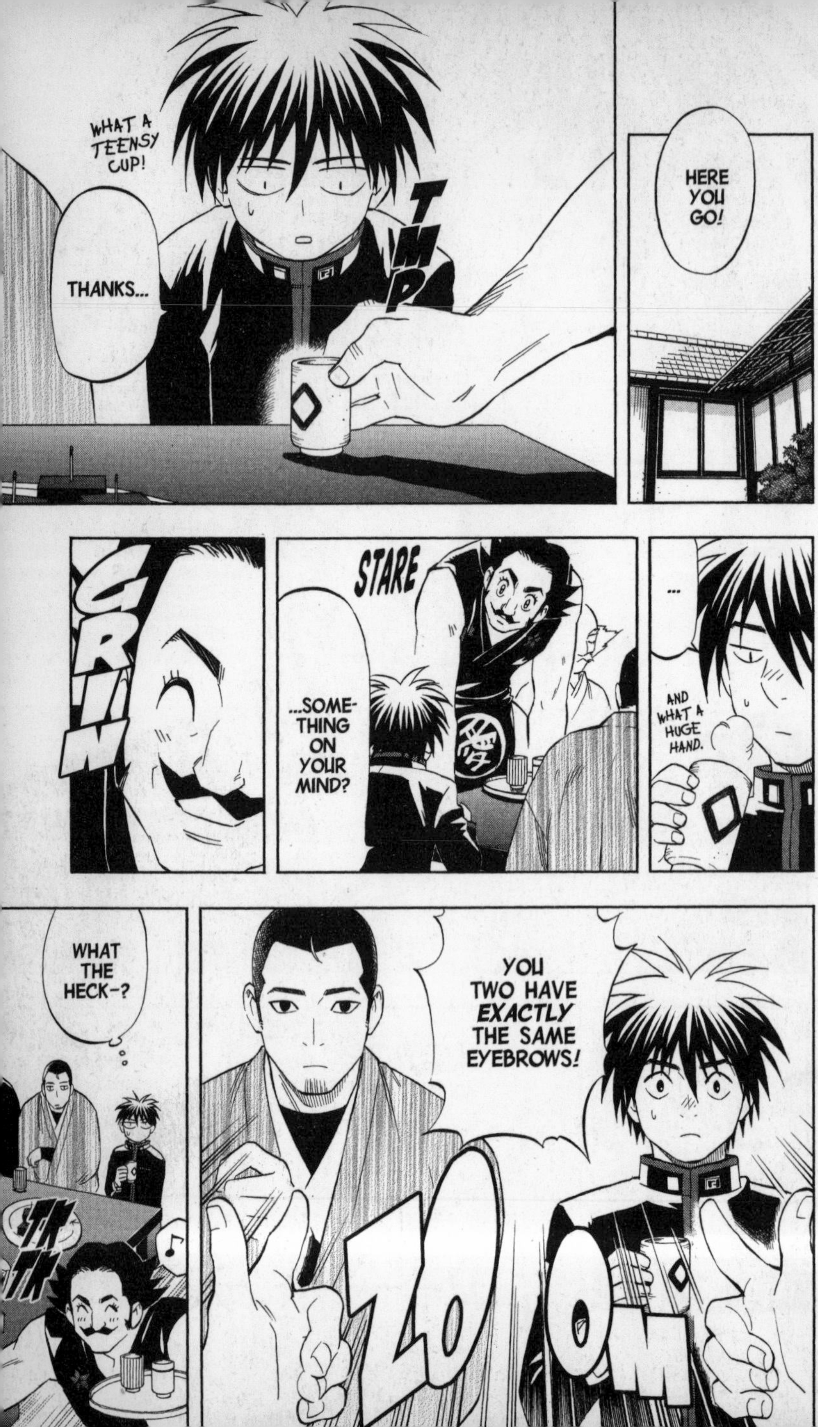
HERE YOU GO!
WHAT A TEENSY CUP!
THANKS...
TMP
...
AND WHAT A HUGE HAND.
STARE
...SOMETHING ON YOUR MIND?
GRIN
YOU TWO HAVE *EXACTLY* THE SAME EYEBROWS!
ZOOM
WHAT THE HECK-?

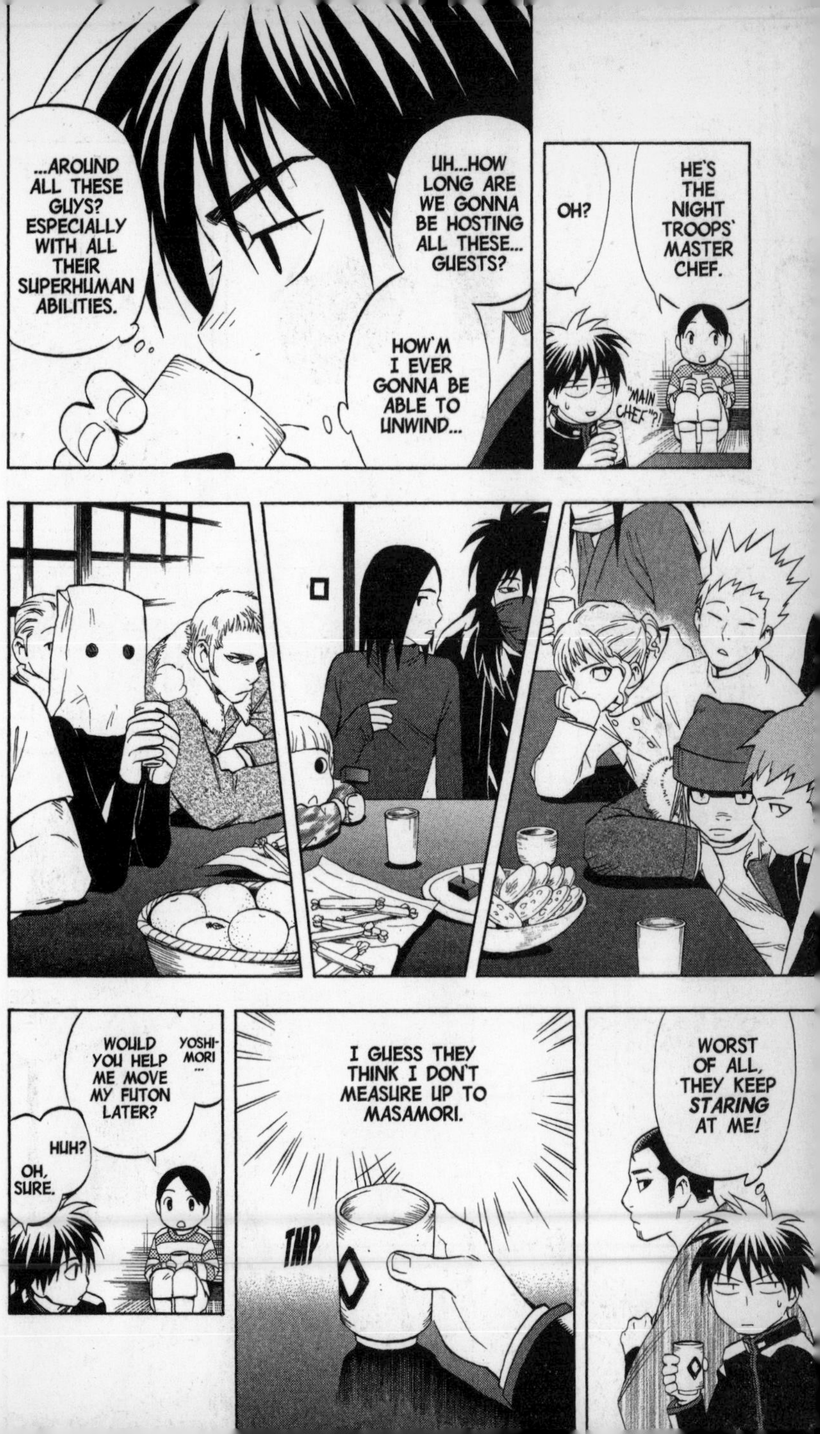
OH?
HE'S THE NIGHT TROOPS' MASTER CHEF.
"MAIN CHEF"?!
UH...HOW LONG ARE WE GONNA BE HOSTING ALL THESE... GUESTS?
HOW'M I EVER GONNA BE ABLE TO UNWIND...
...AROUND ALL THESE GUYS? ESPECIALLY WITH ALL THEIR SUPERHUMAN ABILITIES.
WORST OF ALL, THEY KEEP *STARING* AT ME!
I GUESS THEY THINK I DON'T MEASURE UP TO MASAMORI.
TMP
YOSHIMORI...
WOULD YOU HELP ME MOVE MY FUTON LATER?
HUH?
OH, SURE.

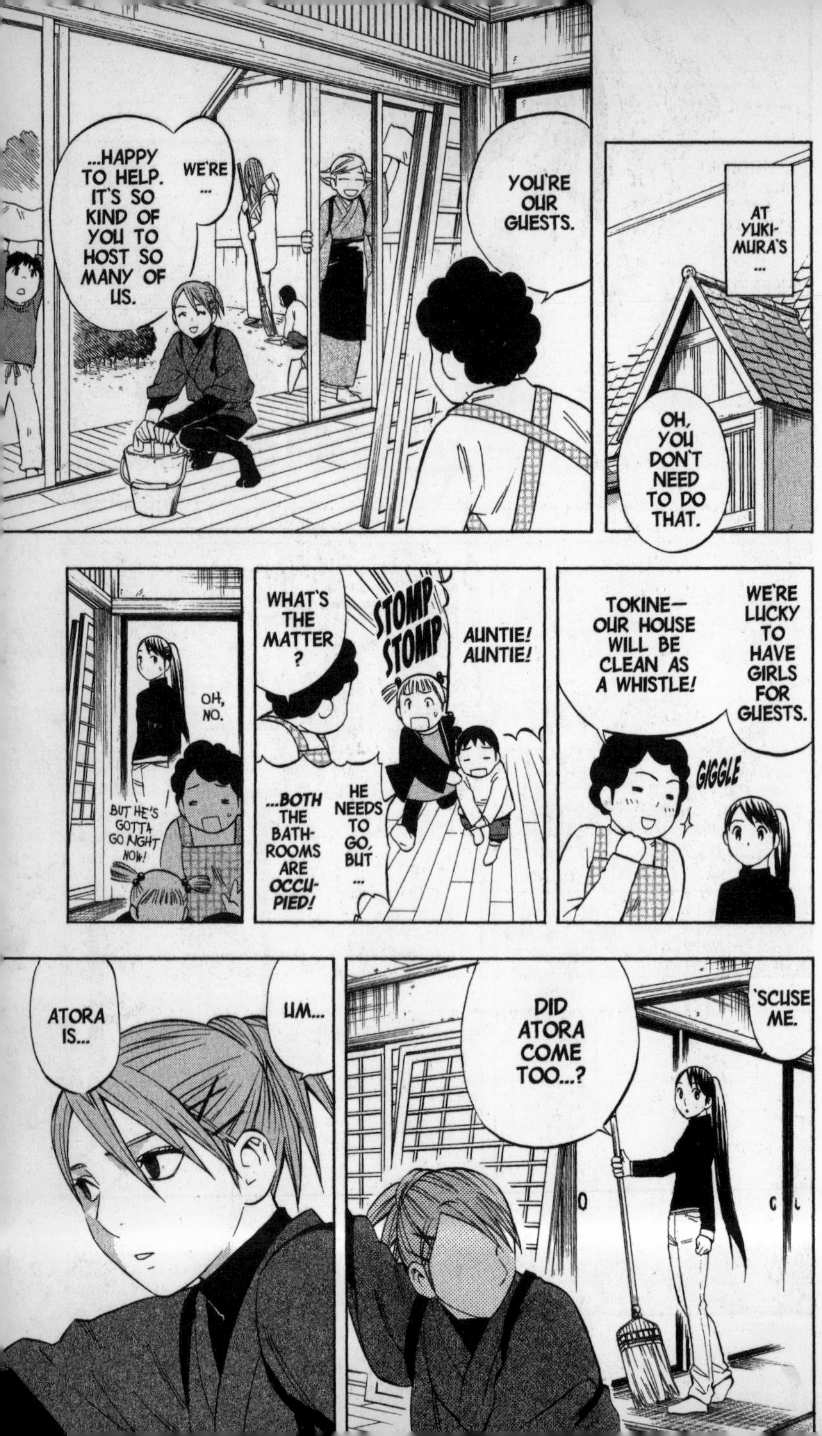
AT YUKIMURA'S ...
OH, YOU DON'T NEED TO DO THAT.
YOU'RE OUR GUESTS.
WE'RE ...
...HAPPY TO HELP. IT'S SO KIND OF YOU TO HOST SO MANY OF US.
WE'RE LUCKY TO HAVE GIRLS FOR GUESTS.
TOKINE— OUR HOUSE WILL BE CLEAN AS A WHISTLE!
GIGGLE
AUNTIE! AUNTIE!
STOMP STOMP
WHAT'S THE MATTER?
HE NEEDS TO GO, BUT ...
...BOTH THE BATHROOMS ARE OCCUPIED!
OH, NO.
BUT HE'S GOTTA GO RIGHT NOW!
'SCUSE ME.
DID ATORA COME TOO...?
UM...
ATORA IS...

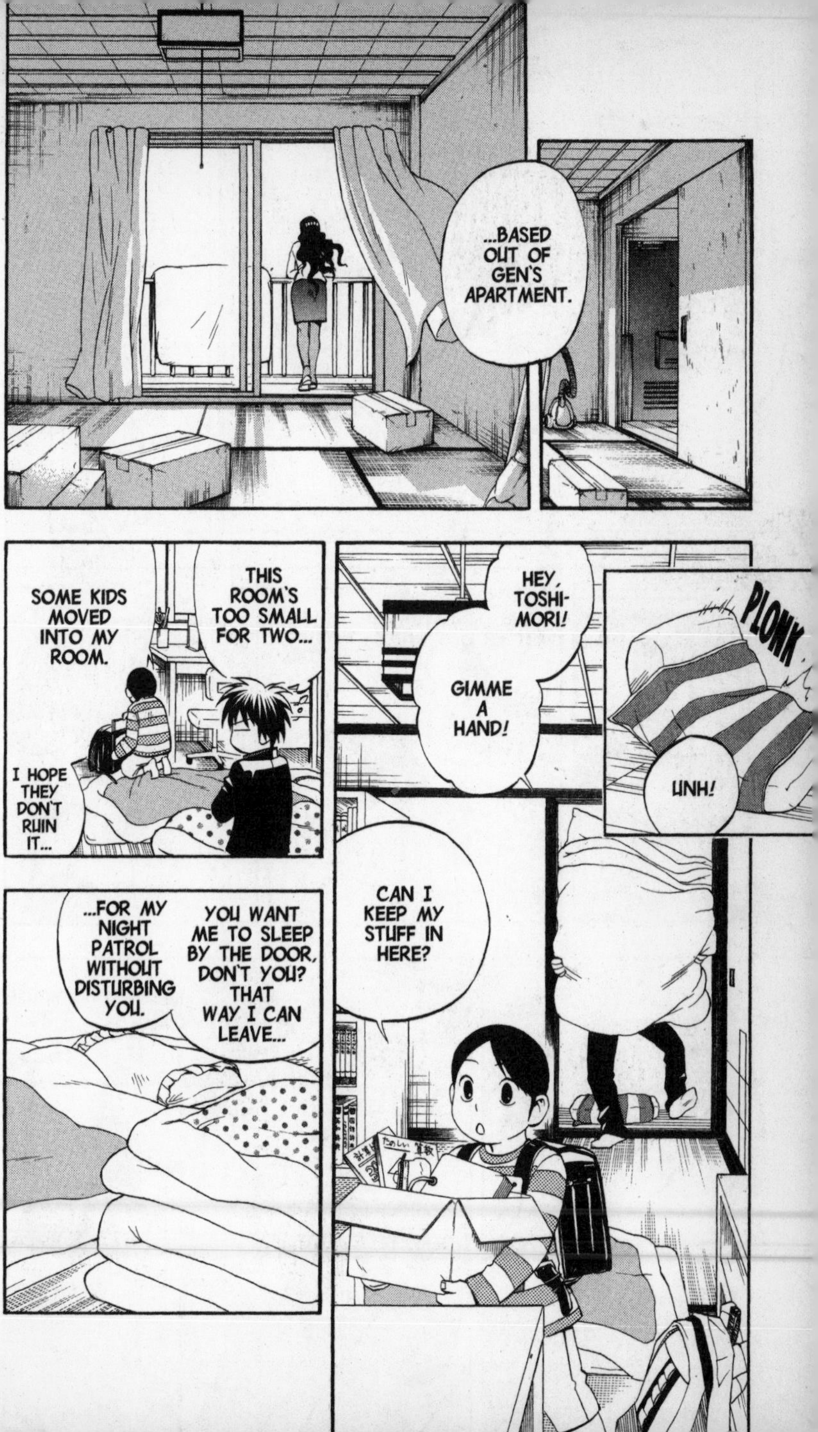
...BASED OUT OF GEN'S APARTMENT.
PLONK
UNH!
HEY, TOSHI-MORI!
GIMME A HAND!
THIS ROOM'S TOO SMALL FOR TWO...
SOME KIDS MOVED INTO MY ROOM.
I HOPE THEY DON'T RUIN IT...
CAN I KEEP MY STUFF IN HERE?
YOU WANT ME TO SLEEP BY THE DOOR, DON'T YOU? THAT WAY I CAN LEAVE...
...FOR MY NIGHT PATROL WITHOUT DISTURBING YOU.

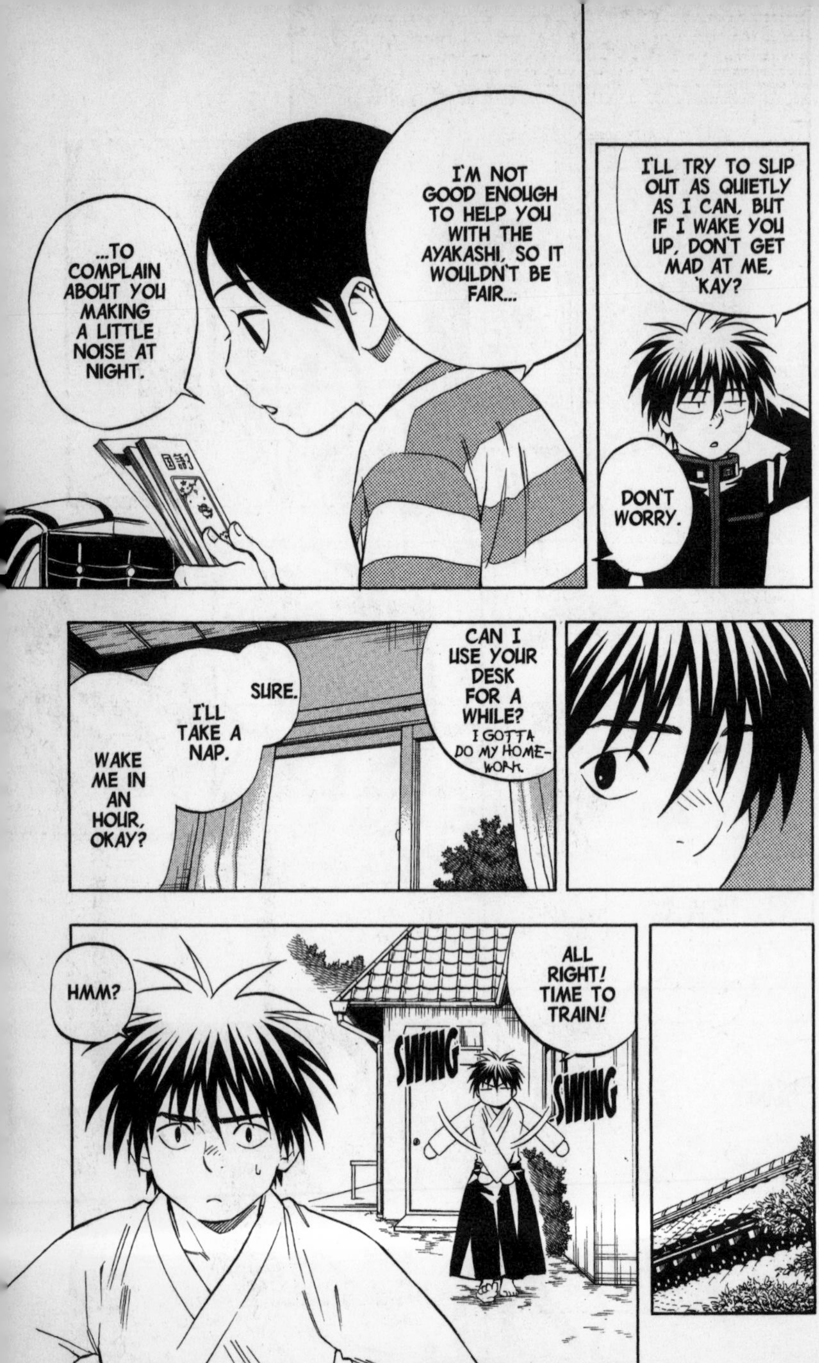
I'LL TRY TO SLIP OUT AS QUIETLY AS I CAN, BUT IF I WAKE YOU UP, DON'T GET MAD AT ME, 'KAY?
DON'T WORRY.
I'M NOT GOOD ENOUGH TO HELP YOU WITH THE AYAKASHI, SO IT WOULDN'T BE FAIR...
...TO COMPLAIN ABOUT YOU MAKING A LITTLE NOISE AT NIGHT.
CAN I USE YOUR DESK FOR A WHILE?
I GOTTA DO MY HOMEWORK.
SURE.
I'LL TAKE A NAP.
WAKE ME IN AN HOUR, OKAY?
ALL RIGHT! TIME TO TRAIN!
SWING
SWING
HMM?

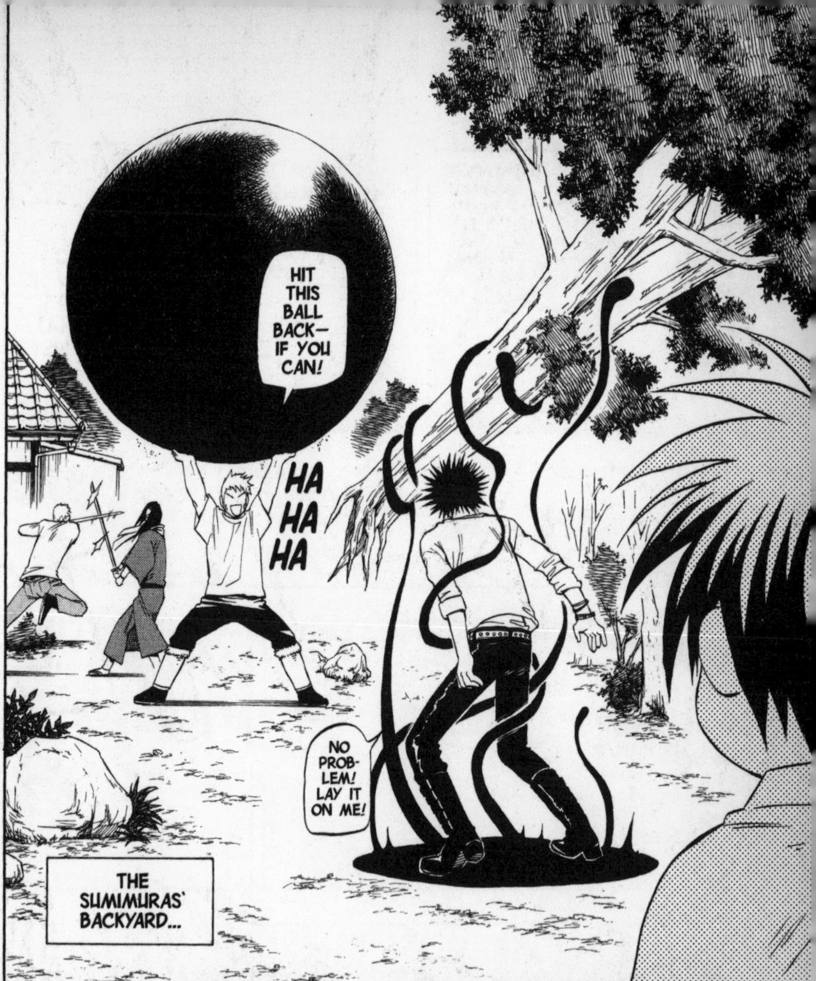
THE SUMIMURAS' BACKYARD...
HIT THIS BALL BACK—IF YOU CAN!
HA HA HA
NO PROB-LEM! LAY IT ON ME!

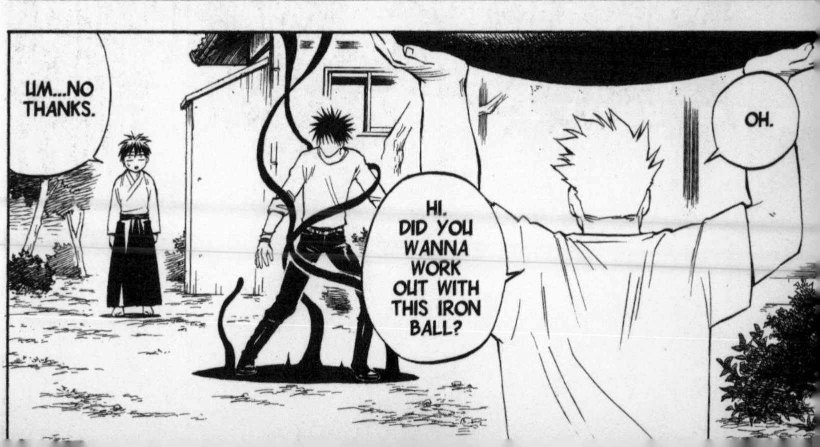
HI. DID YOU WANNA WORK OUT WITH THIS IRON BALL?
OH.
UM...NO THANKS.

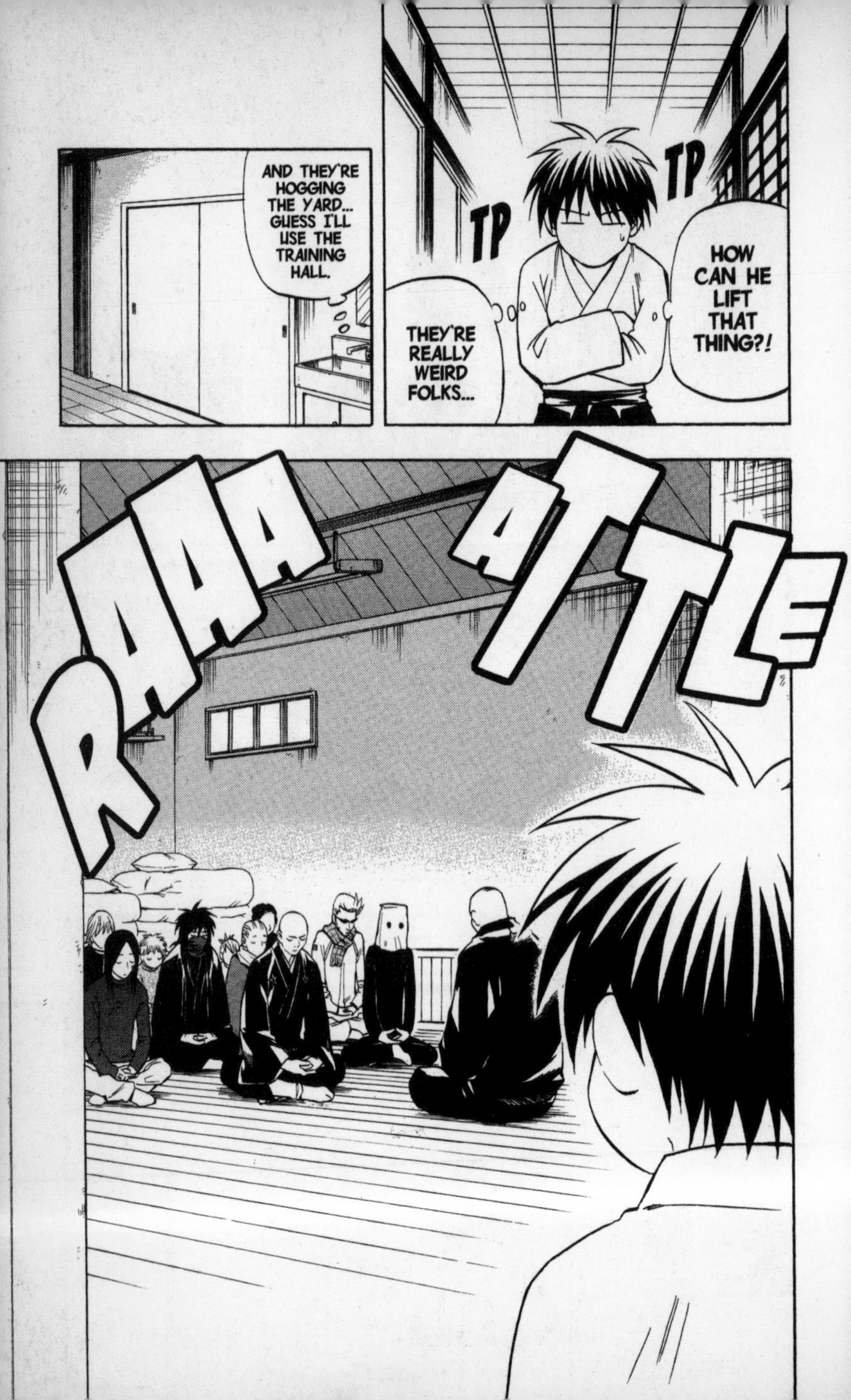

TP
HOW CAN HE LIFT THAT THING?!
TP
THEY'RE REALLY WEIRD FOLKS...
AND THEY'RE HOGGING THE YARD... GUESS I'LL USE THE TRAINING HALL.
RAAA ATTLE

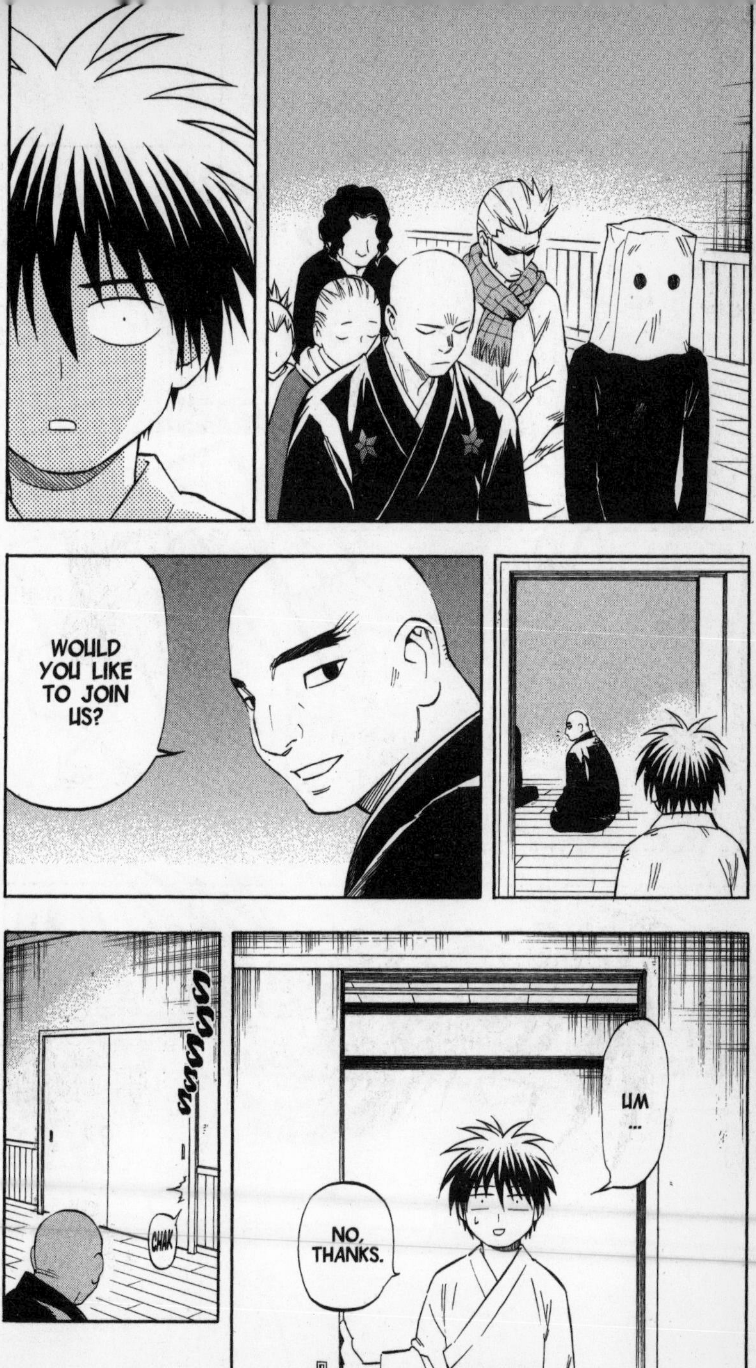
WOULD YOU LIKE TO JOIN US?
UM ...
NO, THANKS.
CHAK

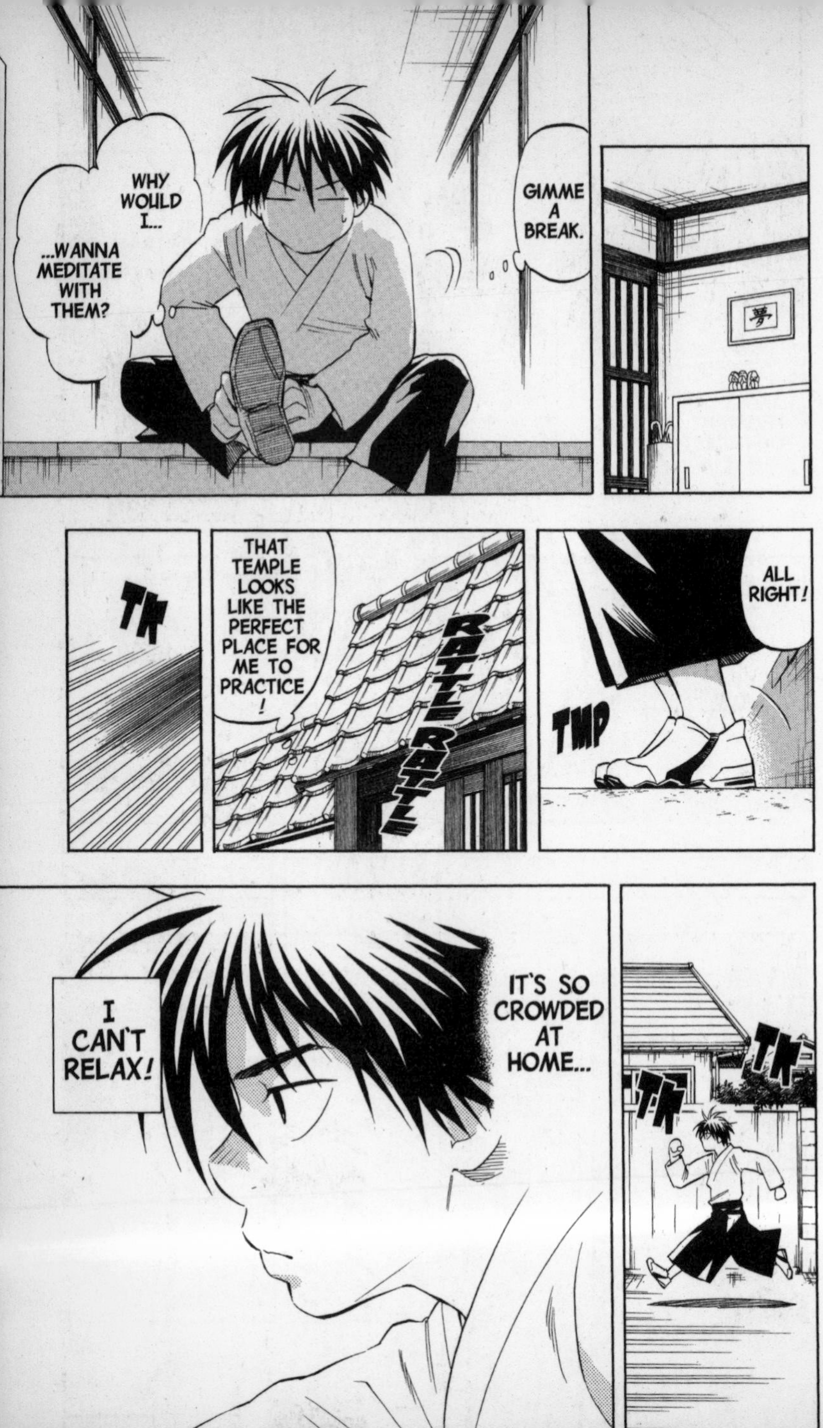
GIMME A BREAK.
WHY WOULD I...
...WANNA MEDITATE WITH THEM?
ALL RIGHT!
TMP
THAT TEMPLE LOOKS LIKE THE PERFECT PLACE FOR ME TO PRACTICE!
RATTLE RATTLE
TK
TK
TK
IT'S SO CROWDED AT HOME...
I CAN'T RELAX!

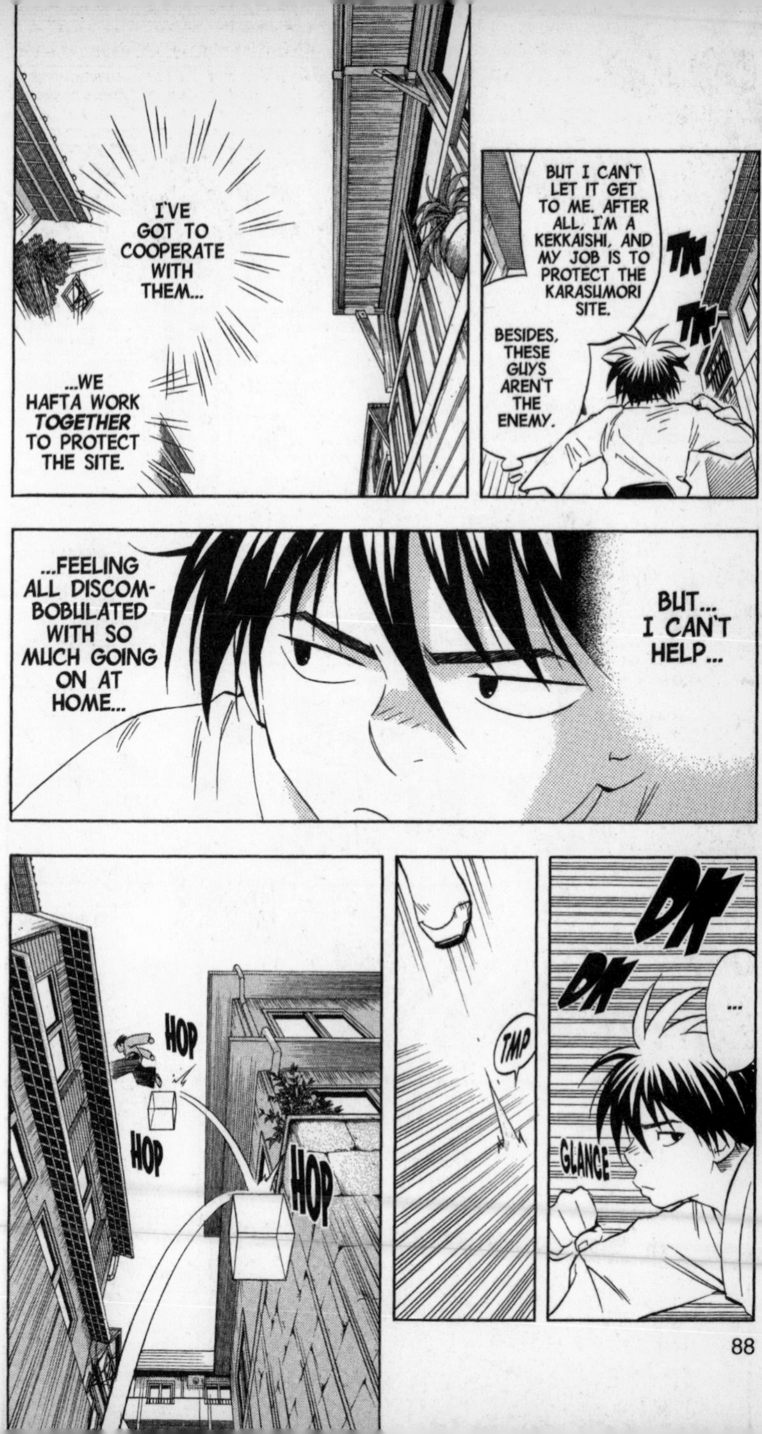
BUT I CAN'T LET IT GET TO ME. AFTER ALL, I'M A KEKKAISHI, AND MY JOB IS TO PROTECT THE KARASUMORI SITE.
TK
TK
BESIDES, THESE GUYS AREN'T THE ENEMY.
I'VE GOT TO COOPERATE WITH THEM...
...WE HAFTA WORK *TOGETHER* TO PROTECT THE SITE.
BUT... I CAN'T HELP...
...FEELING ALL DISCOM-BOBULATED WITH SO MUCH GOING ON AT HOME...
DK
DK
...
GLANCE
TMP
HOP
HOP
HOP

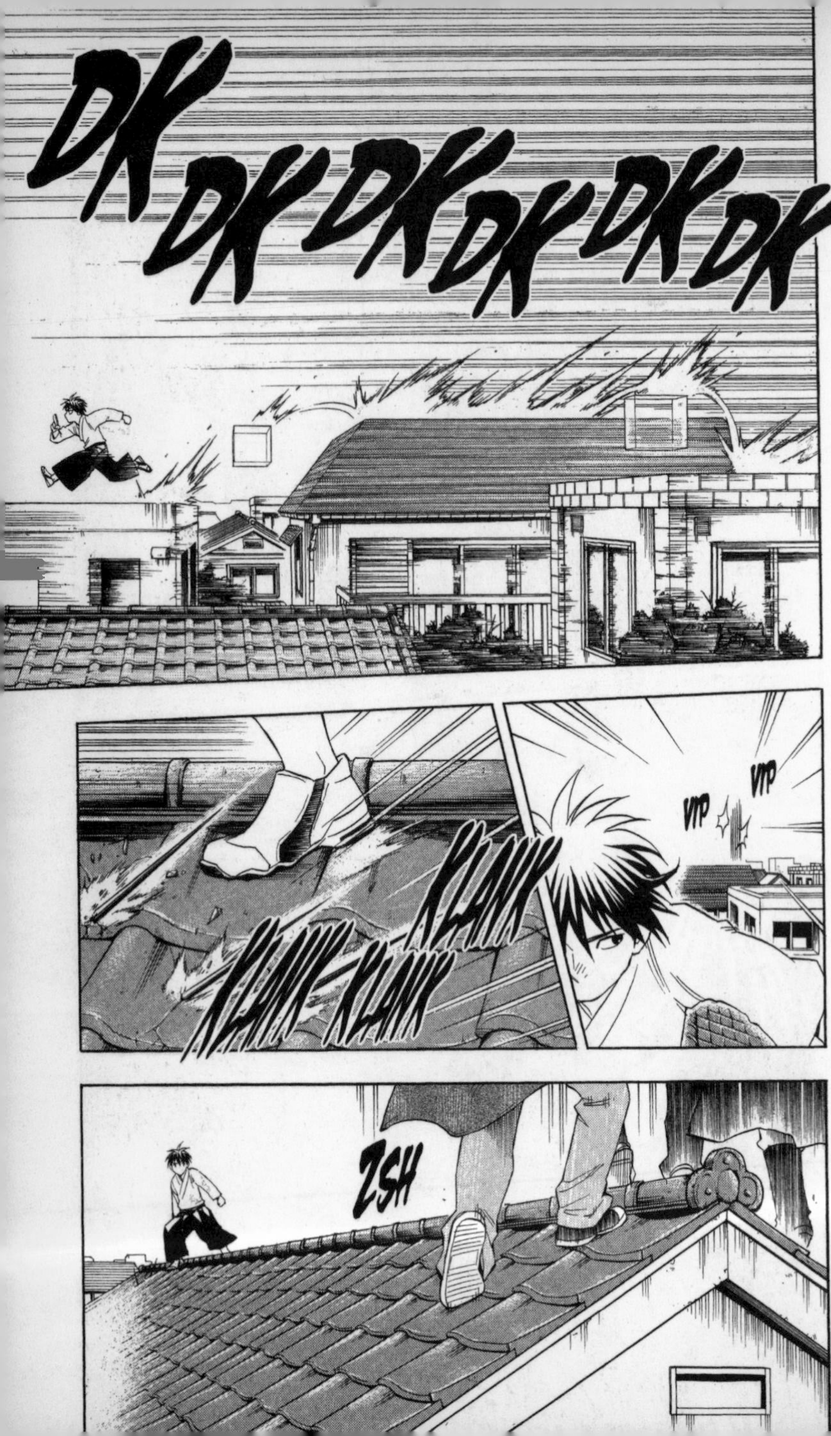
DK DK DK DK DK DK
VIP VIP
KLANK KLANK KLANK KLANK
ZSH

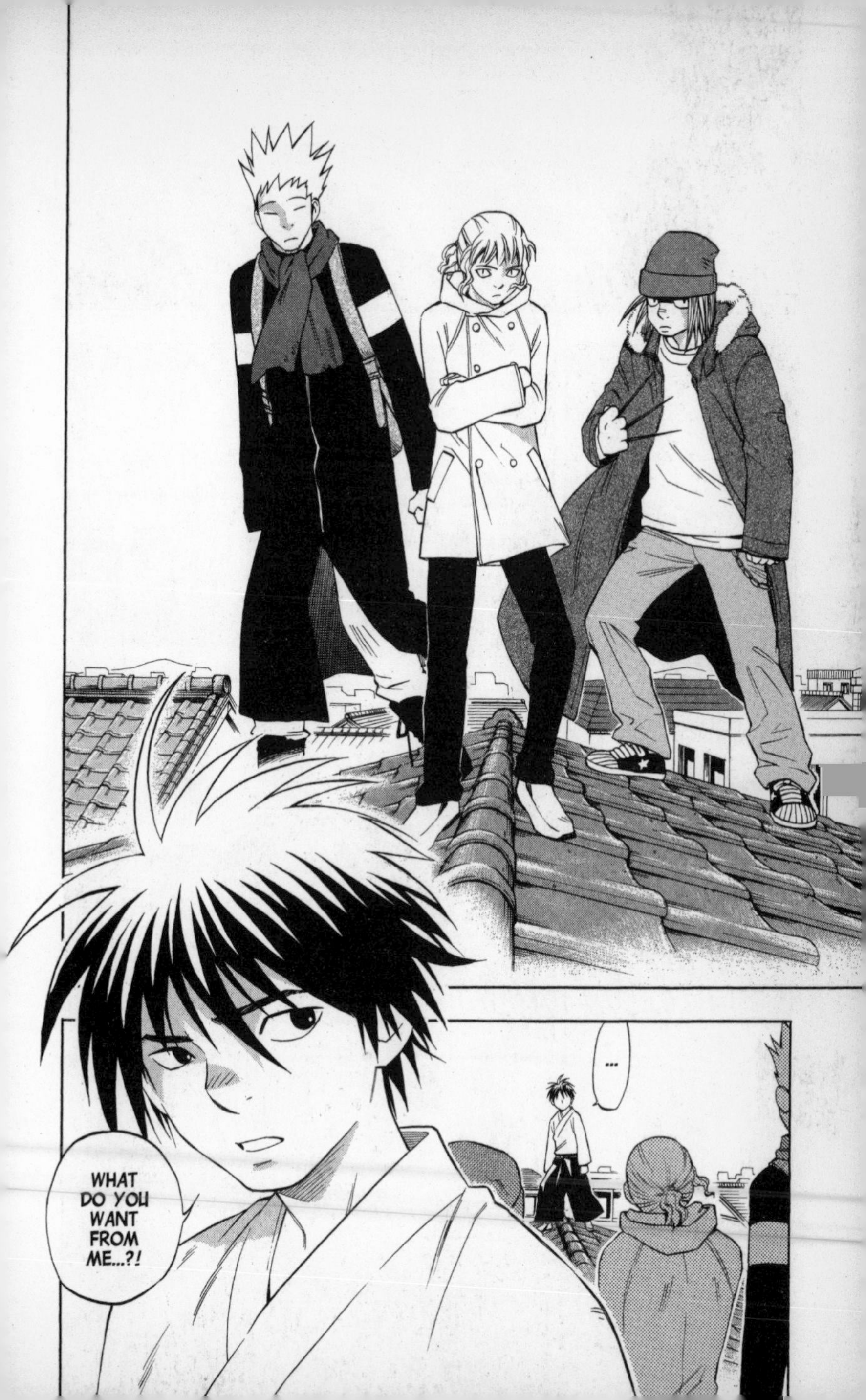
...
WHAT DO YOU WANT FROM ME...?!

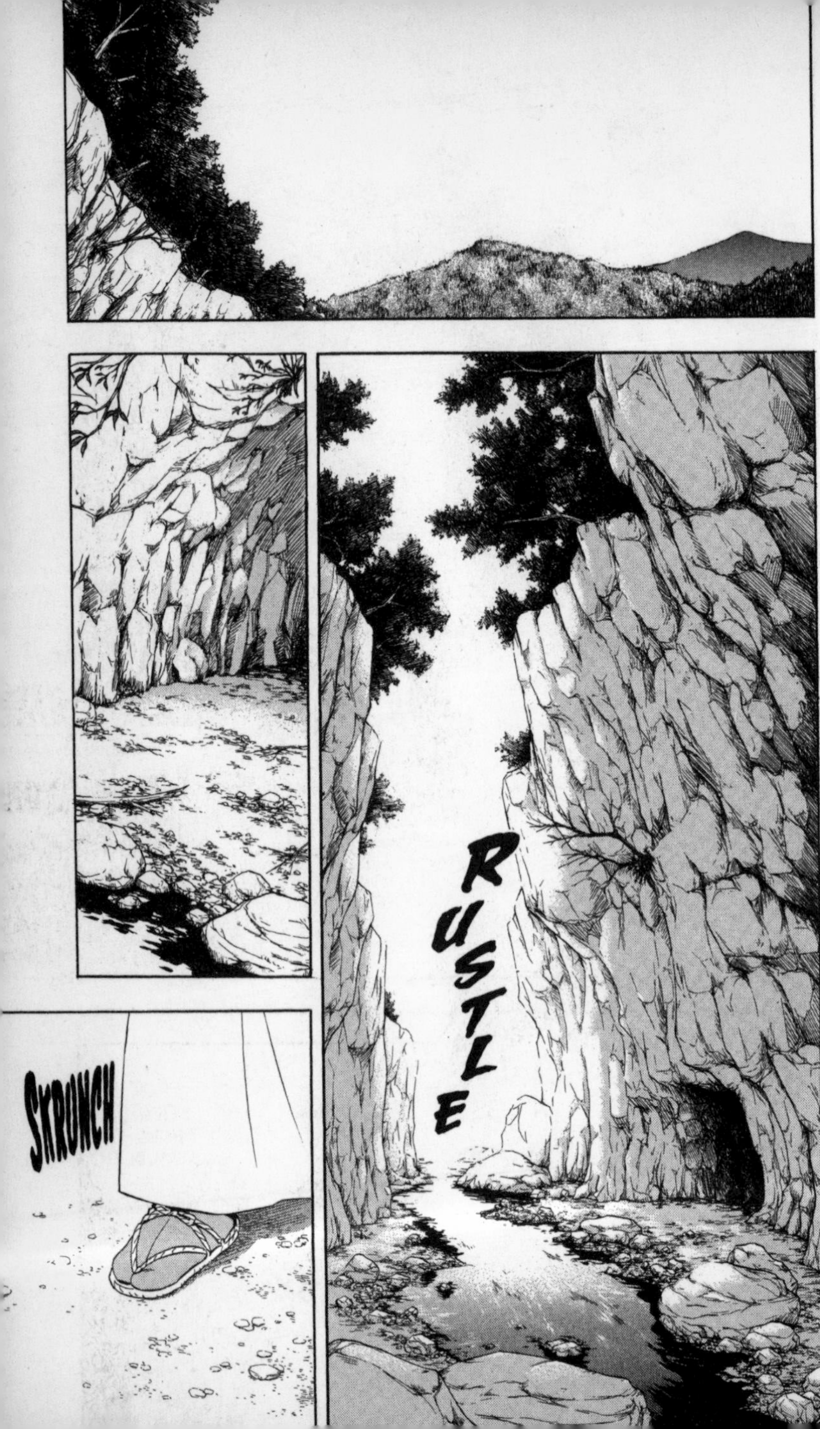
RUSTLE
SKRUNCH

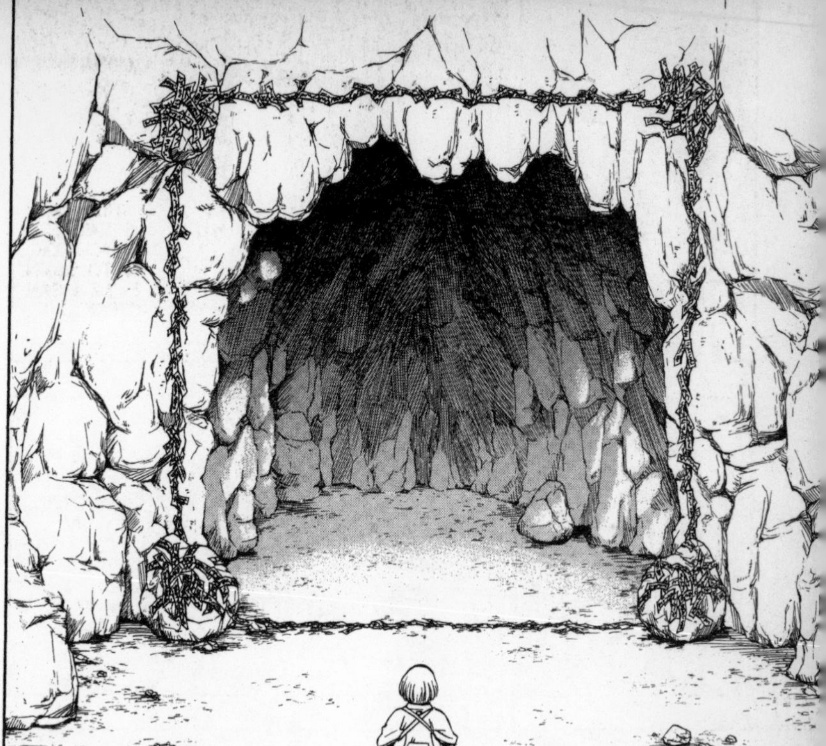

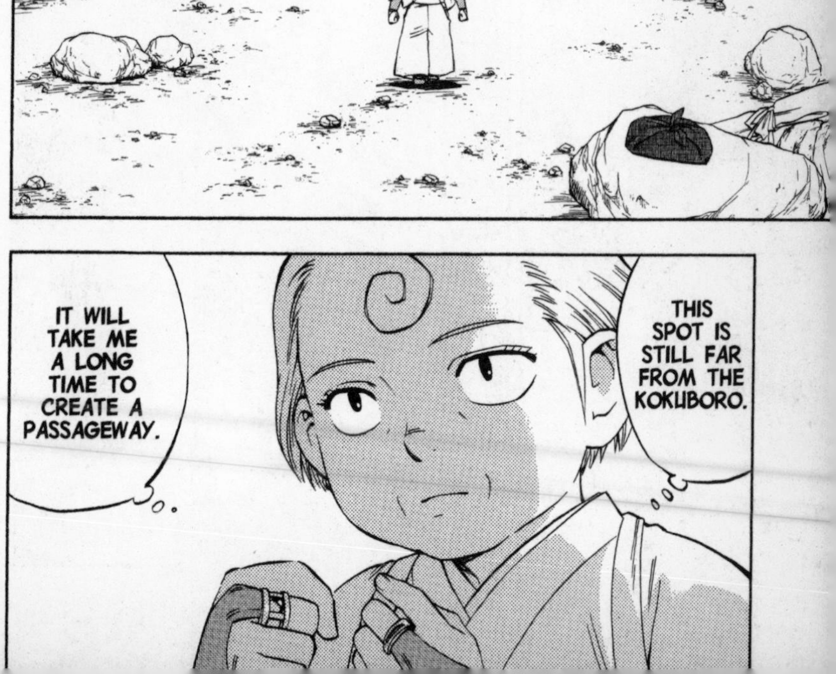
THIS SPOT IS STILL FAR FROM THE KOKUBORO.
IT WILL TAKE ME A LONG TIME TO CREATE A PASSAGEWAY.

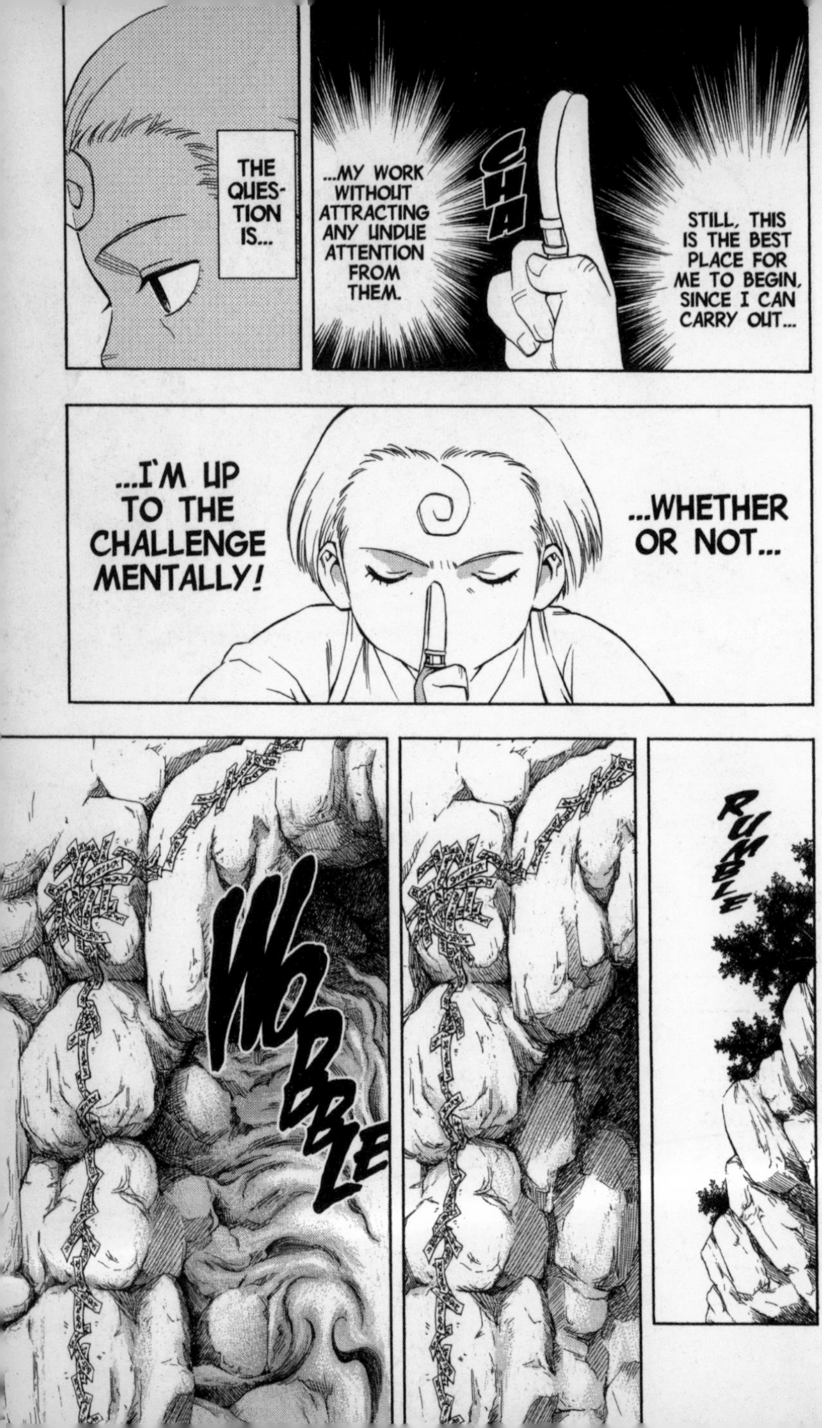
STILL, THIS IS THE BEST PLACE FOR ME TO BEGIN, SINCE I CAN CARRY OUT...
CHA
...MY WORK WITHOUT ATTRACTING ANY UNDUE ATTENTION FROM THEM.
THE QUES-TION IS...
...WHETHER OR NOT...
...I'M UP TO THE CHALLENGE MENTALLY!
RUMBLE
WOBBLE

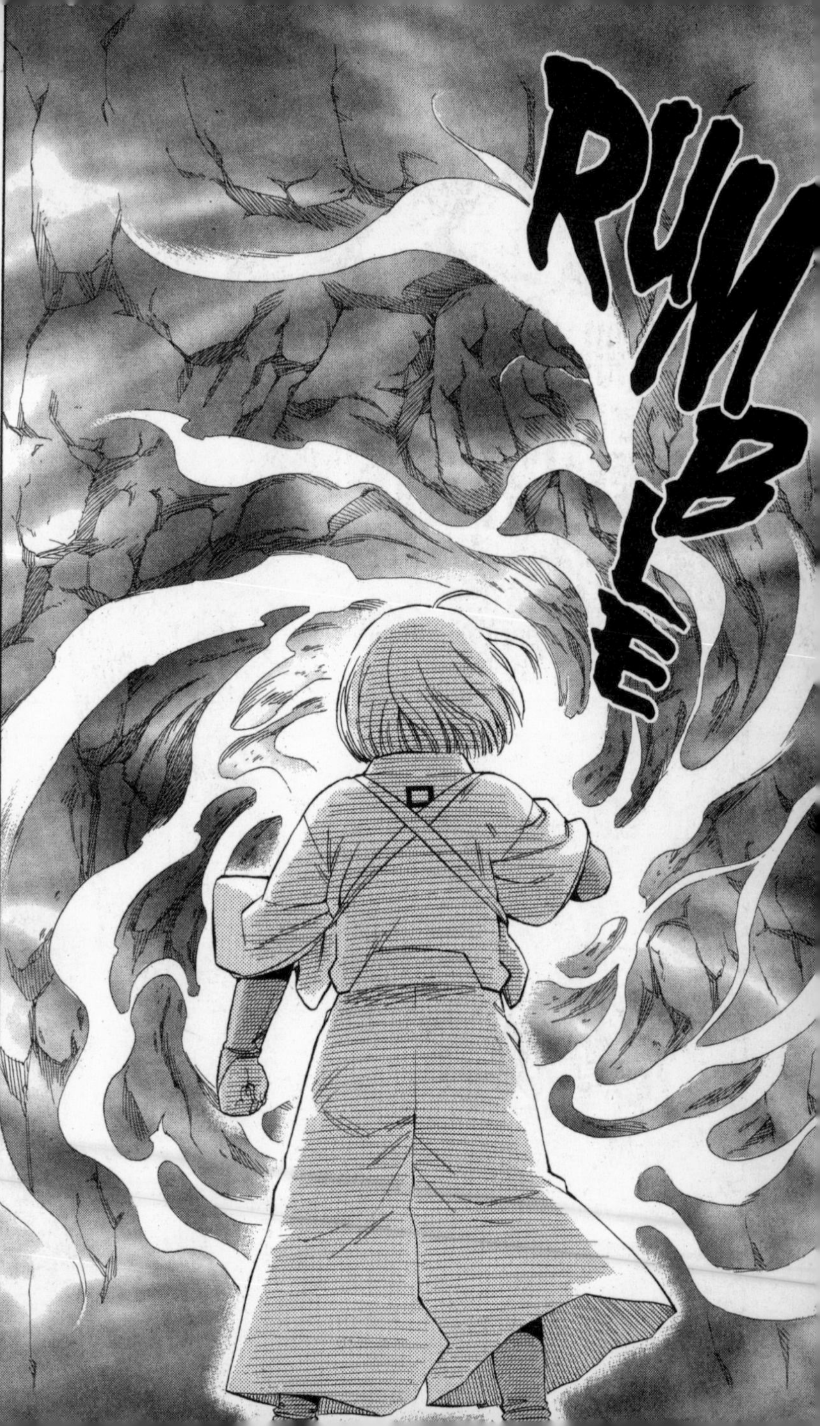
RUMBLE

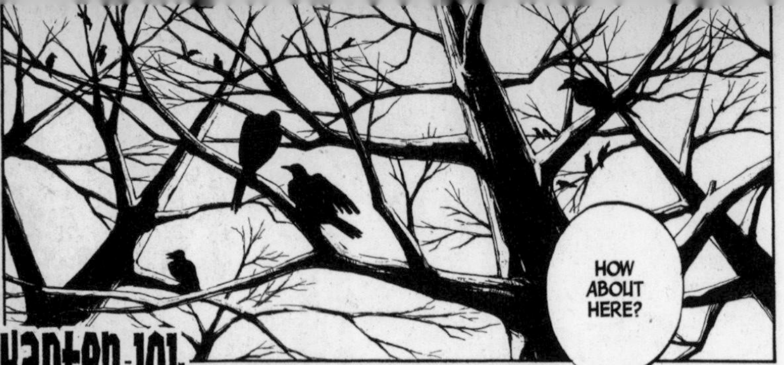
HOW ABOUT HERE?

Chapter 101: Skirmishes

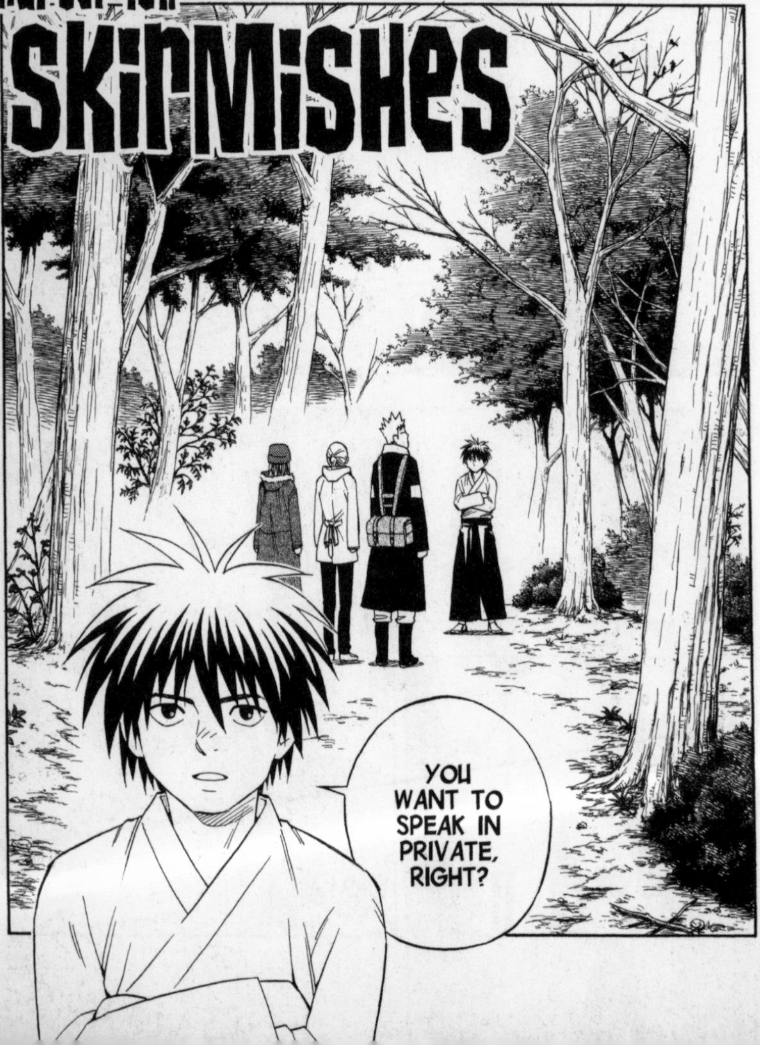
YOU WANT TO SPEAK IN PRIVATE, RIGHT?

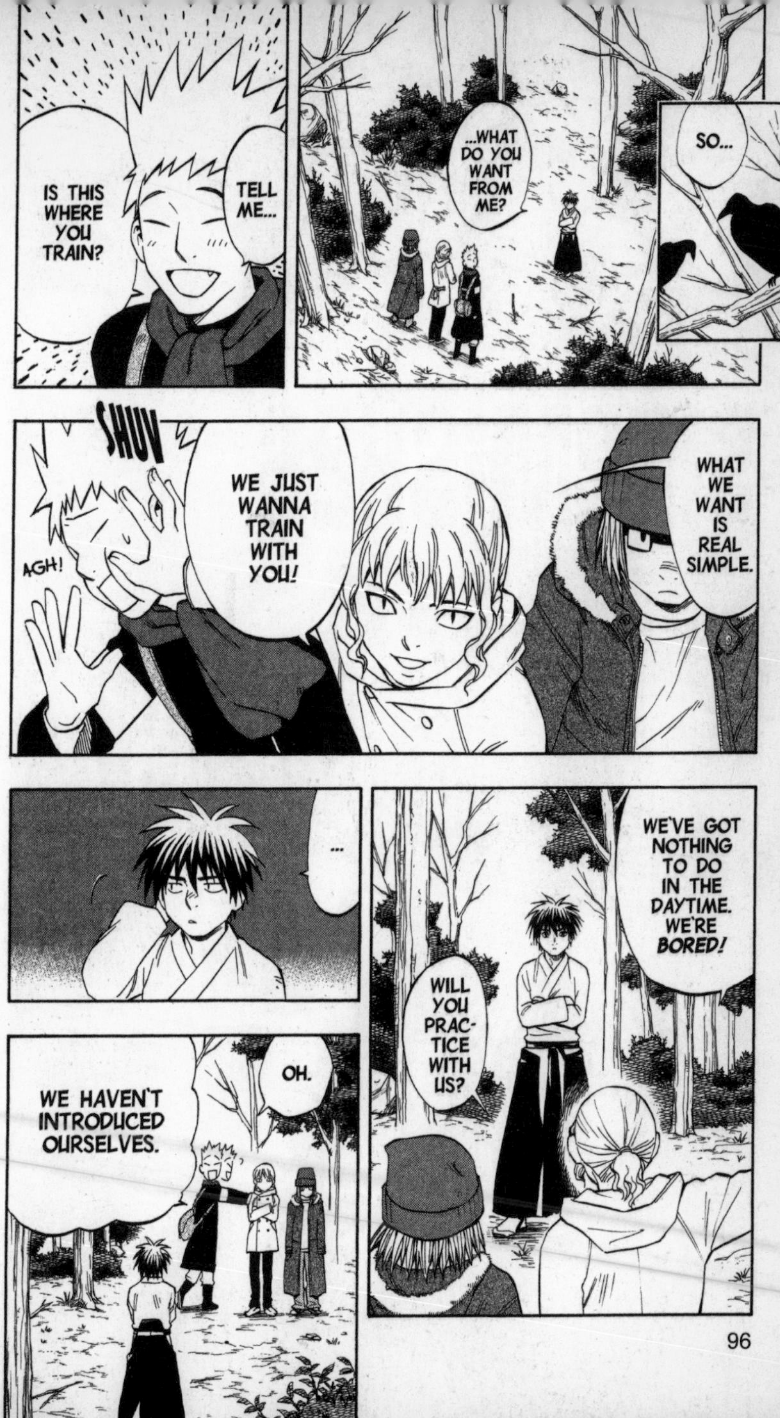
SO...
...WHAT DO YOU WANT FROM ME?
TELL ME...
IS THIS WHERE YOU TRAIN?
WHAT WE WANT IS REAL SIMPLE.
WE JUST WANNA TRAIN WITH YOU!
SHUV
AGH!
WE'VE GOT NOTHING TO DO IN THE DAYTIME. WE'RE *BORED!*
WILL YOU PRACTICE WITH US?
...
OH.
WE HAVEN'T INTRODUCED OURSELVES.

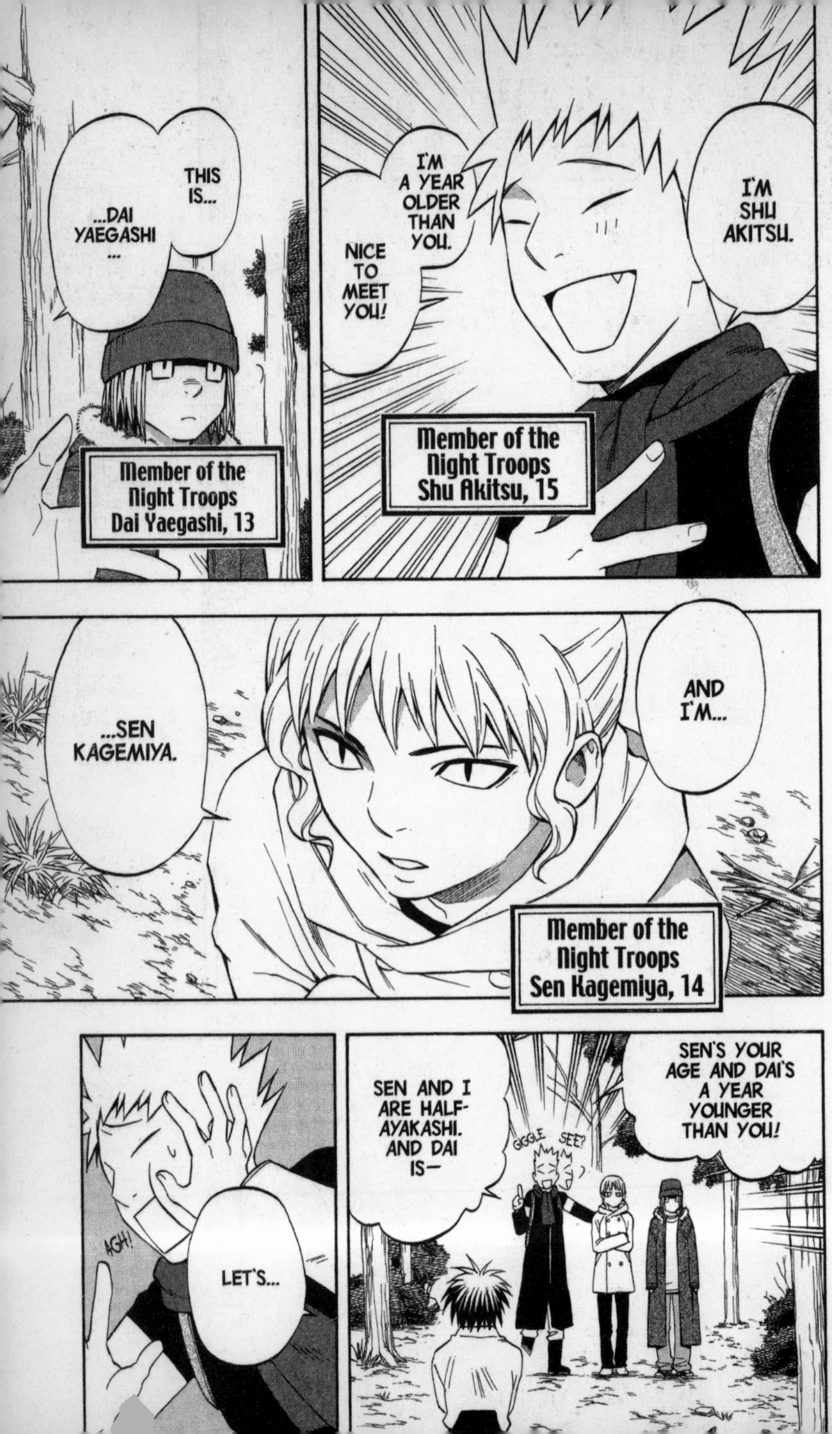
I'M SHU AKITSU.
I'M A YEAR OLDER THAN YOU.
NICE TO MEET YOU!
Member of the Night Troops Shu Akitsu, 15
THIS IS...
...DAI YAEGASHI ...
Member of the Night Troops Dai Yaegashi, 13
AND I'M...
...SEN KAGEMIYA.
Member of the Night Troops Sen Kagemiya, 14
SEN'S YOUR AGE AND DAI'S A YEAR YOUNGER THAN YOU!
GIGGLE
SEE?
SEN AND I ARE HALF-AYAKASHI. AND DAI IS—
AGH!
LET'S...

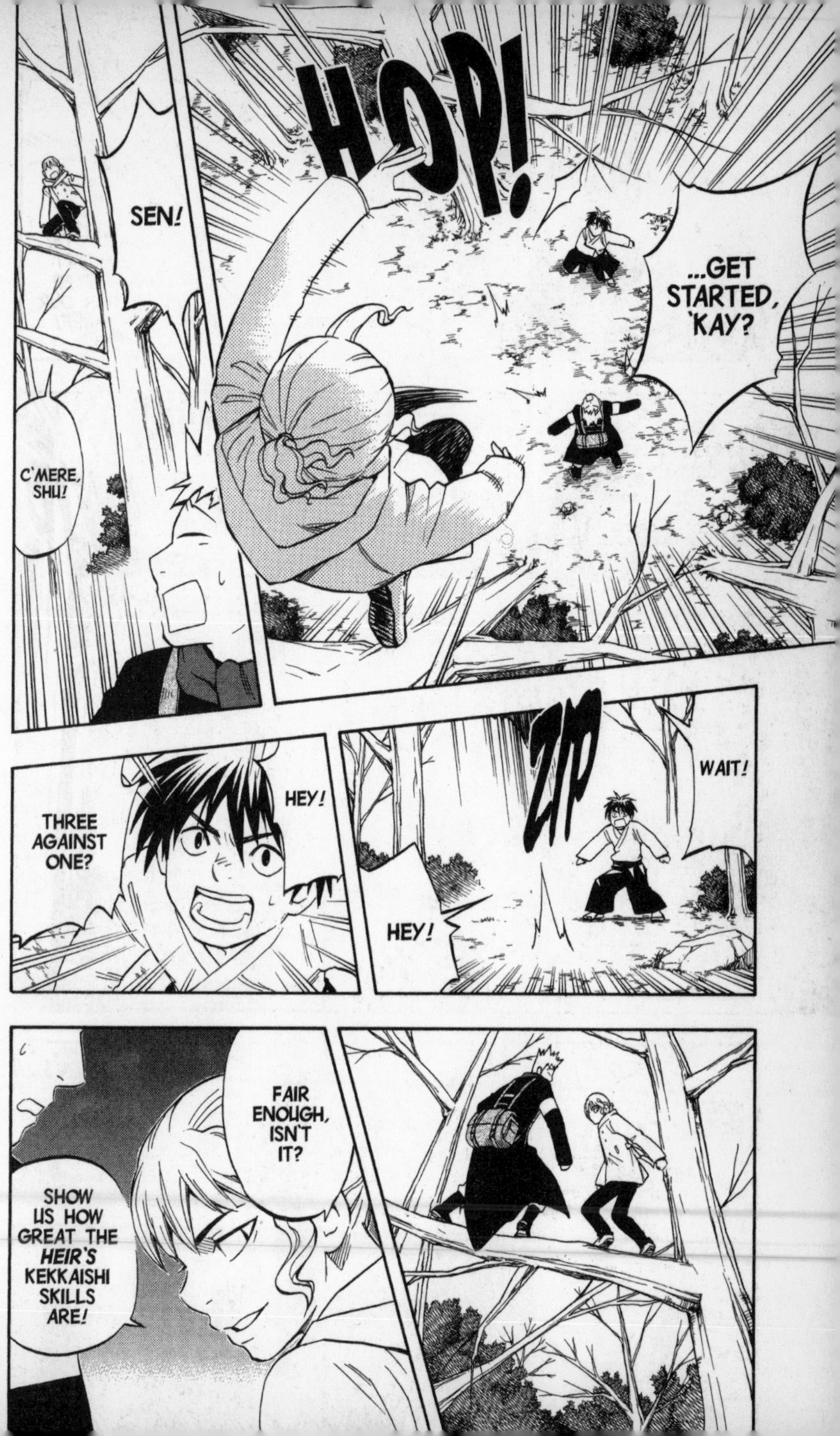
HOP!
...GET STARTED, 'KAY?
SEN!
C'MERE, SHU!
WAIT!
ZIP
HEY!
HEY!
THREE AGAINST ONE?
FAIR ENOUGH, ISN'T IT?
SHOW US HOW GREAT THE *HEIR'S* KEKKAISHI SKILLS ARE!

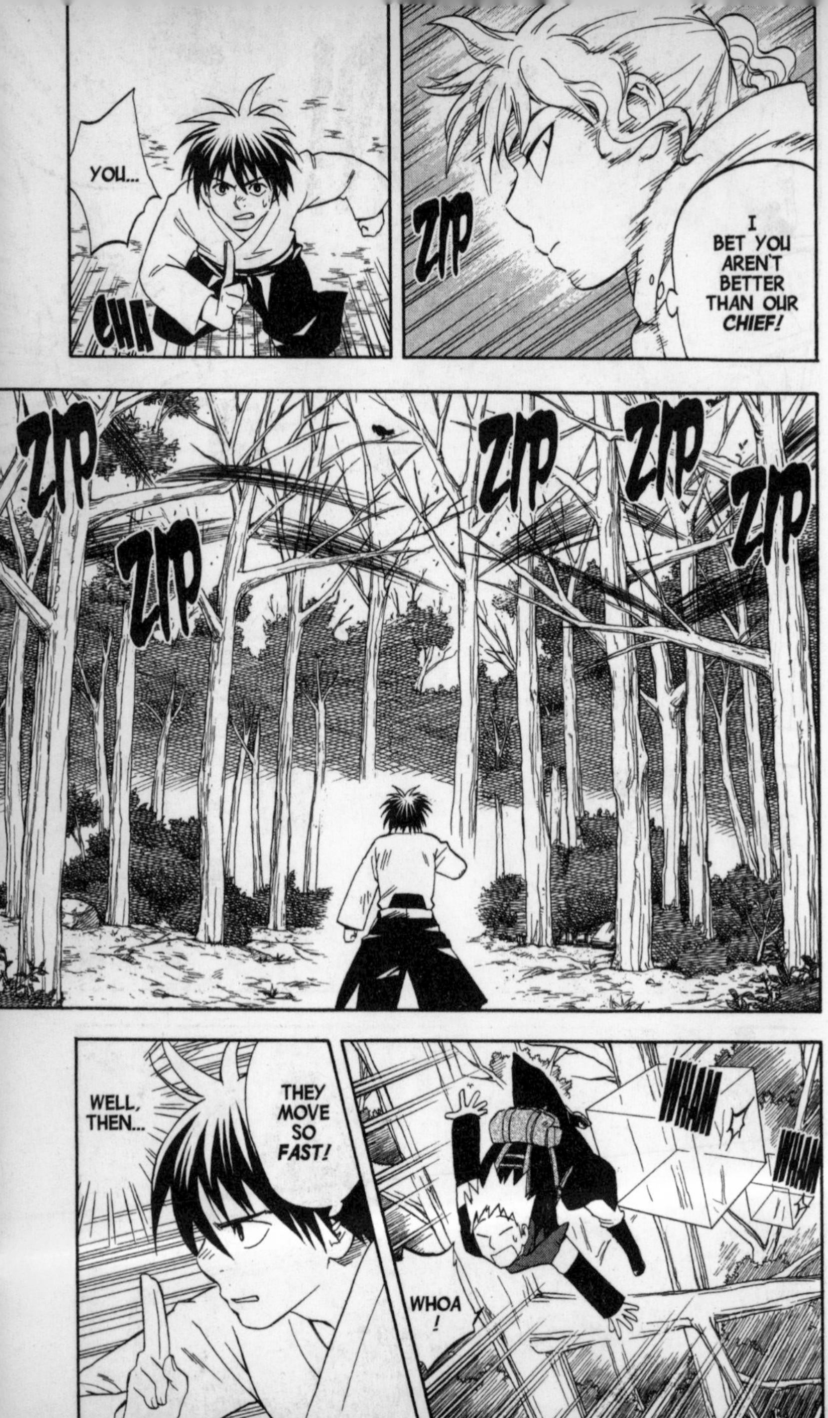
ZIP
I BET YOU AREN'T BETTER THAN OUR CHIEF!
YOU...
CHA
ZIP
ZIP
ZIP
ZIP
ZIP
ZIP
WHAM
WHAM
WHOA!
THEY MOVE SO FAST!
WELL, THEN...

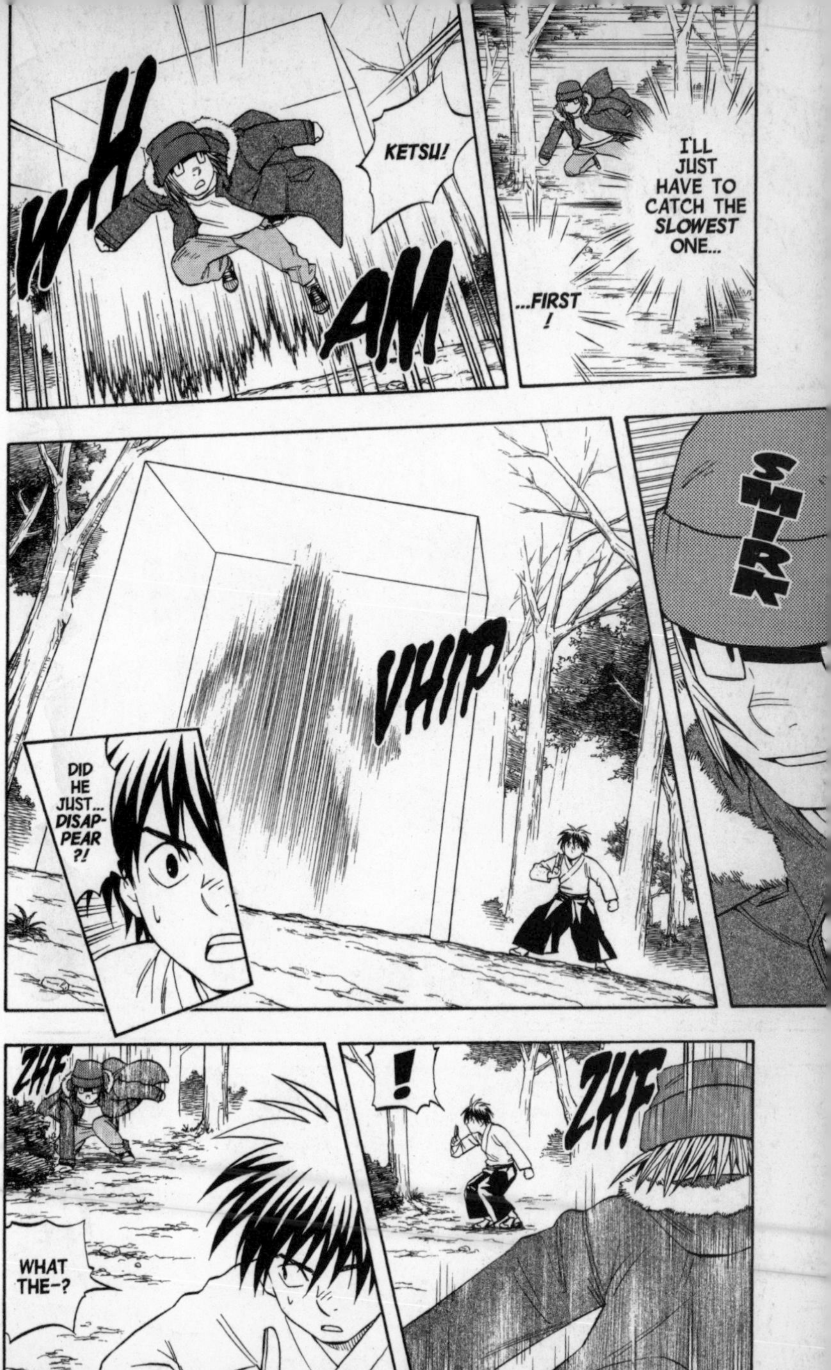
I'LL JUST HAVE TO CATCH THE SLOWEST ONE...
...FIRST!
KETSU!
WHAM
SMIRK
VHIP
DID HE JUST... DISAPPEAR?!
!
ZHF
ZHF
WHAT THE-?

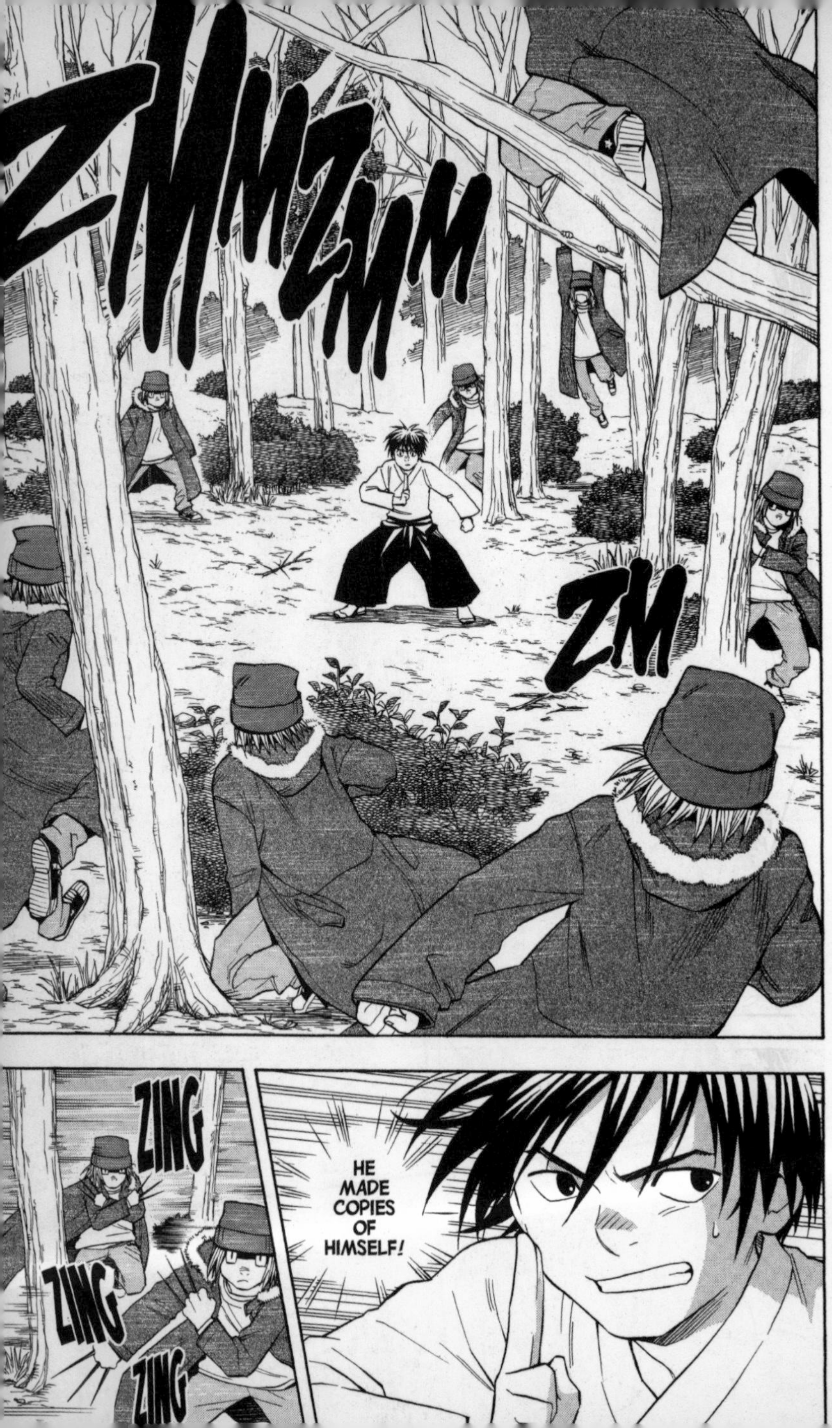
ZMMZMM
ZM
HE MADE COPIES OF HIMSELF!
ZING
ZING
ZING

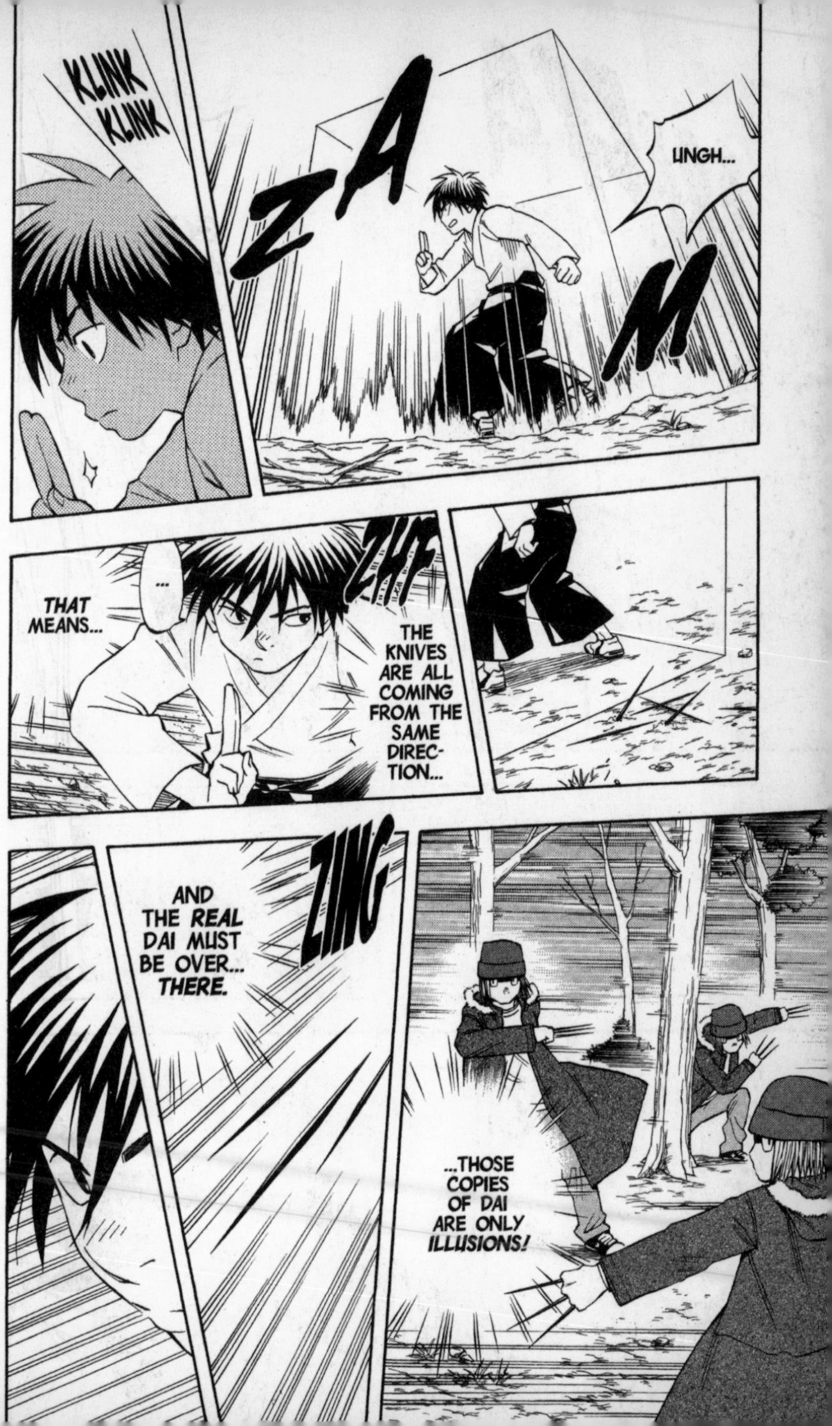
ZA
M
UNGH...
KLINK
KLINK
ZHF
...
THE KNIVES ARE ALL COMING FROM THE SAME DIREC-TION...
THAT MEANS...
...THOSE COPIES OF DAI ARE ONLY *ILLUSIONS!*
ZING
AND THE *REAL* DAI MUST BE OVER... *THERE.*

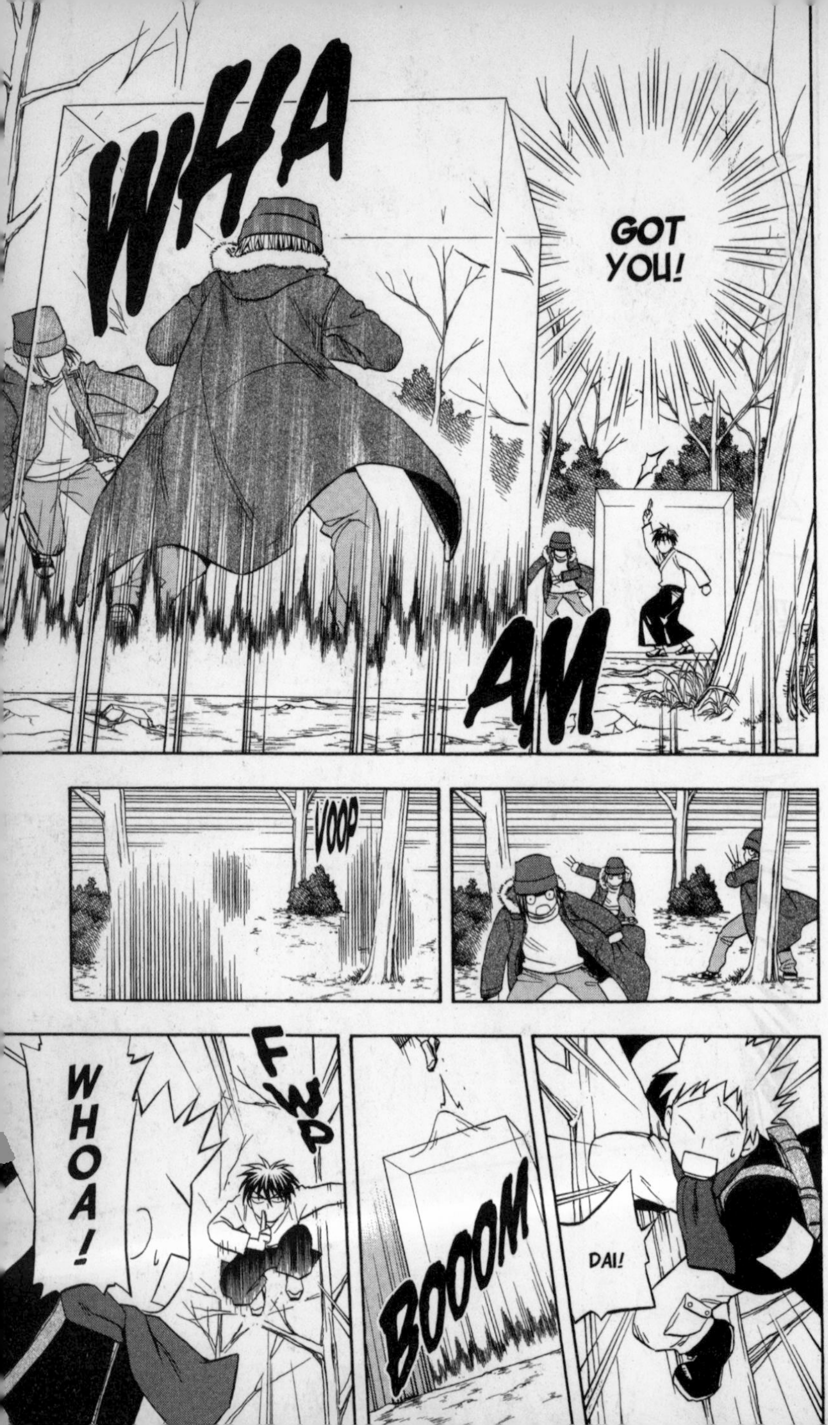
GOT YOU!
WHA
AM
VOOP
DAI!
BOOOM
FWP
WHOA!

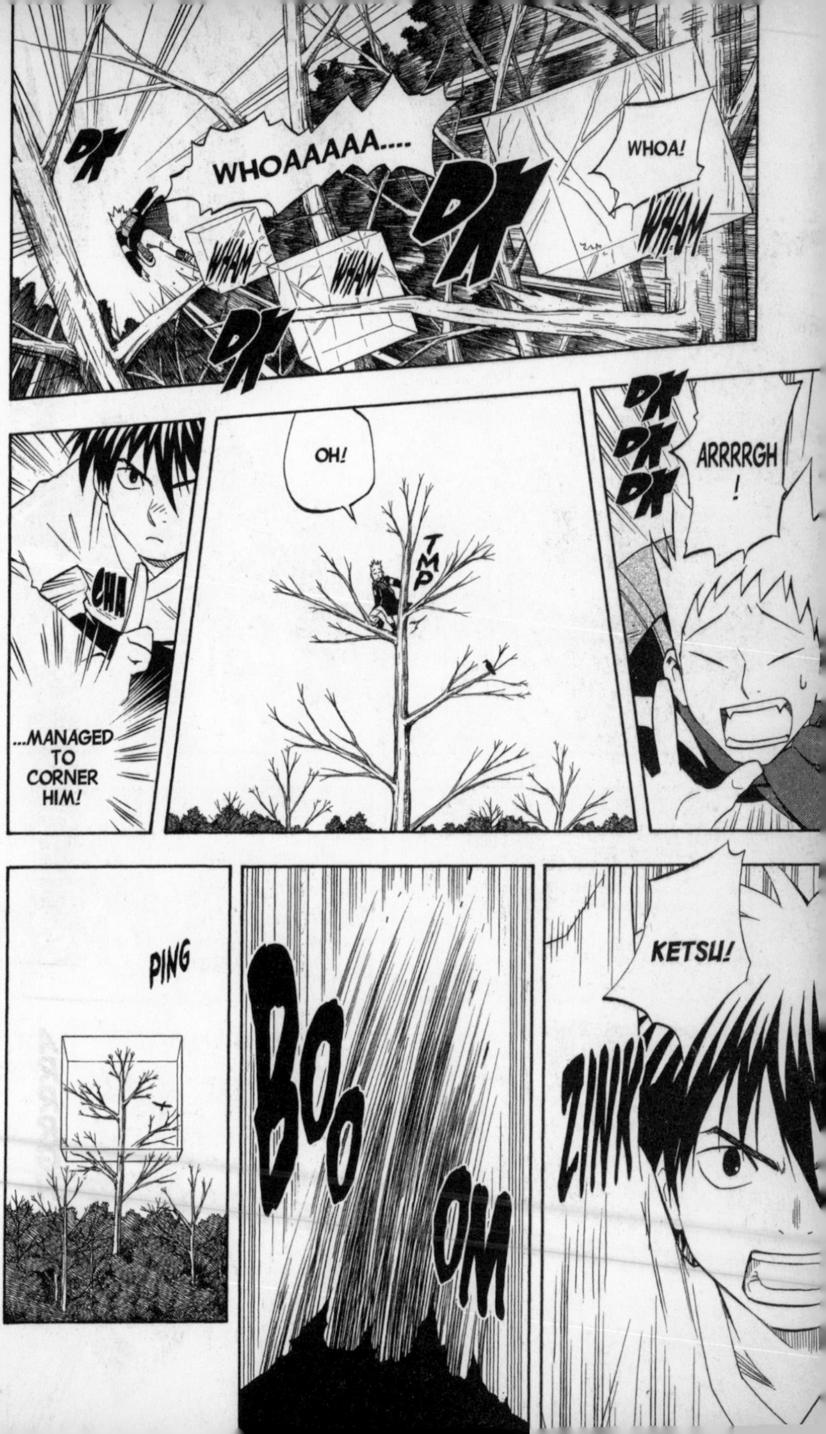
WHOA!
WHAM
DK
WHOAAAAA....
DK
WHAM
WHAM
DK
DK DK DK
ARRRRGH!
OH!
TMP
CHA
...MANAGED TO CORNER HIM!
KETSU!
ZINK
BOOOM
PING

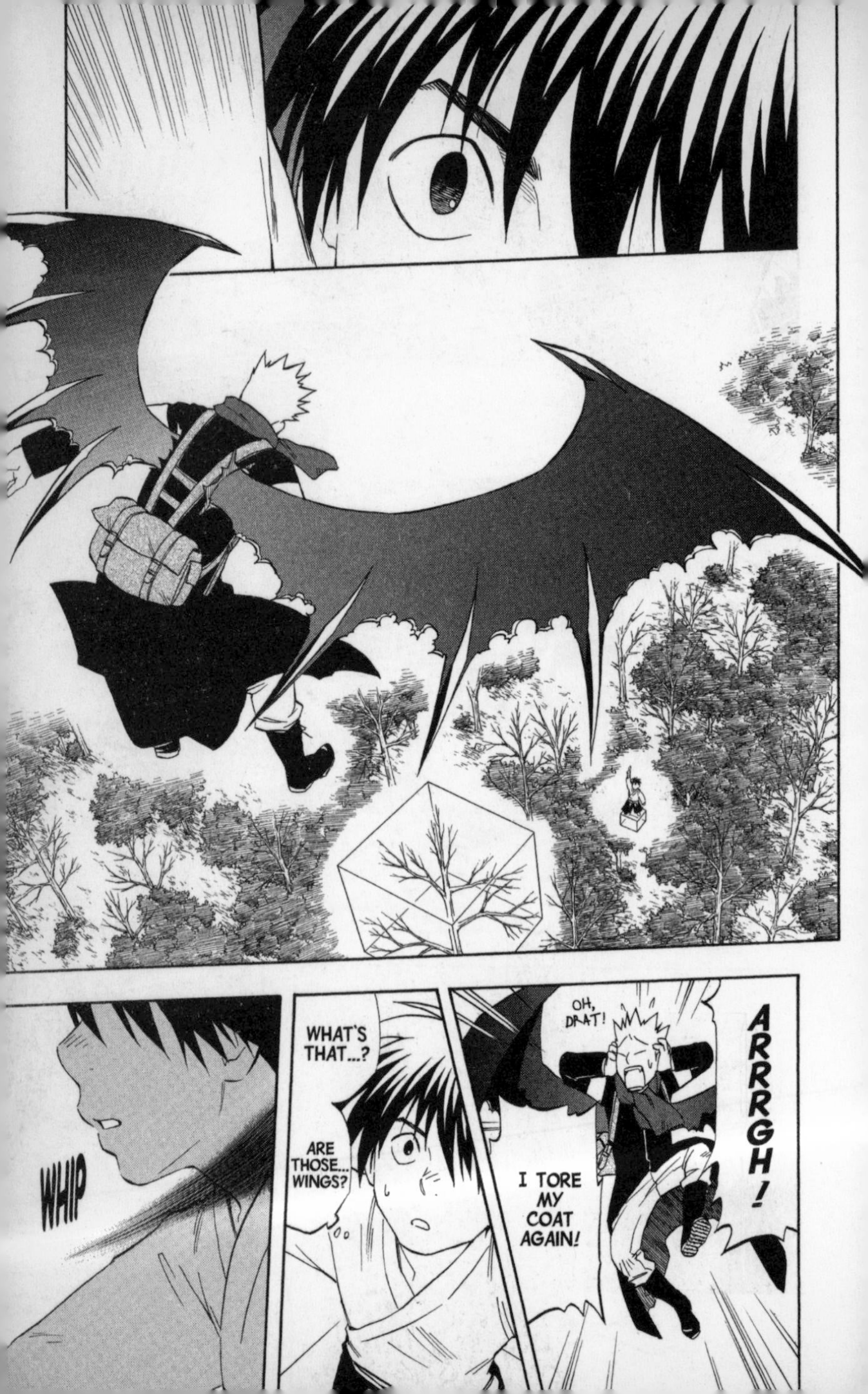
ARRRGH!
OH, DRAT!
I TORE MY COAT AGAIN!
WHAT'S THAT...?
ARE THOSE... WINGS?
WHIP

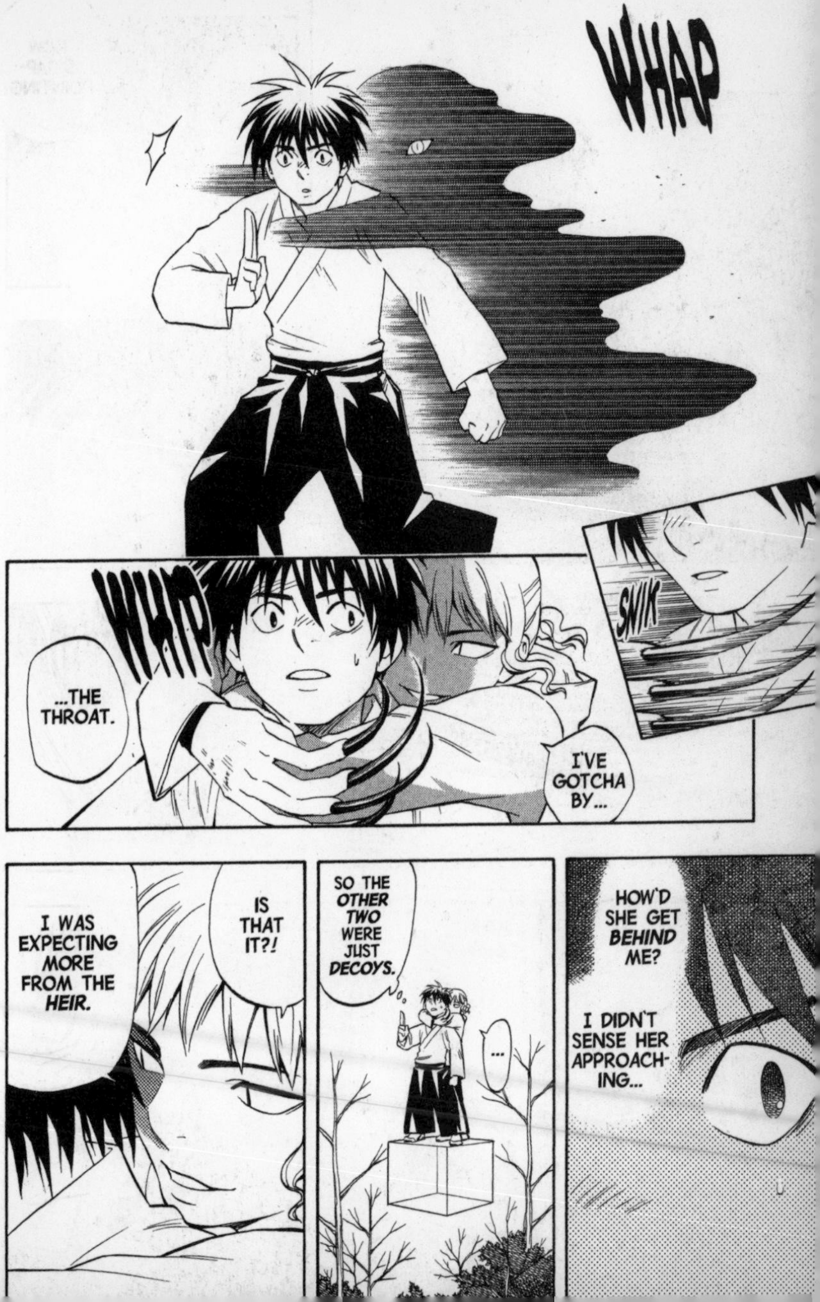
WHAP
SNIK
WHAP
I'VE GOTCHA BY...
...THE THROAT.
HOW'D SHE GET BEHIND ME?
I DIDN'T SENSE HER APPROACHING...
SO THE OTHER TWO WERE JUST DECOYS.
...
IS THAT IT?!
I WAS EXPECTING MORE FROM THE HEIR.

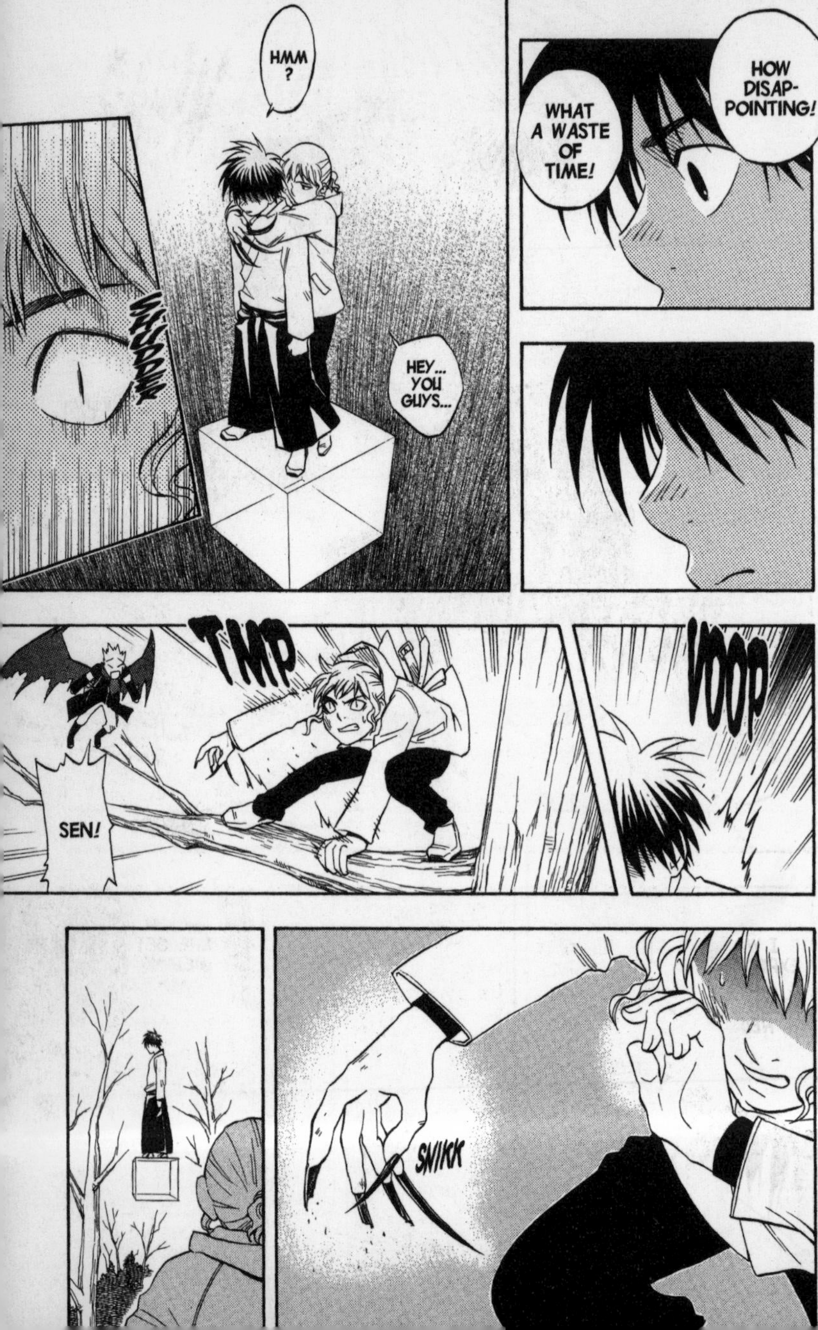
HOW DISAP-POINTING!
WHAT A WASTE OF TIME!
HMM ?
HEY... YOU GUYS...
SHUDDER
VOOP
TMP
SEN!
SNIKK

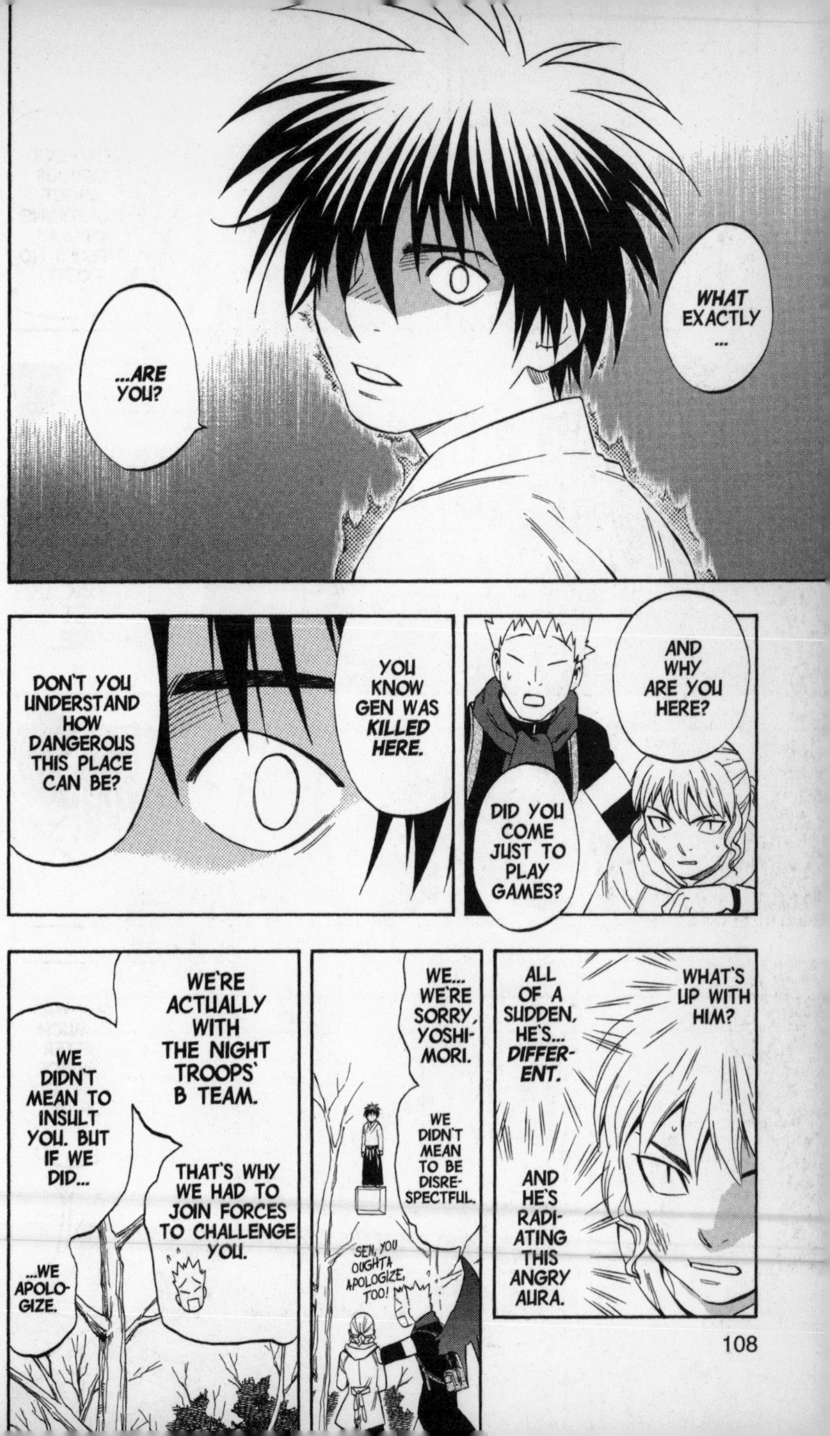
WHAT EXACTLY ...
...ARE YOU?
AND WHY ARE YOU HERE?
DID YOU COME JUST TO PLAY GAMES?
YOU KNOW GEN WAS KILLED HERE.
DON'T YOU UNDERSTAND HOW DANGEROUS THIS PLACE CAN BE?
WHAT'S UP WITH HIM?
ALL OF A SUDDEN, HE'S... DIFFERENT.
AND HE'S RADIATING THIS ANGRY AURA.
WE... WE'RE SORRY, YOSHIMORI.
WE DIDN'T MEAN TO BE DISRESPECTFUL.
SEN, YOU OUGHTA APOLOGIZE, TOO!
WE'RE ACTUALLY WITH THE NIGHT TROOPS' B TEAM.
THAT'S WHY WE HAD TO JOIN FORCES TO CHALLENGE YOU.
WE DIDN'T MEAN TO INSULT YOU. BUT IF WE DID...
...WE APOLOGIZE.

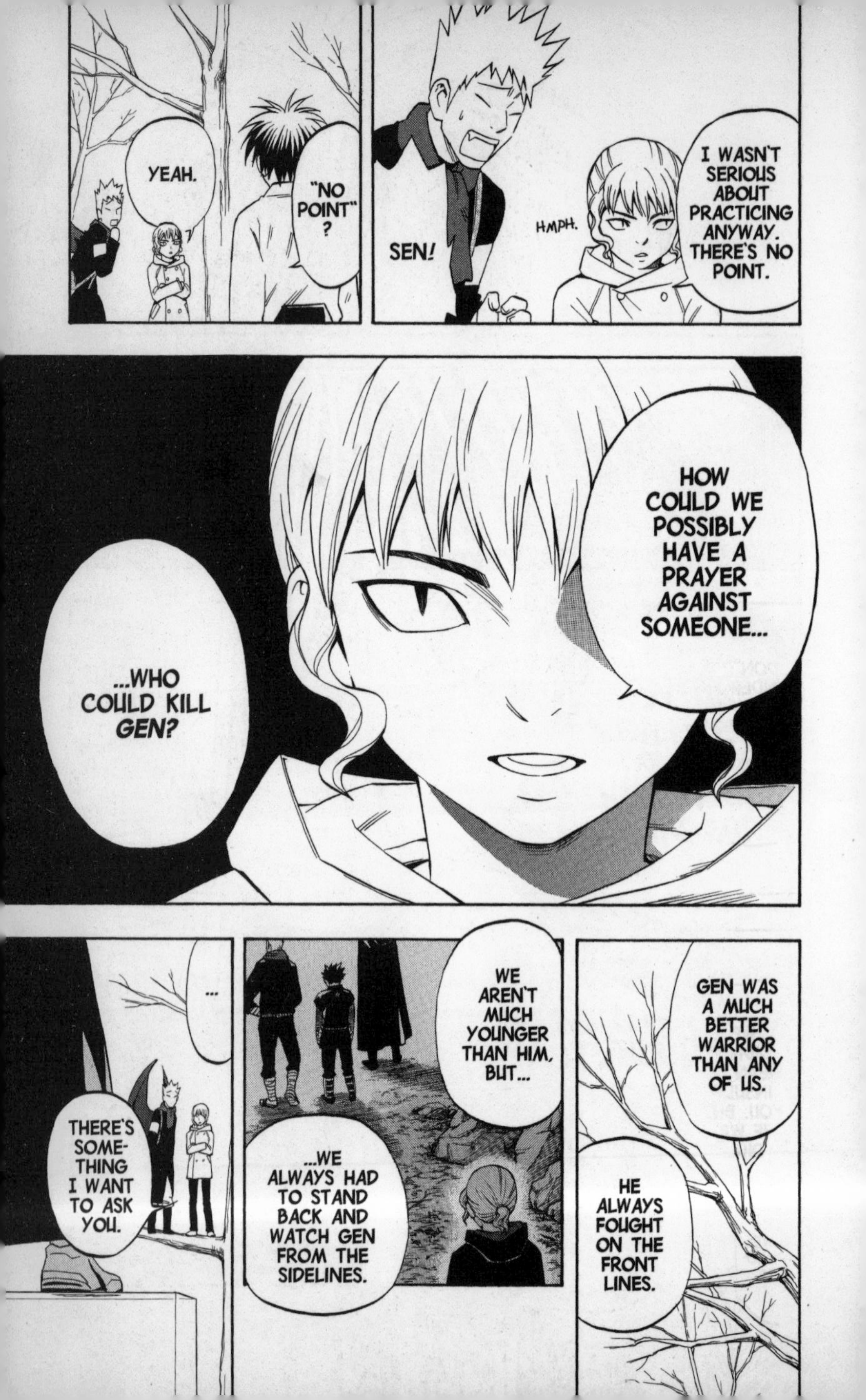
I WASN'T SERIOUS ABOUT PRACTICING ANYWAY. THERE'S NO POINT.
HMPH.
SEN!
"NO POINT"?
YEAH.
HOW COULD WE POSSIBLY HAVE A PRAYER AGAINST SOMEONE...
...WHO COULD KILL *GEN*?
GEN WAS A MUCH BETTER WARRIOR THAN ANY OF US.
HE ALWAYS FOUGHT ON THE FRONT LINES.
WE AREN'T MUCH YOUNGER THAN HIM, BUT...
...WE ALWAYS HAD TO STAND BACK AND WATCH GEN FROM THE SIDELINES.
...
THERE'S SOME-THING I WANT TO ASK YOU.

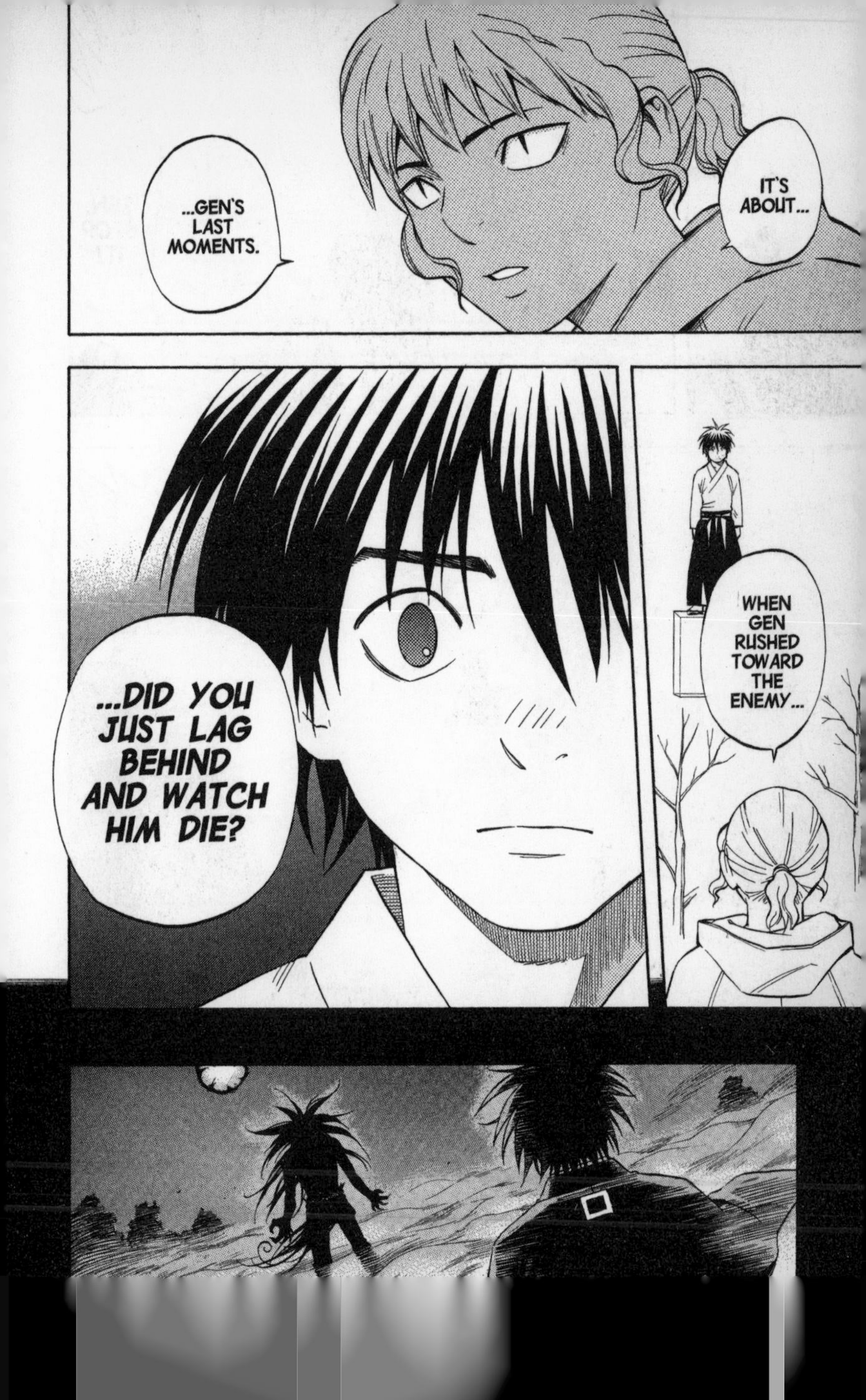
IT'S ABOUT...
...GEN'S LAST MOMENTS.
WHEN GEN RUSHED TOWARD THE ENEMY...
...DID YOU JUST LAG BEHIND AND WATCH HIM DIE?

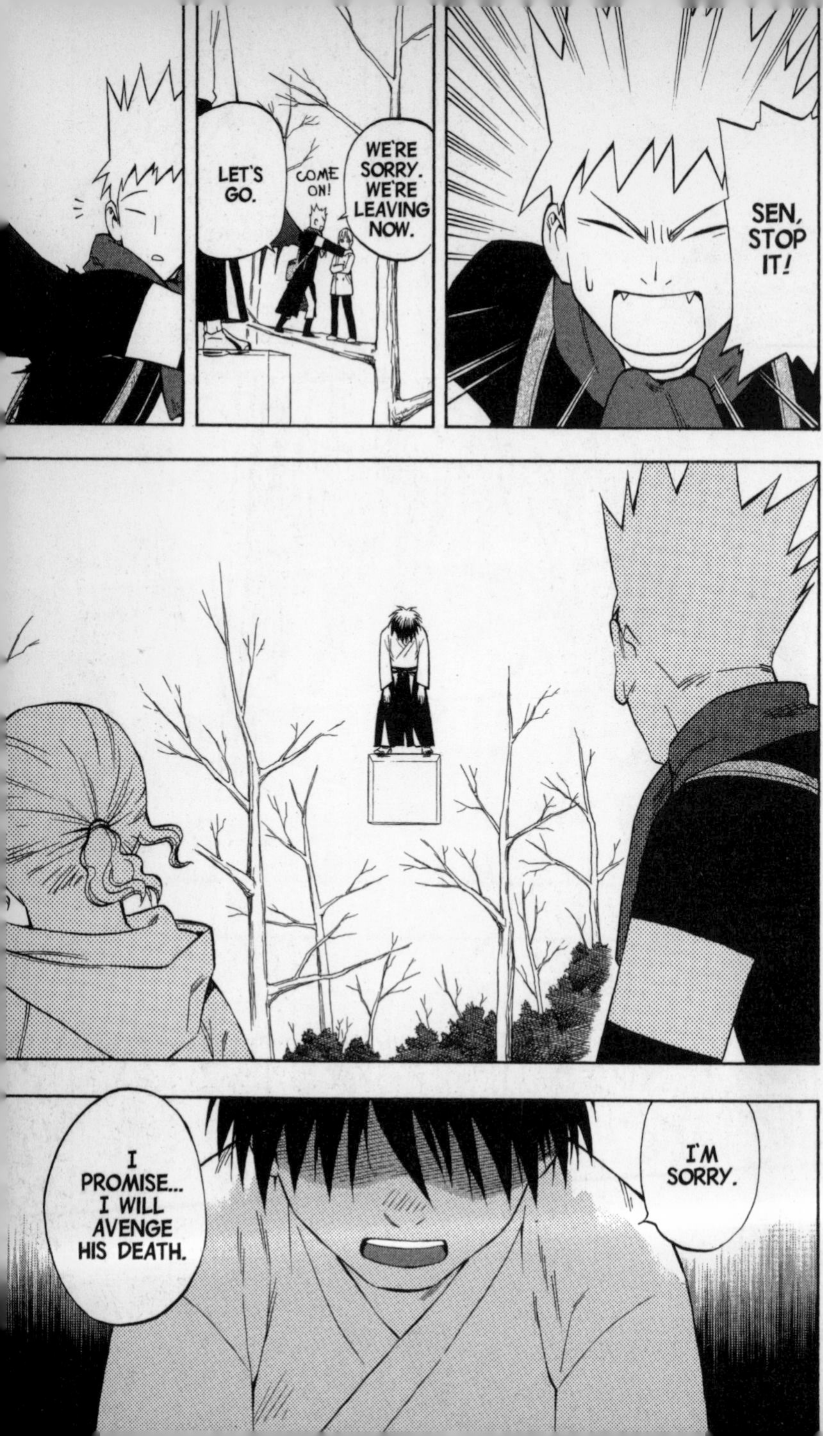
SEN, STOP IT!
WE'RE SORRY. WE'RE LEAVING NOW.
COME ON!
LET'S GO.
I'M SORRY.
I PROMISE... I WILL AVENGE HIS DEATH.

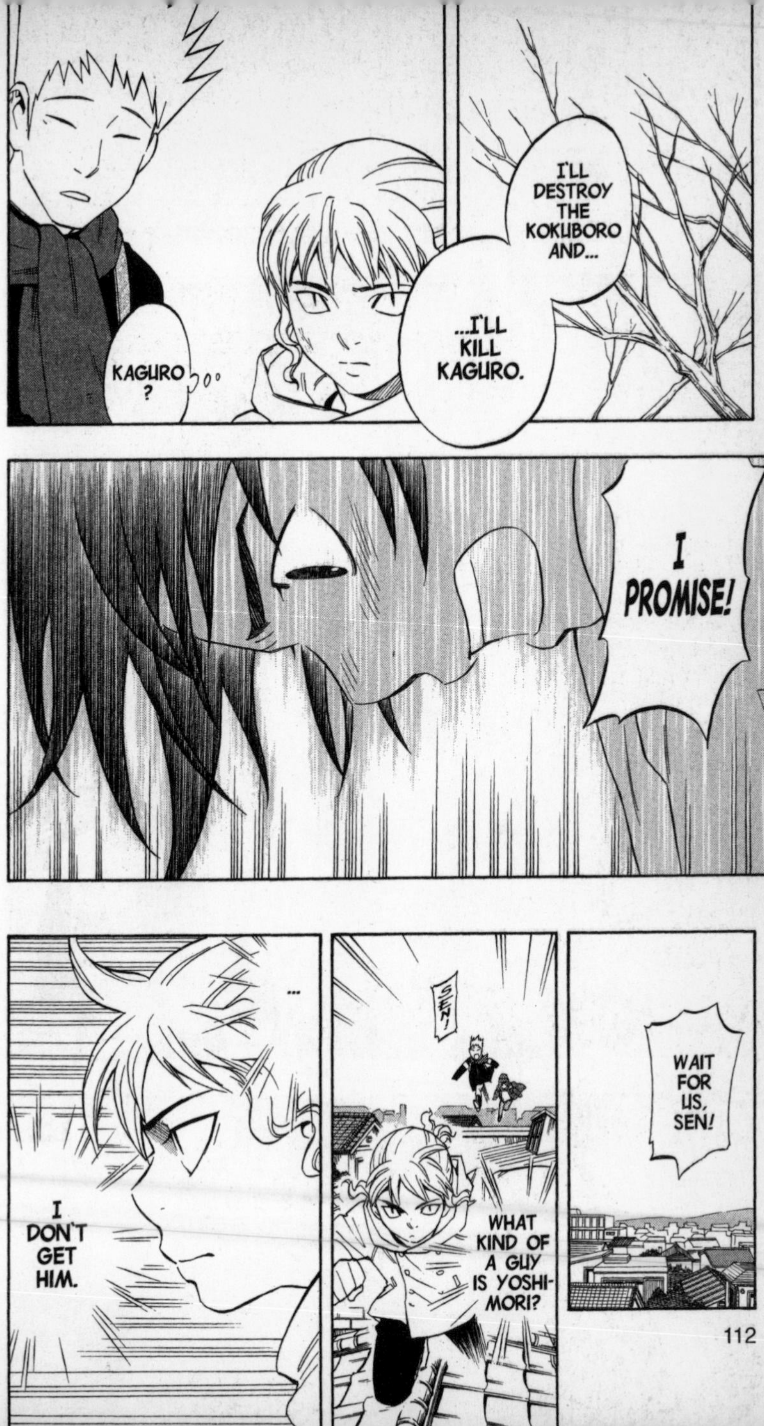
I'LL DESTROY THE KOKUBORO AND...
...I'LL KILL KAGURO.
KAGURO?
I PROMISE!
WAIT FOR US, SEN!
SEN!
WHAT KIND OF A GUY IS YOSHIMORI?
...
I DON'T GET HIM.

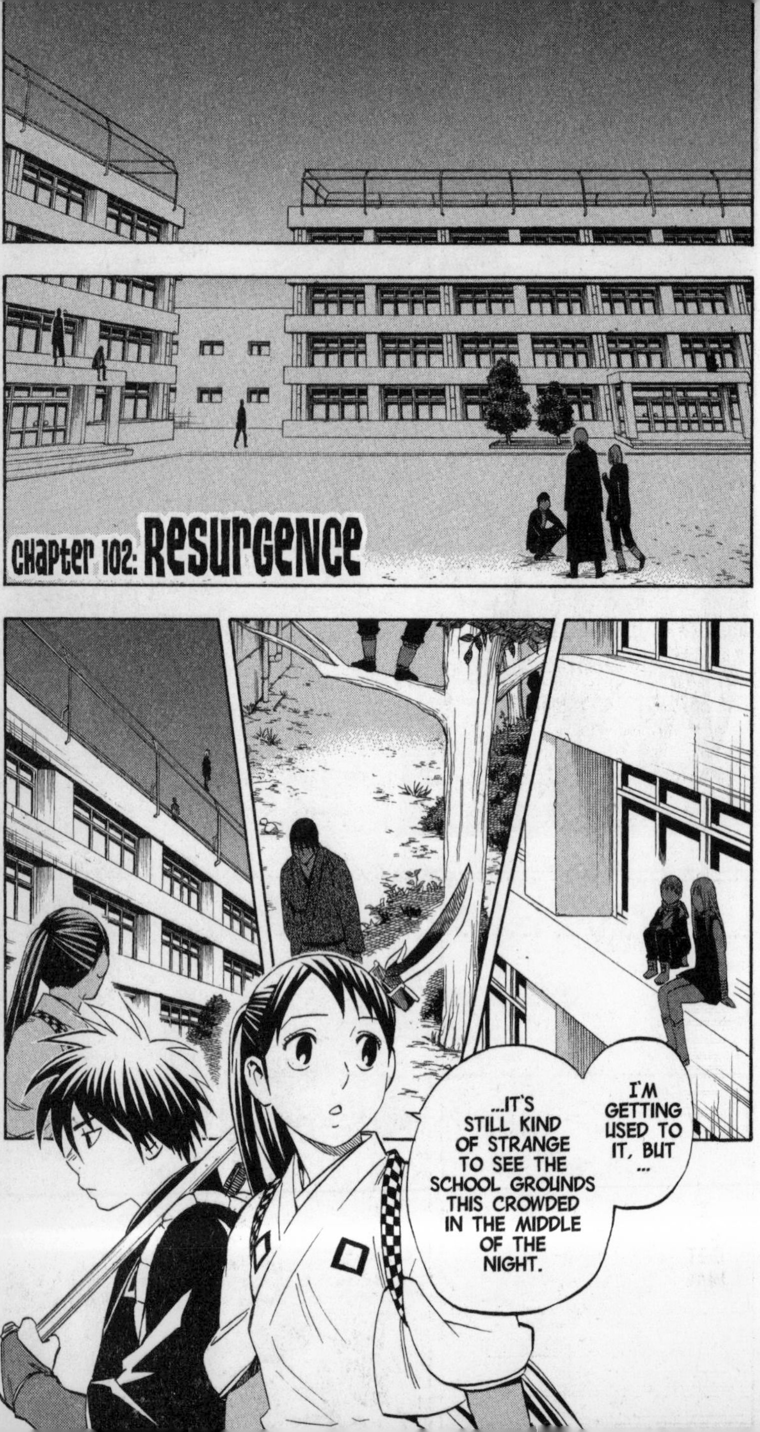
Chapter 102: Resurgence
I'M GETTING USED TO IT, BUT ...
...IT'S STILL KIND OF STRANGE TO SEE THE SCHOOL GROUNDS THIS CROWDED IN THE MIDDLE OF THE NIGHT.

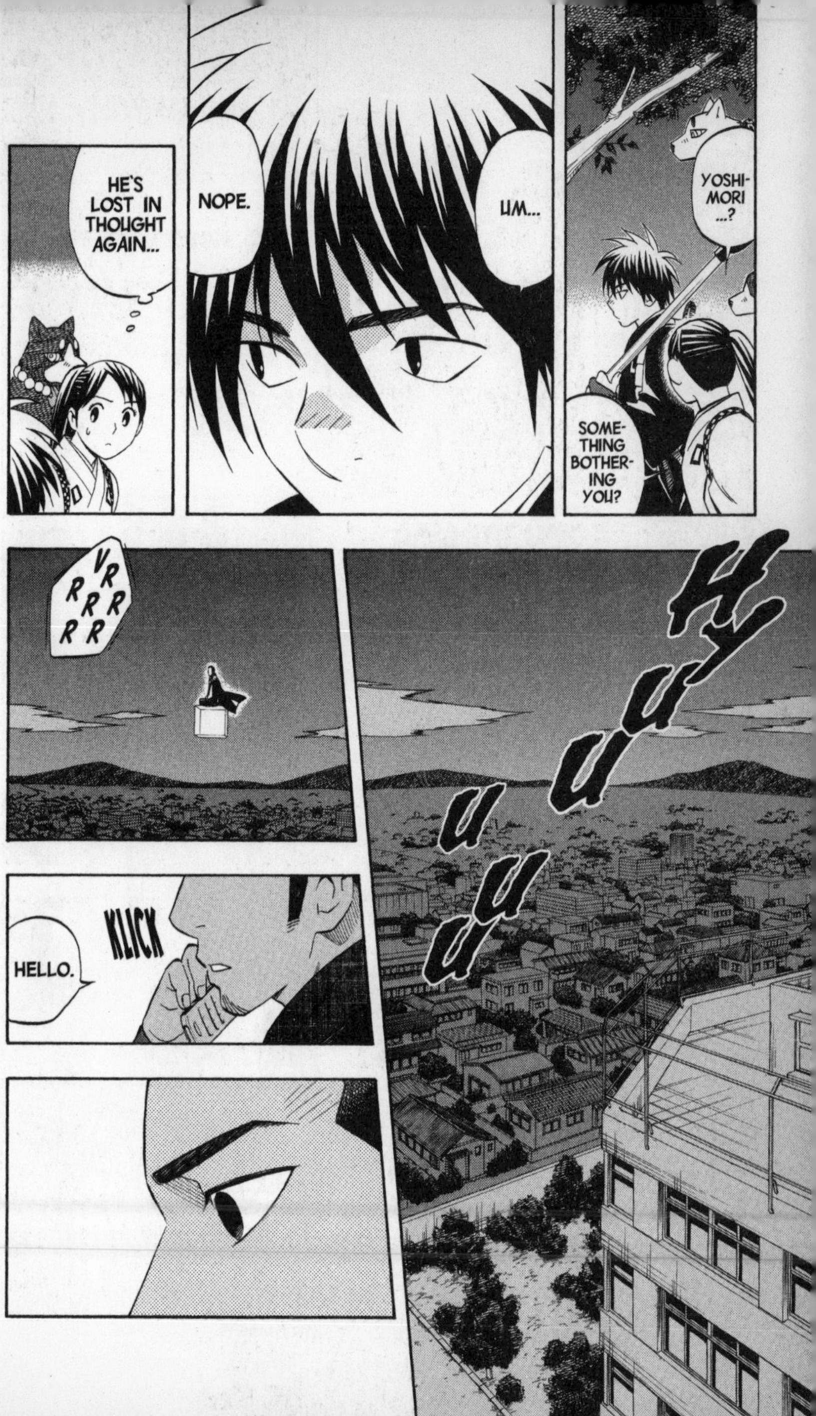
YOSHI-MORI ...?
SOMETHING BOTHERING YOU?
UM...
NOPE.
HE'S LOST IN THOUGHT AGAIN...
HYUUUUUUU
VRRRRRRRR
KLICK
HELLO.

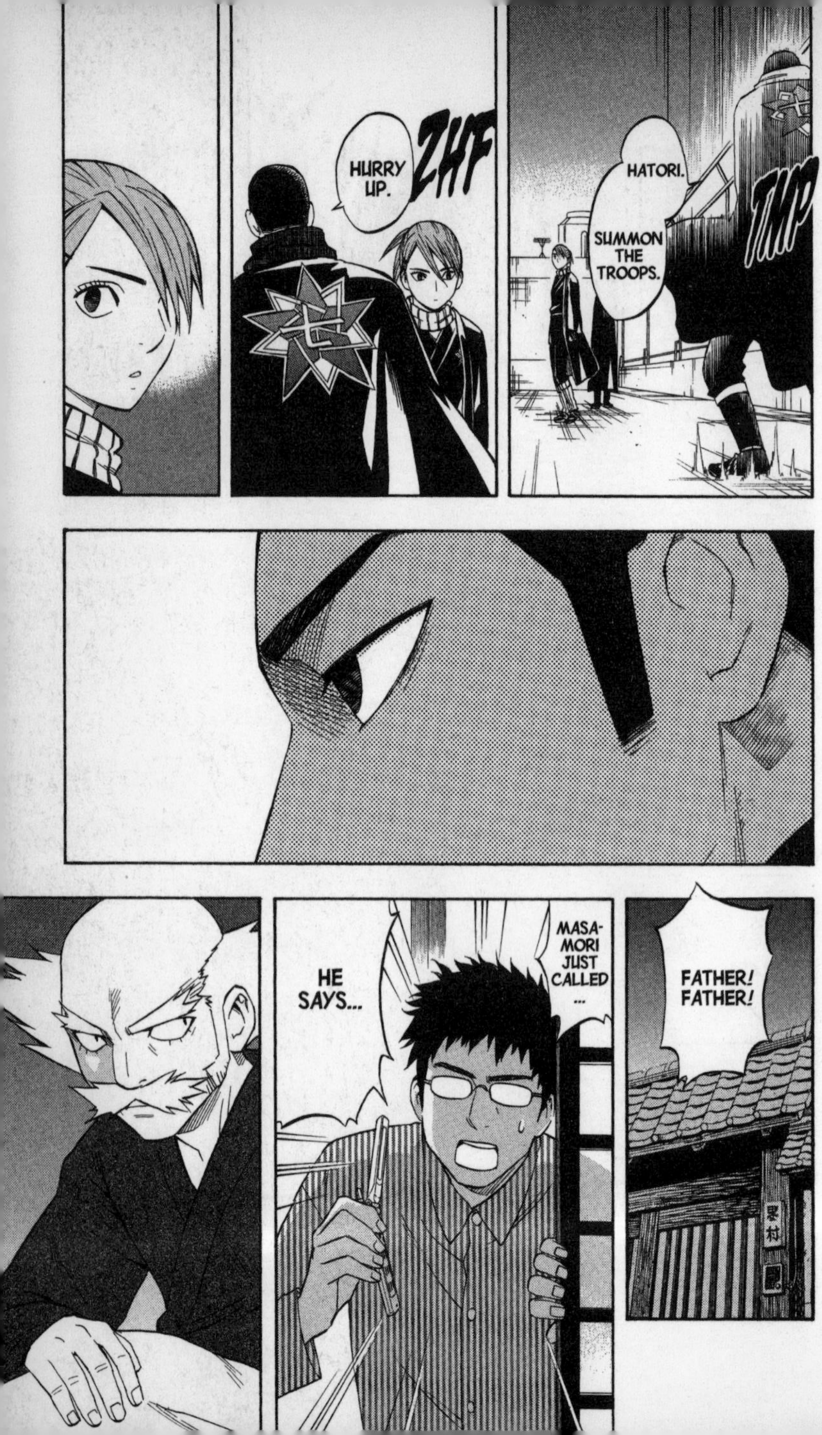
HATORI.
SUMMON THE TROOPS.
TMP
HURRY UP.
ZHF
FATHER! FATHER!
MASAMORI JUST CALLED...
HE SAYS...

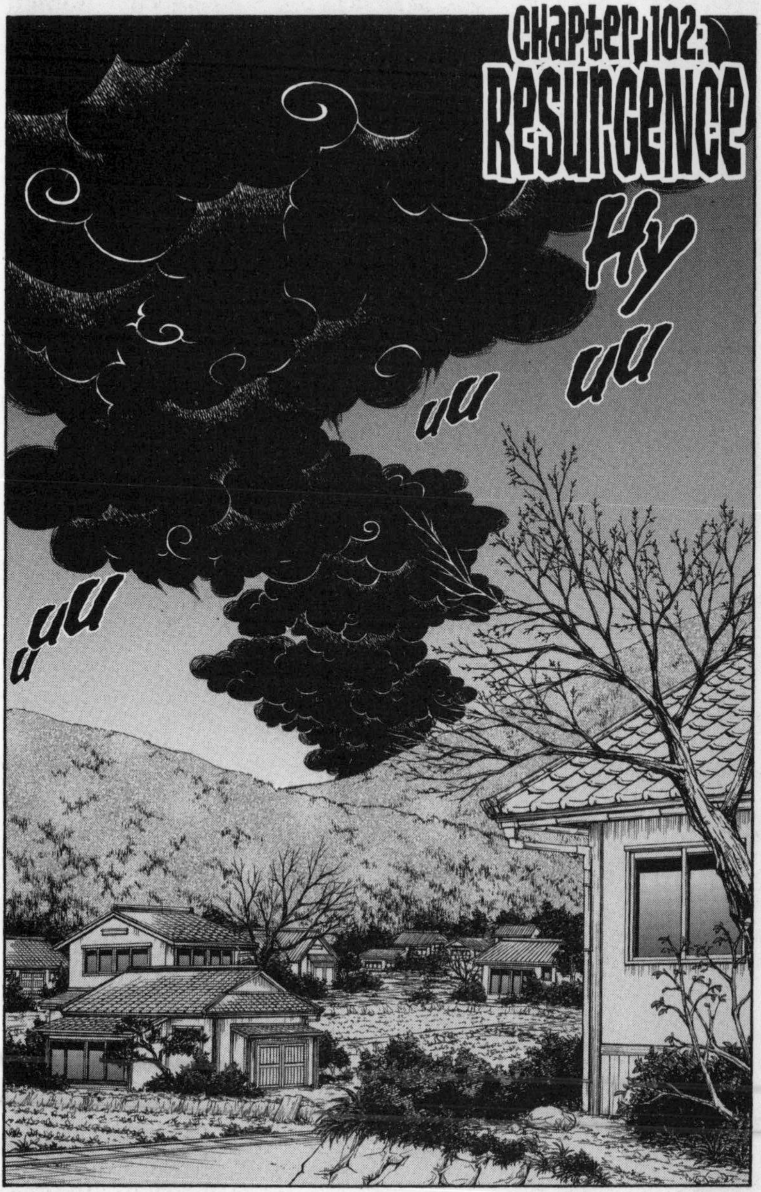
Chapter 102:
Resurgence
Hy
uu
uu
uu

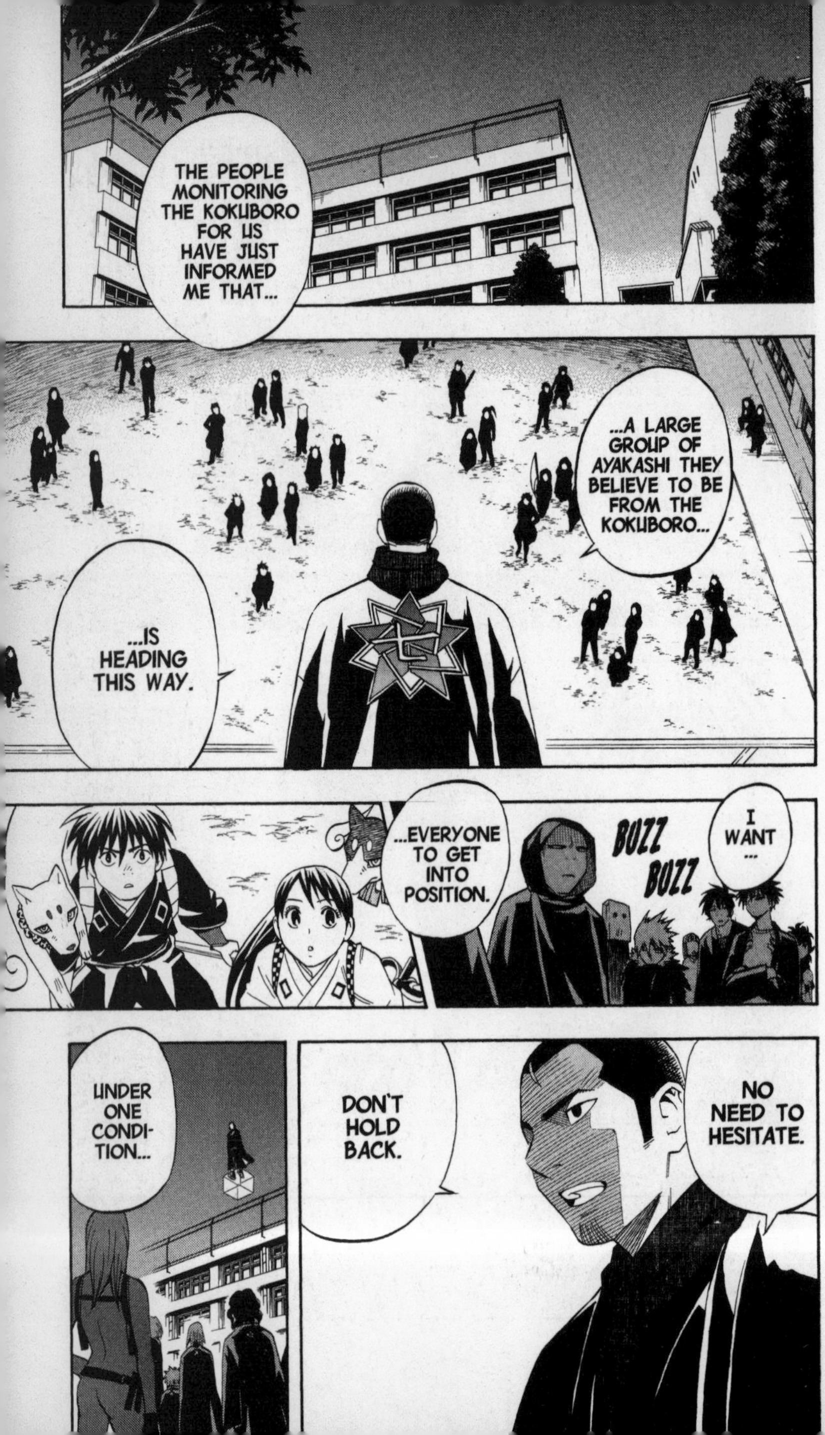
THE PEOPLE MONITORING THE KOKUBORO FOR US HAVE JUST INFORMED ME THAT...
...A LARGE GROUP OF AYAKASHI THEY BELIEVE TO BE FROM THE KOKUBORO...
...IS HEADING THIS WAY.
I WANT ...
BUZZ BUZZ
...EVERYONE TO GET INTO POSITION.
NO NEED TO HESITATE.
DON'T HOLD BACK.
UNDER ONE CONDI- TION...

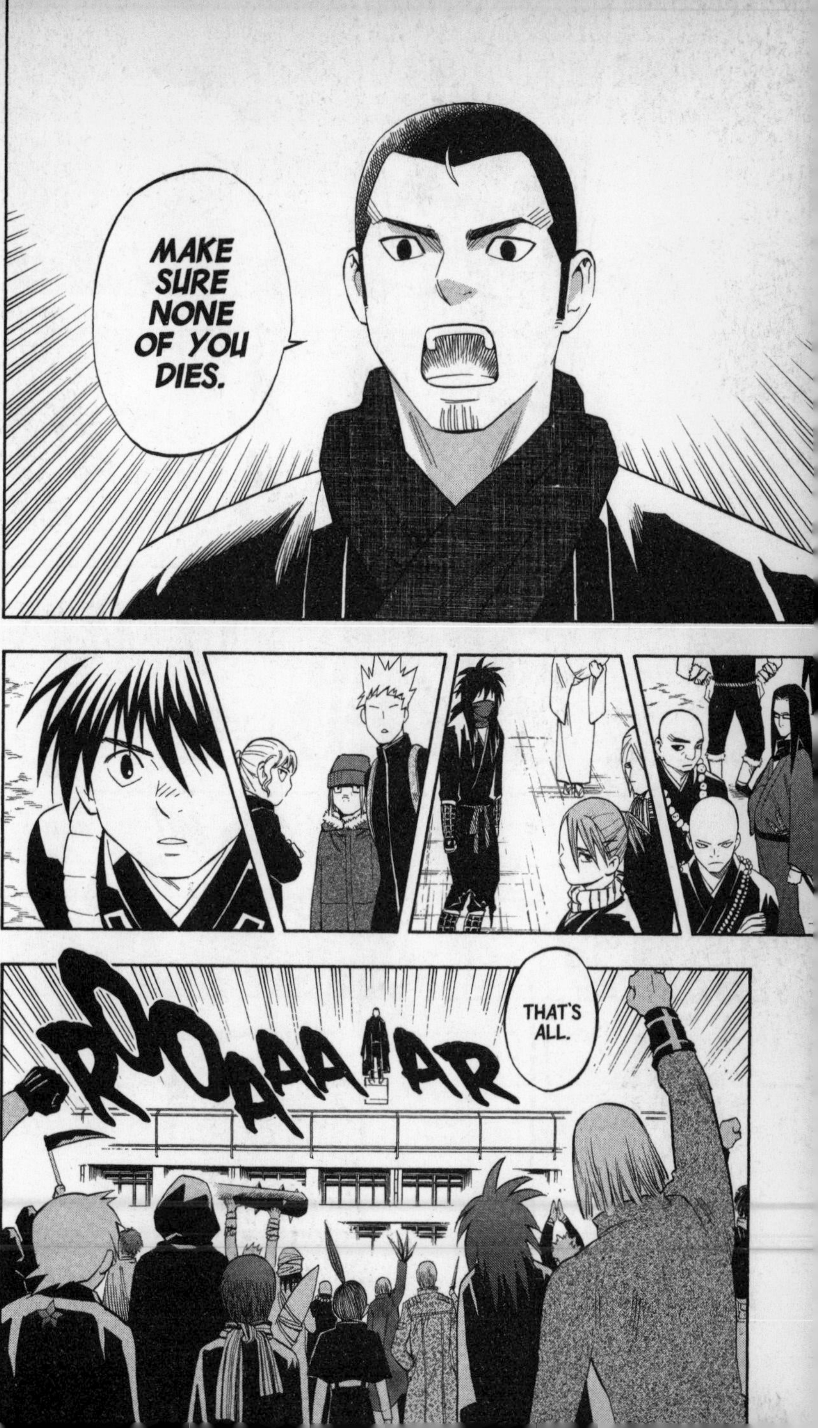
MAKE SURE NONE OF YOU DIES.
THAT'S ALL.
ROOAAAAR

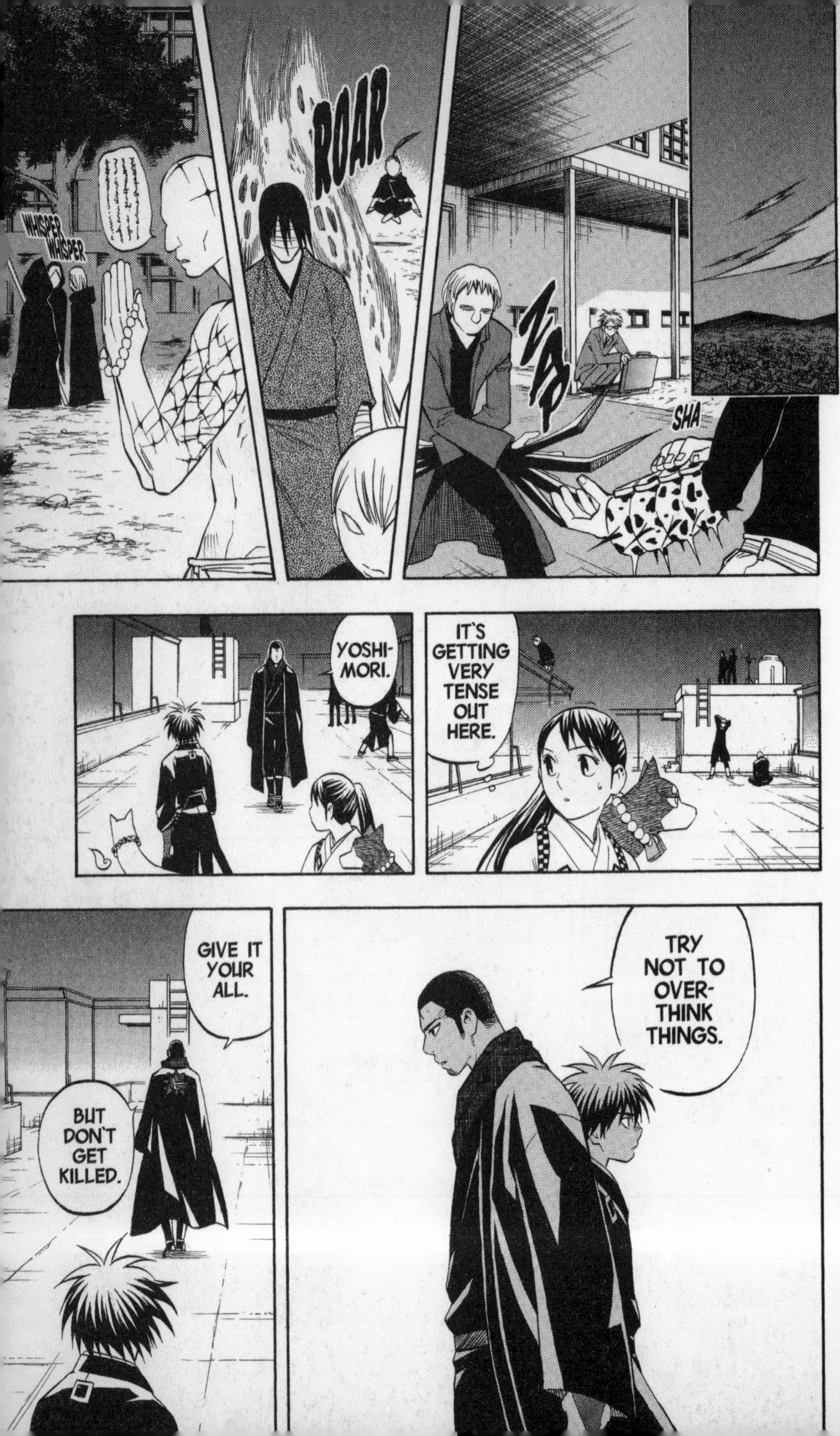
SHA
ROAR
WHISPER WHISPER
IT'S GETTING VERY TENSE OUT HERE.
YOSHI-MORI.
TRY NOT TO OVER-THINK THINGS.
GIVE IT YOUR ALL.
BUT DON'T GET KILLED.

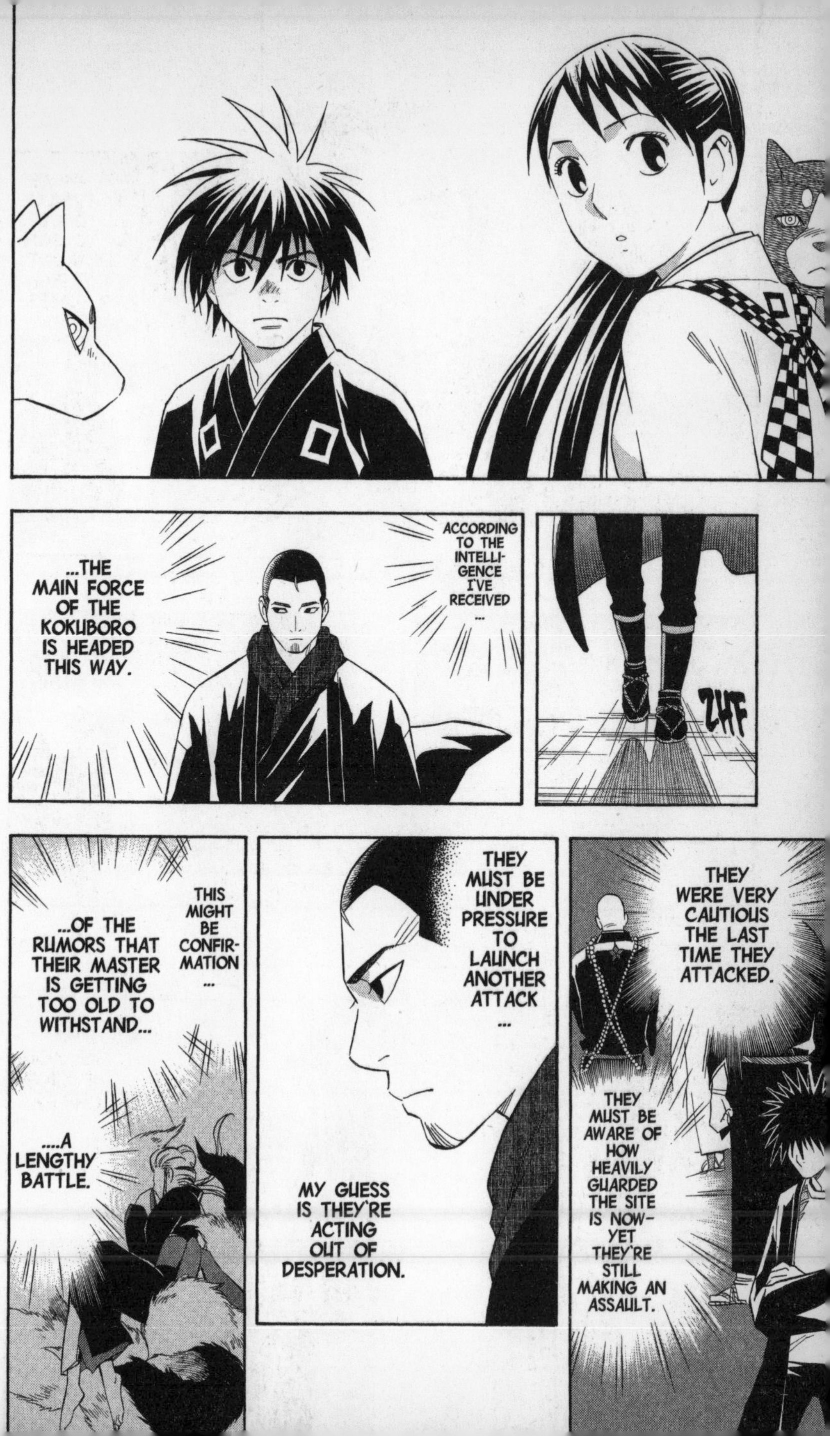
ZHF
ACCORDING TO THE INTELLIGENCE I'VE RECEIVED...
...THE MAIN FORCE OF THE KOKUBORO IS HEADED THIS WAY.
THEY WERE VERY CAUTIOUS THE LAST TIME THEY ATTACKED.
THEY MUST BE AWARE OF HOW HEAVILY GUARDED THE SITE IS NOW—YET THEY'RE STILL MAKING AN ASSAULT.
THEY MUST BE UNDER PRESSURE TO LAUNCH ANOTHER ATTACK...
MY GUESS IS THEY'RE ACTING OUT OF DESPERATION.
THIS MIGHT BE CONFIRMATION...
...OF THE RUMORS THAT THEIR MASTER IS GETTING TOO OLD TO WITHSTAND...
....A LENGTHY BATTLE.

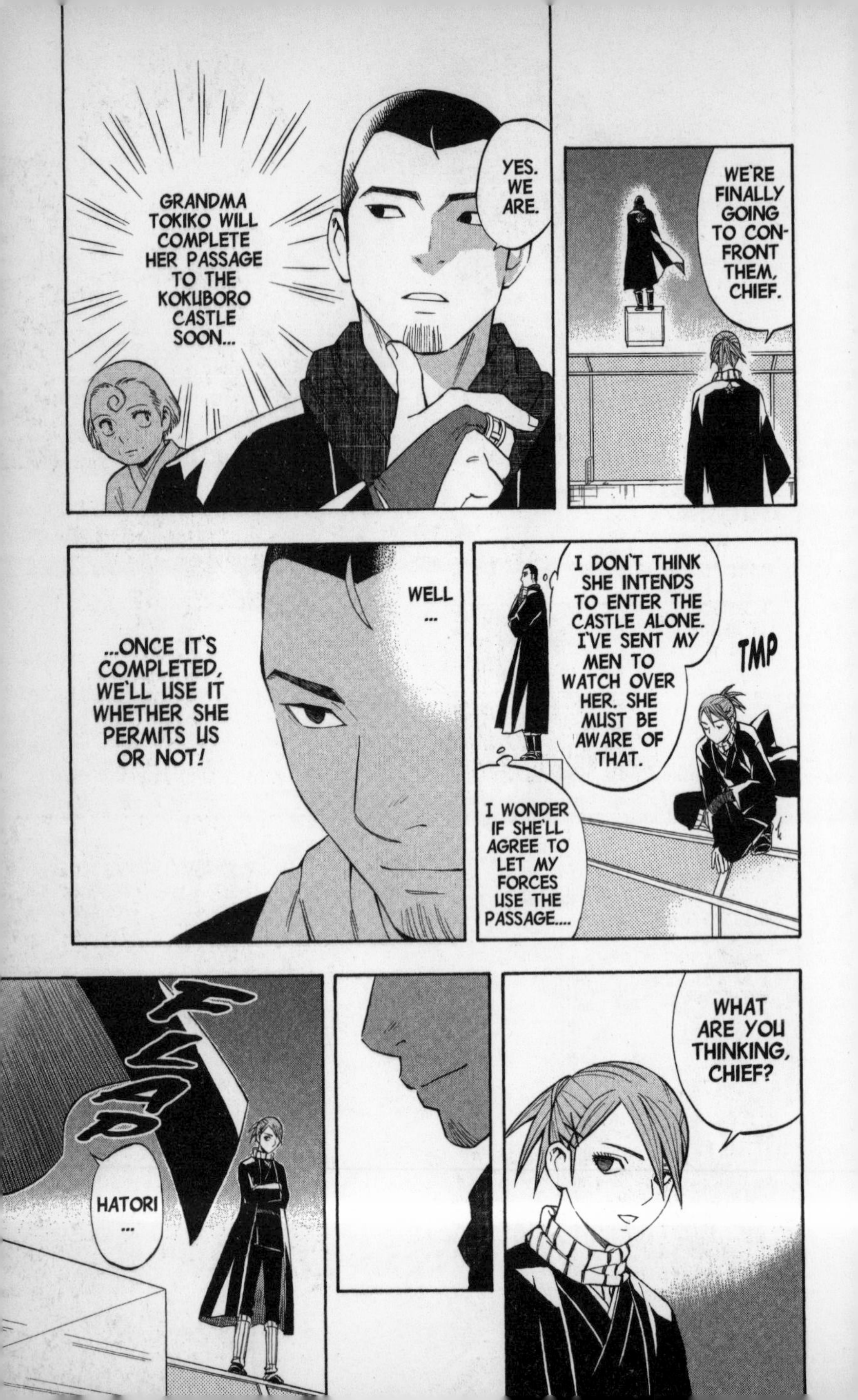
WE'RE FINALLY GOING TO CON- FRONT THEM, CHIEF.
YES. WE ARE.
GRANDMA TOKIKO WILL COMPLETE HER PASSAGE TO THE KOKUBORO CASTLE SOON...
I DON'T THINK SHE INTENDS TO ENTER THE CASTLE ALONE. I'VE SENT MY MEN TO WATCH OVER HER. SHE MUST BE AWARE OF THAT.
TMP
I WONDER IF SHE'LL AGREE TO LET MY FORCES USE THE PASSAGE....
WELL ...
...ONCE IT'S COMPLETED, WE'LL USE IT WHETHER SHE PERMITS US OR NOT!
WHAT ARE YOU THINKING, CHIEF?
FLAP
HATORI ...

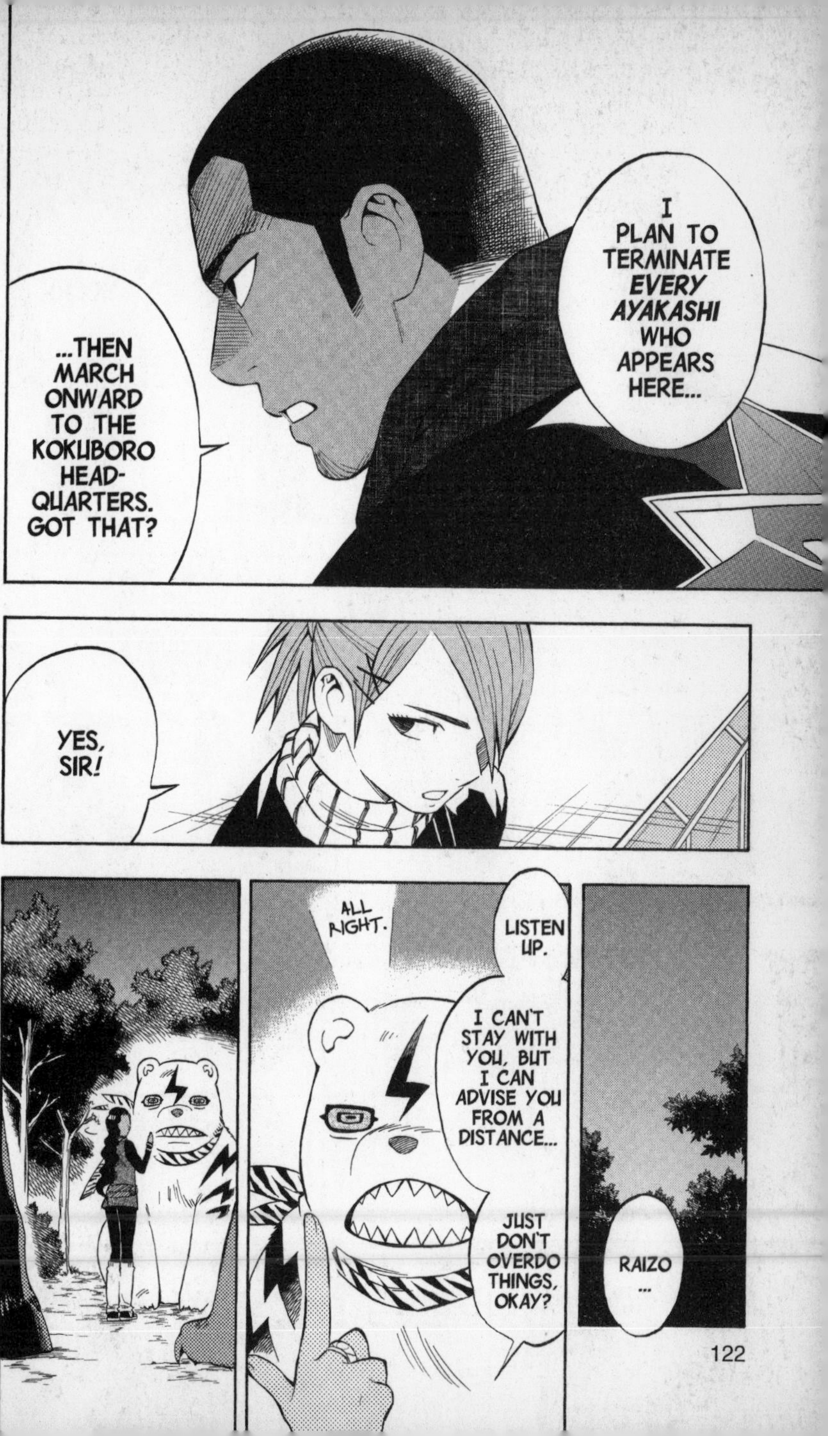
I PLAN TO TERMINATE *EVERY AYAKASHI* WHO APPEARS HERE...
...THEN MARCH ONWARD TO THE KOKUBORO HEAD-QUARTERS. GOT THAT?
YES, SIR!
RAIZO ...
LISTEN UP.
ALL RIGHT.
I CAN'T STAY WITH YOU, BUT I CAN ADVISE YOU FROM A DISTANCE...
JUST DON'T OVERDO THINGS, OKAY?

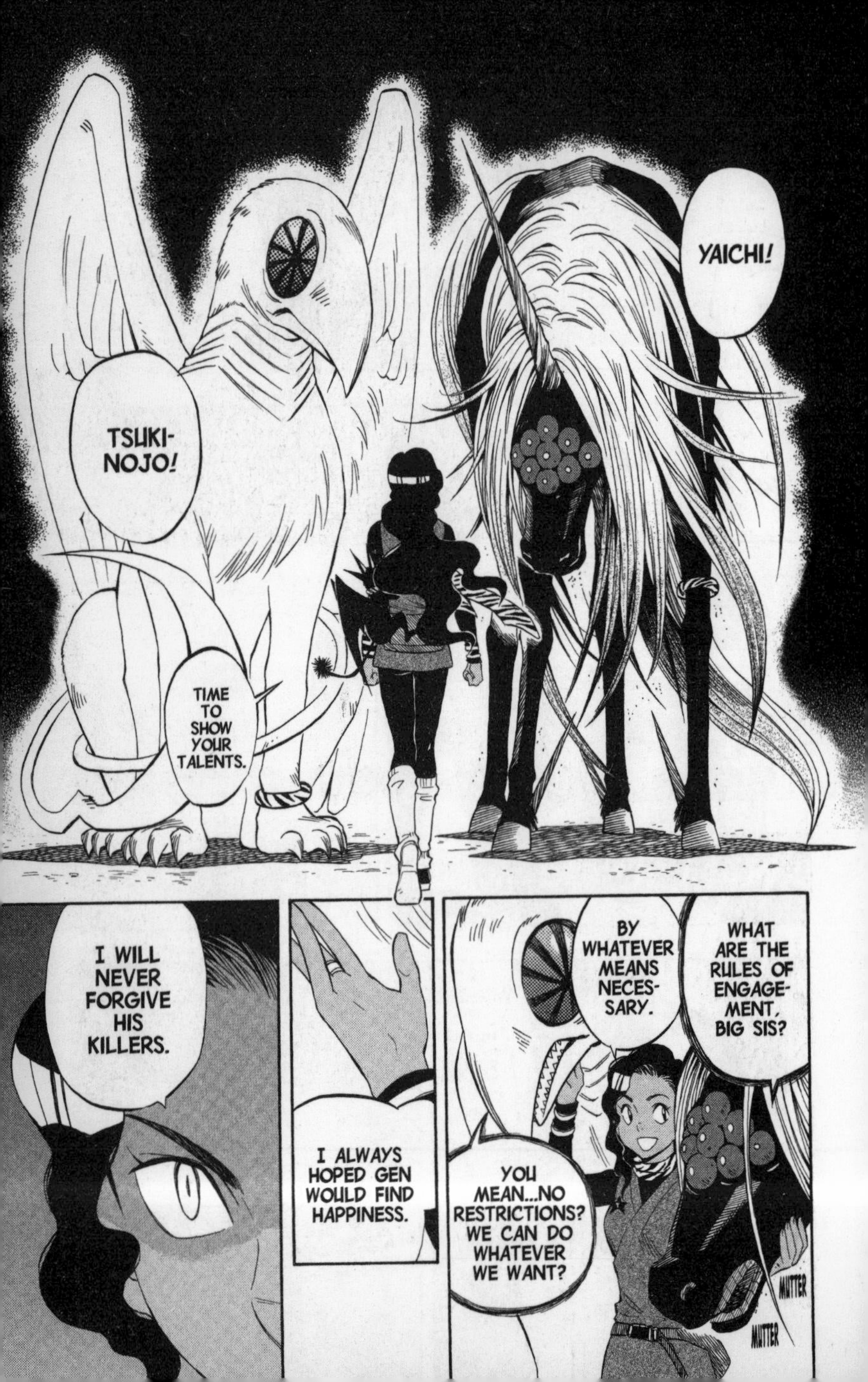
YAICHI!
TSUKI-NOJO!
TIME TO SHOW YOUR TALENTS.
WHAT ARE THE RULES OF ENGAGE-MENT, BIG SIS?
BY WHATEVER MEANS NECES-SARY.
YOU MEAN...NO RESTRICTIONS? WE CAN DO WHATEVER WE WANT?
MUTTER
MUTTER
I ALWAYS HOPED GEN WOULD FIND HAPPINESS.
I WILL NEVER FORGIVE HIS KILLERS.

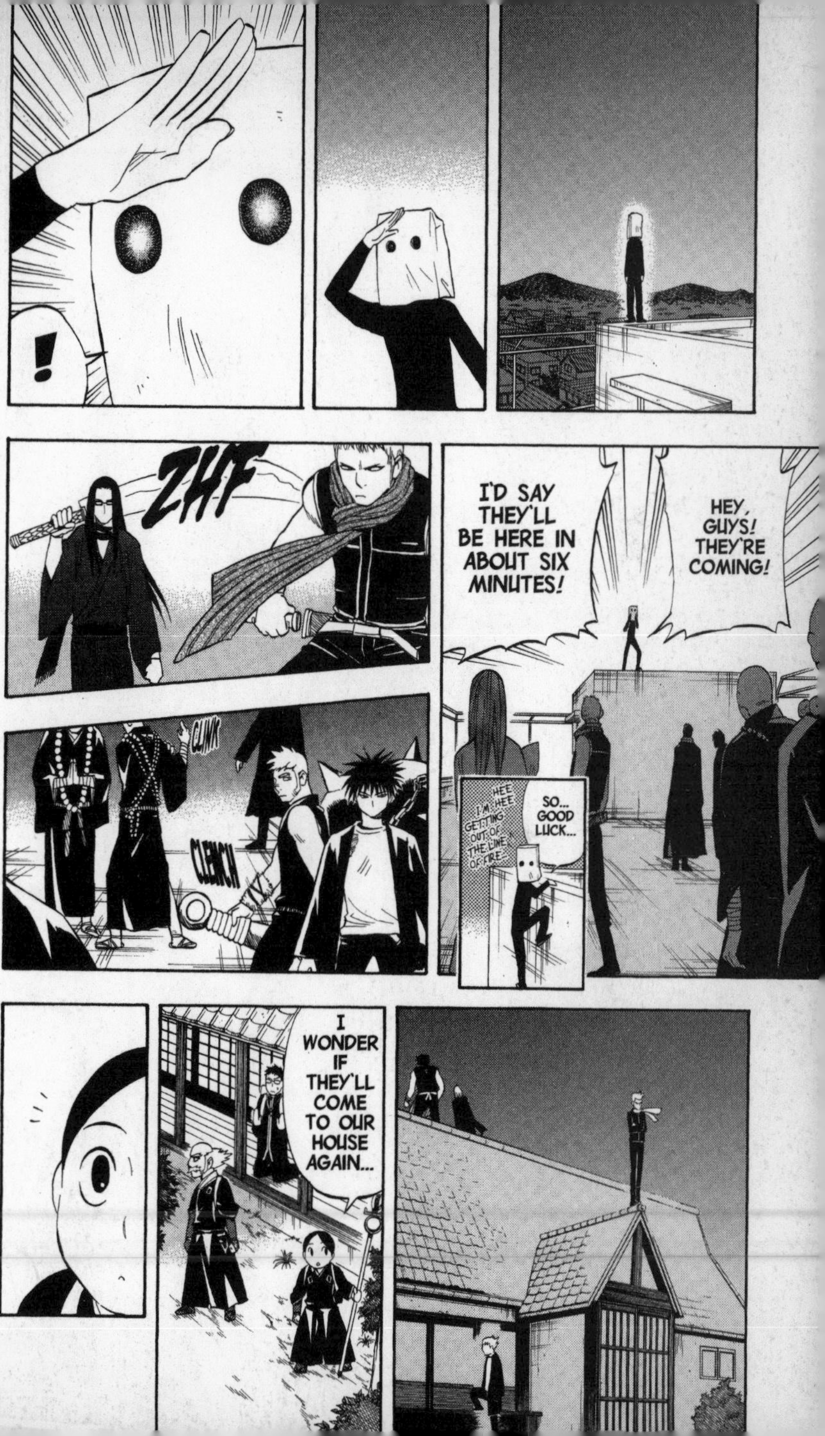
!
HEY, GUYS! THEY'RE COMING!
I'D SAY THEY'LL BE HERE IN ABOUT SIX MINUTES!
SO... GOOD LUCK...
HEE HEE I'M GETTING OUT OF THE LINE OF FIRE...
ZHF
CLINK
CLENCH
I WONDER IF THEY'LL COME TO OUR HOUSE AGAIN...

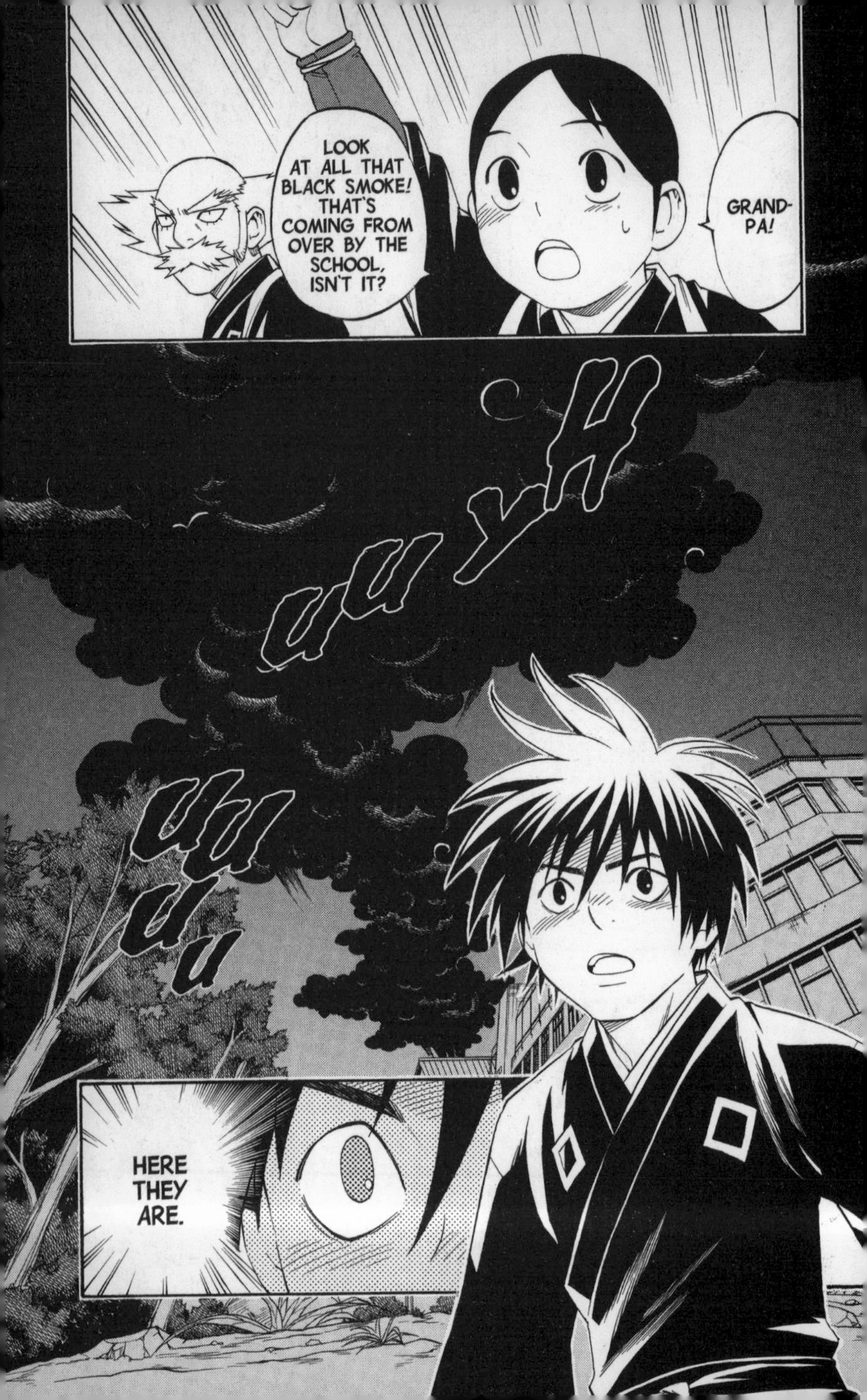
GRAND-PA!
LOOK AT ALL THAT BLACK SMOKE! THAT'S COMING FROM OVER BY THE SCHOOL, ISN'T IT?
HRRMMM
UUUU
HERE THEY ARE.

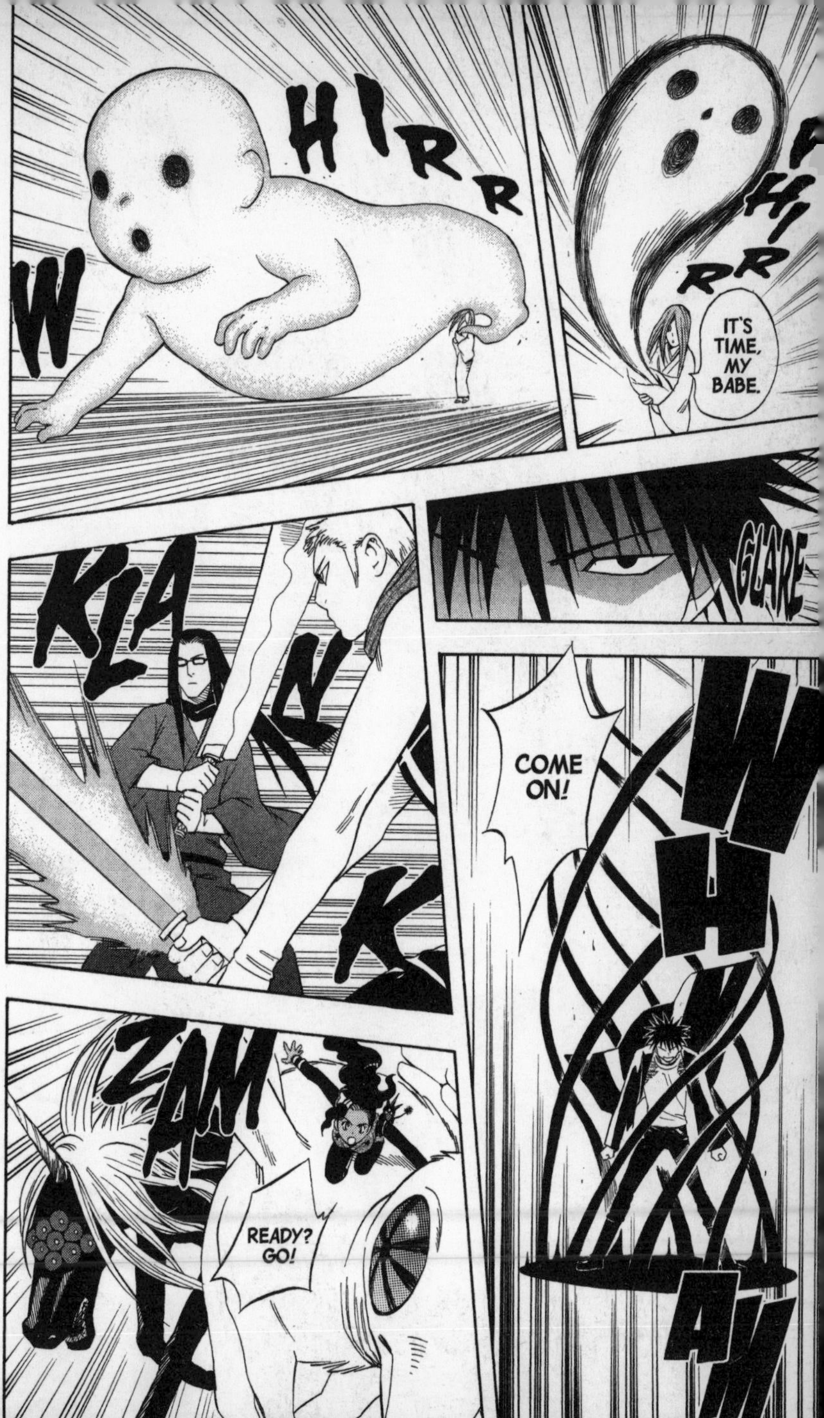
HIRRR
IT'S TIME, MY BABE.
WHIRRR
GLARE
COME ON!
WHAH
KLANK
ZAM
READY? GO!

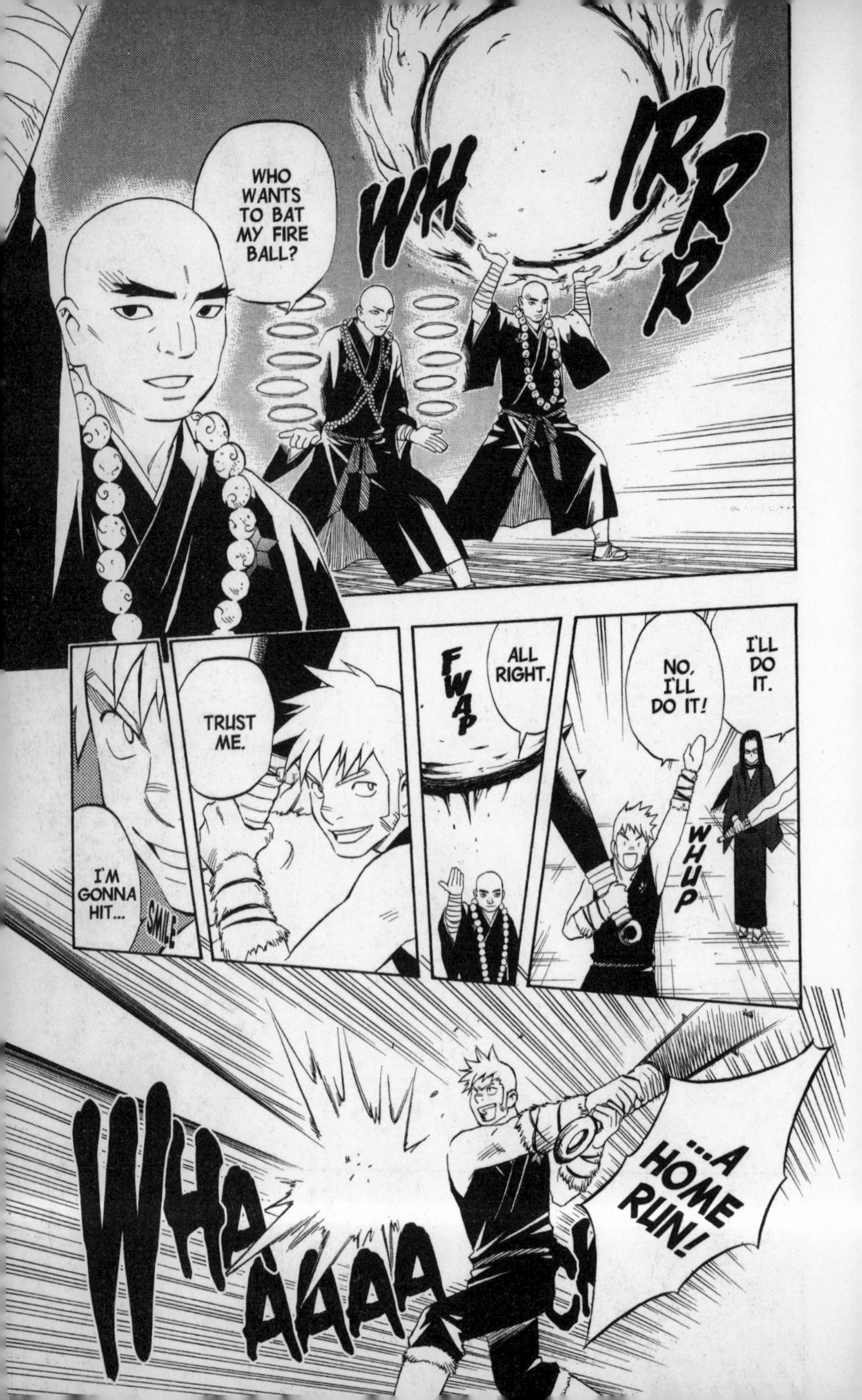
WHIRRR
WHO WANTS TO BAT MY FIRE BALL?
I'LL DO IT.
NO, I'LL DO IT!
WHUP
ALL RIGHT.
FWAP
TRUST ME.
I'M GONNA HIT...
SMILE
...A HOME RUN!
WHAAAAAC!

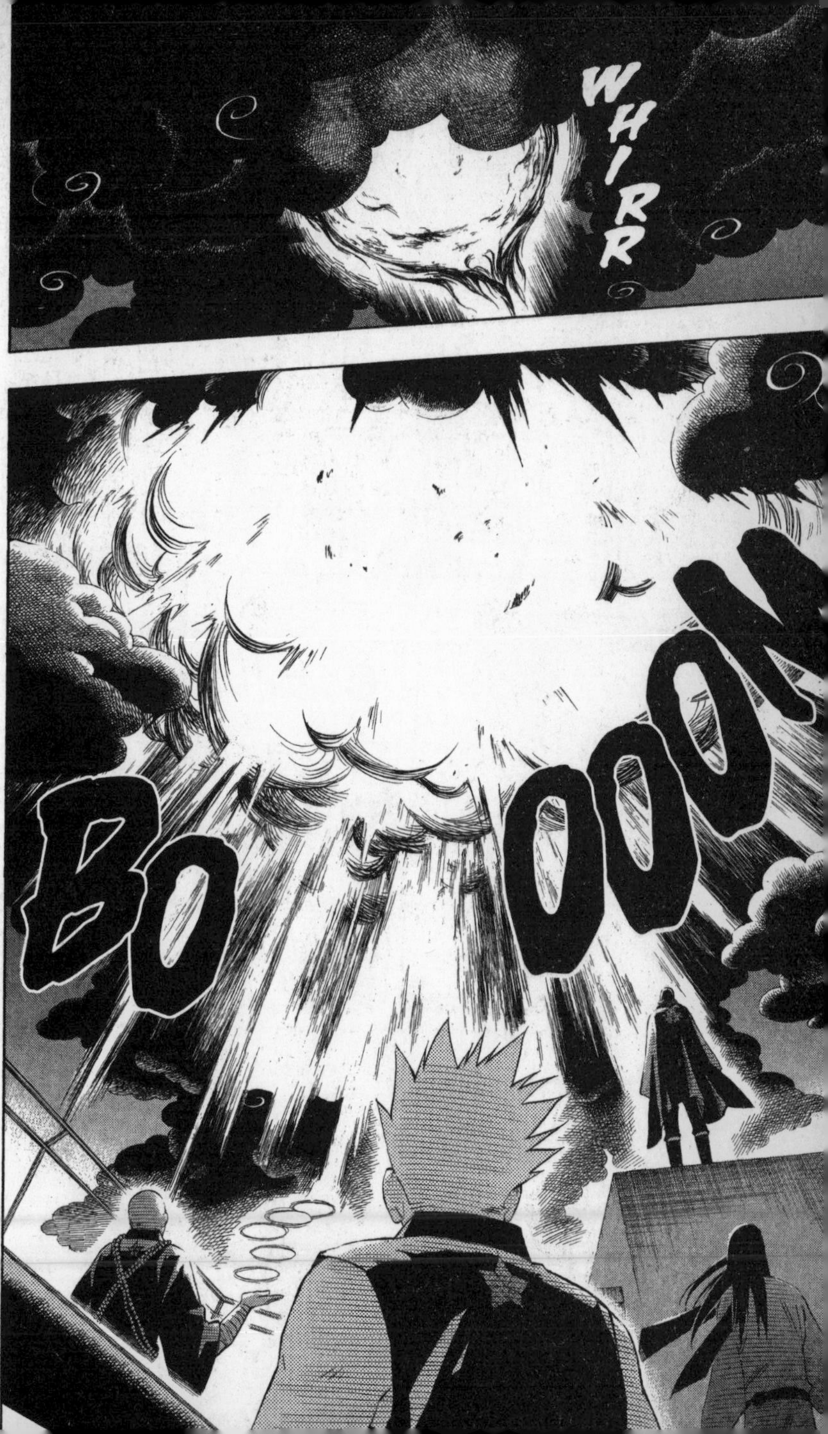
WHIRR
BOOOOM

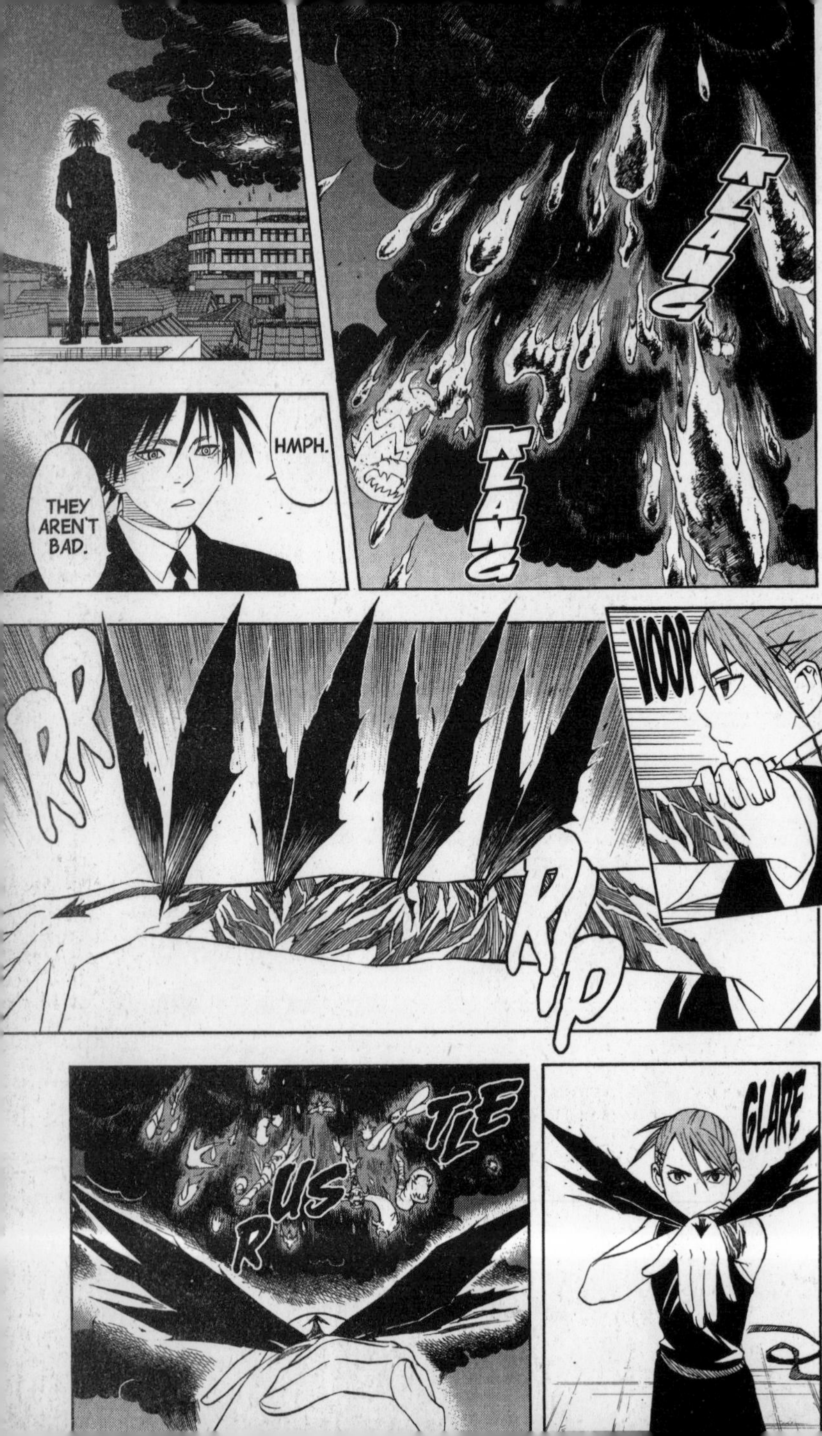
KLANG
KLANG
HMPH.
THEY AREN'T BAD.
VOOP
RR
RIP
GLARE
RUSTLE

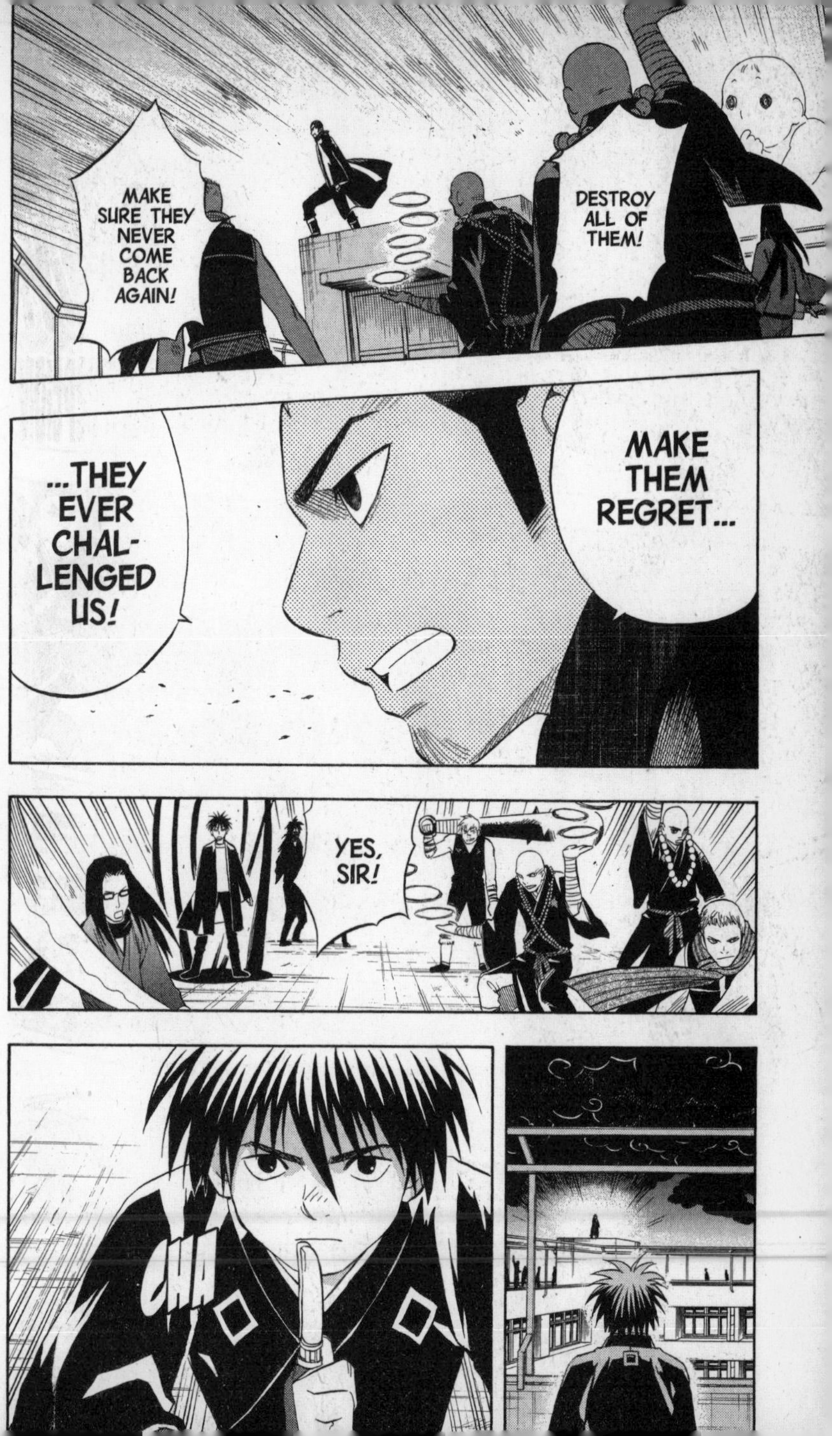
DESTROY ALL OF THEM!
MAKE SURE THEY NEVER COME BACK AGAIN!
MAKE THEM REGRET...
...THEY EVER CHALLENGED US!
YES, SIR!
CHA

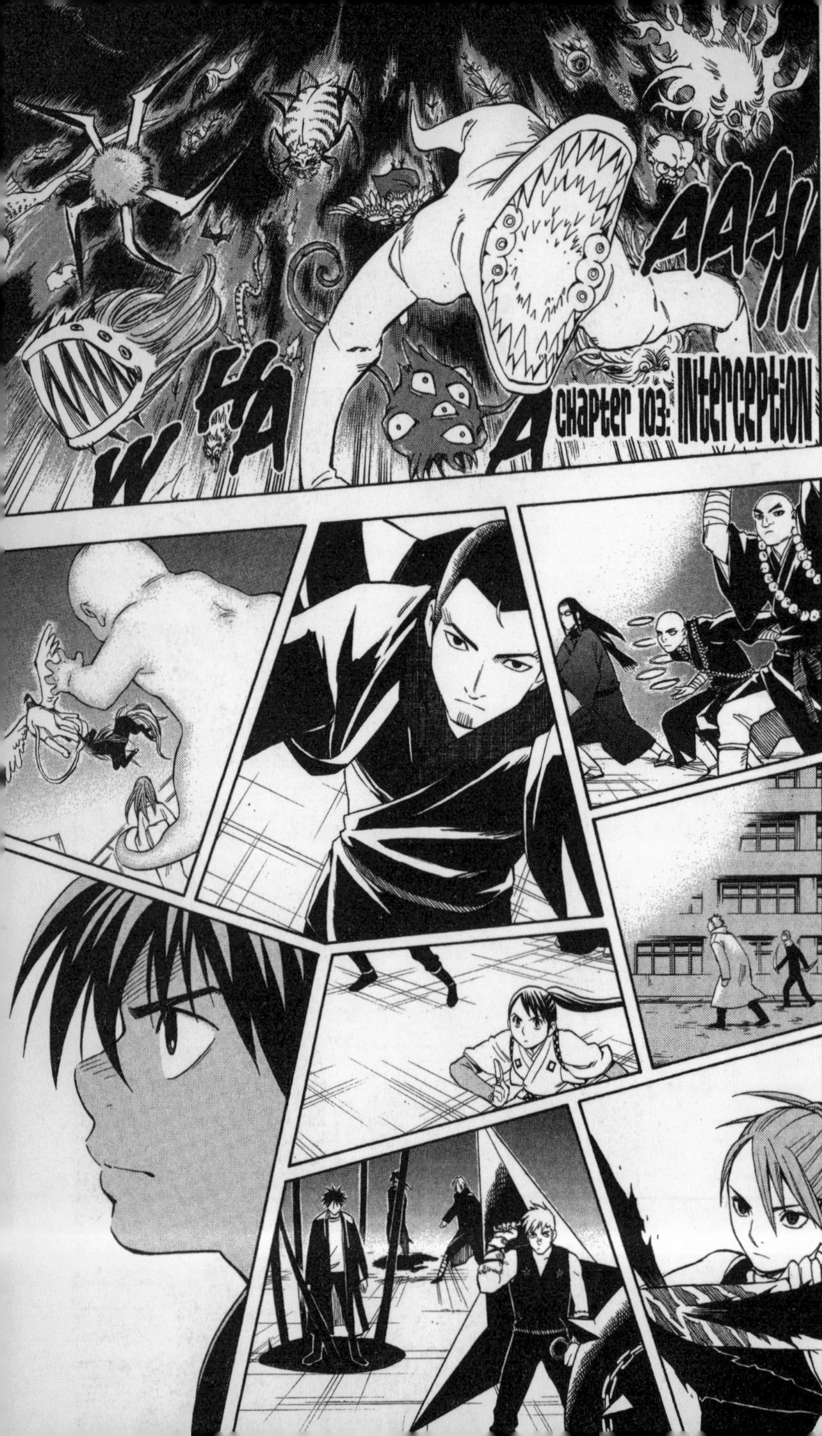
AAAH
Chapter 103: Interception
W HA A

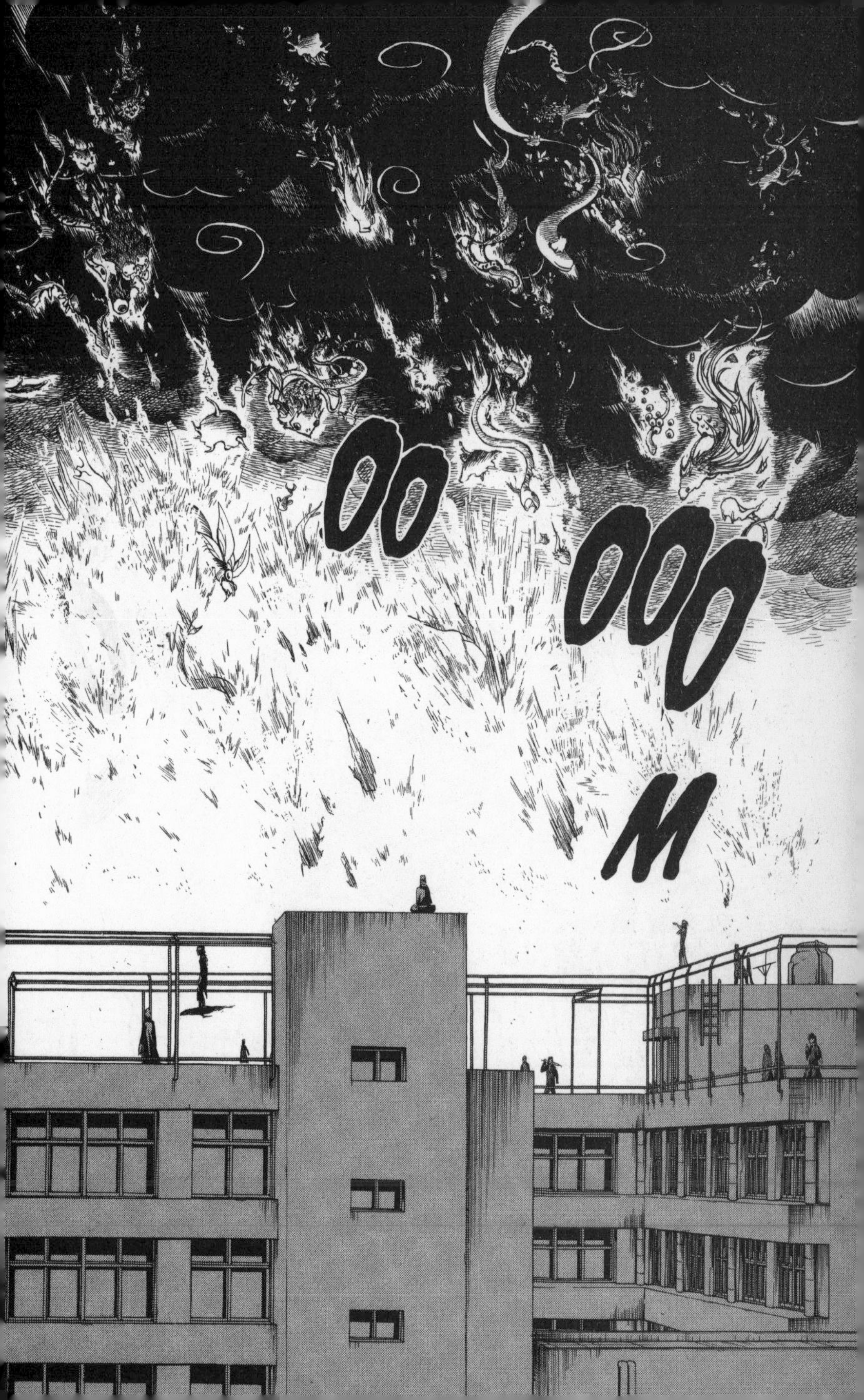
OOOOOM

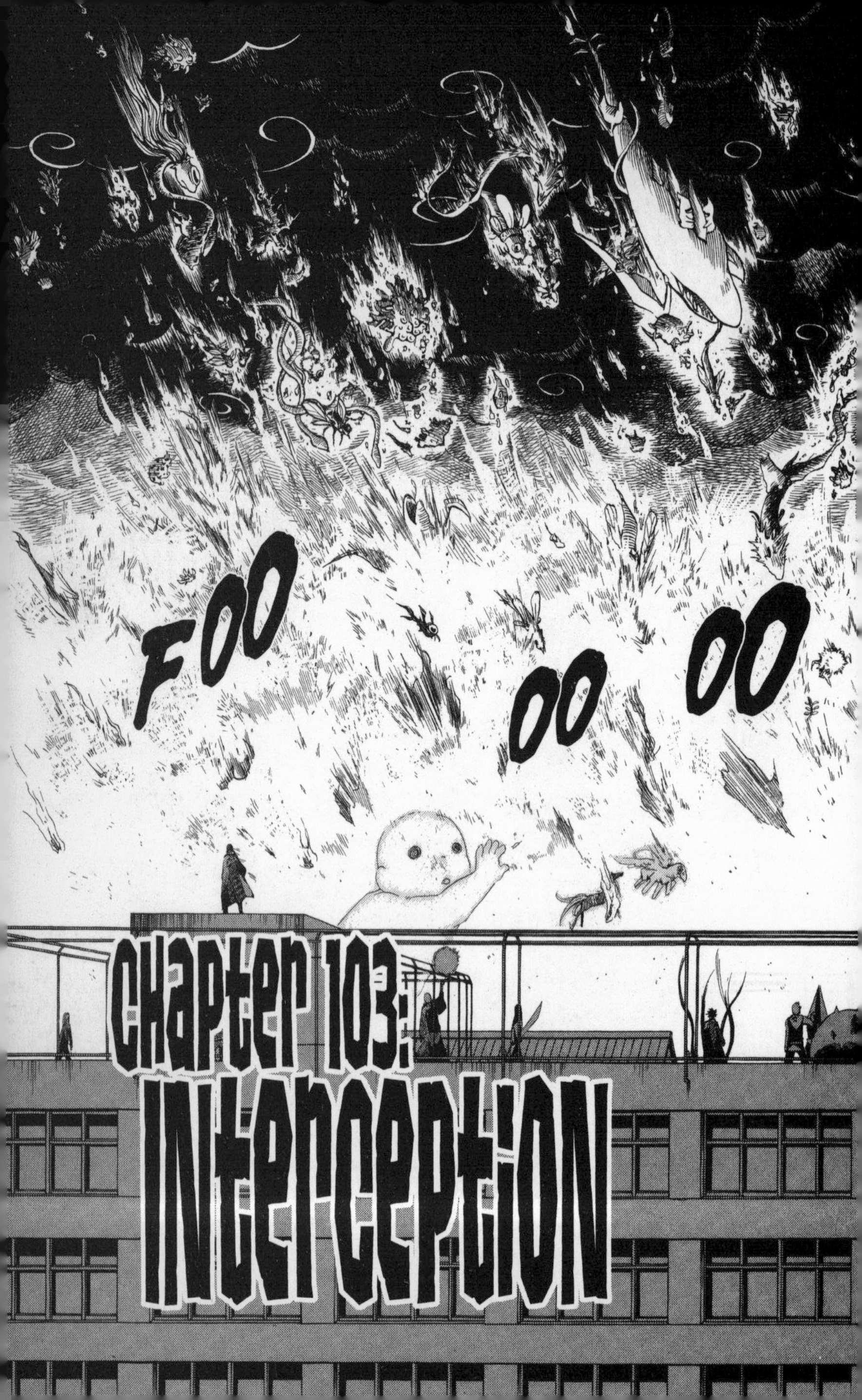
FOO
OO
OO
CHAPTER 103:
INTERCEPTION

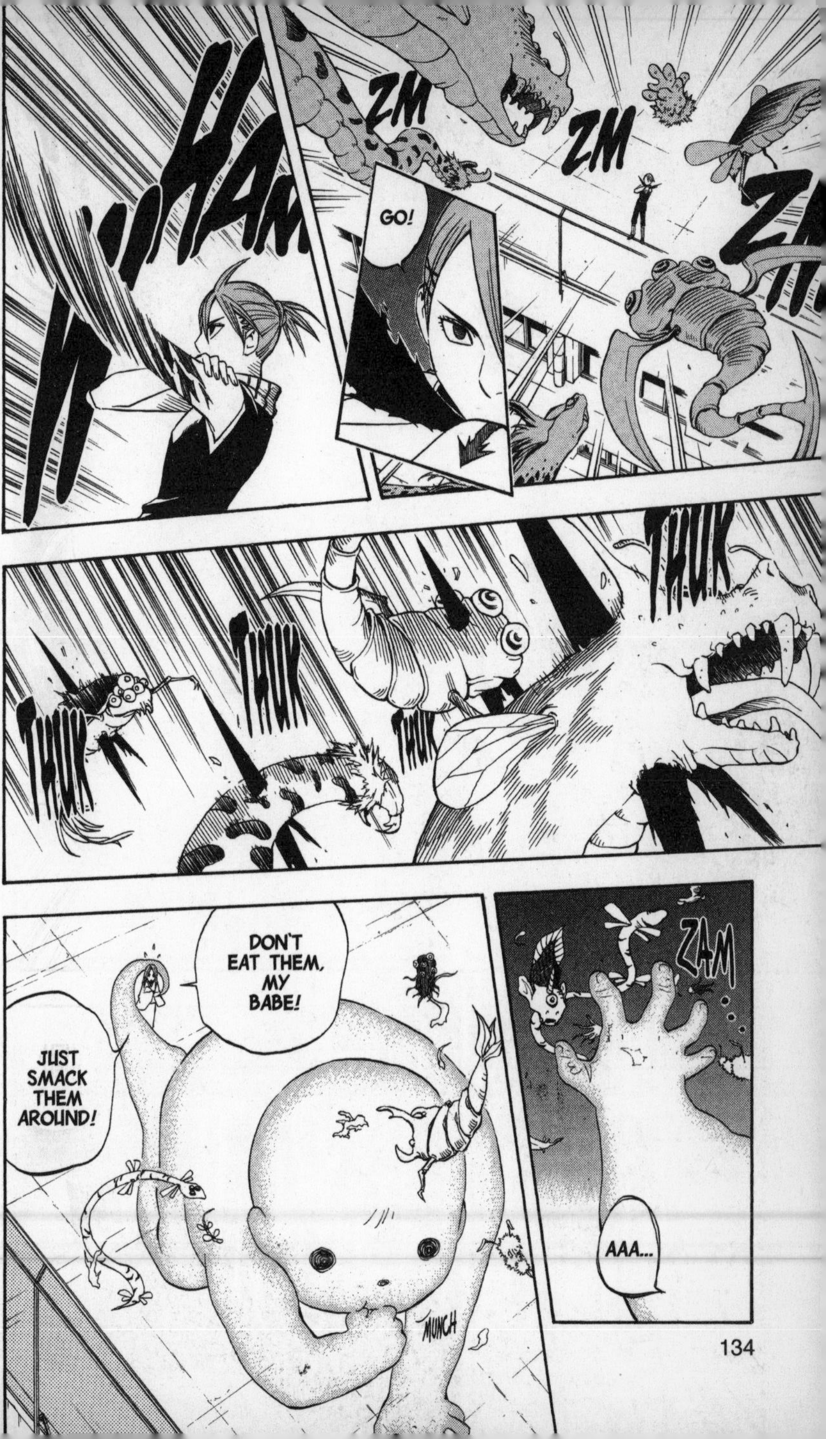

ZM
ZM
GO!
THUK
THUK
THUK
THUK
ZAM
AAA...
DON'T EAT THEM, MY BABE!
JUST SMACK THEM AROUND!
MUNCH

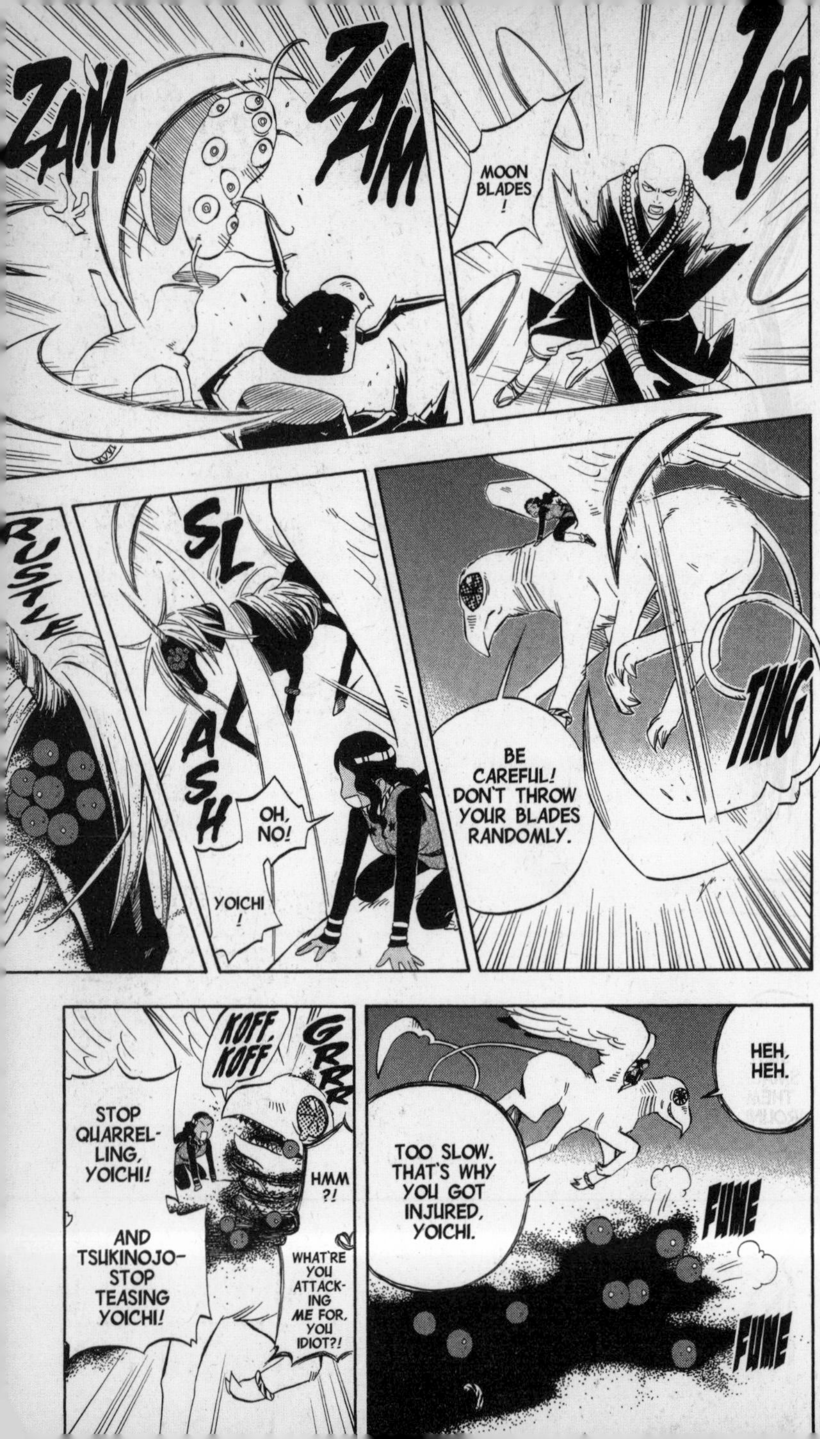
ZIP
MOON BLADES!
ZAM
ZAM
SLASH
TING
BE CAREFUL! DON'T THROW YOUR BLADES RANDOMLY.
OH, NO!
YOICHI!
RUSTLE
HEH, HEH.
TOO SLOW. THAT'S WHY YOU GOT INJURED, YOICHI.
FUME
FUME
GRRR
KOFF, KOFF
STOP QUARRELLING, YOICHI!
HMM?!
AND TSUKINOJO-STOP TEASING YOICHI!
WHAT'RE YOU ATTACKING ME FOR, YOU IDIOT?!

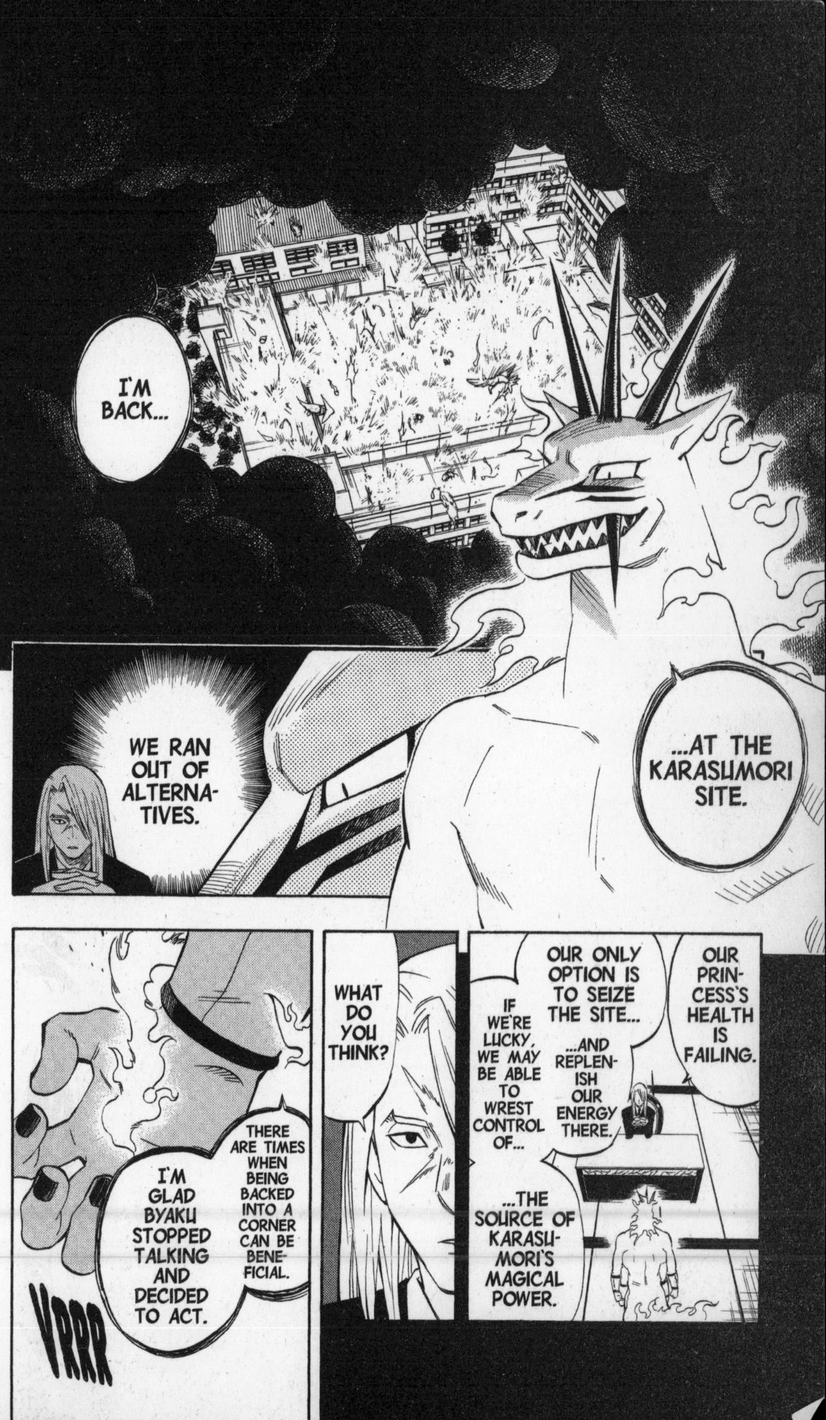
I'M BACK...
...AT THE KARASUMORI SITE.
WE RAN OUT OF ALTERNATIVES.
OUR PRINCESS'S HEALTH IS FAILING.
OUR ONLY OPTION IS TO SEIZE THE SITE...
...AND REPLENISH OUR ENERGY THERE.
IF WE'RE LUCKY, WE MAY BE ABLE TO WREST CONTROL OF...
...THE SOURCE OF KARASUMORI'S MAGICAL POWER.
WHAT DO YOU THINK?
THERE ARE TIMES WHEN BEING BACKED INTO A CORNER CAN BE BENEFICIAL.
I'M GLAD BYAKU STOPPED TALKING AND DECIDED TO ACT.
VRRR

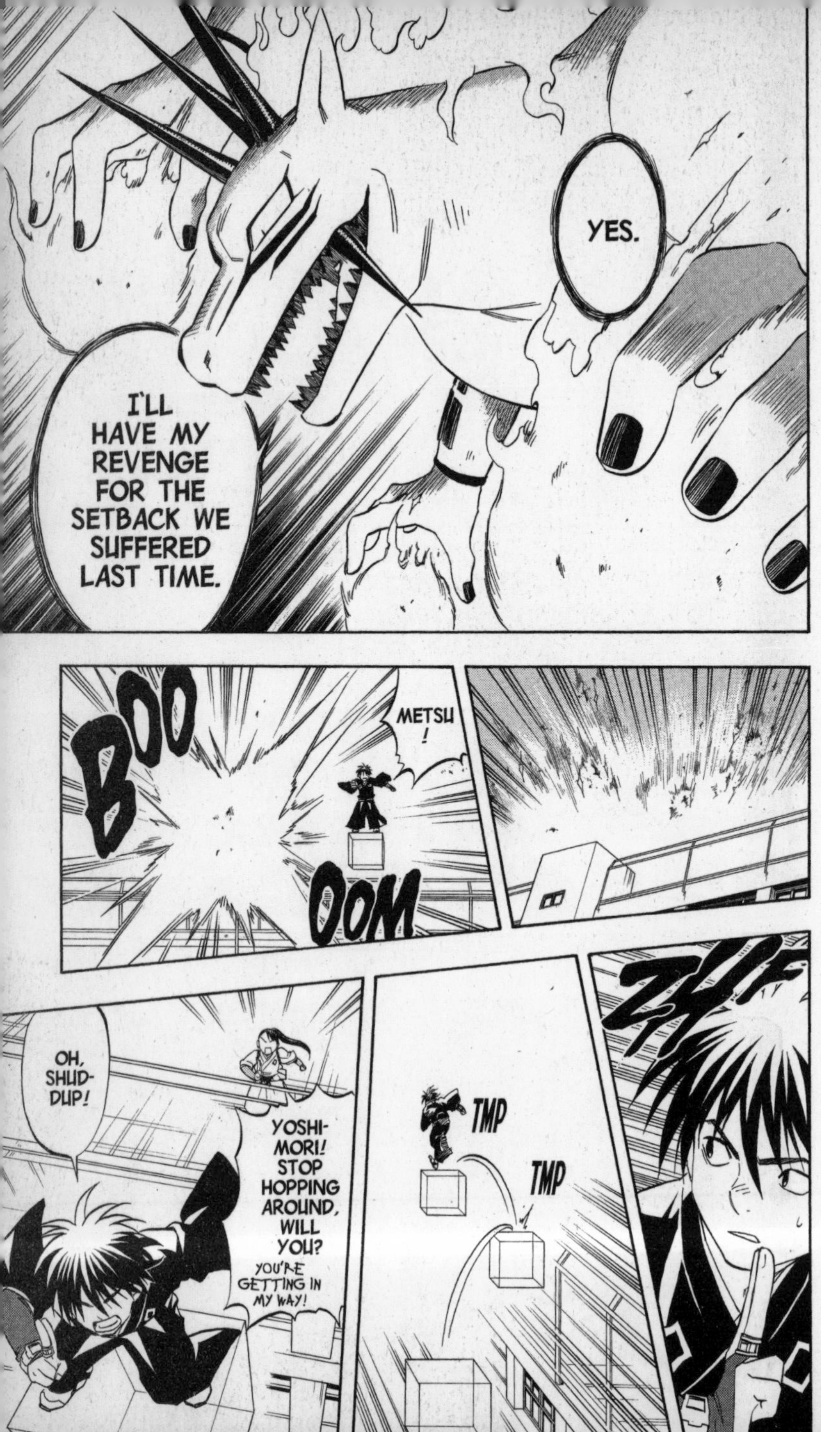
YES.
I'LL HAVE MY REVENGE FOR THE SETBACK WE SUFFERED LAST TIME.
METSU!
BOO
OOM
ZHF
TMP
TMP
YOSHIMORI! STOP HOPPING AROUND, WILL YOU?
YOU'RE GETTING IN MY WAY!
OH, SHUDDUP!

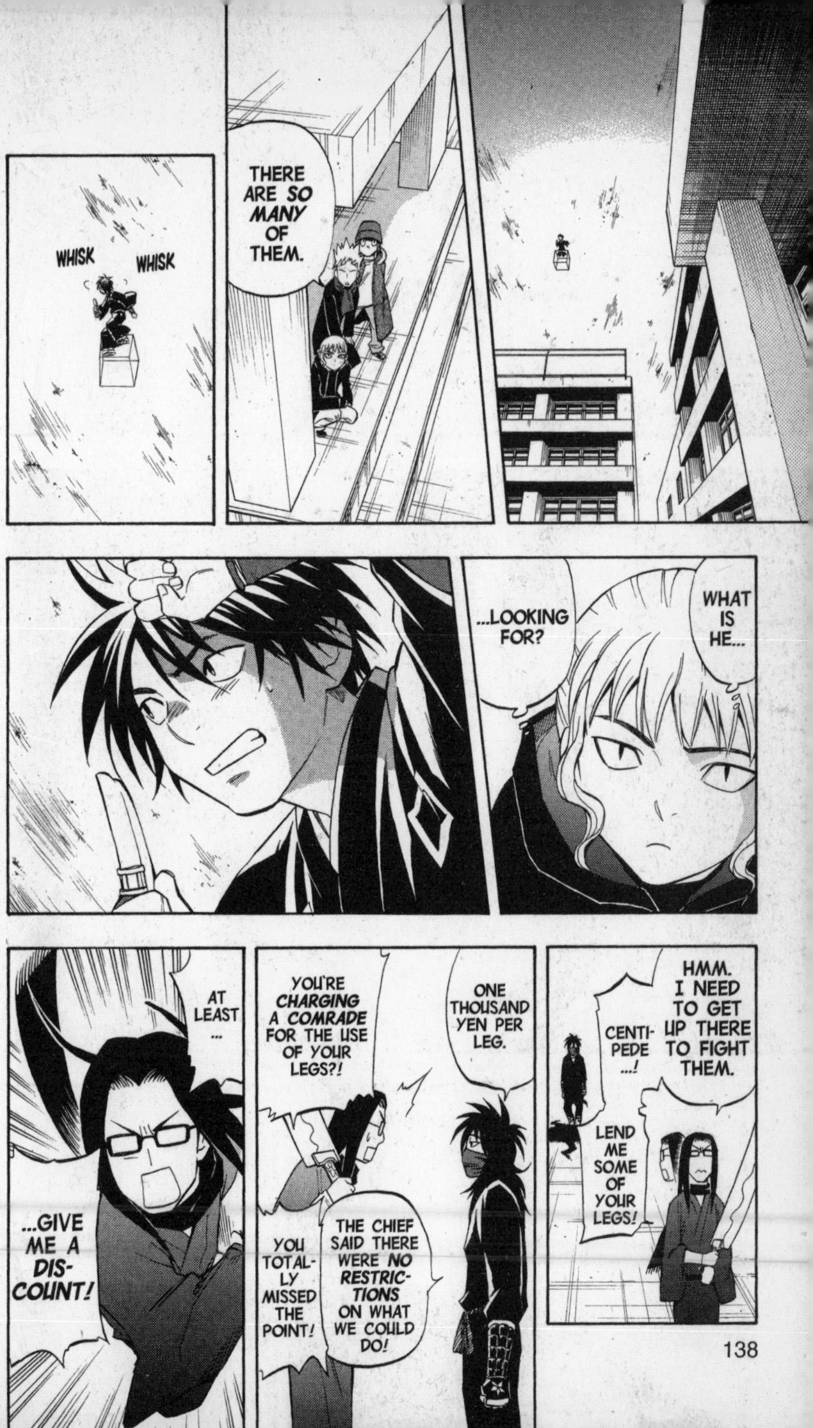
THERE ARE SO *MANY* OF THEM.
WHISK
WHISK
WHAT IS HE...
...LOOKING FOR?
HMM. I NEED TO GET UP THERE TO FIGHT THEM.
CENTI-PEDE ...!
LEND ME SOME OF YOUR LEGS!
ONE THOUSAND YEN PER LEG.
YOU'RE *CHARGING* A *COMRADE* FOR THE USE OF YOUR LEGS?!
THE CHIEF SAID THERE WERE *NO RESTRICTIONS* ON WHAT WE COULD DO!
YOU TOTAL-LY MISSED THE POINT!
AT LEAST ...
...GIVE ME A *DIS-COUNT!*

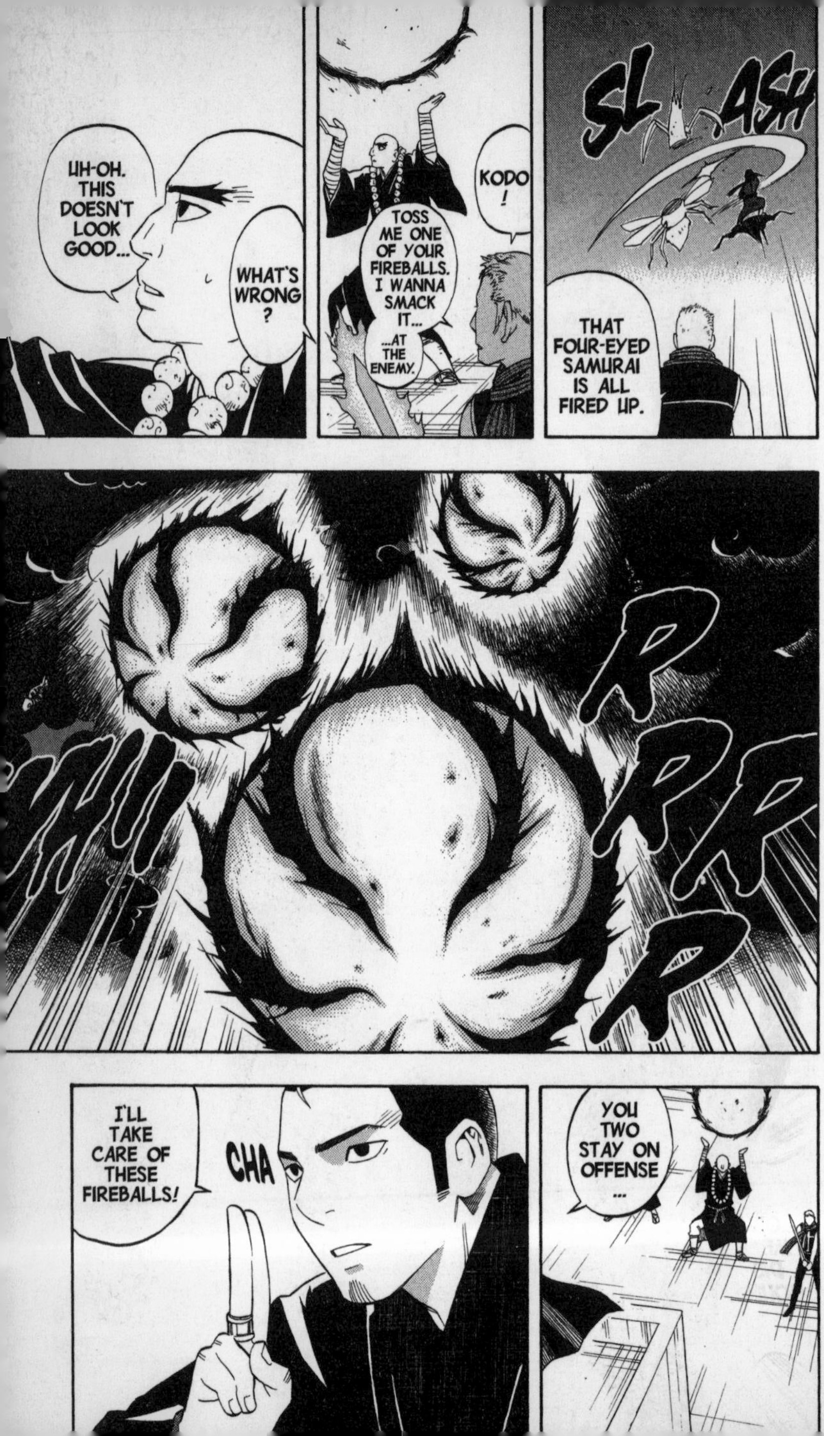
SLASH
THAT FOUR-EYED SAMURAI IS ALL FIRED UP.
KODO!
TOSS ME ONE OF YOUR FIREBALLS. I WANNA SMACK IT...
...AT THE ENEMY.
UH-OH. THIS DOESN'T LOOK GOOD...
WHAT'S WRONG?
RRRRR
YOU TWO STAY ON OFFENSE...
CHA
I'LL TAKE CARE OF THESE FIREBALLS!

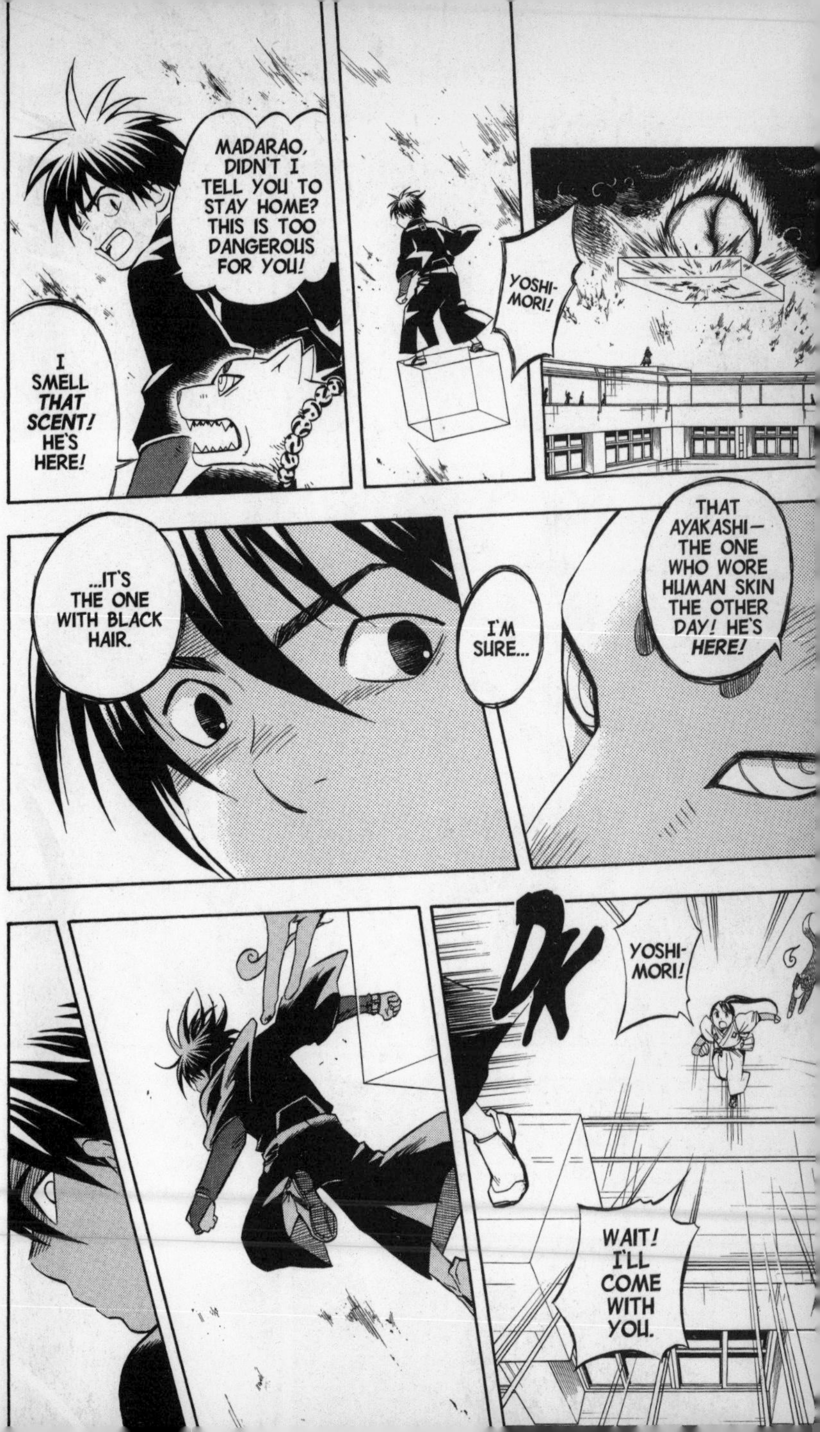
YOSHI-MORI!
MADARAO, DIDN'T I TELL YOU TO STAY HOME? THIS IS TOO DANGEROUS FOR YOU!
I SMELL THAT SCENT! HE'S HERE!
THAT AYAKASHI—THE ONE WHO WORE HUMAN SKIN THE OTHER DAY! HE'S HERE!
I'M SURE...
...IT'S THE ONE WITH BLACK HAIR.
DK
YOSHI-MORI!
WAIT! I'LL COME WITH YOU.

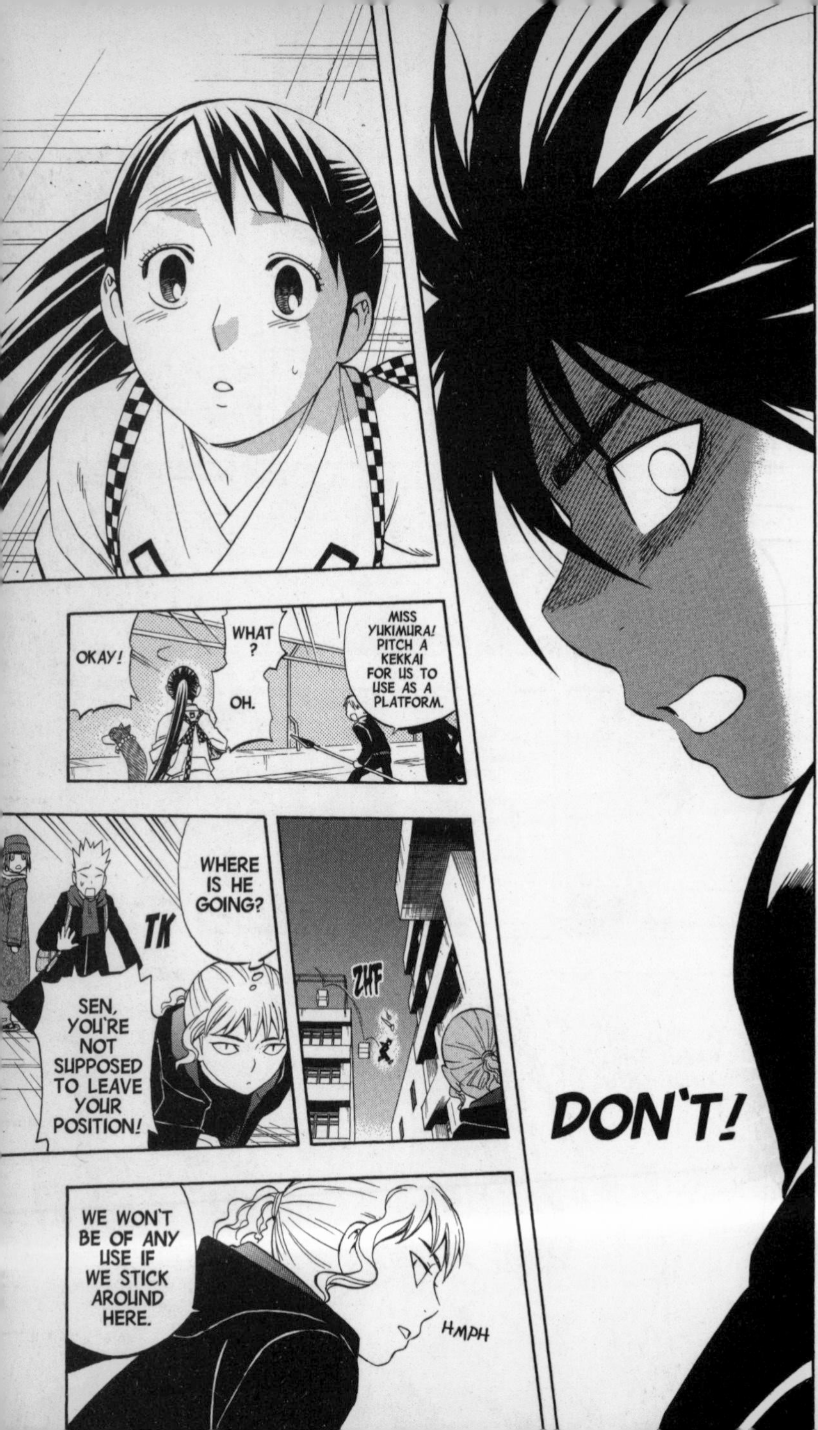
DON'T!
MISS YUKIMURA! PITCH A KEKKAI FOR US TO USE AS A PLATFORM.
WHAT? OH.
OKAY!
ZHF
WHERE IS HE GOING?
TK
SEN, YOU'RE NOT SUPPOSED TO LEAVE YOUR POSITION!
WE WON'T BE OF ANY USE IF WE STICK AROUND HERE.
HMPH

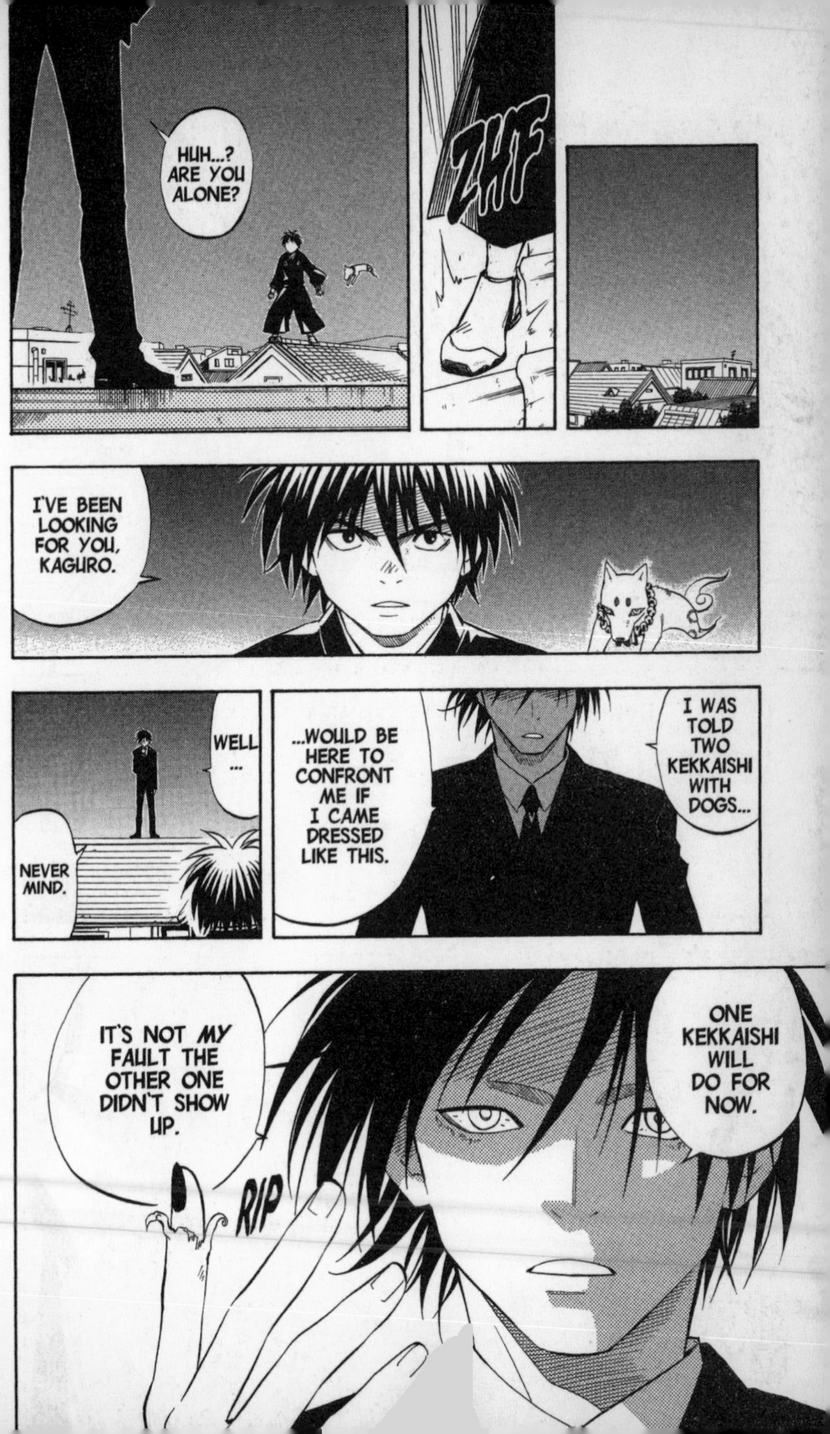
ZHF
HUH...? ARE YOU ALONE?
I'VE BEEN LOOKING FOR YOU, KAGURO.
I WAS TOLD TWO KEKKAISHI WITH DOGS...
...WOULD BE HERE TO CONFRONT ME IF I CAME DRESSED LIKE THIS.
WELL...
NEVER MIND.
ONE KEKKAISHI WILL DO FOR NOW.
IT'S NOT *MY* FAULT THE OTHER ONE DIDN'T SHOW UP.
RIP

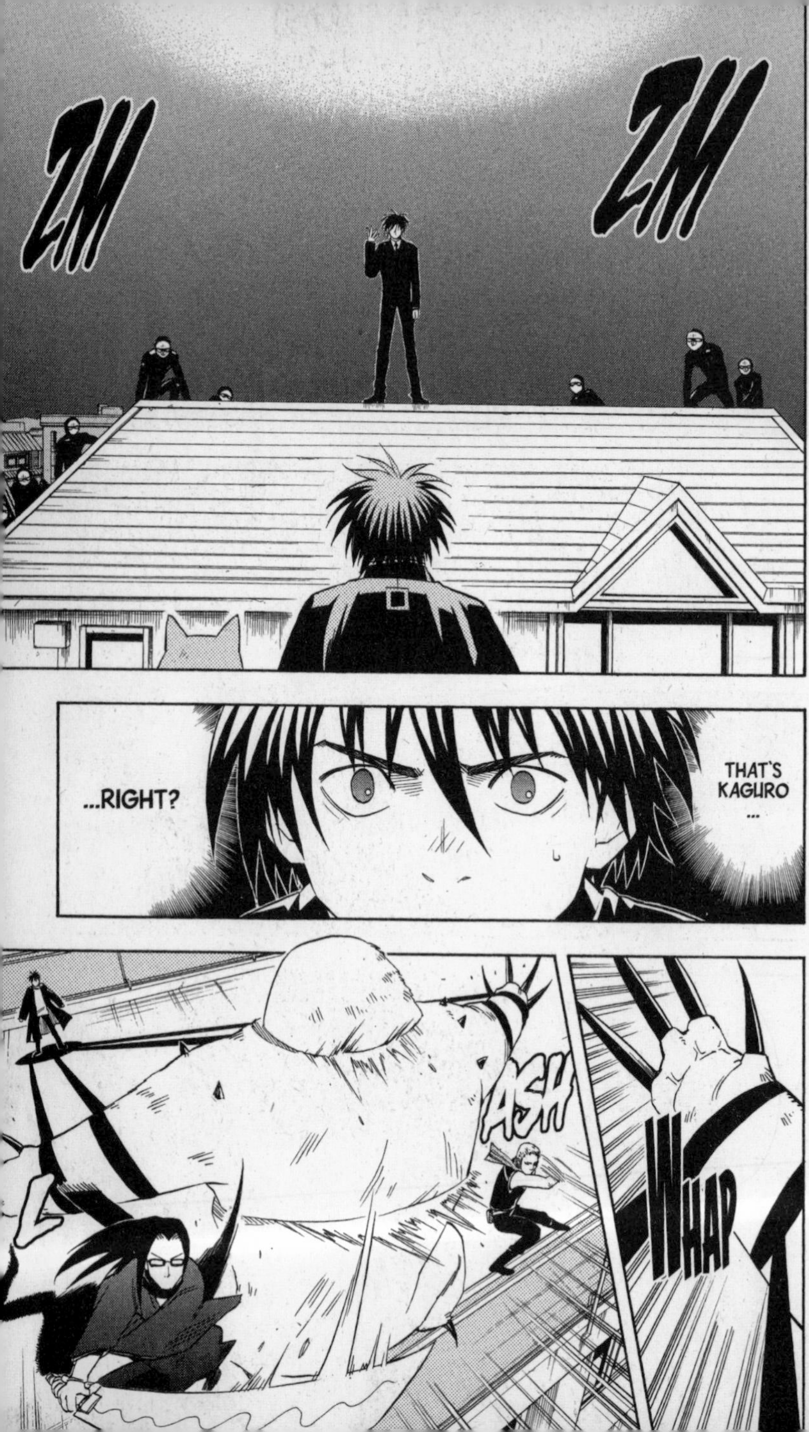
ZM
ZM
THAT'S KAGURO ...
...RIGHT?
WHAP
ASH

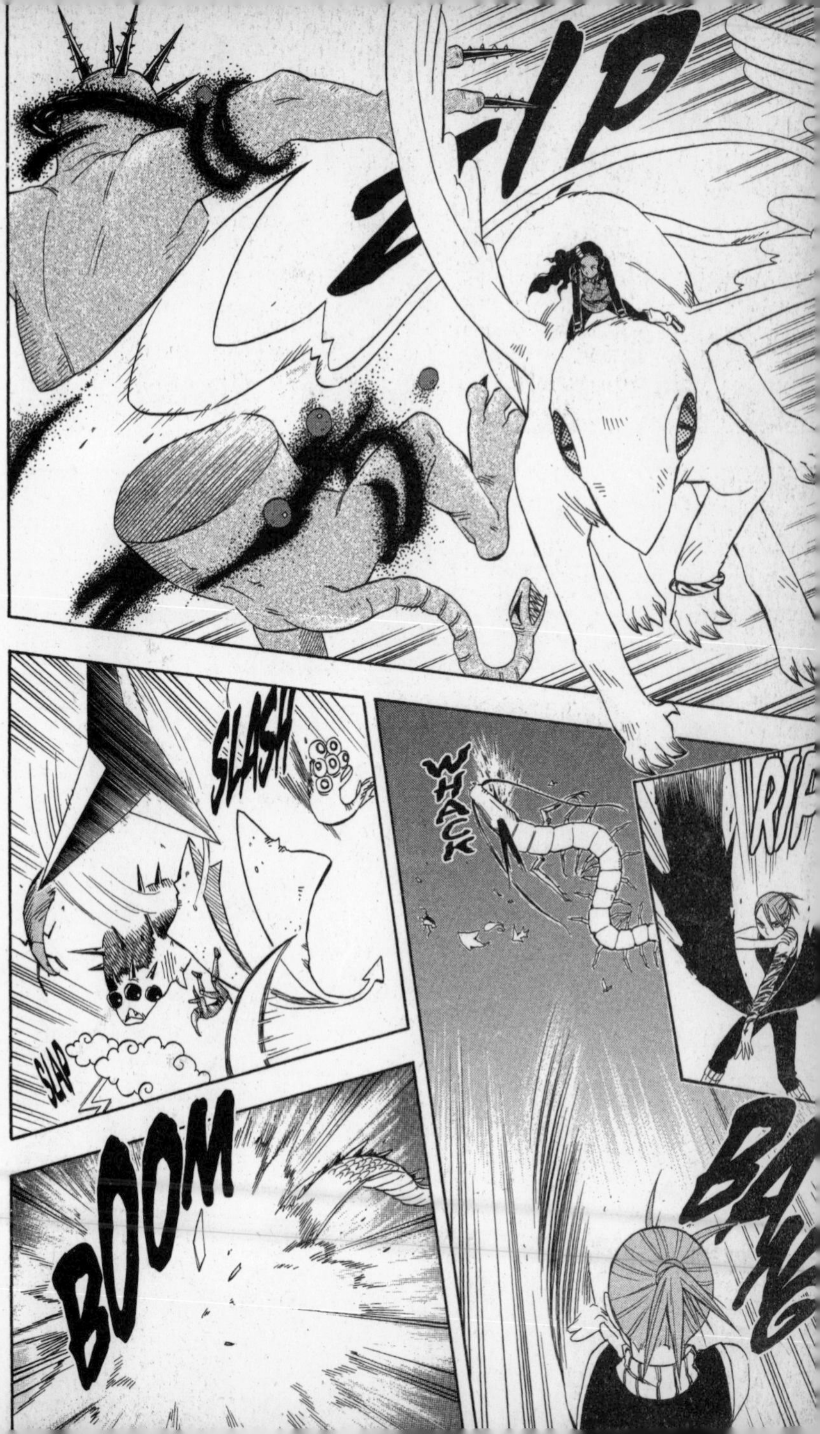

RIP
WHACK
SLASH
SLAP
BANG
BOOM

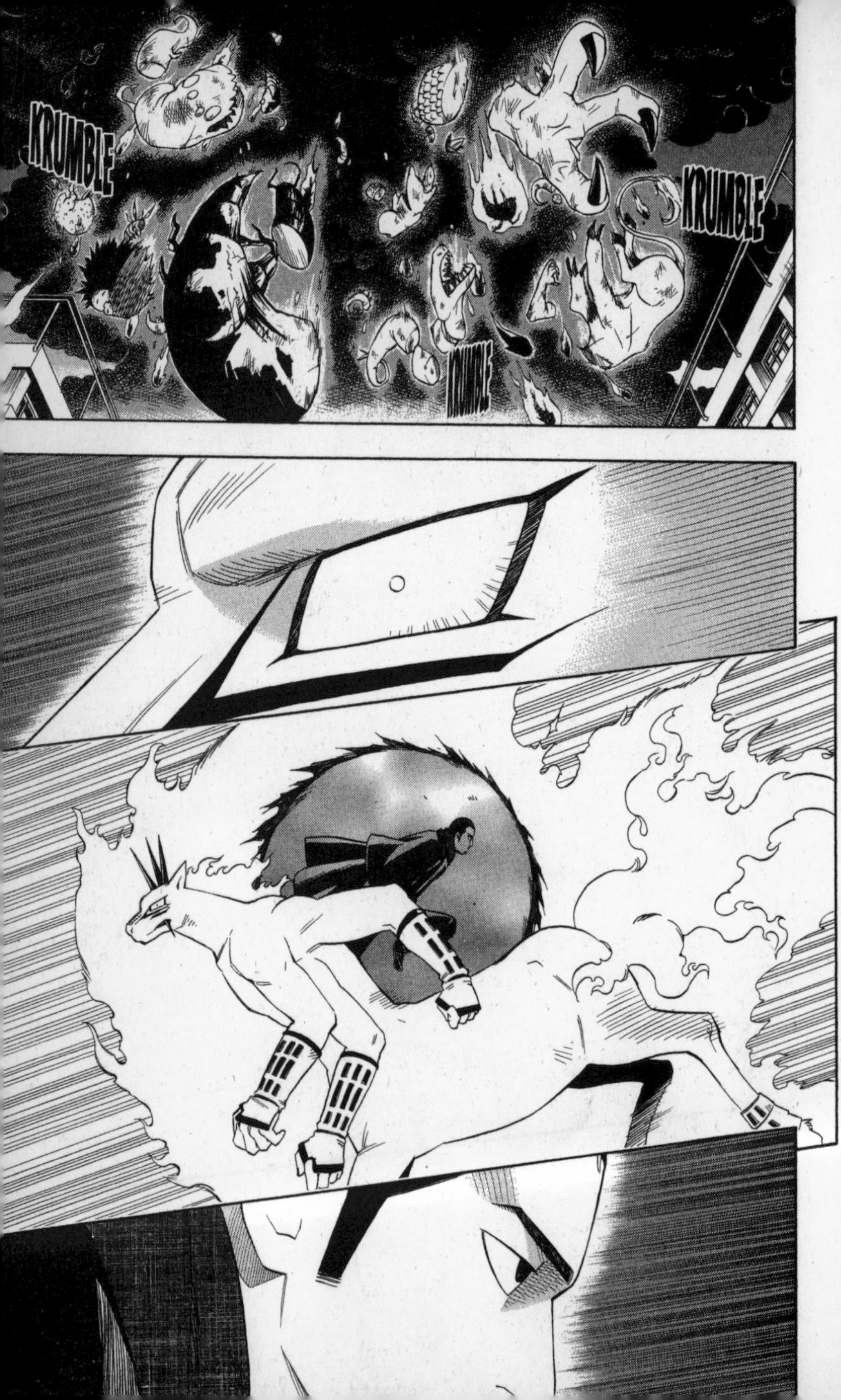
KRUMBLE
KRUMBLE
KRUMBLE

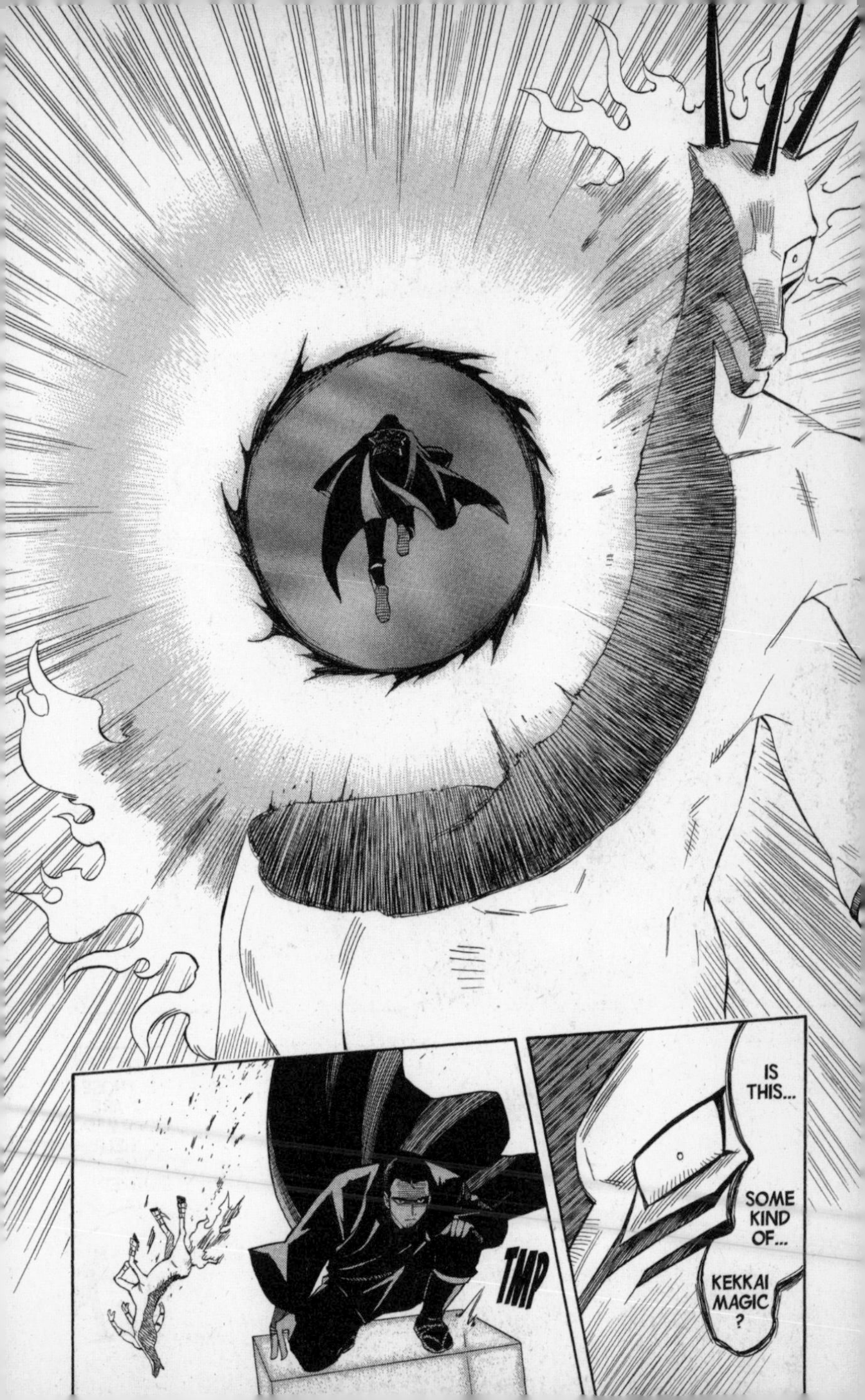
IS THIS...
SOME KIND OF...
KEKKAI MAGIC?
TMP

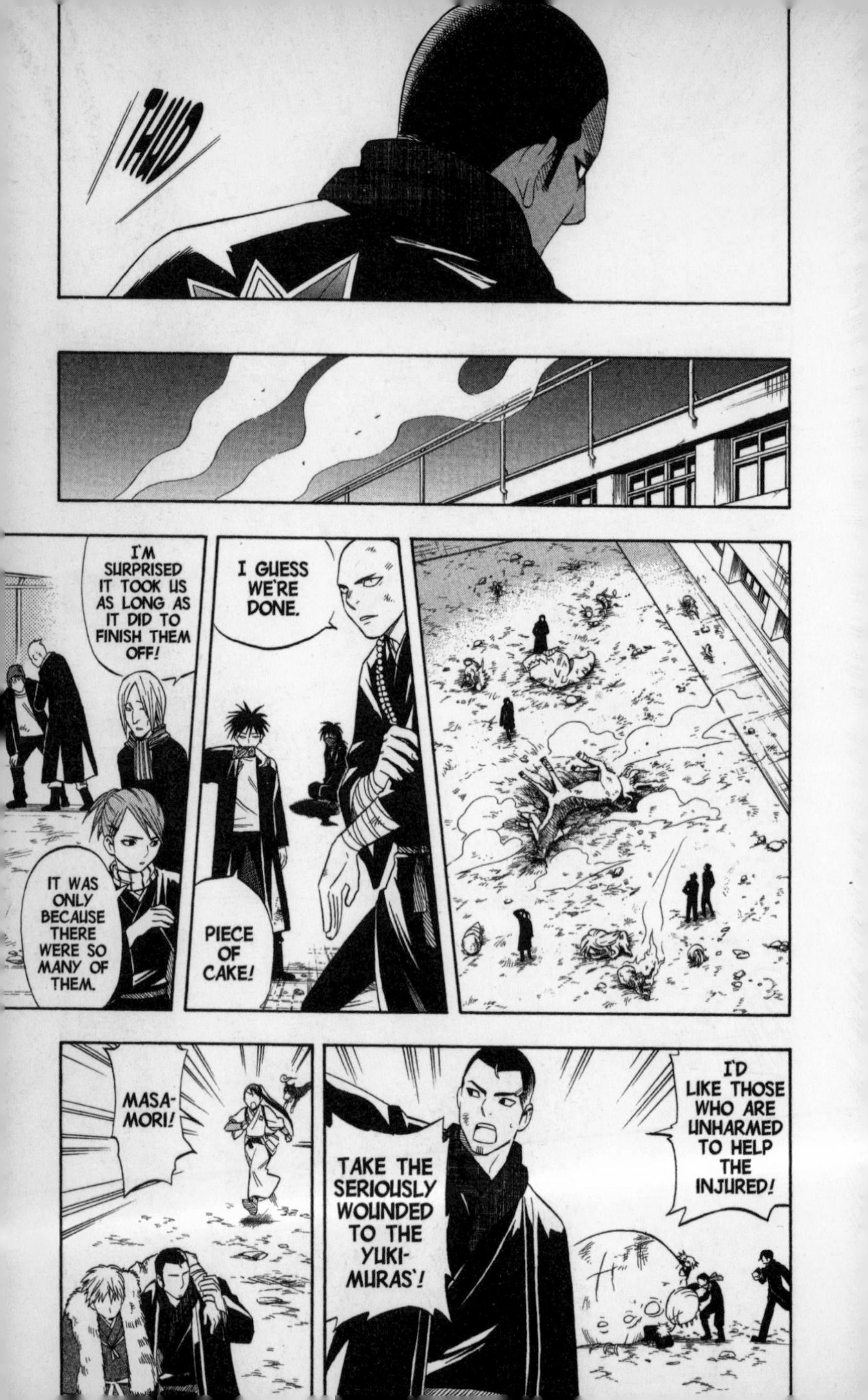
THUD
I GUESS WE'RE DONE.
PIECE OF CAKE!
I'M SURPRISED IT TOOK US AS LONG AS IT DID TO FINISH THEM OFF!
IT WAS ONLY BECAUSE THERE WERE SO MANY OF THEM.
I'D LIKE THOSE WHO ARE UNHARMED TO HELP THE INJURED!
TAKE THE SERIOUSLY WOUNDED TO THE YUKI-MURAS'!
MASA-MORI!

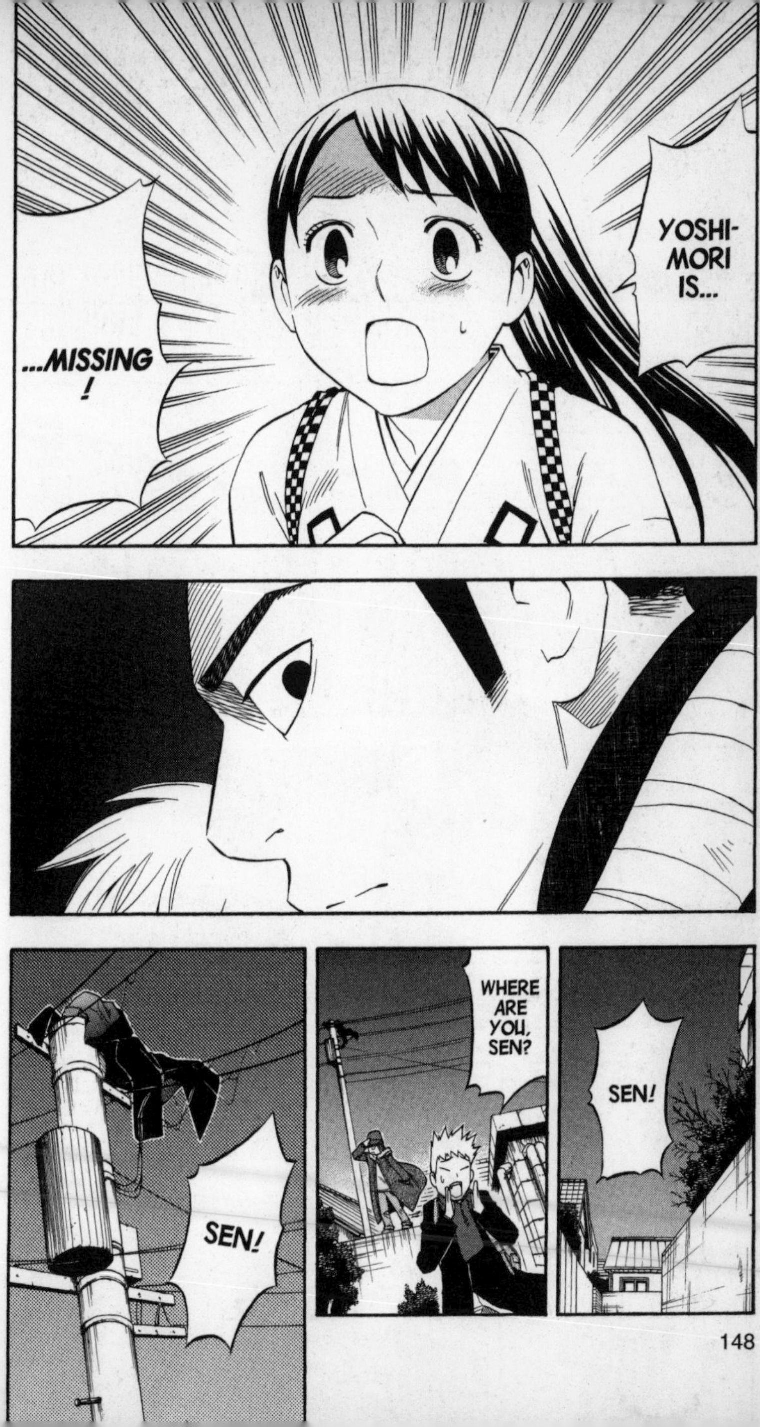
YOSHI-MORI IS...
...MISSING!
SEN!
WHERE ARE YOU, SEN?
SEN!

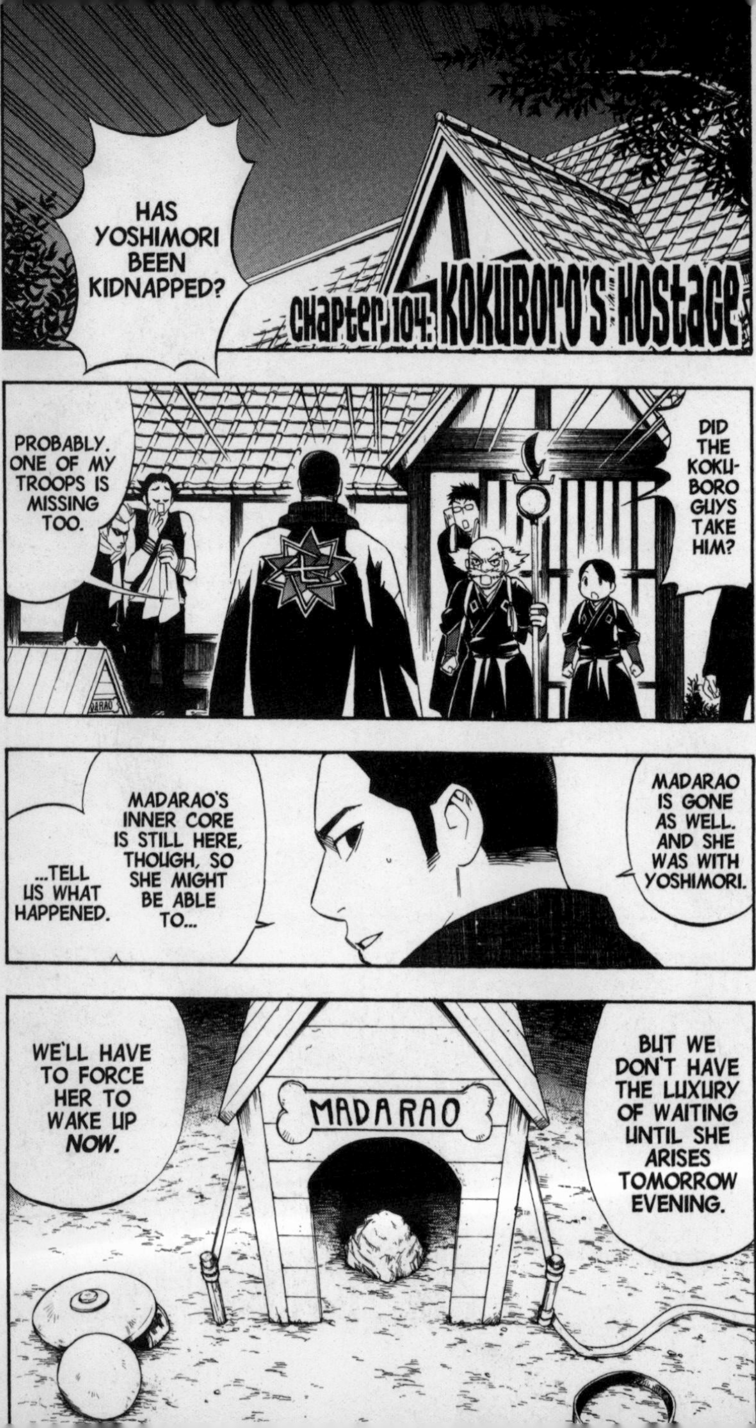
HAS YOSHIMORI BEEN KIDNAPPED?
Chapter 104: Kokuboro's Hostage
DID THE KOKU-BORO GUYS TAKE HIM?
PROBABLY. ONE OF MY TROOPS IS MISSING TOO.
MADARAO
MADARAO IS GONE AS WELL. AND SHE WAS WITH YOSHIMORI.
MADARAO'S INNER CORE IS STILL HERE, THOUGH, SO SHE MIGHT BE ABLE TO...
...TELL US WHAT HAPPENED.
BUT WE DON'T HAVE THE LUXURY OF WAITING UNTIL SHE ARISES TOMORROW EVENING.
MADARAO
WE'LL HAVE TO FORCE HER TO WAKE UP *NOW*.

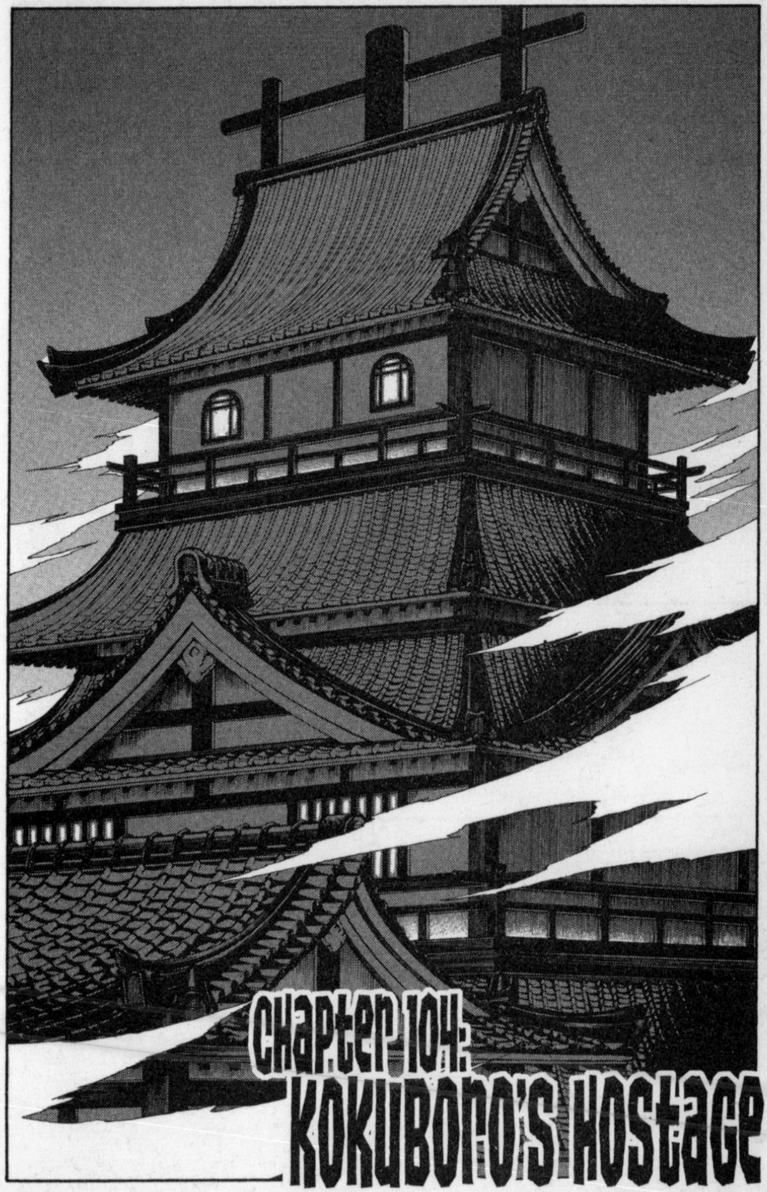
Chapter 104:
Kokuboro's Hostage

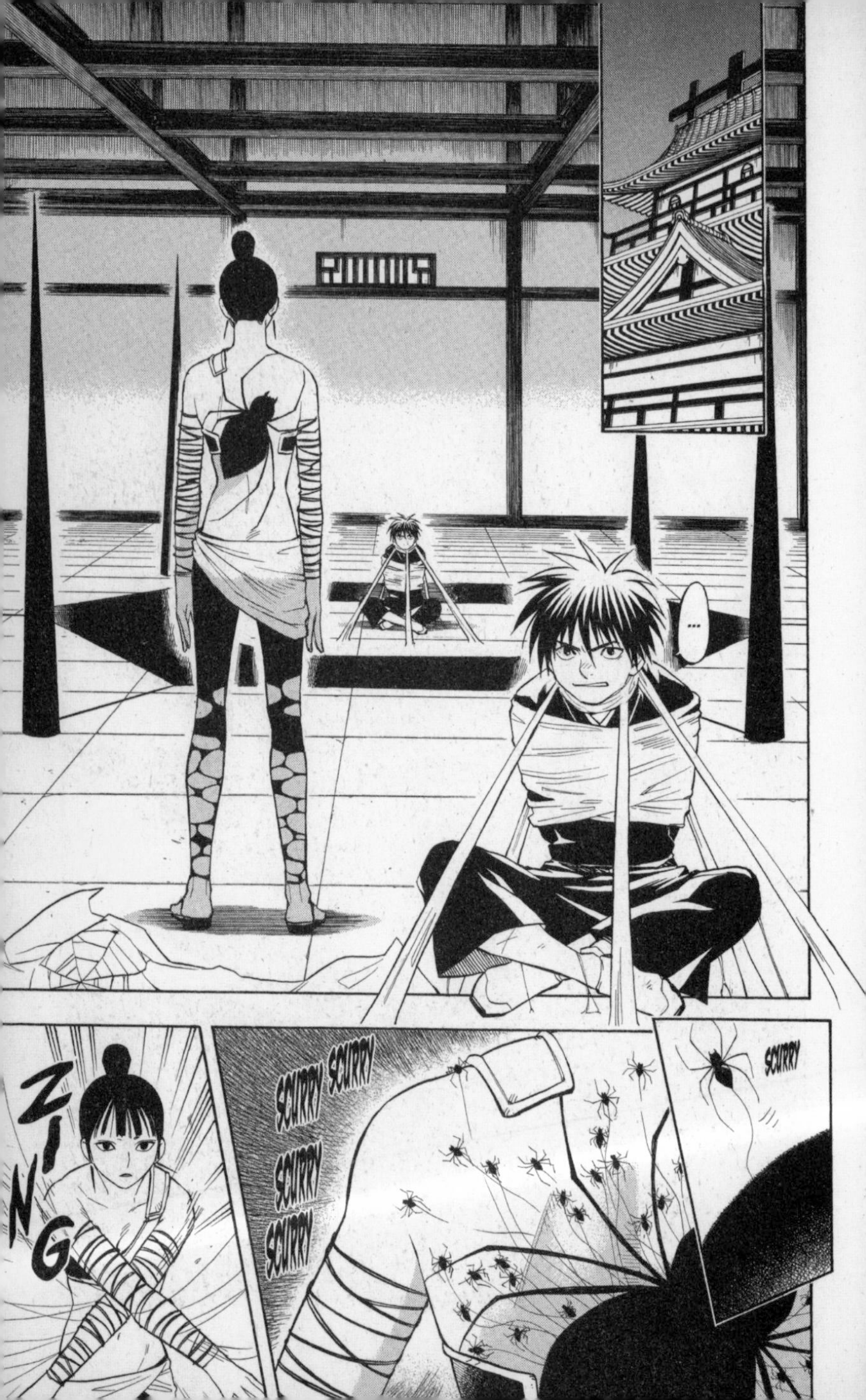
...
SCURRY
SCURRY
SCURRY
SCURRY
SCURRY
SCURRY
ZING

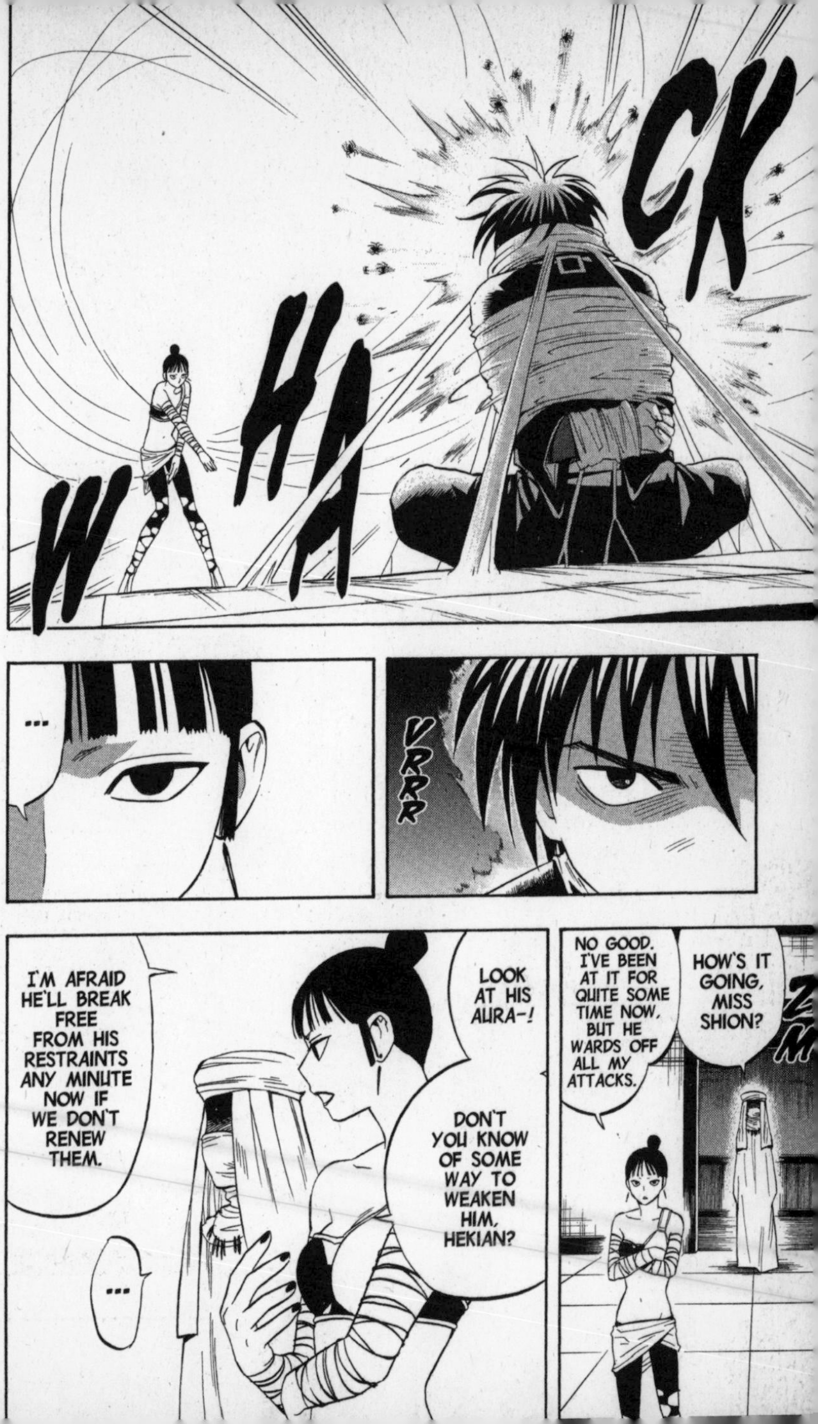
WHACK
VRRR
...
HOW'S IT GOING, MISS SHION?
NO GOOD. I'VE BEEN AT IT FOR QUITE SOME TIME NOW, BUT HE WARDS OFF ALL MY ATTACKS.
LOOK AT HIS AURA-!
DON'T YOU KNOW OF SOME WAY TO WEAKEN HIM, HEKIAN?
I'M AFRAID HE'LL BREAK FREE FROM HIS RESTRAINTS ANY MINUTE NOW IF WE DON'T RENEW THEM.
...

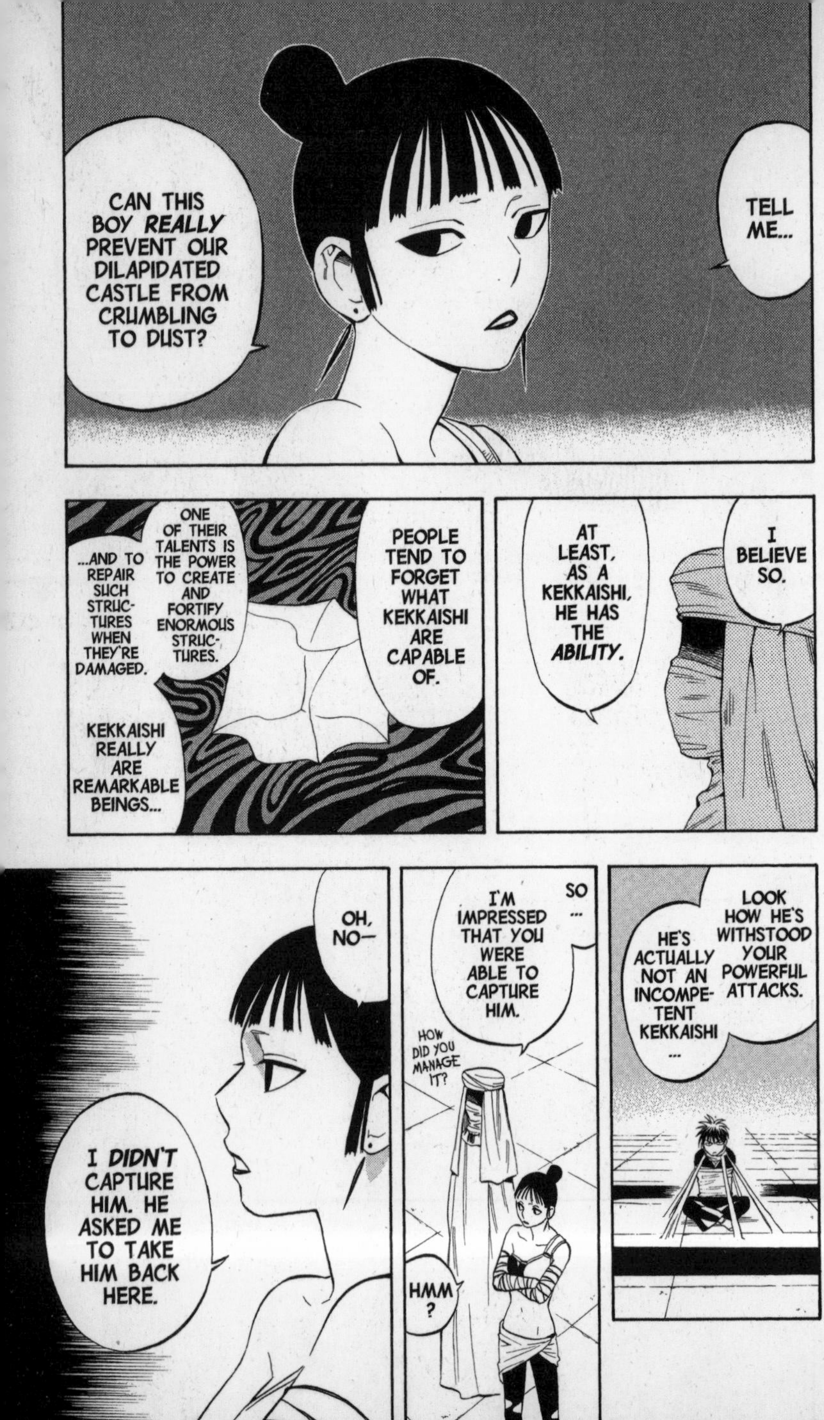
TELL ME...
CAN THIS BOY *REALLY* PREVENT OUR DILAPIDATED CASTLE FROM CRUMBLING TO DUST?
I BELIEVE SO.
AT LEAST, AS A KEKKAISHI, HE HAS THE *ABILITY*.
PEOPLE TEND TO FORGET WHAT KEKKAISHI ARE CAPABLE OF.
ONE OF THEIR TALENTS IS THE POWER TO CREATE AND FORTIFY ENORMOUS STRUCTURES.
...AND TO REPAIR SUCH STRUCTURES WHEN THEY'RE DAMAGED.
KEKKAISHI REALLY ARE REMARKABLE BEINGS...
LOOK HOW HE'S WITHSTOOD YOUR POWERFUL ATTACKS.
HE'S ACTUALLY NOT AN INCOMPETENT KEKKAISHI...
SO...
I'M IMPRESSED THAT YOU WERE ABLE TO CAPTURE HIM.
HOW DID YOU MANAGE IT?
HMM?
OH, NO—
I *DIDN'T* CAPTURE HIM. HE ASKED ME TO TAKE HIM BACK HERE.

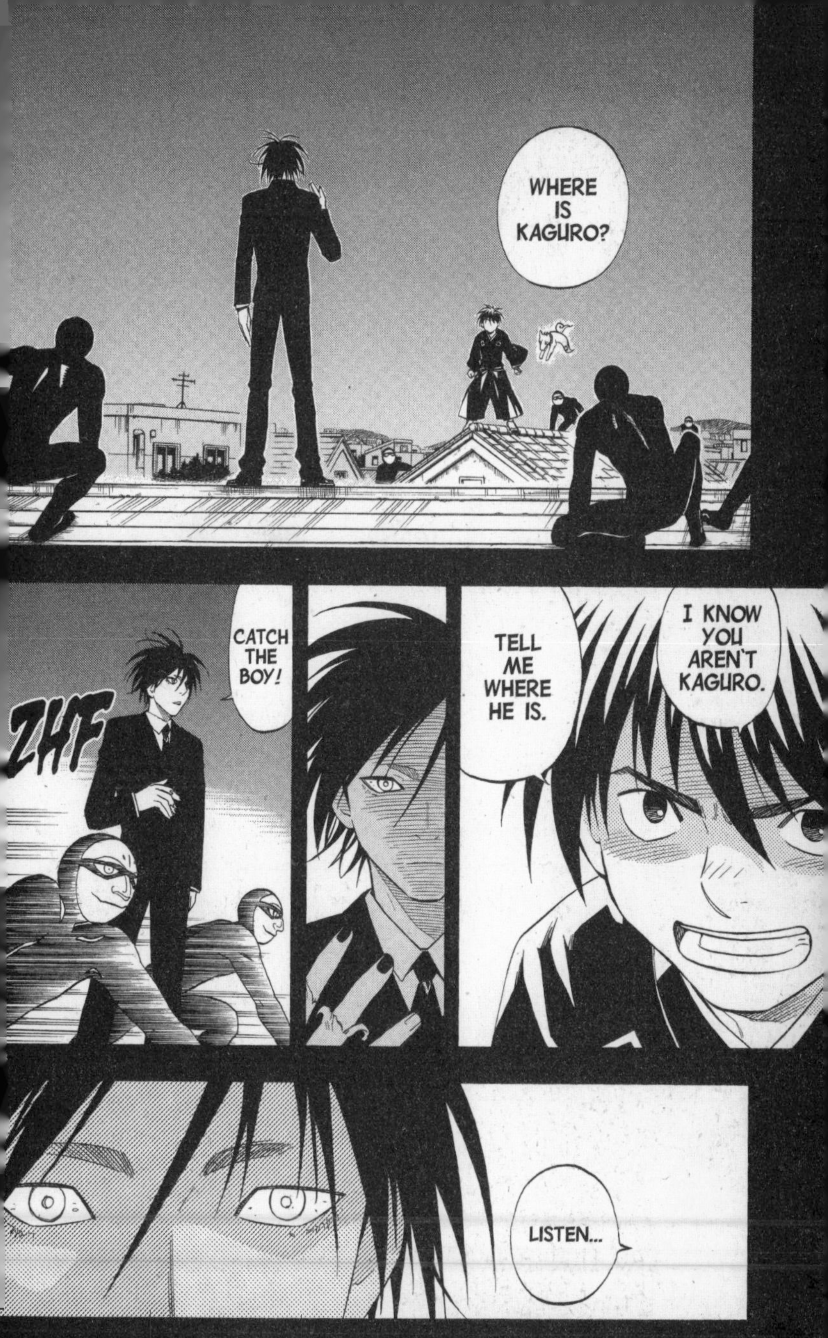
WHERE IS KAGURO?
I KNOW YOU AREN'T KAGURO.
TELL ME WHERE HE IS.
CATCH THE BOY!
ZHF
LISTEN...

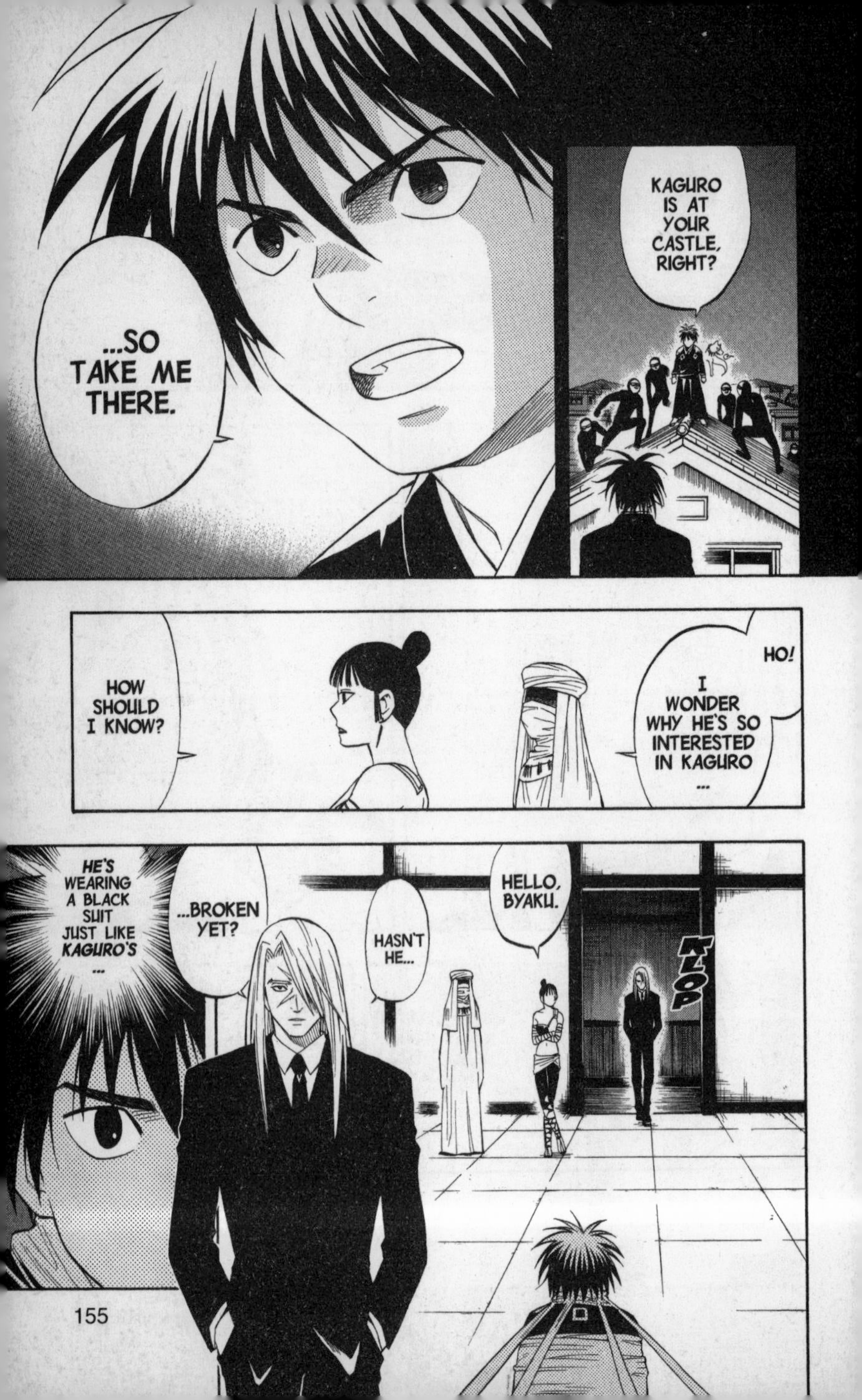
KAGURO IS AT YOUR CASTLE, RIGHT?
...SO TAKE ME THERE.
HO!
I WONDER WHY HE'S SO INTERESTED IN KAGURO ...
HOW SHOULD I KNOW?
KLOP
HELLO, BYAKU.
HASN'T HE...
...BROKEN YET?
HE'S WEARING A BLACK SUIT JUST LIKE KAGURO'S ...

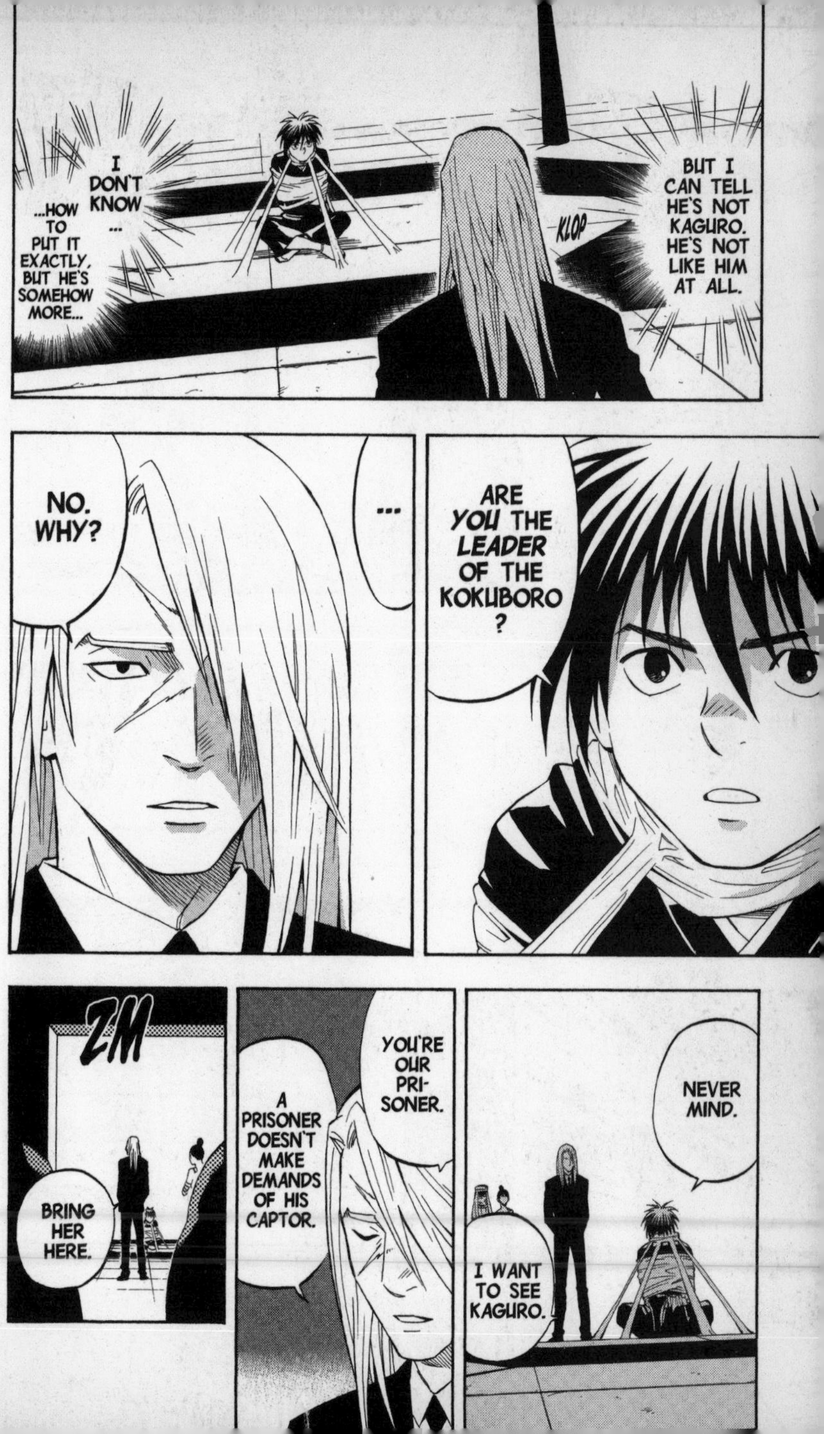
BUT I CAN TELL HE'S NOT KAGURO. HE'S NOT LIKE HIM AT ALL.
KLOP
I DON'T KNOW ...
...HOW TO PUT IT EXACTLY, BUT HE'S SOMEHOW MORE...
ARE YOU THE LEADER OF THE KOKUBORO ?
...
NO. WHY?
NEVER MIND.
I WANT TO SEE KAGURO.
YOU'RE OUR PRI-SONER.
A PRISONER DOESN'T MAKE DEMANDS OF HIS CAPTOR.
ZM
BRING HER HERE.

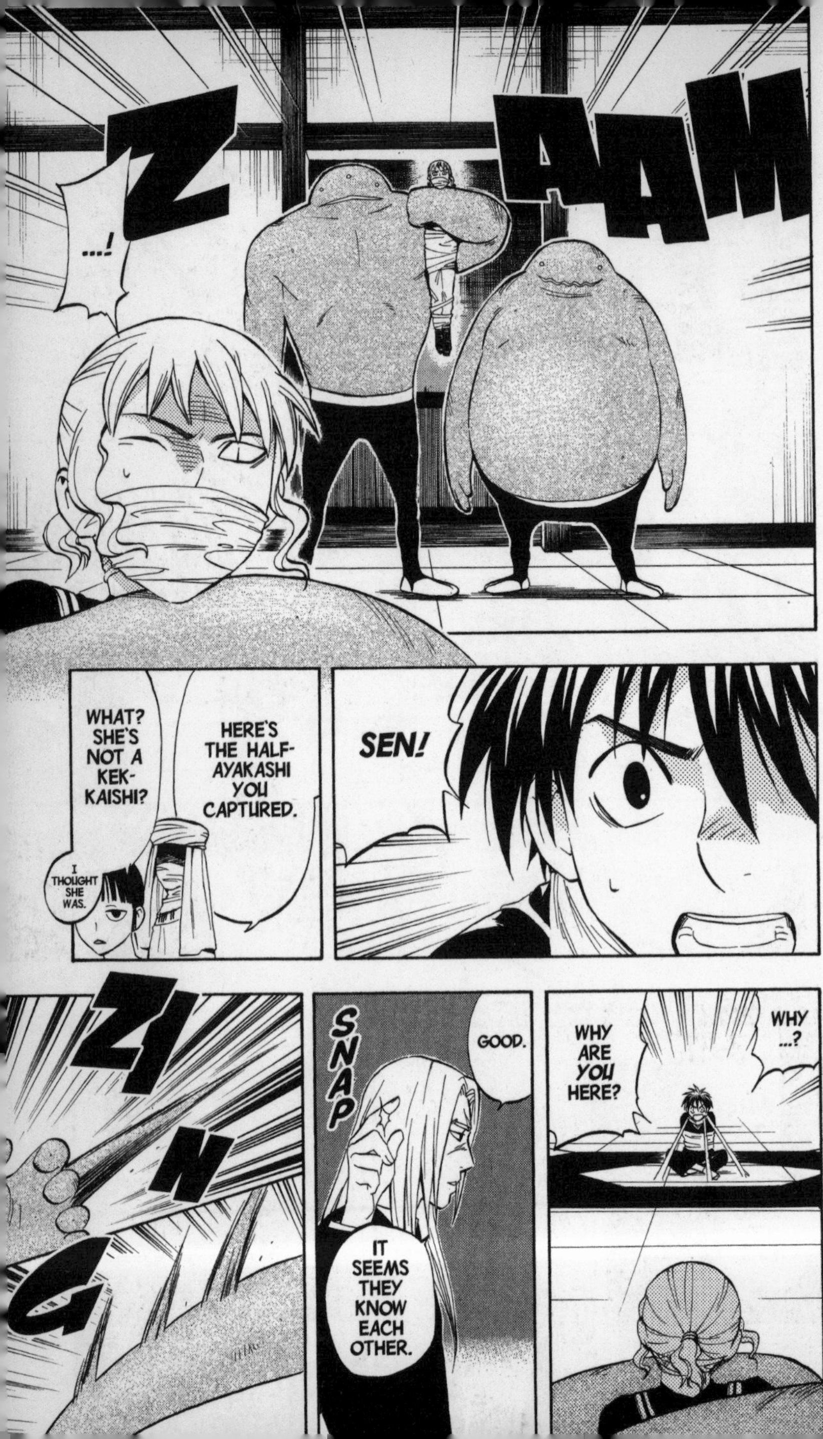
ZAAM
...!
SEN!
HERE'S THE HALF-AYAKASHI YOU CAPTURED.
WHAT? SHE'S NOT A KEK-KAISHI?
I THOUGHT SHE WAS.
WHY ...?
WHY ARE YOU HERE?
GOOD.
SNAP
IT SEEMS THEY KNOW EACH OTHER.
ZING

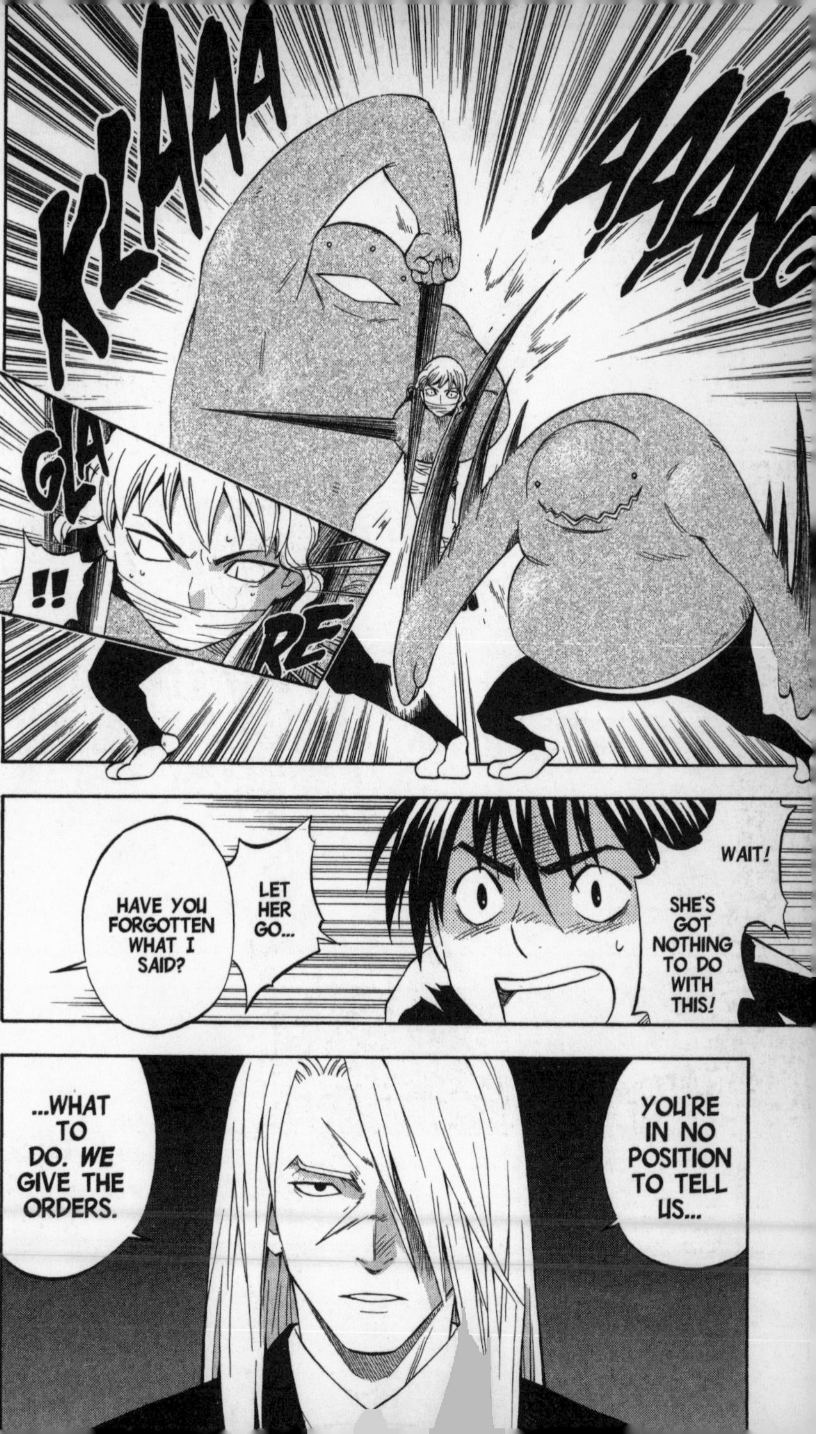
KLAAA
AAANG
GLA
RE
!!
WAIT!
SHE'S GOT NOTHING TO DO WITH THIS!
LET HER GO...
HAVE YOU FORGOTTEN WHAT I SAID?
YOU'RE IN NO POSITION TO TELL US...
...WHAT TO DO. WE GIVE THE ORDERS.

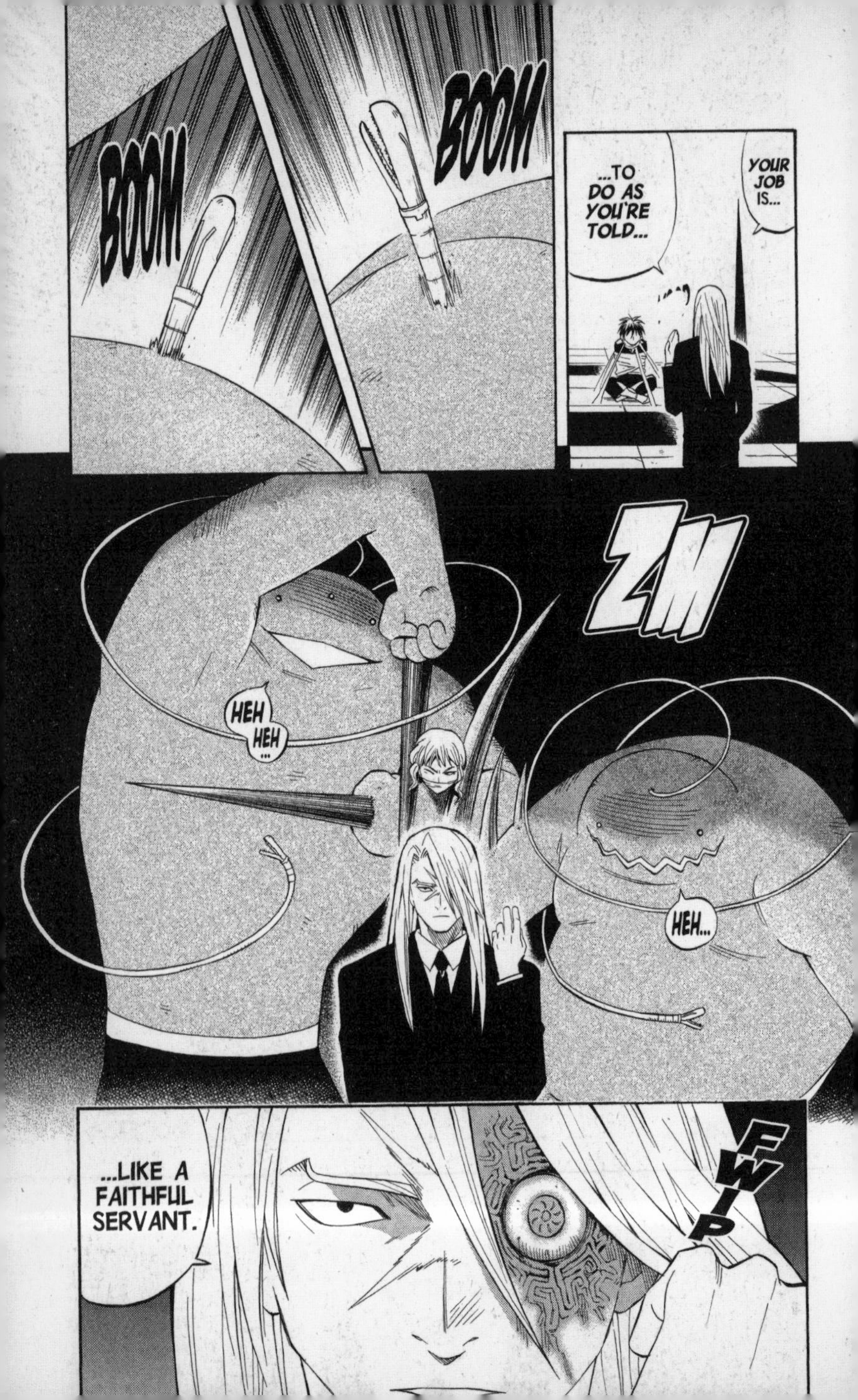

YOUR JOB IS...
...TO DO AS YOU'RE TOLD...
BOOM
BOOM
ZM
HEH HEH...
HEH...
FWIP
...LIKE A FAITHFUL SERVANT.

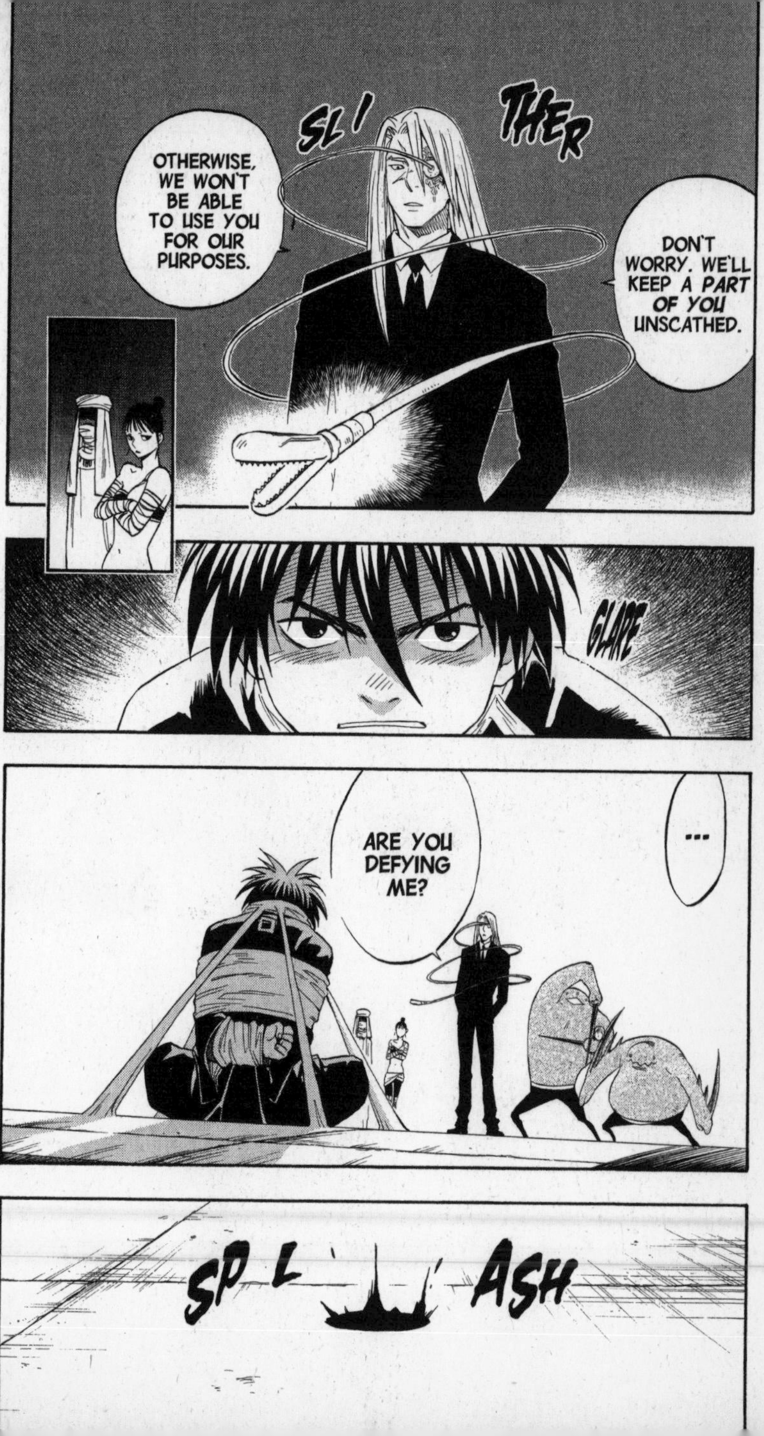
SLITHER
DON'T WORRY. WE'LL KEEP A *PART* OF YOU UNSCATHED.
OTHERWISE, WE WON'T BE ABLE TO USE YOU FOR OUR PURPOSES.
GLARE
...
ARE YOU DEFYING ME?
SPLASH

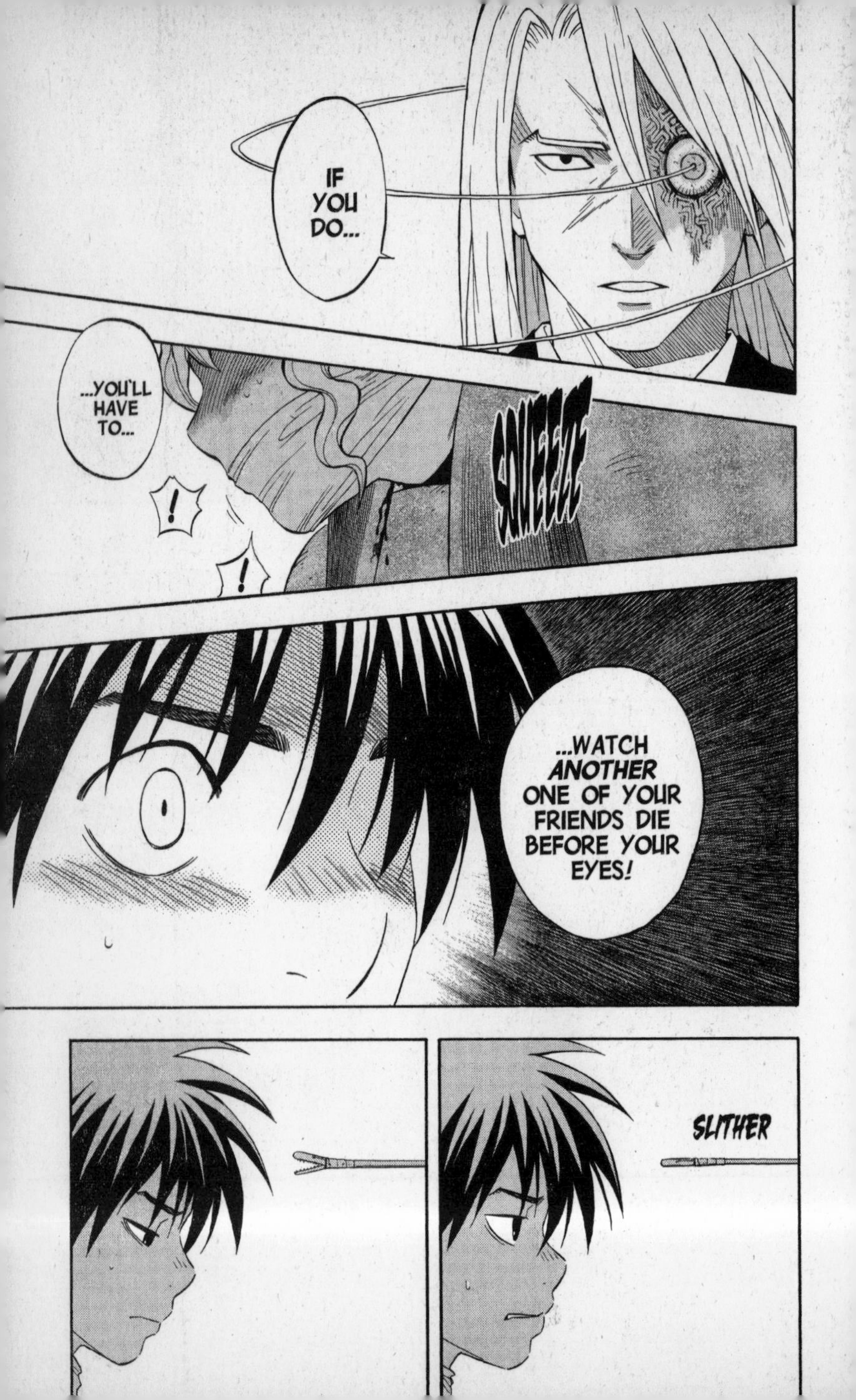
IF YOU DO...
...YOU'LL HAVE TO...
!
!
SQUEEZE
...WATCH *ANOTHER* ONE OF YOUR FRIENDS DIE BEFORE YOUR EYES!
SLITHER

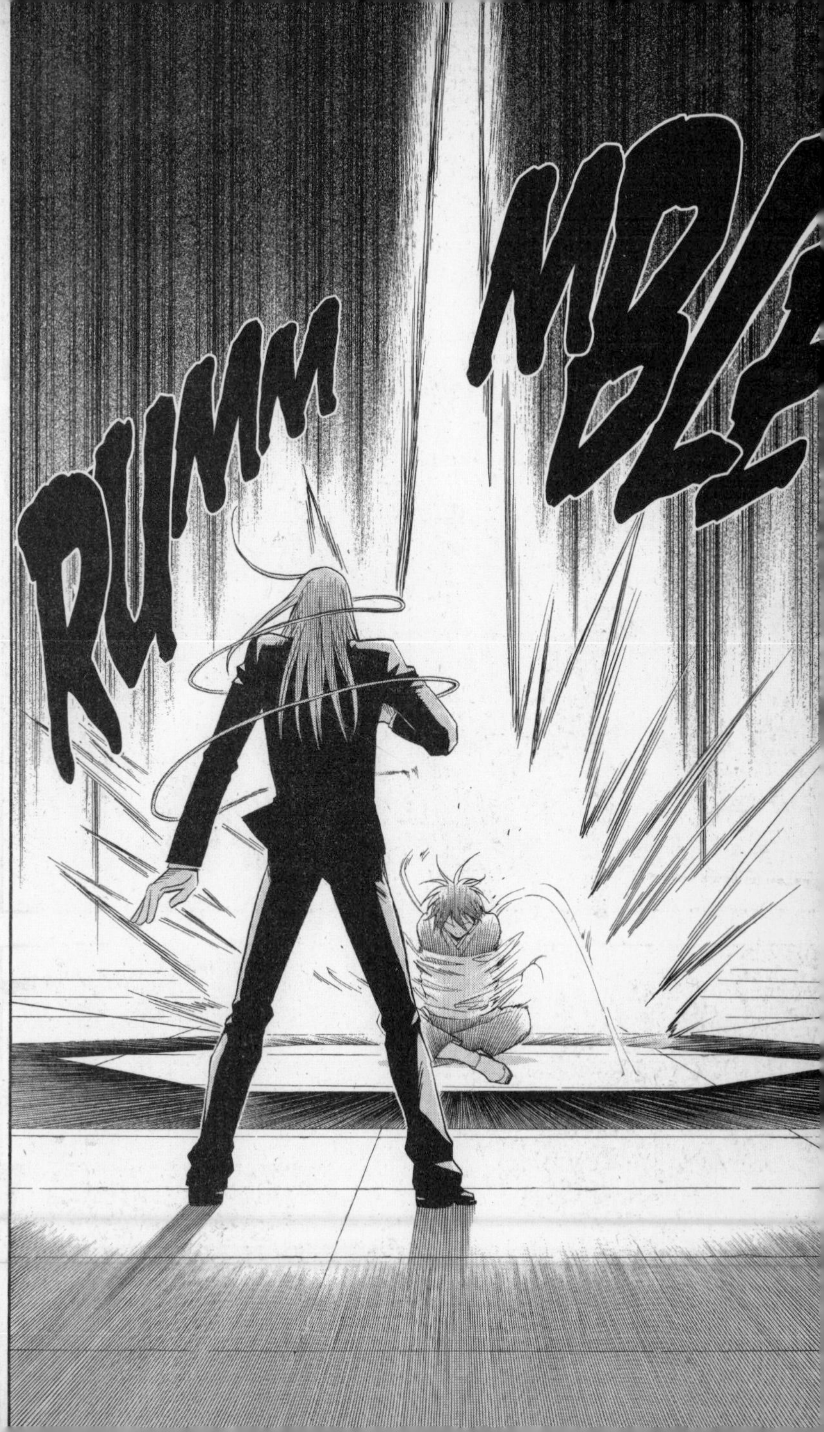
RUMM MBLE

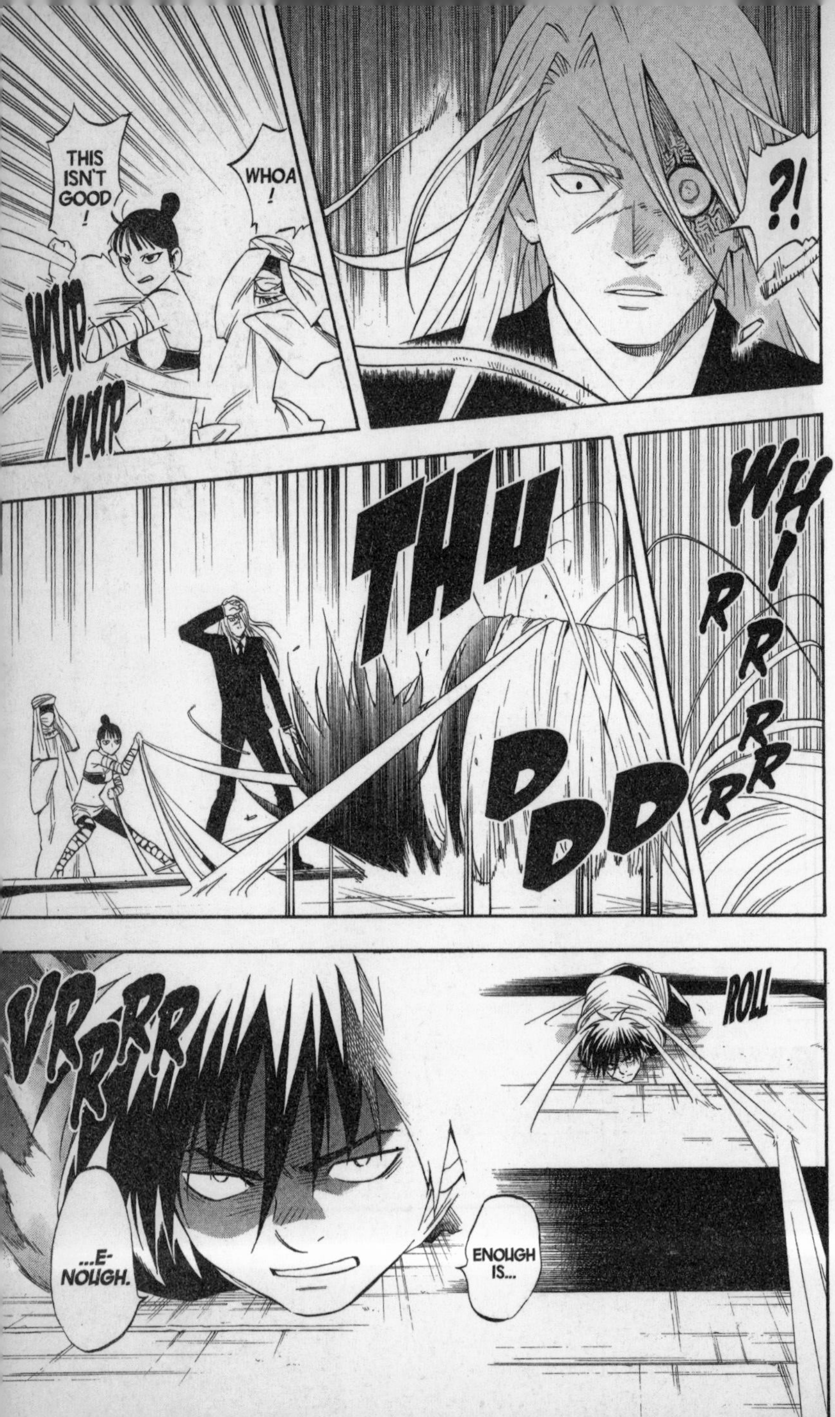
?!
WHOA!
THIS ISN'T GOOD!
WUP
WUP
WHIRRRRR
THUDDD
ROLL
VRRRR
ENOUGH IS...
...E-NOUGH.

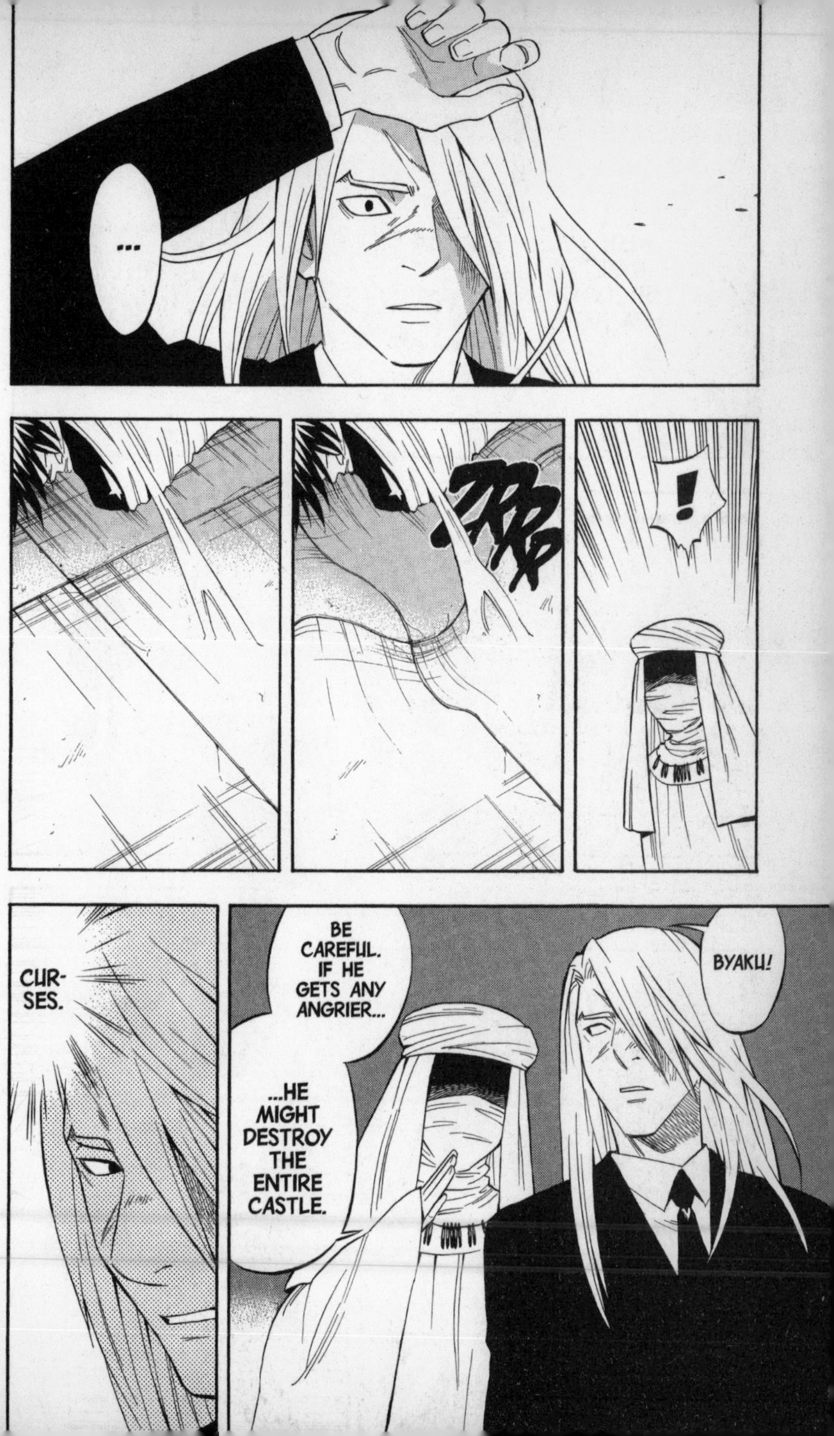
...
!
ZRRP
BYAKU!
BE CAREFUL. IF HE GETS ANY ANGRIER...
...HE MIGHT DESTROY THE ENTIRE CASTLE.
CUR-
SES.

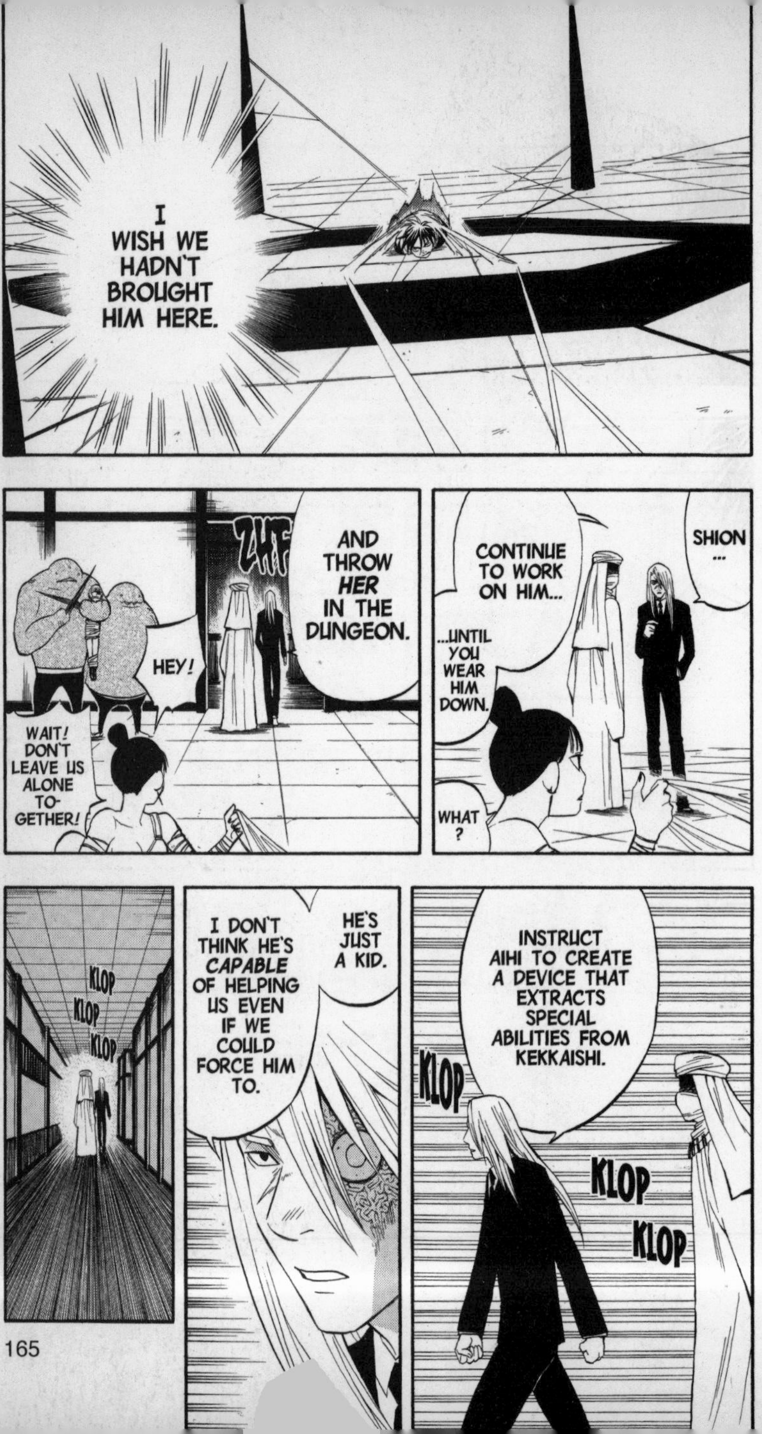
I WISH WE HADN'T BROUGHT HIM HERE.
SHION ...
CONTINUE TO WORK ON HIM...
...UNTIL YOU WEAR HIM DOWN.
WHAT?
AND THROW *HER* IN THE DUNGEON.
ZHF
HEY!
WAIT! DON'T LEAVE US ALONE TO-GETHER!
INSTRUCT AIHI TO CREATE A DEVICE THAT EXTRACTS SPECIAL ABILITIES FROM KEKKAISHI.
KLOP
KLOP
KLOP
HE'S JUST A KID.
I DON'T THINK HE'S *CAPABLE* OF HELPING US EVEN IF WE COULD FORCE HIM TO.
KLOP
KLOP
KLOP

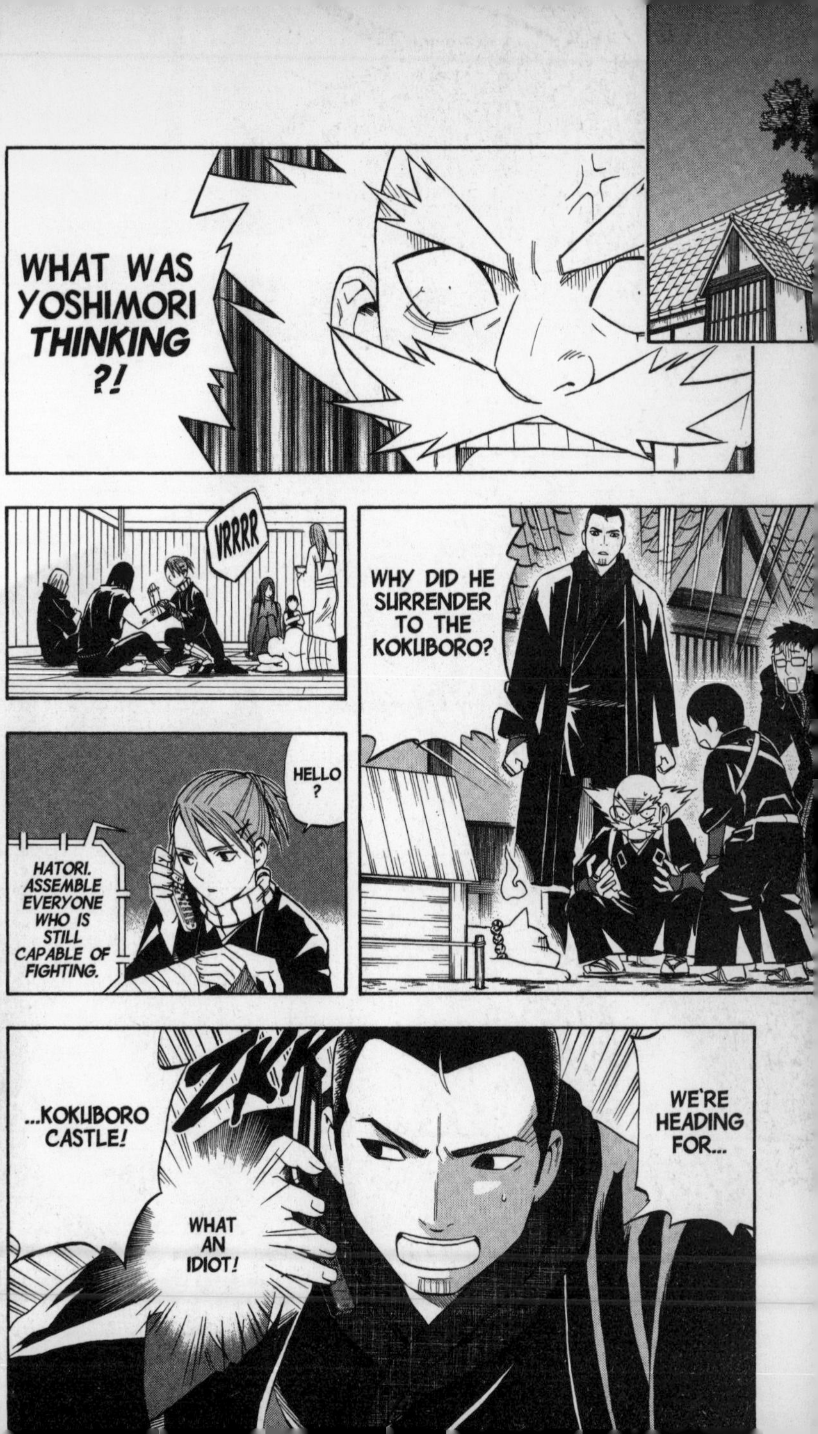
WHAT WAS YOSHIMORI THINKING?!
WHY DID HE SURRENDER TO THE KOKUBORO?
VRRRR
HELLO?
HATORI. ASSEMBLE EVERYONE WHO IS STILL CAPABLE OF FIGHTING.
WE'RE HEADING FOR...
ZKK
...KOKUBORO CASTLE!
WHAT AN IDIOT!

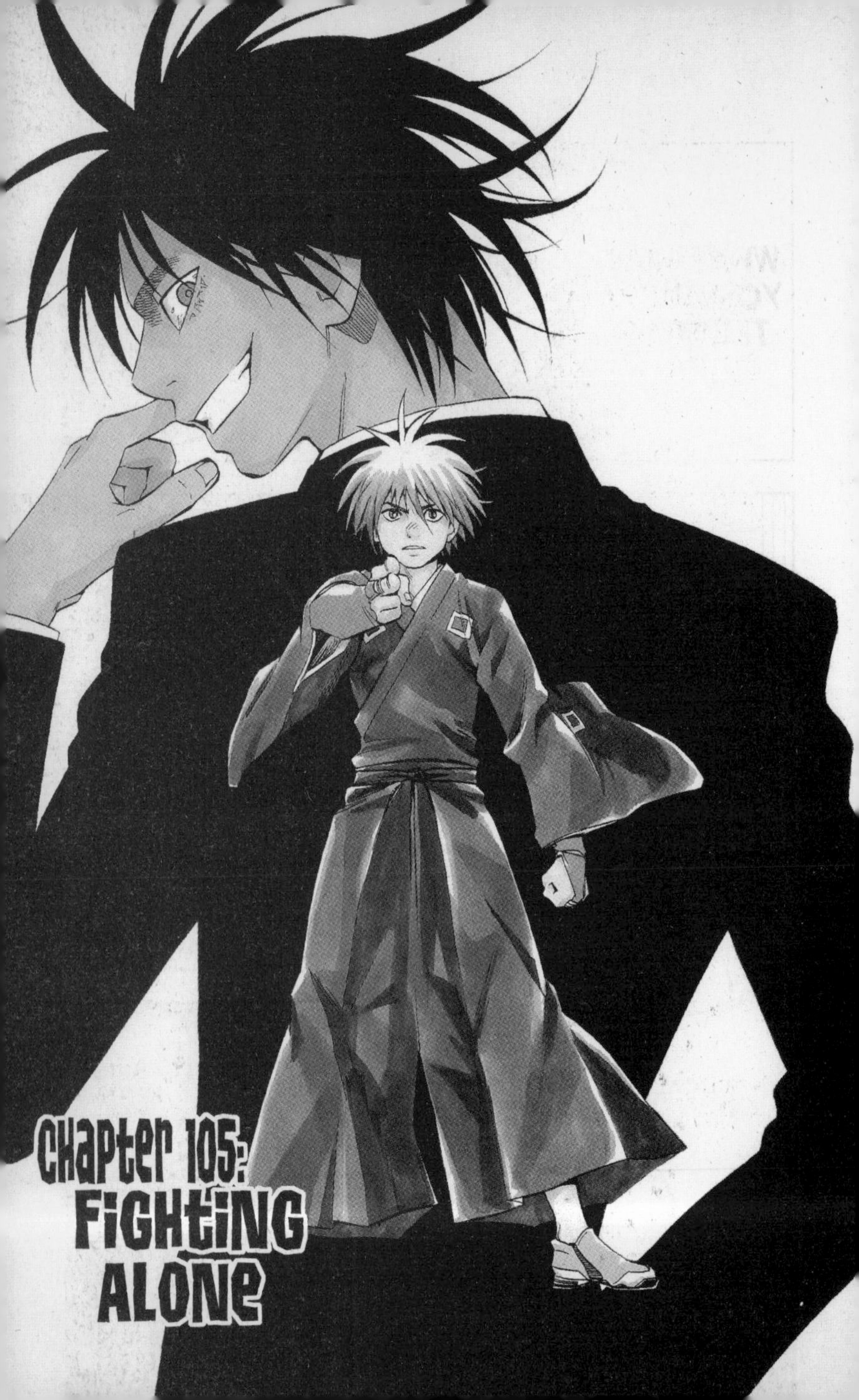
Chapter 105:
Fighting
Alone

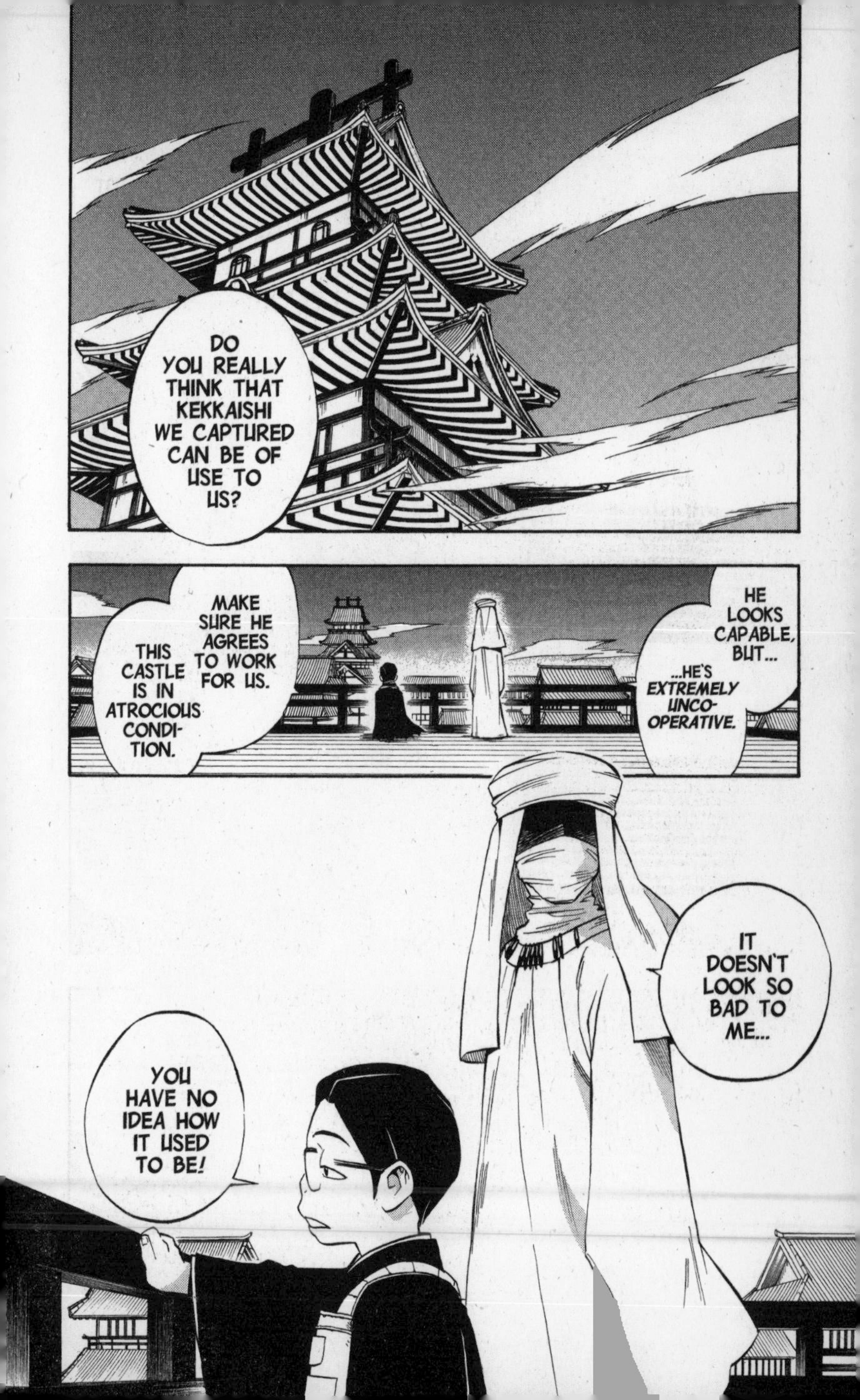
DO YOU REALLY THINK THAT KEKKAISHI WE CAPTURED CAN BE OF USE TO US?
HE LOOKS CAPABLE, BUT...
...HE'S *EXTREMELY UNCO-OPERATIVE.*
MAKE SURE HE AGREES TO WORK FOR US.
THIS CASTLE IS IN ATROCIOUS CONDI-TION.
IT DOESN'T LOOK SO BAD TO ME...
YOU HAVE NO IDEA HOW IT USED TO BE!

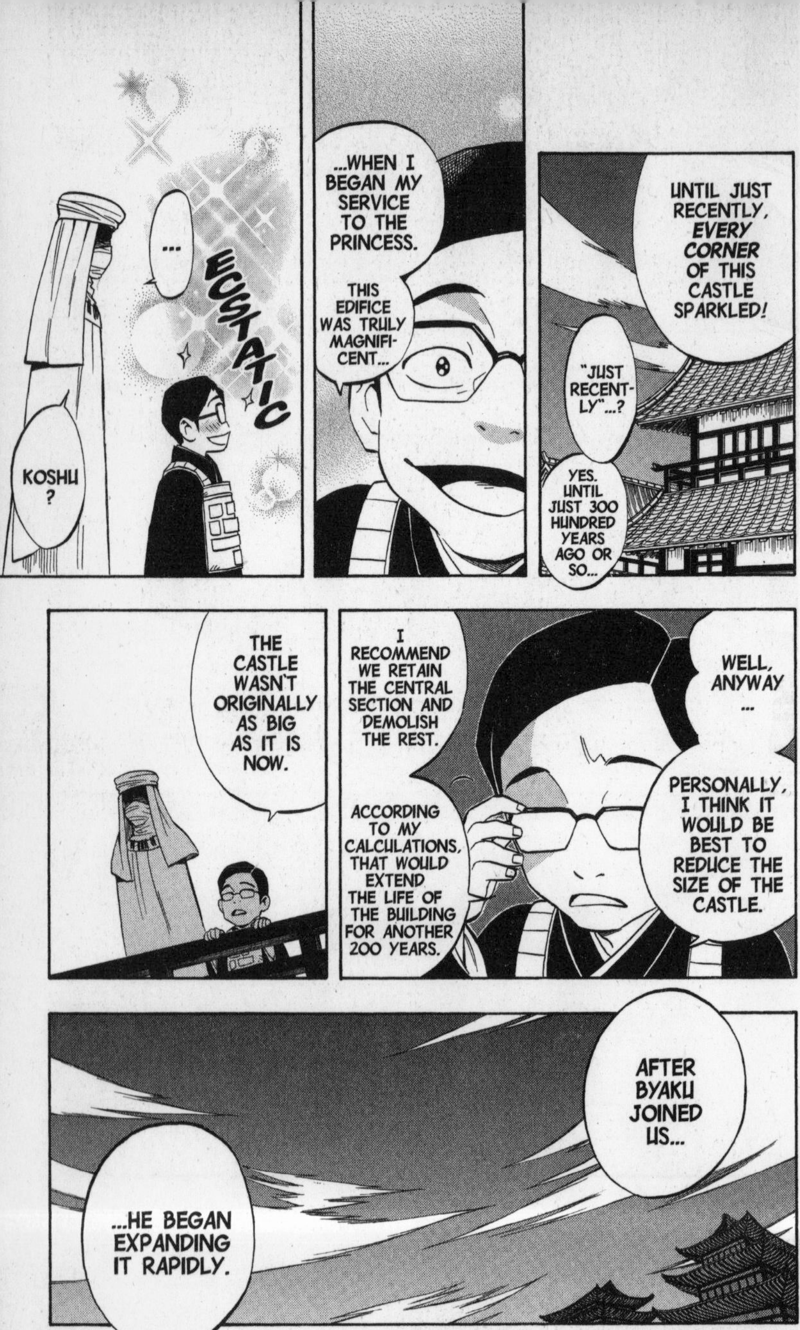
UNTIL JUST RECENTLY, EVERY CORNER OF THIS CASTLE SPARKLED!
"JUST RECENTLY"...?
YES. UNTIL JUST 300 HUNDRED YEARS AGO OR SO...
...WHEN I BEGAN MY SERVICE TO THE PRINCESS.
THIS EDIFICE WAS TRULY MAGNIFI-CENT...
...
ECSTATIC
KOSHU?
WELL, ANYWAY...
PERSONALLY, I THINK IT WOULD BE BEST TO REDUCE THE SIZE OF THE CASTLE.
I RECOMMEND WE RETAIN THE CENTRAL SECTION AND DEMOLISH THE REST.
ACCORDING TO MY CALCULATIONS, THAT WOULD EXTEND THE LIFE OF THE BUILDING FOR ANOTHER 200 YEARS.
THE CASTLE WASN'T ORIGINALLY AS BIG AS IT IS NOW.
AFTER BYAKU JOINED US...
...HE BEGAN EXPANDING IT RAPIDLY.

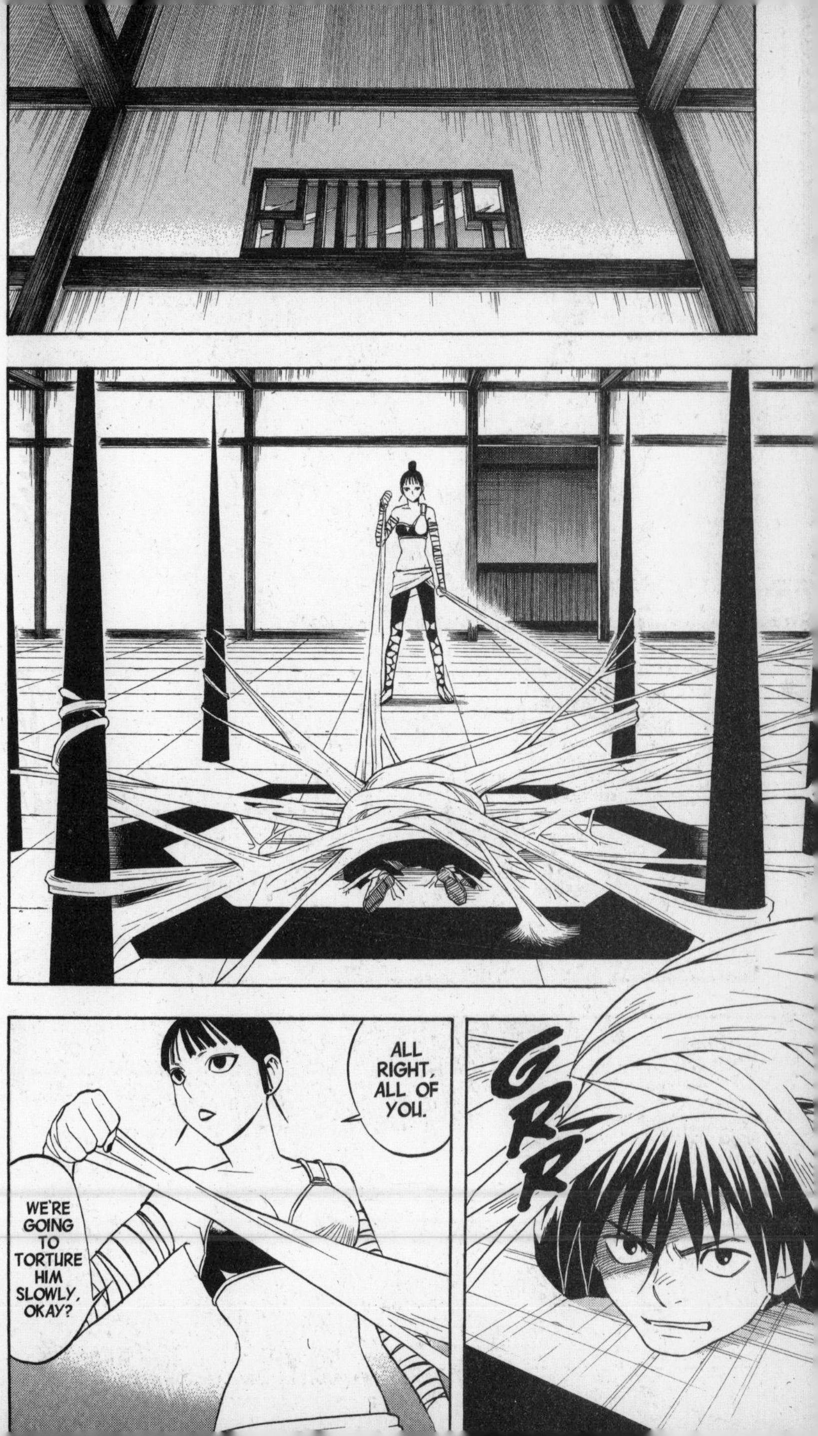
GRR
ALL RIGHT, ALL OF YOU.
WE'RE GOING TO TORTURE HIM SLOWLY, OKAY?

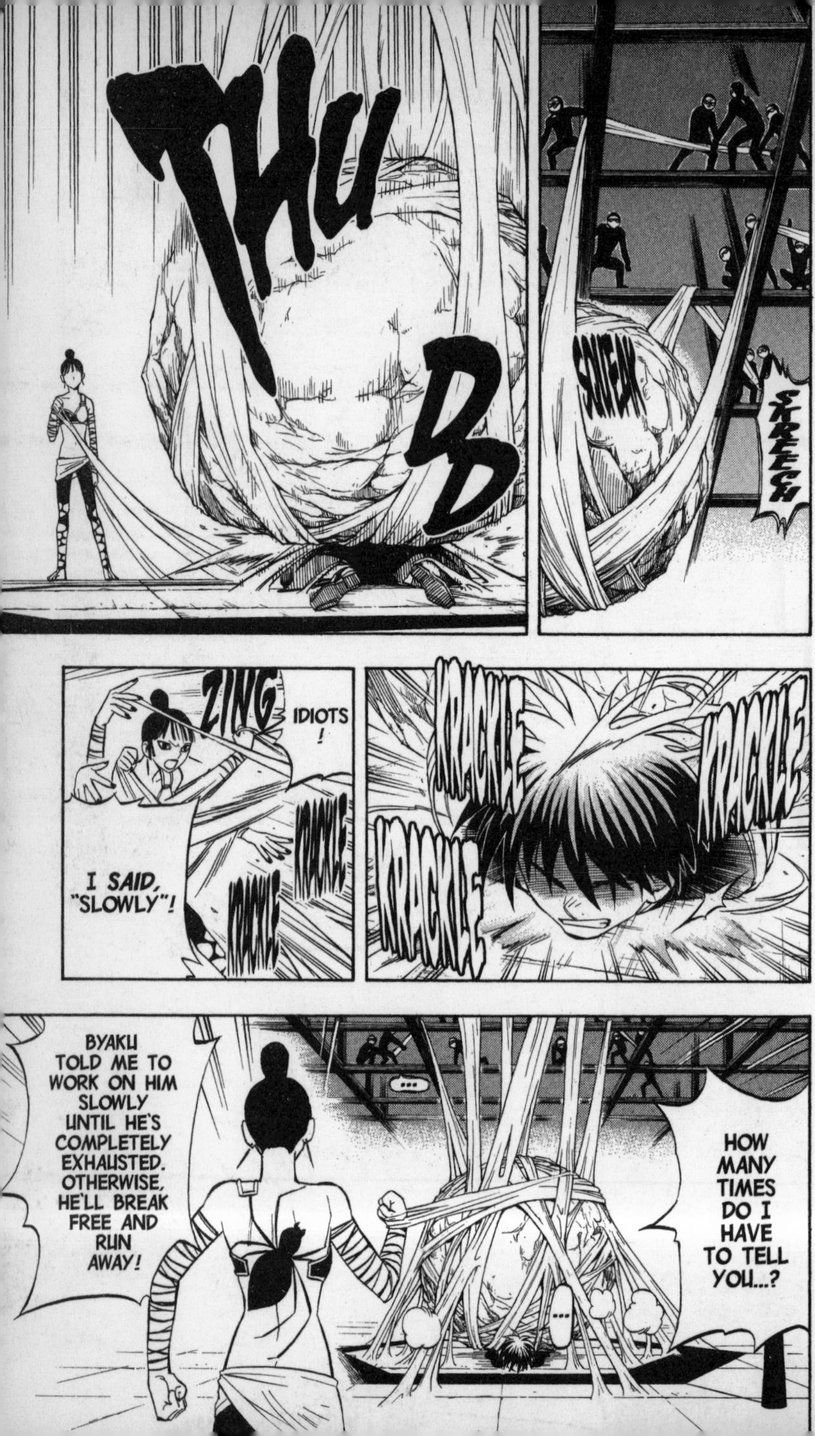
SQUEAK
SKREECH
THUB
KRACKLE
KRACKLE
KRACKLE
ZING
IDIOTS!
KRACKLE
KRACKLE
I SAID, "SLOWLY"!
HOW MANY TIMES DO I HAVE TO TELL YOU...?
...
...
BYAKU TOLD ME TO WORK ON HIM SLOWLY UNTIL HE'S COMPLETELY EXHAUSTED. OTHERWISE, HE'LL BREAK FREE AND RUN AWAY!

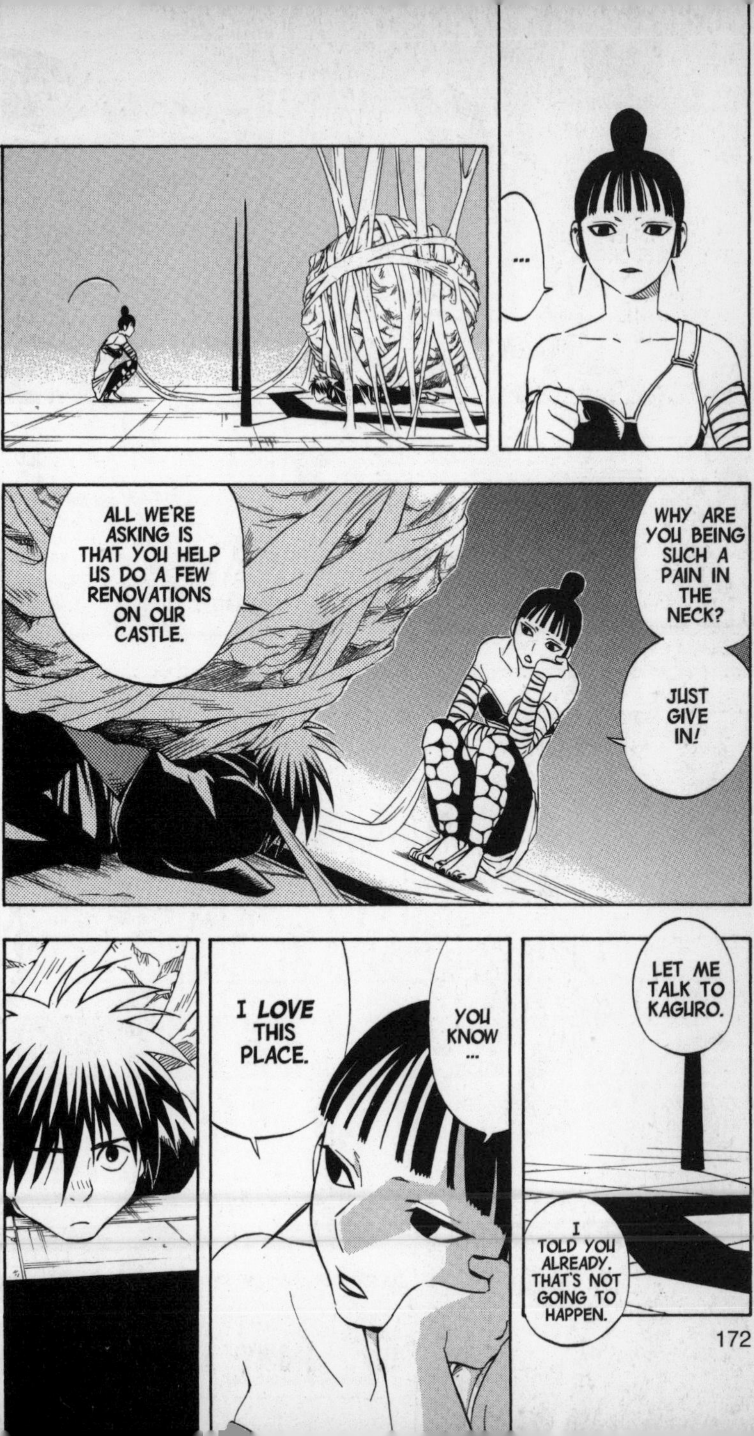
...
WHY ARE YOU BEING SUCH A PAIN IN THE NECK?
JUST GIVE IN!
ALL WE'RE ASKING IS THAT YOU HELP US DO A FEW RENOVATIONS ON OUR CASTLE.
LET ME TALK TO KAGURO.
I TOLD YOU ALREADY. THAT'S NOT GOING TO HAPPEN.
YOU KNOW ...
I *LOVE* THIS PLACE.

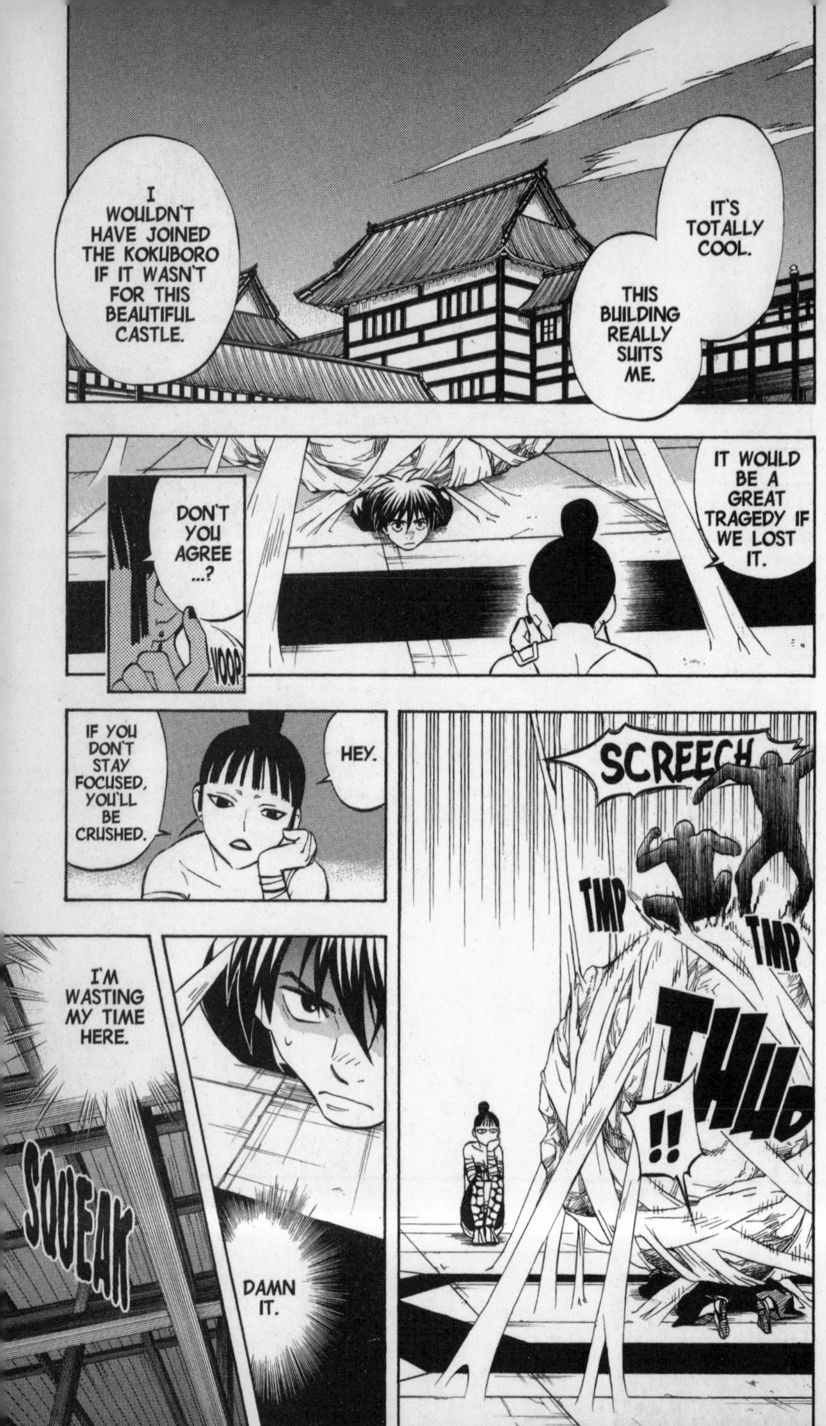
IT'S TOTALLY COOL.
THIS BUILDING REALLY SUITS ME.
I WOULDN'T HAVE JOINED THE KOKUBORO IF IT WASN'T FOR THIS BEAUTIFUL CASTLE.
IT WOULD BE A GREAT TRAGEDY IF WE LOST IT.
DON'T YOU AGREE ...?
VOOP
SCREECH
TMP
TMP
THUD
!!
HEY.
IF YOU DON'T STAY FOCUSED, YOU'LL BE CRUSHED.
I'M WASTING MY TIME HERE.
SQUEAK
DAMN IT.

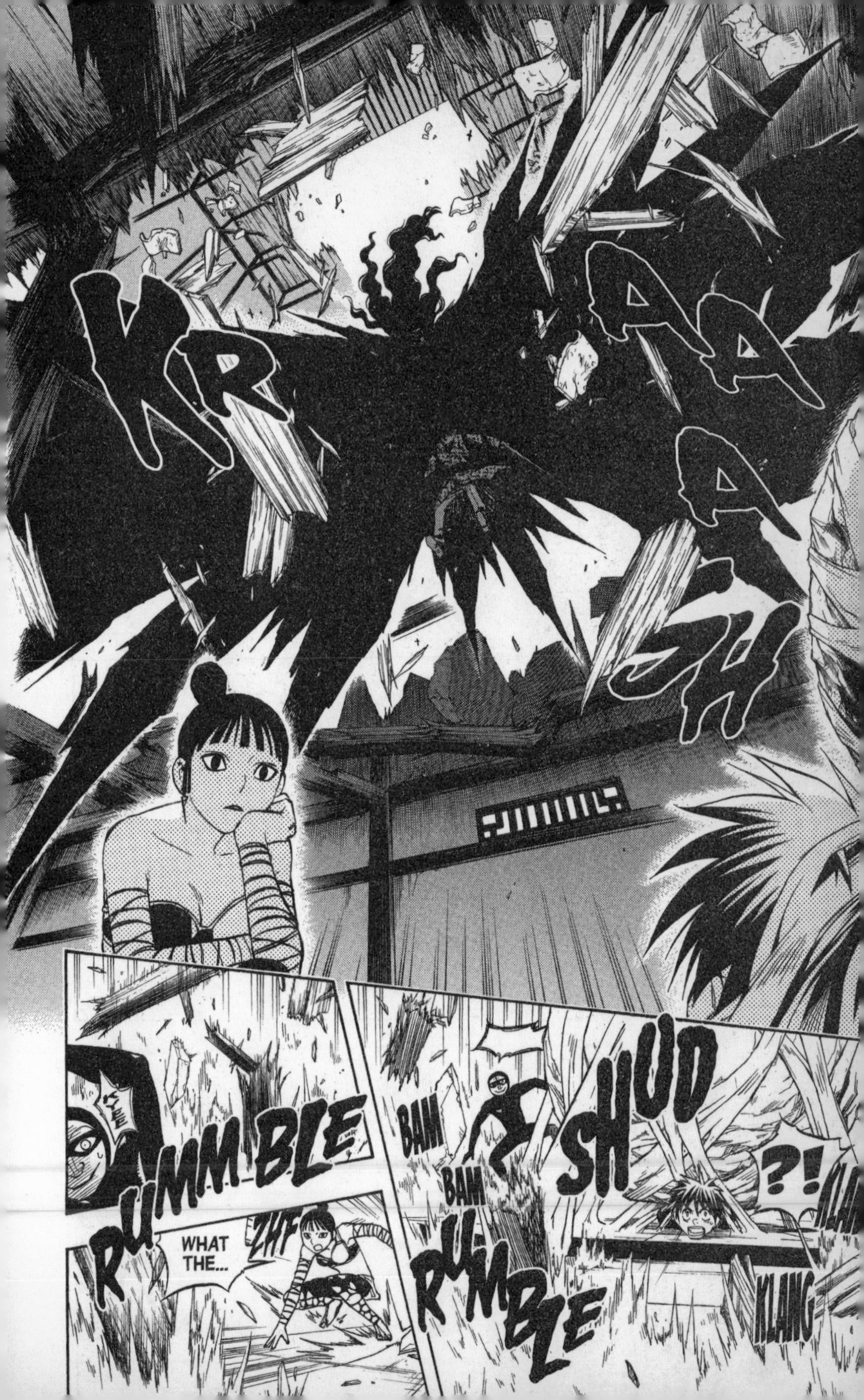
KRAAASH
SHUD
?!
KLANG
BAM
BAM
RUMBLE
KYEE
RUMMBLE
WHAT THE...
ZHF

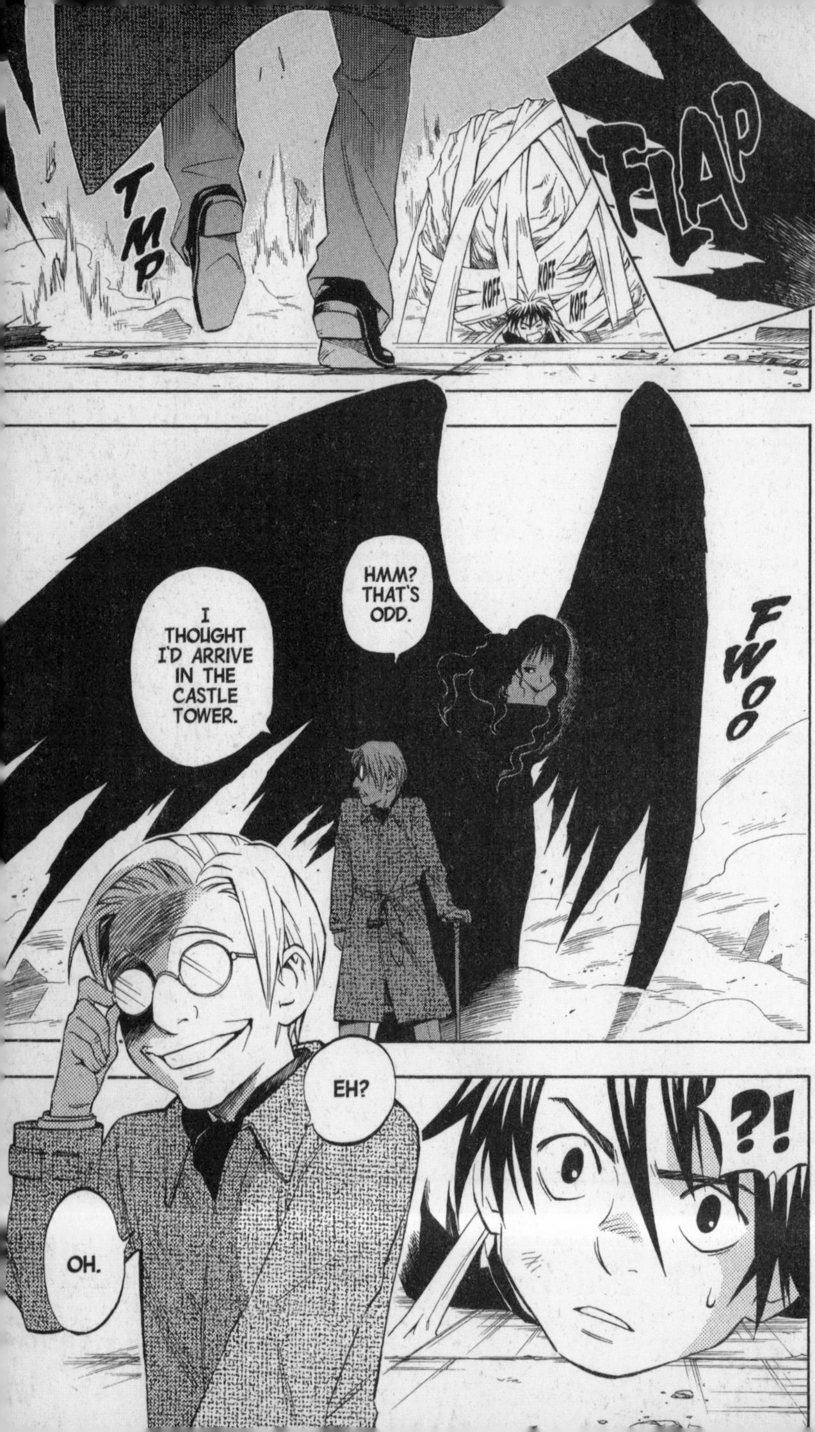
FLAP
KOFF
KOFF
KOFF
TMP
FWOO
HMM? THAT'S ODD.
I THOUGHT I'D ARRIVE IN THE CASTLE TOWER.
?!
EH?
OH.

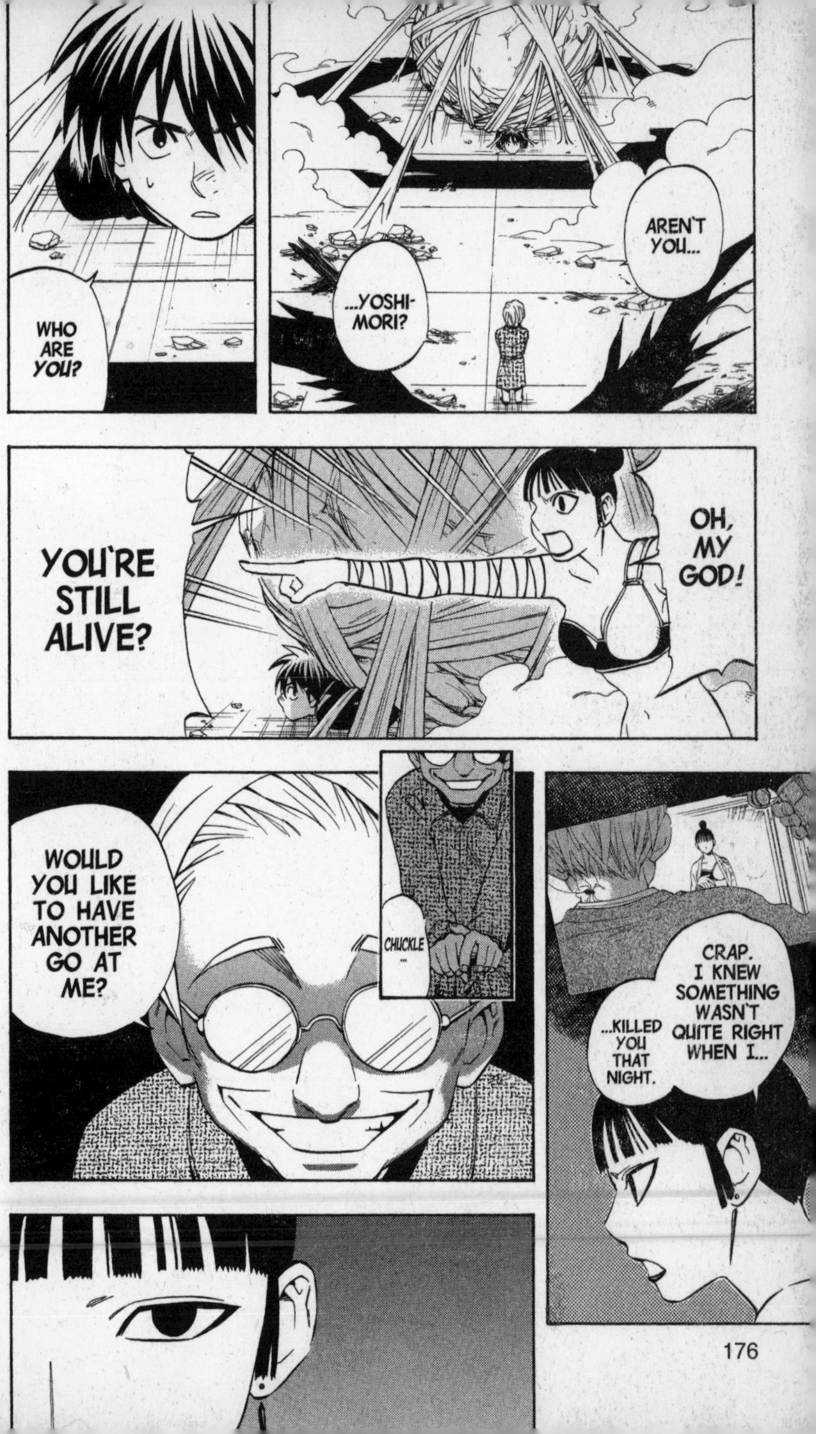
AREN'T YOU...
...YOSHI-MORI?
WHO ARE YOU?
OH, MY GOD!
YOU'RE STILL ALIVE?
CRAP. I KNEW SOMETHING WASN'T QUITE RIGHT WHEN I...
...KILLED YOU THAT NIGHT.
CHUCKLE...
WOULD YOU LIKE TO HAVE ANOTHER GO AT ME?

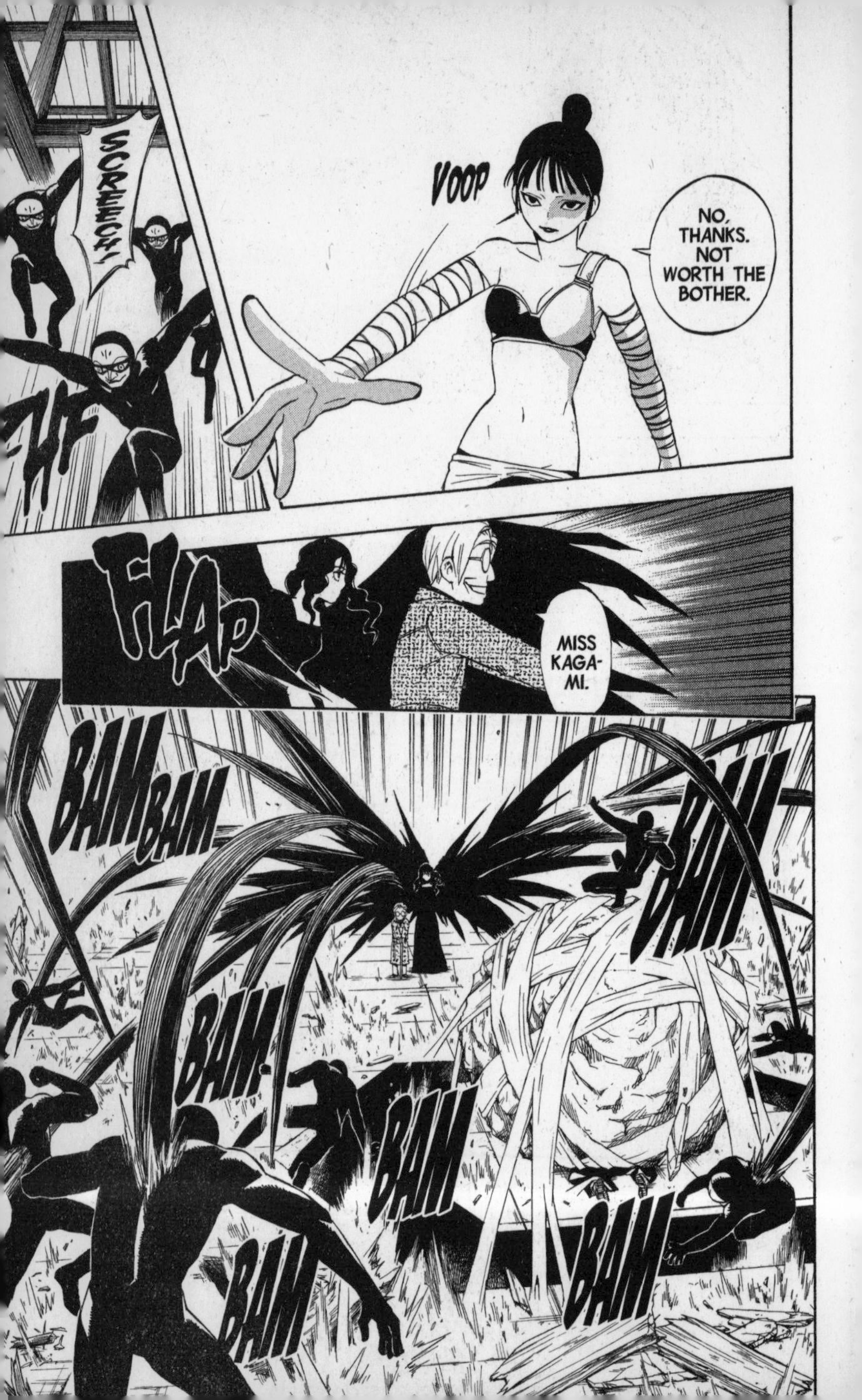
NO, THANKS. NOT WORTH THE BOTHER.
VOOP
SCREEECH!
MISS KAGAMI.
FLAP
BAM
BAM
BAM BAM
BAM
BAM
BAM
BAM

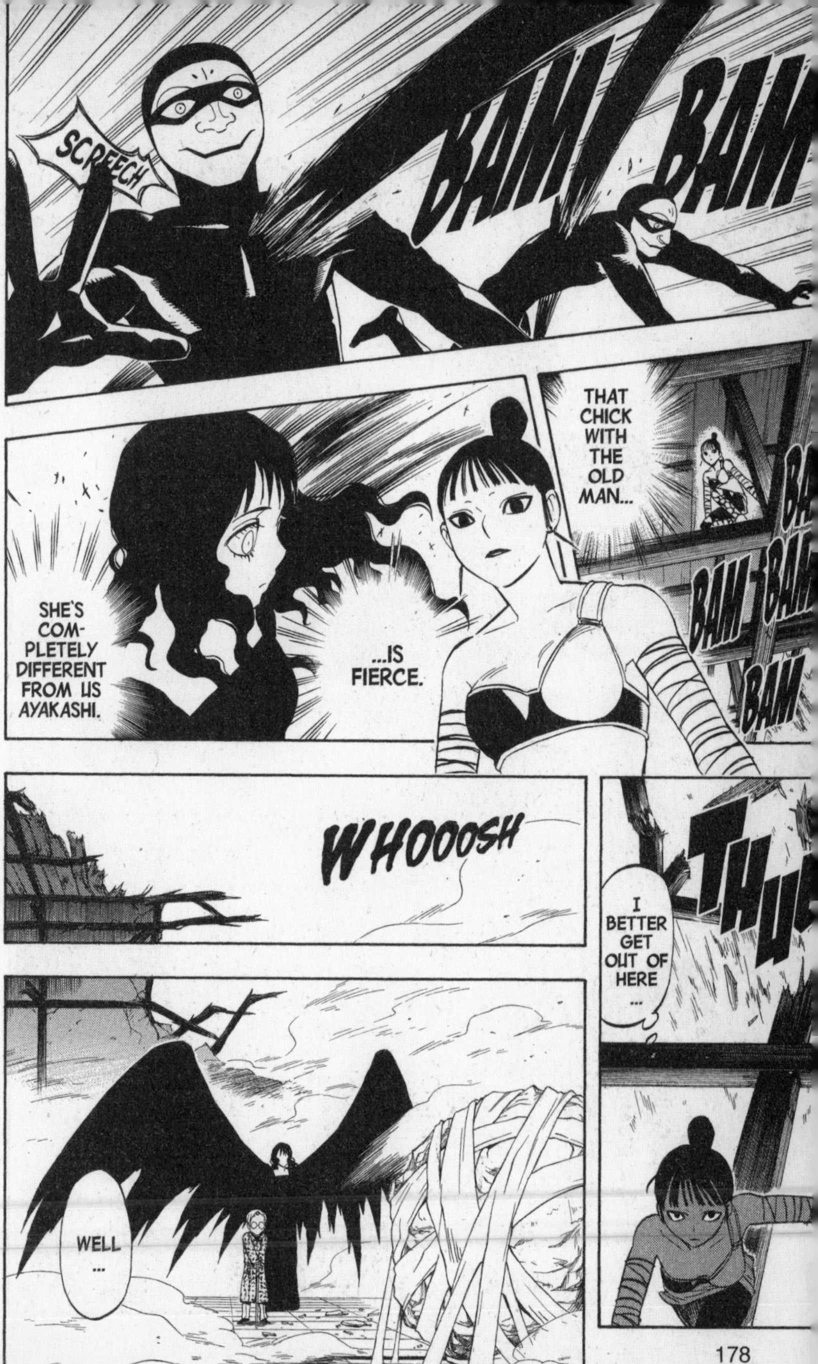
BAM
BAM
SCREECH
THAT CHICK WITH THE OLD MAN...
BAM
BAM
BAM
BAM
BAM
...IS FIERCE.
SHE'S COM-PLETELY DIFFERENT FROM US AYAKASHI.
THUD
I BETTER GET OUT OF HERE...
WHOOOSH
WELL...

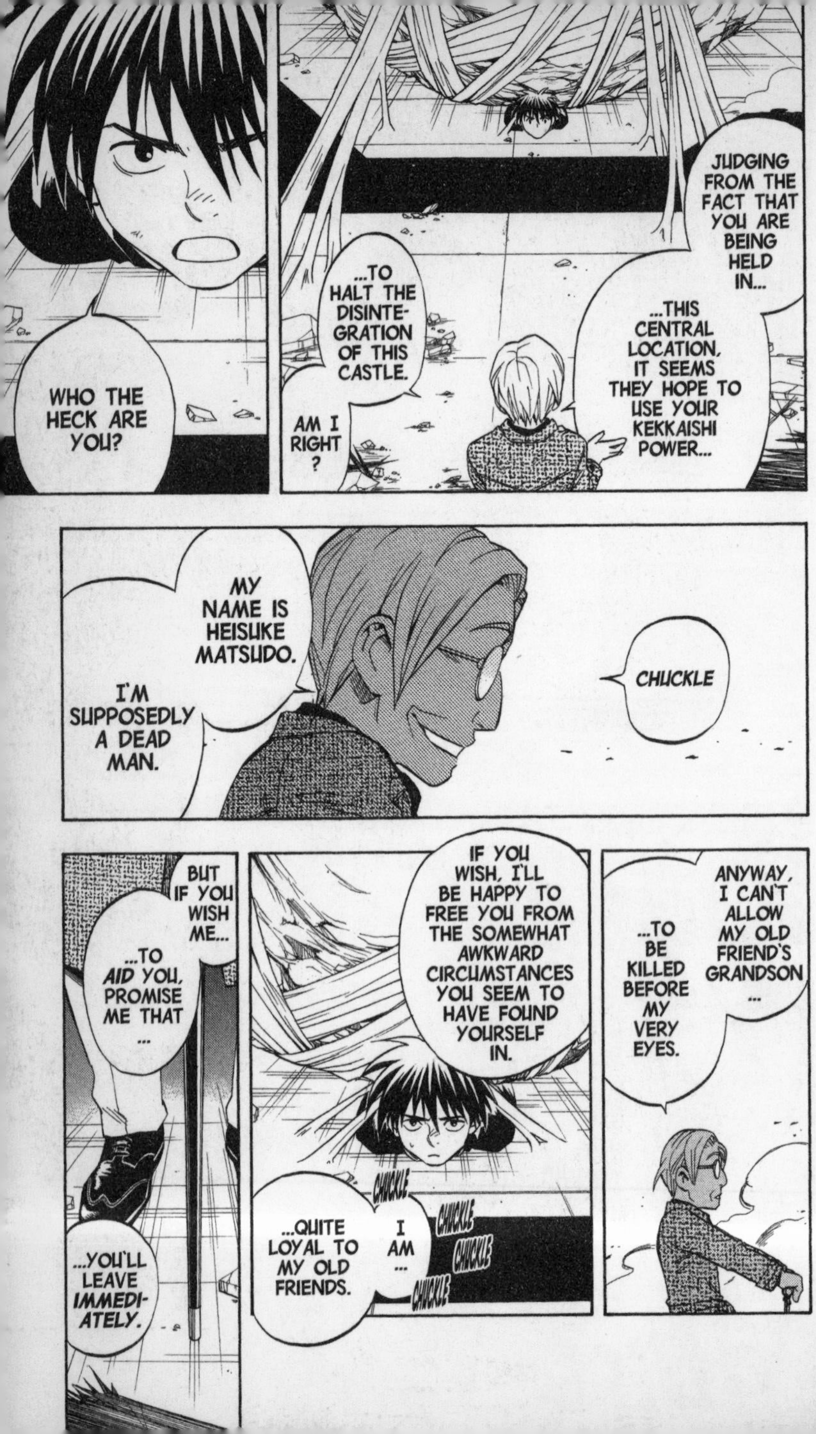
JUDGING FROM THE FACT THAT YOU ARE BEING HELD IN...
...THIS CENTRAL LOCATION, IT SEEMS THEY HOPE TO USE YOUR KEKKAISHI POWER...
...TO HALT THE DISINTEGRATION OF THIS CASTLE.
AM I RIGHT?
WHO THE HECK ARE YOU?
CHUCKLE
MY NAME IS HEISUKE MATSUDO.
I'M SUPPOSEDLY A DEAD MAN.
ANYWAY, I CAN'T ALLOW MY OLD FRIEND'S GRANDSON...
...TO BE KILLED BEFORE MY VERY EYES.
IF YOU WISH, I'LL BE HAPPY TO FREE YOU FROM THE SOMEWHAT AWKWARD CIRCUMSTANCES YOU SEEM TO HAVE FOUND YOURSELF IN.
I AM...
...QUITE LOYAL TO MY OLD FRIENDS.
CHUCKLE
CHUCKLE
CHUCKLE
CHUCKLE
BUT IF YOU WISH ME...
...TO AID YOU, PROMISE ME THAT...
...YOU'LL LEAVE IMMEDIATELY.

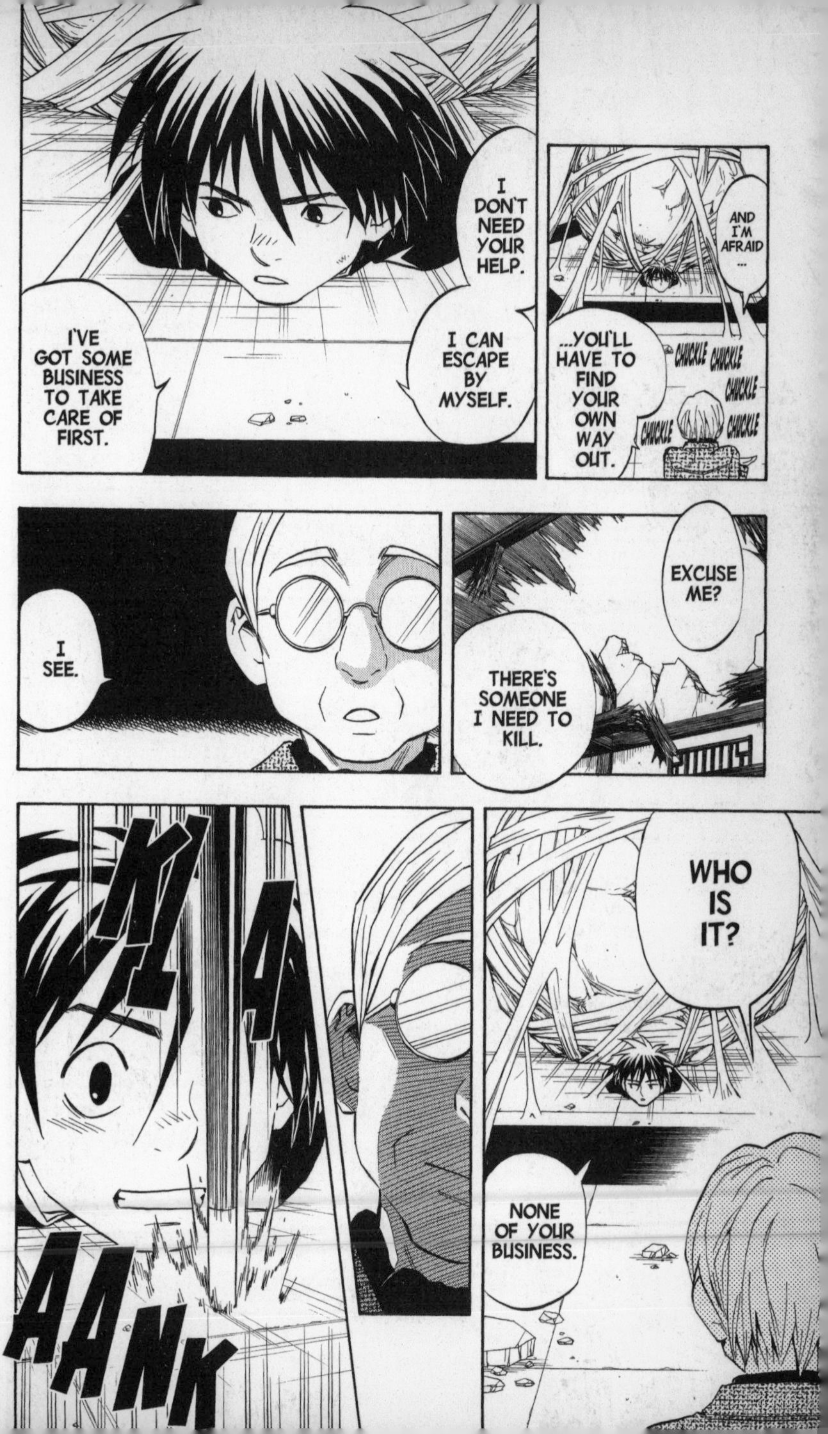
AND I'M AFRAID...
...YOU'LL HAVE TO FIND YOUR OWN WAY OUT.
CHUCKLE CHUCKLE CHUCKLE CHUCKLE CHUCKLE
I DON'T NEED YOUR HELP.
I CAN ESCAPE BY MYSELF.
I'VE GOT SOME BUSINESS TO TAKE CARE OF FIRST.
EXCUSE ME?
THERE'S SOMEONE I NEED TO KILL.
I SEE.
WHO IS IT?
NONE OF YOUR BUSINESS.
WA
AANK

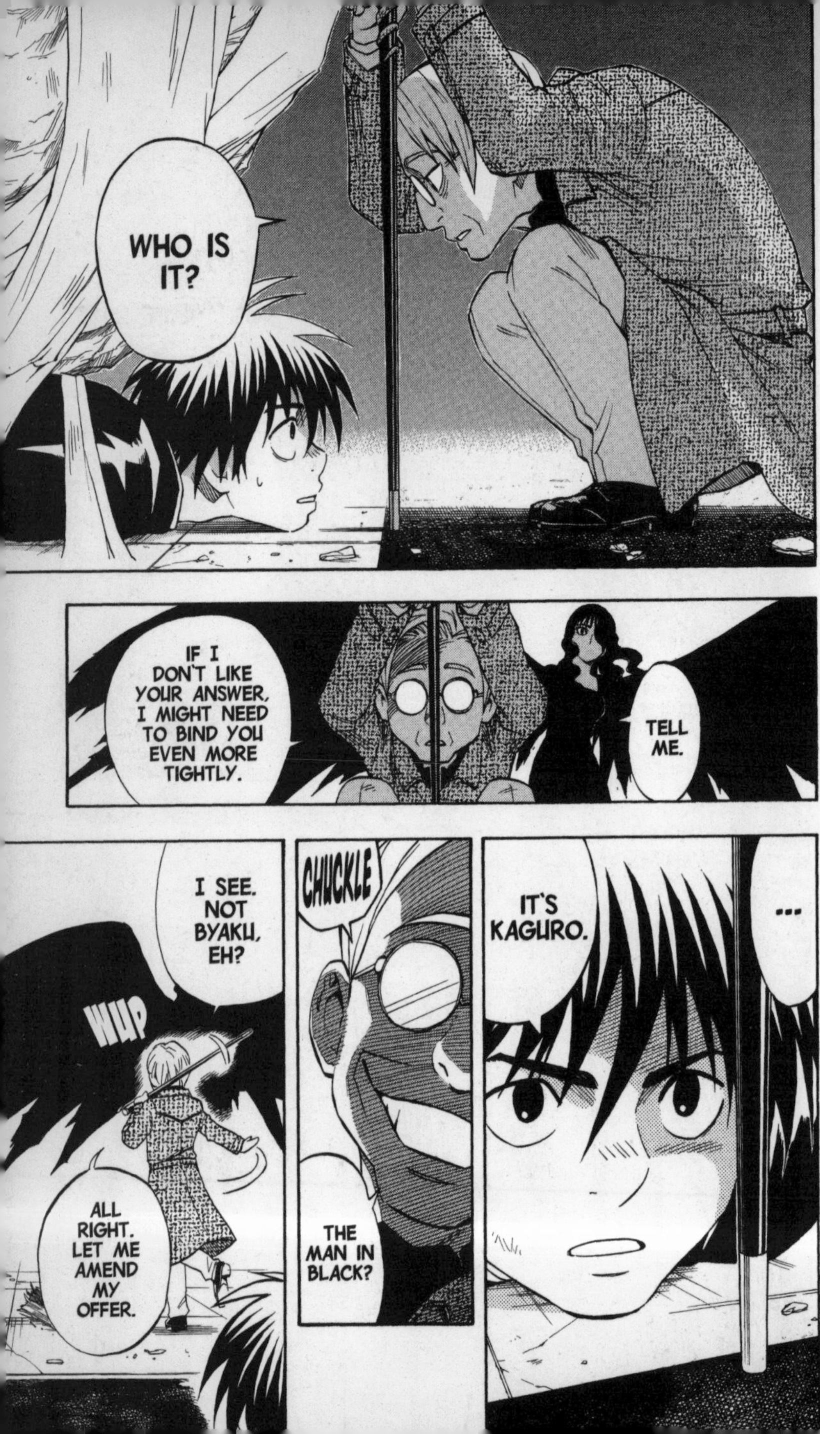
WHO IS IT?
TELL ME.
IF I DON'T LIKE YOUR ANSWER, I MIGHT NEED TO BIND YOU EVEN MORE TIGHTLY.
...
IT'S KAGURO.
CHUCKLE
THE MAN IN BLACK?
I SEE. NOT BYAKU, EH?
WUP
ALL RIGHT. LET ME AMEND MY OFFER.

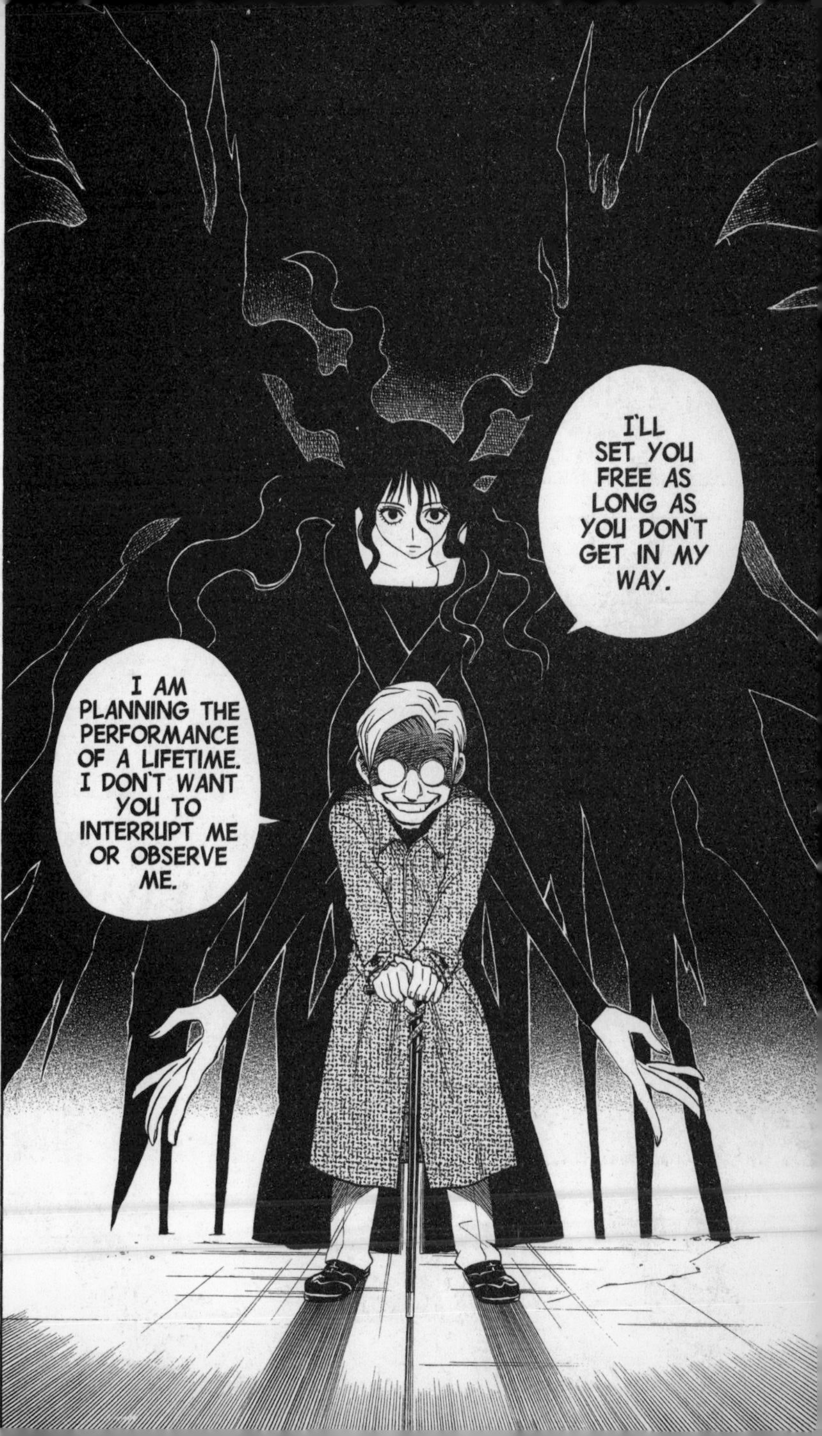
I'LL SET YOU FREE AS LONG AS YOU DON'T GET IN MY WAY.
I AM PLANNING THE PERFORMANCE OF A LIFETIME. I DON'T WANT YOU TO INTERRUPT ME OR OBSERVE ME.

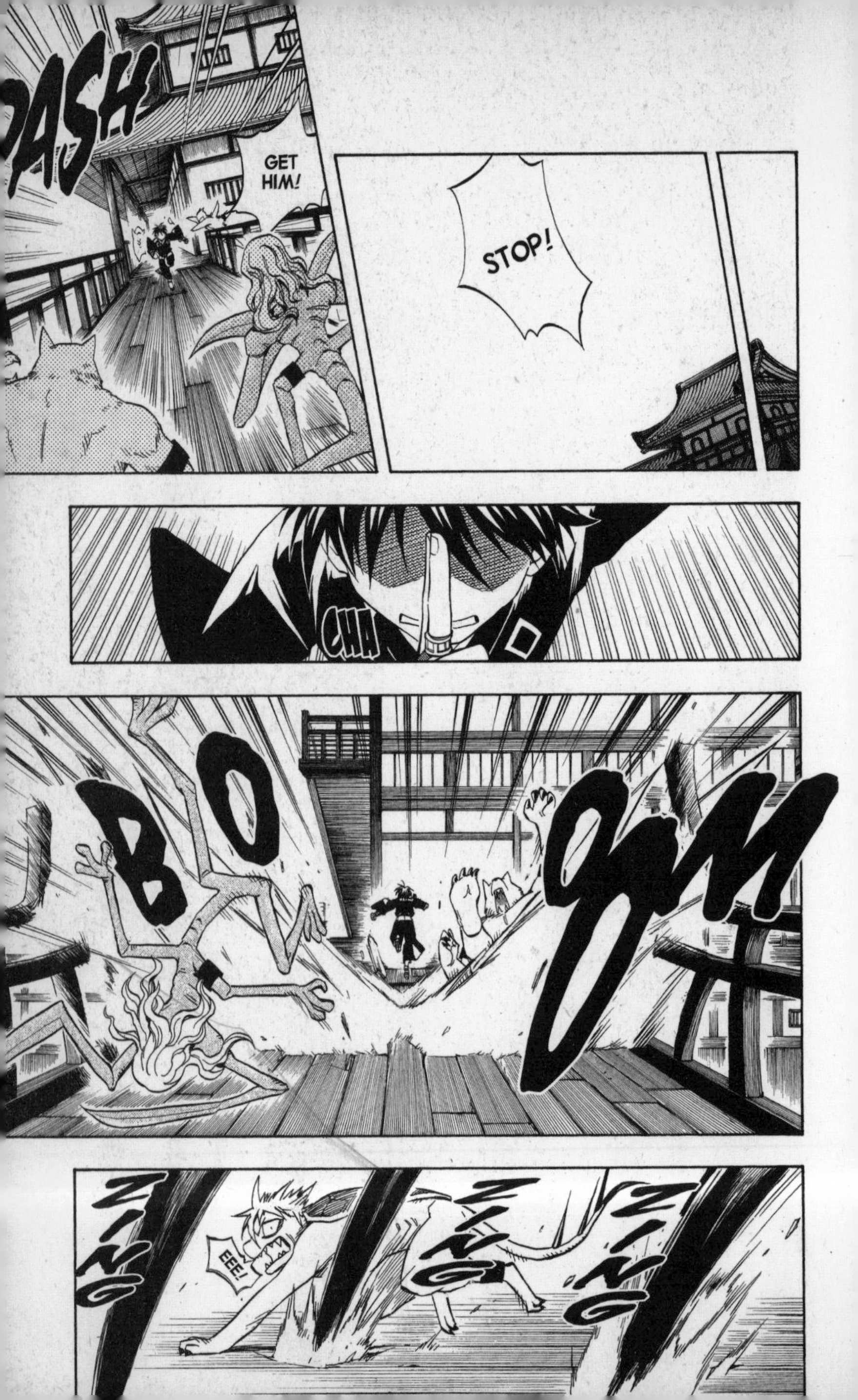
STOP!
DASH
GET HIM!
CHA
BOOM
ZING
ZING
ZING
EEE!

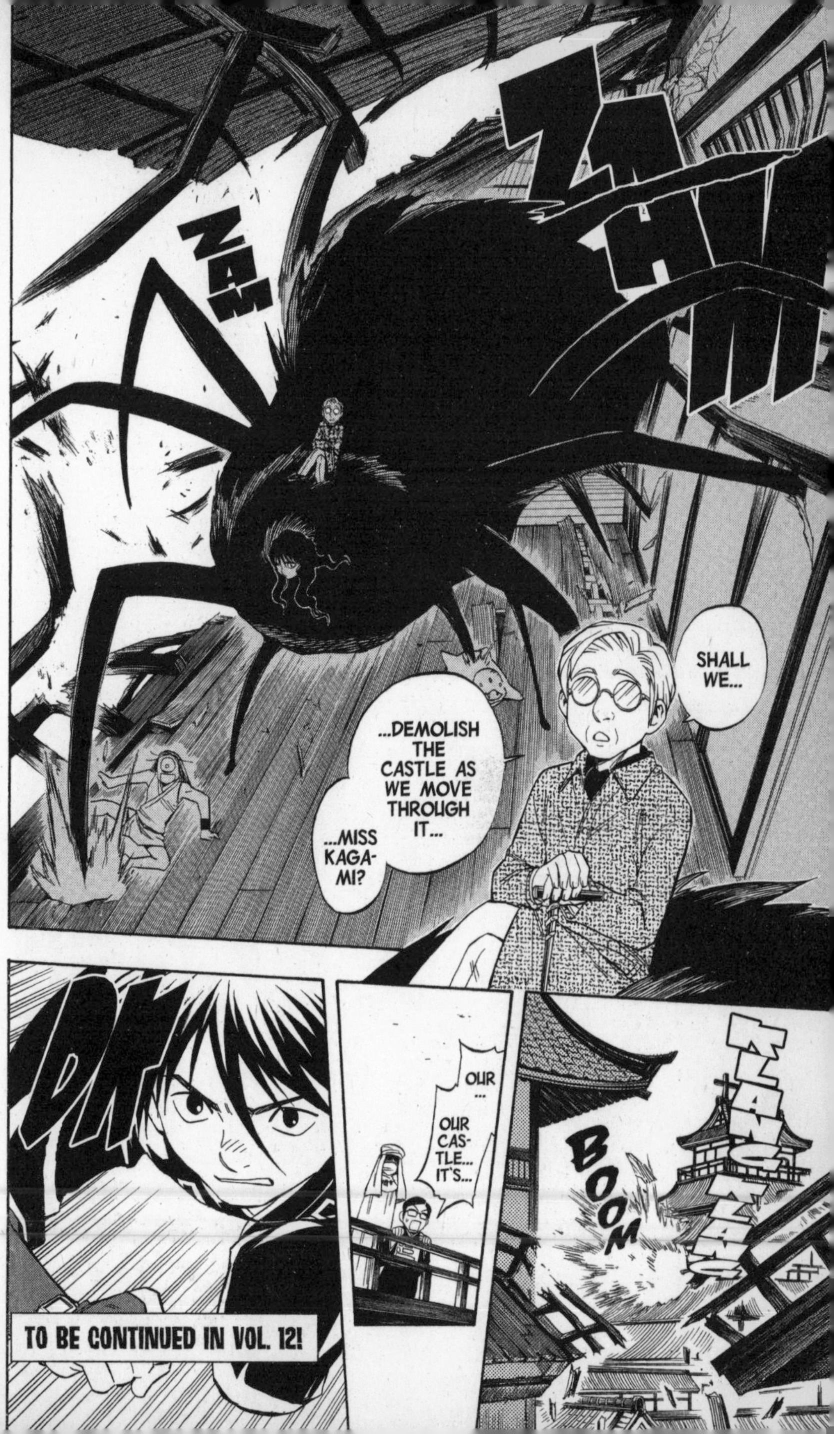
ZAM
SHALL WE...
...DEMOLISH THE CASTLE AS WE MOVE THROUGH IT...
...MISS KAGA-MI?
KLANG KLANG
BOOM
OUR ...
OUR CAS-TLE... IT'S...
TO BE CONTINUED IN VOL. 12!

FWAP

結界師

I got an eye patch.

I thought it would be fun to wear, but it turns out to be very inconvenient.

MESSAGE FROM YELLOW TANABE

I've got a sty in my eye.
A sty is a bacterial infection you're prone to acquiring when you're physically vulnerable, say from fatigue and lack of sleep.
It's not a serious problem, but it sure dampens my spirits.

Schnorrr
Nngh...

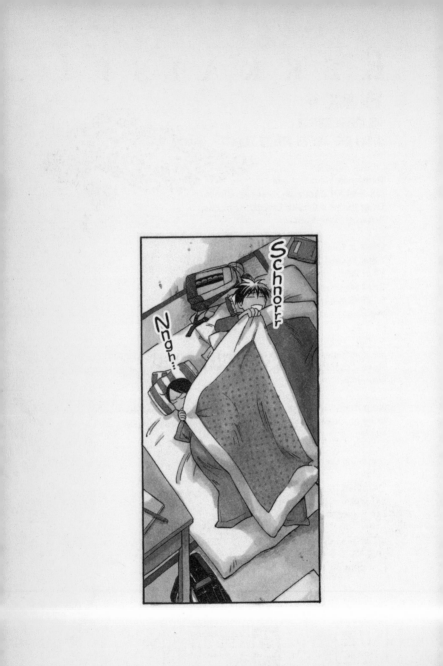

KEKKAISHI

VOLUME 11
VIZ MEDIA EDITION
STORY AND ART BY YELLOW TANABE

Translation/Yuko Sawada
Touch-up Art & Lettering/Stephen Dutro
Cover Design & Graphic Layout/Izumi Evers
Editor/Annette Roman

Editor in Chief, Books/Alvin Lu
Editor in Chief, Magazines/Marc Weidenbaum
VP of Publishing Licensing/Rika Inouye
VP of Sales/Gonzalo Ferreyra
Sr. VP of Marketing/Liza Coppola
Publisher/Hyoe Narita

Printed in the U.S.A.

Published by VIZ Media, LLC
P.O. Box 77010
San Francisco, CA 94107

VIZ Media Edition
10 9 8 7 6 5 4 3 2 1
First printing, November 2007

www.viz.com

store.viz.com